ROD STEWART

THE NEW BIOGRAPHY

ROD STEWART

THE NEW BIOGRAPHY

TIM EWBANK AND STAFFORD HILDRED

PORTRAIT

Visit the Portrait website!

Portrait publishes a wide range of non-fiction, including biography, history, science, music, popular culture and sport.

Visit our website to:

- read descriptions of our popular titles
- buy our books over the internet
- take advantage of our special offers
- enter our monthly competition
- learn more about your favourite Portrait authors

VISIT OUR WEBSITE AT: www.portraitbooks.com

Copyright © 2003 by Tim Ewbank and Stafford Hildred

First published in 2003 by Portrait, an imprint
of Piatkus Books Limited
5 Windmill Street
London W1T 2JA
e-mail: info@piatkus.co.uk

Reprinted 2003

This edition published in 2004

The moral right of the author has been asserted

Some of the material in this book appeared in a different form in *Rod Stewart* by
the same authors published by Headline, 1991.

A catalogue record for this book is available from the British Library

ISBN 0 7499 5027 7

This book has been printed on paper manufactured with respect for
the environment using wood from managed sustainable resources

Data manipulation by Phoenix Photosetting, Chatham, Kent
Printed and bound in Great Britain by
Mackays Ltd, Chatham, Kent

CONTENTS

ACKNOWLEDGEMENTS

The authors wish to express their deep gratitude to the many individuals who have made this book possible. Heartfelt thanks go to all those who have figured in Rod Stewart's life who agreed to be interviewed for this book. They are too many to mention but they include girlfriends, lovers, relatives, musicians, mentors, friends, band members, songwriters, roadies, promoters and record executives.

For their co-operation, help and encouragement, special thanks go to: Roy Addison, Lou Adler, Keith Altham, Ian Armit, Brian Auger, Martine Aupetit, John Baker, Brenda Barton, Dave and Sue Batchelor, Simon Bates, Moira Bellas, The Biography Channel, John Blake, Cindy 'Hot Legs' Blanchflower, Cecil, Kim and Rachael Booker, Bebe Buell, Roy Carr, Phil Chen, Nickie Clarke, Rodney Collins, Louise Court, Jim Cregan, Sally Croft, Keith Cronshaw, Carrie Davies at the Halfmoon in Putney, Albert Dempster, Tom Dowd, Julie Driscoll, Ken Eastaugh, Jane Ennis, Rod and Joy Gilchrist, Richard Hall, Phil and Ann Hammond, Bob Harris, Jim and Jorma Hampshire of Canterbury Rock, Dee Harrington, Stuart Higgins, Kathryn Holcombe, Lorinda Holness, Mike Hope, Jimmy Horowitz, Clive Jackson, Jerry Johns, Hilary Johnston, Richard Johnston, Shona Johnston, Steven Johnston, Paula Jones, Wizz Jones, Pat and Nick Justice, Fergus Kelly, Barry Kernon, Alan Kingston, Simon Kinnersley, Fiona Knight, Moira Marr, Bryan and Vicki Marshall, Sarita Martin, Fraser Massey, Mandy McCaffer, Ian McLagan, Charles McCutcheon, David and Sarah Mertens, The Misfits, Rene and Miranda Moolenaar, Yvonne and Richard Partridge, Helen and Peter Pasea, Garth Pearce, John Peel, John Pigeon, Jackie Poole, Sean and Debbie Poulley, Jimmy Powell, Martin Quittenton, Peter Radford, Liz and Rory Ramsden, Lou Reizner, Keith Richmond, Alasdair Riley, the late Lloyd Turner, Keith Skues, Alison and Paul Tissington, Jane Virgo, Johnny Walker, Mickey Waller, Denis Weymouth, The Rollin' Stoned, Jane Teckman and Leopard Films.

The authors would like to acknowledge as important sources: BBC Radio 2, BBC TV, *Zig Zag*, *NME*, *Melody Maker*, *News of the World*, the *Sun*, the *Mirror*, the *Sunday Mirror*, the *Sunday Times*, *The Times*, *Q* magazine, *GQ*, *Arena*, *Uncut*, *Now*, *True Britt* by Britt Ekland, and *Rebel Heart* by Bebe Buell with Victor Bockris.

Special thanks must go to Maddy Bisoni and VH1 whose programmes *Rod Stewart Revealed*, and *Behind the Music* provided a valuable source of information. Also to John Gray, whose excellent Smiler fan club magazines also provided vital insights and helped the efforts of the authors make the book as accurate as possible.

Tim Ewbank would especially like to thank his guitar teacher Rob Urbino for his patience, knowledge, and infectious enthusiasm. And Tim also wishes to thank his old Aberdeen University backing group of Doug McKenzie, Brian Mott, Geoff Hickman, Bert Munro, Dave Cairns and John Seaton for sharing the joys of R 'n' B.

Stafford: To Janet, Claire and Rebecca
Tim: To my mother Joy, Emma, Oliver and Carole Anne

PROLOGUE

Monte Carlo: May 2003

The nod of approval was accompanied by a smile and a cheery 'Go for it!' The setting was the exclusive Jimmy'z nightclub in Monte Carlo 2003. The smile on the face of beautiful blonde Penny Lancaster was broad and uninhibited. Rock star Rod Stewart was happily leaving the limelight to someone else for once and encouraging his lover as the sexy, fun-loving girl stepped up to deliver a raunchy, 30-minute dance routine that had the ultra-sophisticated audience roaring with acclaim. Dressed in a skimpy white dress which showed off her remarkable 6ft 1in figure, Penny posed and strutted and danced her way through a series of numbers including, inevitably, Rod's classic hit 'Da Ya Think I'm Sexy'. Two men sat and applauded with most enthusiasm – her lover Rod and her father Graham, who at 57 is by a year the younger man.

'Penny really went for it,' said a friend. 'She really loves Rod and she wanted to dance for him. And it helped that she knew she was looking pretty good as well.' But it was the conclusion of an evening that had begun uncertainly. Penny and Rod had arrived at a welcoming gala for the prestigious Laureus Sports Awards only to find they were sitting virtually next to his ex, Rachel Hunter. Polite exchanges were made but Penny was still left feeling strangely vulnerable. The encounter reminded her of the first time she met Rod, four and a half years previously at London's Dorchester Hotel. Then she was an unknown photographer asking for an autograph for a friend and Rachel was still the glamorous, headline-hitting international model and rock star bride Mrs Rod Stewart.

Rachel has quite a presence. And for some time Penny felt in awe of her. But Rod is friendly with almost all of the women he has lived with. 'It's because I'm an old softie,' he says. 'I give them everything they want.' And he has certainly stayed close to Rachel in spite of the split. They have two children together, ten-year-old Renee and Liam who is eight. Both Rod and Rachel are keen to give them as down-to-earth an upbringing as they can manage in the celebrity circumstances.

But Penny has a powerful personality of her own and after the meeting with Rachel she was keen to leave her own impression on the evening. So after she and Rod and her father left the glittering ceremony for a more relaxed celebration in the famous nightclub it felt only natural for Penny to leap to her feet and put on a show for the two most important men in her life. But before she did she looked to Rod for a hint of encouragement which quickly came. 'For once Rod was happy to be just a spectator,' said a friend. 'It's unusual for him but he lapped it up.'

But then, Rod Stewart is an unusual rock star in many ways. His voice is so individual and so natural it sustains a major and lasting talent. His songwriting ability is remarkable in its range and its originality and he has penned far more of his classic hits than is widely recognised. His capacity to reinvent himself is now almost legendary in the business. His appetite for beautiful women is well known but he also has an unusual talent for maintaining strong and lasting friendships with most of the former lovers who no longer spend time in his bedroom.

And most unusual of all, in an industry packed with tortured egos, fragile personalities, and all-round weirdos who regularly make visits to psychiatrists and drying-out clinics, Rod Stewart thoroughly enjoys being a rich and famous rock star and healthily steers clear of chemical assistance.

Underneath that eccentric exterior is a man largely at ease with himself and his world. 'I've never really worried too much about my career to be honest,' says Rod. 'I have been so really lucky that I've never been one to turn to drink or drugs or suffer from deep depression. I use the word "nonchalant". I've always been pretty casual about it. I've never taken it for granted, but if it happens it happens, if it don't it don't.'

From the moment Rod was overheard playing the harmonica on Twickenham railway station by early mentor Long John Baldry there has always been good fortune in his life. 'I'm a lucky guy,' says Rod. 'Sometimes it's best not to worry too much when something good happens, just get on and enjoy it is my philosophy.' The long career is full of moments of sublime good fortune but part of Rod's strength is that he is not pretending to be anyone else. The talent is genuine and so is the all-important personal style. Most people remember where they were when President Kennedy was shot, and Rod Stewart recalls he was buying his first leather overcoat. Clothes have always been very important to image-conscious Rod.

And he handles the fame better than most. Actress Joanna Lumley was an early lover and she was highly impressed by the way that Rod could use his stardom instead of being a slave to it. Rod showed her he could create attention if he wanted it by arriving in a limo and having security guards causing a scene. 'But he could also behave perfectly normally and not get bothered,' said Joanna. 'He was very together.'

One of Rod's early breaks was the highly successful tour of America with the Jeff Beck Group in 1967. It was the first time Rod went to America and the band was given a standing ovation at the Fillmore East in New York. Close friend Ronnie Wood recalled recently: 'It was very interesting. We had a write-up from the *New York Times* by Robert Sheldon and he likened the interplay between Jeff's guitar and Rod's voice to a Harold Pinter play. The review was on the front page of the *New York Times*.'

Rod didn't know Harold Pinter from Harold Steptoe but he knew good news when he saw it. The band had the rave review copied and sent ahead of them round the States. Typically, Rod remembers the concert differently. 'I remember Janis Joplin chasing me and Ronnie round backstage at the Fillmore East saying, "I'm going to have one of you cute boys." But she didn't get either of us, we disappeared together. We were both just so scared. It didn't happen in Britain; women didn't come on to you aggressively like they did in the States. It scared the living daylights out of us little British boys.'

Laughter always plays a huge part in Rod's make-up. He is one of the funniest guys in the rock business. And even though Ronnie Wood famously described his pal as 'tighter than two coats of paint', Rod's legendary meanness is often more of a running joke than a genuine reluctance to spend his money.

Rod's rise and rise has taken none of that down-to-earth realism and good humour from him. He is well aware of how fortunate he has been. 'Singing has changed my whole life,' says Rod. 'Coming from a council house in north London and now having three houses around the world and looking for a fourth in the south of France. I'm a lucky little bugger, aren't I? I've tried to remain as grounded as I can. I don't really have good close friends in show business. Most of my friends are people who have been in my band or people I play football with. And my family are tremendously grounding too. My two brothers, my sister, they keep me grounded.'

Family is still the most important thing in Rod's life and he is proud that he is on good terms with all of his five children and almost all of his previous wives and lovers. 'The kids see this, and it's good for them,' says Rod. 'They see we're a united family.'

From all of his long success Rod still believes his finest hour was the amazing 'Maggie May', which reached the top of the charts on both sides of the Atlantic. Rod still believes that the best moment of his career was: 'My mum and dad's faces when I told them "Maggie May" was number one. They were always firm believers in me. They always encouraged me and I never heard the words "get a decent job" or "it's all going to fade away" so their gleaming faces when I finally made it were a picture.' Now Penny has become part of that large and happy family, it's definitely something to dance about.

CHAPTER ONE

THE BOY CAN'T HELP IT

When I left school, the only ambition I had was to play football. But somewhere along the line I must have fallen in with the wrong people, who turned out to be the right people in the long run, and turned to music. I haven't regretted anything I've done. Rod Stewart

Before the man who was to become a leading contender for the title of the world's greatest hell-raiser was allowed out for the night which was to change his life, his mother had something to say.

Rod Stewart was just three days away from his 19th birthday when his forceful mother, Elsie, telephoned her son's newly found musical mentor Long John Baldry, and firmly warned him to have her young son home in time for bed. Long John was surprised that the lusty youth still answered to his mum on matters of bedtime, but had already seen enough star potential to agree to this strange request.

That initial jam session in a dingy cellar in the depths of Soho was perhaps the real beginning of the musical education of Rod Stewart, the first step on the road to understanding fully the remarkable talents of the shy and nervous stand-in singer and harmonica player.

And more than once in the weeks and months that followed, having been driven back across the city by Baldry to his humble north London home long after the deadline, Rod would stumble up the path to the sound of Elsie yelling, 'Is that you, Roddy? I'll pay you! I'll pay you!'

But the Rod Stewart story really began in January 1945, as the war in Europe was grinding to its grim conclusion and London was far from swinging. Huge areas had been devastated by the Luftwaffe, food was rationed and in desperately short supply, and the winter was bitterly cold. But there were still some warm celebrations long into the night of 10 January, in the household of expatriate Scot Robert Stewart from Leith and his Cockney wife Elsie, when they added a chubby baby boy to their already chirpy brood of two sons and two daughters. Robert gave him his first name, Roderick, after there had been some debate in the family as to whether to call him Rodney. Robert Stewart is said to have won the day when he prophetically pronounced: 'I have a feeling he'll never want for anything if we call him Roderick.' Rod's sister Mary, who had been sent out to play on her roller skates while Rod arrived in the world, gave him his second name, David, when she returned home after his delivery.

The baby's safe arrival was a huge relief to Rod's parents, who had spent many an anxious hour leading up to the birth huddled together with their four children in a brick bomb shelter, while the Germans launched a heavy 'doodlebug' rocket attack. The family clung together as they listened fearfully for the rockets' engines to stop, and waited for the inevitable explosions that would follow.

Just thirty minutes before Rod was born, a German V2 rocket made a direct hit on Highgate Police Station. Rod was to reflect, years later: 'I've always thought that I was very lucky because that bomb fell just a stone's throw from where I lived. I've sort of had a feeling that I nearly didn't make it.'

Robert Stewart came from King's Port in Edinburgh. He was just 14 when he ran away to sea, but by the time he had reached his late teens he had washed up on dry land in London. He began his land-bound career as a plumber's apprentice but eventually worked his way up to become a master builder. Rod's mother, Elsie, came from Upper Holloway, north London. She fell for the fast-talking young Scot, the couple married in 1928 and the Stewart clan began to appear soon afterwards. Mary, Don, Bob and Peggy were born in quick succession and the happy family moved to 507 Archway Road, Highgate, where, after a gap of eight years, young Roderick was born.

Bob senior retired from the building trade at 65, but family funds were never large enough to make for a relaxed retirement, and so he opened a newsagent's shop when Rod was in his early teens.

Rod's earliest recollections are of a lively, laughing family. The main preoccupations of the male members were football and music, in that order. Now he says, simply: 'I came from a very poor family, but I was extremely well fed and extremely happy. I was incredibly spoilt as the youngest of five kids. I had a fantastically happy childhood.'

Rod was in fact spoilt even before he was born. His sister Mary worked as a seamstress five minutes from the family home and as Rod's birth approached, Mary's work colleagues each generously put a few coins into a money box every week, which eventually realised enough cash to buy a new cot. Rod's arrival had been all the more eagerly anticipated as his mother Elsie was 39, quite an advanced age to have a baby in those days, and it had been eight years since she had produced her last child, Peggy.

Perhaps because he now speaks from a personal perspective of immense wealth, Rod is inclined to exaggerate the poverty of his childhood. Certainly the Stewarts were by no means well off, but their small business selling sweets, cigarettes and tobacco and newspapers brought in enough to keep the large family in reasonable comfort. Good times or bad, on Tuesdays Bob and Elsie would regularly go out to the cinema, and on Saturdays they went for a drink at the local, leaving Mary to dote over little Roddy.

Respect for his father, based on a very strong bond of love and founded in those early years, was to last Rod into his own middle age: 'The only thing I worry about,' he would say, 'is my dad. If I upset my dad, then I'm really in trouble. He's dearer to me than anything.'

Neither of his parents are still alive. But from his mother Rod inherited a love of a good party, and from his father he inherited a respect for loyalty and honesty. He always put that down to his 'good Scottish roots', and once described his father as 'an interesting guy – rotund, about five foot ten, and he had just one tooth because he didn't believe in going to the dentist. A lot of Scots haven't got too many teeth – it's something to do with the water. He was very, very thoughtful, fairly puritanical and a quiet man. My mum was much more outgoing than Dad. She loved to get the family round and give them a drink and make everyone get up and sing a song. She was a very, very good mother.' Rod's own loyalty to his family has become legendary over the years, as he has done his best to protect them from some of the more unpleasant and intrusive aspects of having a famous pop star for a son and brother.

Rod's father and his two elder brothers were great soccer enthusiasts. Although his father was 42 when Rod was born, he was still playing for a local amateur side. Rod remembers as a small child seeing his dad play a rather over-enthusiastic game of football, and break his leg as a result: 'He was playing a bit too tough, and he had to spend Christmas in hospital with his leg in plaster. An absolute soccer nut,' he says with pride. And the stars of the Stewarts' spiritual home were their heroes. In spite of being born in London, both Don and Bob had their bedroom walls covered with pictures of Scottish football stars like George Young of Rangers, and Hibernians' Gordon Smith. Rod's father ran the local Highgate Redwings Football Club, which at its height had three teams chasing all over north London every weekend. As amateur facilities were somewhat basic in those days, this frequently meant anything up to 33 mud-spattered players using the house as a changing room on a Saturday afternoon.

Not surprisingly, a lifelong enthusiasm for football was instilled in Rod at a very early age. He loved kicking a ball around in the street with his friends – his father even painted a tennis ball white so he could go on playing after dark – and he was a keen supporter of local north London team Arsenal. Generally regarded as the most talented footballer in the family, even as a youngster Rod plunged into the game with enormous enthusiasm, and with a style of play that relied as much on his considerable natural skill as on an almost reckless aggression.

At secondary school Rod's footballing skills were perhaps more highly regarded than his scholastic abilities. He rose through the junior teams to become school soccer captain, and went on to play for Middlesex Schoolboys as centre-half. As a useful all-rounder, he also became cricket captain, but football was always his real love.

After football the great enthusiasm of the Stewart family was music, which generally expressed itself as good old-fashioned house parties with assorted inebriated relations, much singing around the piano, and good times being enjoyed by all. All the Stewarts enjoyed a good party, and the immediate post-war euphoria prompted many a celebration at their Edwardian home. When the war ended, Bob Stewart was able to take down the wooden boards he had nailed across the windows, so frequently shattered by exploding bombs. At last he could replace the glass which soon collected a film of dirt from the lorries that thundered past. But, in every way, the gloom of the war years was lifted, and the Stewarts' home was often packed with relations and friends singing and dancing. On such occasions, Bob Stewart would carefully erect scaffolding and planks of wood in the cellar to prop up the sitting room floor, to make sure it could take the weight of dancing feet.

'We are a very close family,' said Bob Stewart, in a rare interview in 1977. 'If you hurt one of us you hurt the lot. We never heard Rod singing at home, you know. Only when he was helping out in my shop.'

Rod fondly recalls the warmth and laughter of those family parties. His favourite moments were spent as a young boy curled up underneath the piano, wondering which of his older brothers would be the first to drop a sixpence on the floor in front of his Uncle John, just to find out exactly what a Scotsman did wear under his kilt. When he was 11, Rod recalls, his family stood him up on the piano at one of the family parties and he sang 'Underneath the Arches'. His rendering of this old British music-hall song was, of course, greeted with enthusiastic applause, and sowed the first seeds in his mind of a possible show-business career.

Al Jolson, who has often been acclaimed as the most consummate entertainer of the twentieth century, was the family favourite. As a recording artist, Jolson had million-sellers as early as 1912, and as late as 1950. His most famous line was 'You ain't heard nothing yet' from the 1927 film *The Jazz Singer.* 'My Mammy', which Jolson flamboyantly used to sing on bended knee, arms outstretched, was the first song Rod remembers hearing. It would bring tears to his eyes and he still has a great affection for the legendary entertainer, even going so far as to cite Jolson as one of his early musical influences: 'My brother Don is a natural entertainer – the finest impersonator of Al Jolson I'd ever seen. As far back as I can remember, when I was about three or four, my father was an Al Jolson fanatic. Every Saturday night, he'd come back from the pub singing Al Jolson songs.' Don's huge collection of Jolson 78s was a constant source of inspiration to the young Rod. When he was taken to see the two Larry Parkes films *The Jolson Story* and *Jolson Sings Again*, Rod was completely bowled over. 'It's incredible that he had no mike and could reach an audience of 2,000,' says the man who now regularly plays to packed stadiums of 20,000 and more, aided by all the latest sound equipment that modern technology can provide. Jolson was always happiest in front of a live audience, and used to strut down ramps he had specially built in order to be closer to his fans. His melodramatic singing style was complemented by pleading interjections and intensifying gestures – all of which had a profound influence on Rod in later years.

After Jolson, following in big brother Don's footsteps, Rod started listening to Little Richard records after Don came home one day with a copy of the singer's Top Ten hit, 'The Girl Can't Help It', in April 1957. Little Richard, who combined a wild, intense piano style with a screaming, manic falsetto, provided Rod's introduction to rock 'n' roll. In purely stylistic terms, Little Richard was the most influential of the early stars of rock 'n' roll, leaving his mark on Paul McCartney's singing and Jimi Hendrix's stagecraft, as well as on soul singers James Brown and Otis Redding. He also had an impact on the young Rod Stewart: 'I remember trying to sound like Little Richard,' says Rod.

As a schoolboy, Rod's finer moments were clearly spent on the sports field. After failing to distinguish himself at Highgate Primary School, he was still surprised to fail the eleven-plus exam. When he moved on to William Grimshaw Secondary Modern School in Hornsey, known locally as Billy Grim, also numbered among the pupils and alongside Rod in the football team were the brothers Davies, Ray and Dave, and Pete Quaife, later to achieve fame and fortune as the Kinks.

While academic accolades passed him by, Rod did rise to become a prefect, but the honour was summarily removed shortly afterwards, following an incident involving the somewhat unnecessary discharge of a fire extinguisher.

Of course, when he was a schoolboy, Rod's famous spiky hairstyle had still to evolve, but even then he was always very concerned about its appearance. He waged a constant battle against the hair at the back of his head, which, despite his best efforts, insisted on standing up. 'My mother used to spit on her hand and try to make it lie flat, but it still stood up. A cowlick, that's what you call it.' At the age of 14, strongly influenced by an American film he had seen at the cinema – 'something to do with test pilots' – he ceded temporary honourable defeat by opting for a crew cut, with mixed results: 'I looked terrible, all nose and ears.' It wasn't until he reached his late teens that, necessity being the mother of invention, he cultivated the famous 'Rod the Mod' hairstyle that he still sports in an updated form.

Rod's first experience with a musical instrument was no more encouraging. As an alternative to ordinary woodwork lessons, an enlightened teacher coached Rod and a group of other boys in the specialised skills of guitar-making. Rod's instrument looked highly promising until he put on the strings. Then it snapped in two. Partly as compensation and partly, perhaps, because he somehow felt there lurked untapped musical potential within his youngest child, Rod's indulgent father splashed out the then considerable sum of eight pounds fifteen shillings (£8.75) for a replacement, a Zenith acoustic guitar, on Rod's 14th birthday. On that day, 10 January 1959, an American born Harold Jenkins in Arkansas, who had changed his name to Conway Twitty, was top of the British charts with 'It's Only Make

Believe'. And as Bob Stewart presented Rod with the guitar, he said cannily: 'There's going to be some money in this.'

The gift might have been remembered as one of the first significant musical moments in Rod's young life. Instead, Rod recalls his reaction was of initial surprise and some disappointment: 'When I was 14, I remember I had a model railway and I asked my dad to buy me a station. Instead, he went and bought me a guitar, for no apparent reason. I think this was my first personal encounter with music. So what I do now is all my dad's fault.

'I didn't ask for it and I hardly used it. At first I wasn't really interested and I hated music at school – there was this teacher called Mr Wainwright, who seemed to be always picking on me to sing in front of the class. Awful.'

As a youngster Rod displayed little or no indication of his musical potential. In his early teens he was much more interested in model railways, locking himself in his room to make tiny carriages and scaled-down scenery by hand, with painstaking care. 'When I was still at school I had no musical inclination whatsoever,' says Rod. 'And I was very shy to sing.' Very, very shy, but gradually, nurtured by his brothers and sisters, Rod's interest in music developed. He even picked up his guitar and, aged 14, joined his first schoolboy group.

'I used to strum around a bit,' he says, 'and gradually I got involved. The first thing I learned on it was "It Takes A Worried Man To Sing A Worried Song" in the key of E, and then it went to A and B flat.' And so Rod's nascent musical abilities were stirred. Soon afterwards in 1959, he bought, at age 14, his first pop record. In spite of his enthusiasm for Al Jolson, it was 'C'mon Everybody', by American teenage rockabilly star Eddie Cochran, which contained some astonishing guitar work as well as vocal dexterity.

The following year, Rod's brother Don took him to the State, in Kilburn, to see Bill Haley and his Comets; Rod was thrilled to hear Haley playing live one of the biggest hits of the era, 'Rock Around The Clock'. That prompted Rod to join his first proper band, the Kool Kats, on guitar in 1960. Rock 'n' roll having only just reached Britain's shores, they played a lot of skiffle music, made hugely popular at the time by Lonnie Donegan. The Kool Kats consisted of eight guitarists, all strumming like mad, and their repertoire contained such classics as 'Freight Train', then a big hit for Charles McDevitt Skiffle Group featuring Nancy Whiskey on vocals, and Donegan's popular novelty song 'Does Your Chewing Gum Lose Its Flavour'. It was a beginning.

Rod's bedroom, however, was still dominated by his model train set. The Stewart family home was not far from the Highgate shunting yards, where Rod spent many a happy and absorbing hour simply watching the trains. Rod soon developed a passionate interest in model railways, and began building and collecting his own trains and track, which he laid out all around his bed. Rod had even constructed an elaborate tunnel going in and out of one window. If the train came off the tracks in the tunnel, Rod had to climb out through his bedroom window and on to the scullery roof to get it back on the rails. One of Rod's teenage pals, a would-be guitarist and future Rolling Stone named Ronnie 'Woody' Wood, stayed round at Rod's one night. The next morning, a little groggy from the night before, Woody jumped up and cracked his head on the tunnel, almost knocking himself out.

Leaving school at 15, Rod took a job as a silk-screen printer at the Framery in Muswell Hill, just down the road from his parents' home. He had shown some promise during art lessons at William Grimshaw, and, despite his lack of formal qualifications, had nurtured a brief hankering to become a designer. But at the time football was still the only activity for which Rod could muster anything approaching real enthusiasm. Father Bob thought that at last he had produced a real footballer: 'All the boys played, but Roddy was the best. I'd really hoped to see him playing at Wembley.' He believed Rod had the ability to make the grade. West London professional side Brentford thought so too. And so, soon after he started his first job, he dropped his artistic ambitions to sign to them as an apprentice.

But while Rod loved playing football, there were aspects of life as an aspiring pro that he found hard to cope with. He hated getting up at seven o'clock in the morning to travel right across London, to Brentford FC's training ground. And he was even less enthusiastic about the opening task of the day – cleaning the First Team's boots. The physical side of the game was also difficult for Rod in those days, as he found it hard to cope with the club's intensive training routines. When he was 17, Rod was 5 ft 11 in tall, but he weighed only nine stone. Often he pushed himself so hard in training that he was sick at the side of the pitch.

And so, although he played in two months of pre-season fixtures as a lively but lightweight centre-half, Rod Stewart decided he was not going to hang around for a whole season, while the middle-aged men who ran the club made up their minds as to whether he had a future in the game. He was also becoming aware that he had a singing voice.

Rod's decision to abandon a football career naturally came as a great disappointment to his father: 'It was my dad's great dream that I would make it as a professional footballer.' Although good amateurs, neither of Rod's elder brothers had been quite special enough to make the grade as professionals. Bob Stewart had therefore pinned his hopes on his youngest – and most talented – son. But while Rod maybe had the ability, he himself admits that he did not have the necessary dedication: 'I had the skill but not the enthusiasm.'

Luckily for him, he had a choice, as the musical side of his life was beginning to develop promisingly at the same time. 'There wasn't ever really a conscious decision to go either way. Music and football, they're two ways to get out of the streets. I was lucky because I had a shot at both ways,' he says now.

Weighing up the options, Rod decided that a professional musician had a lifestyle far better suited to him than that of a professional footballer. As he put it: 'I thought, well, a musician's life is a lot easier and I can also get drunk and make music, and I can't do that and play football. I plumped for music . . . They're the only things I can do, really, play football and sing.'

However, Rod's greatest asset, whether he wanted to become a footballer or a musician, was his insuperable belief in himself, fostered, perhaps, by his position as the youngest child in a loving and devoted family. He might not have been ready for fame – and in those early days he was unprepared to work for his future – but he most certainly wanted to make it, somehow or other.

Rod frequently insisted that he had no ambition except one day to become famous. Even when he left school, he was convinced he was going to be famous for something, it didn't matter what – medicine, jumping off the Eiffel Tower, anything – he just had to be famous. Rod later reflected that the most important thing to have was the belief in yourself, that you are going to make it sooner or later. He said: 'If it is a half-hearted effort you'll fail. I always wanted to be the centre of attention. It's in my make-up. When I was at school I wanted to be the centre of attention in everything. Some of us are like that and some of us are not. I don't think I've ever been ordinary.'

But, like so many 17-year-olds, Rod had no real clue about his future. After walking out of Brentford, he used a small amount of money his father had given him to make his first trip abroad, to Paris. He hitch-hiked to Dover, and from Calais on to Paris. But he stayed only a couple of nights, sleeping on the Left

Bank and wandering around. The language barrier and an acute shortage of money sent him scuttling home to Mum and Dad. But it was a first taste of the wide world outside north London, and he was to return.

When not playing in the band, Rod worked in the family shop, doing odd jobs and ordering stock. Less successfully he attempted early morning newspaper deliveries. Rod's mother recalls that she would often go to wake him at seven, only to find that he was still fast asleep an hour later. Rod remembers being press-ganged into an early-morning round, when one of the regular boys failed to turn up one morning: 'I was 17 at the time. My dad dragged me up at six in the morning. It was a humiliating sight. All those kids were up to my knees and he pushed me out into the snow, and made me deliver papers. I threw them over the railway and went back to bed.'

Soon afterwards, he took up his best-known job outside the music business, that of grave-digger. It was easily the oddest job he has ever had. He worked for a few weeks only at Highgate Cemetery, last resting-place of Karl Marx. Wielding a shovel in the pouring rain was hardly fun, but Rod had a reason for taking the job other than the minimal financial rewards. As a boy and as a young man Rod Stewart had always felt an almost irrational fear of dying. He had suffered nightmares about death from a very early age and so thought, as an impressionable teenager, that perhaps by getting as close as he could to death, actually digging out holes to be filled by real bodies, he could rid himself of that fear. It was also the only job he could get at the time as, by now, he had grown his recalcitrant locks right the way down his back.

Later he took an equally grim job, working for a north Finchley funeral parlour. There, Rod perhaps got closer to experiencing death than he had initially anticipated: 'One experience that scared the shit out of me was when I first went on the job. What happens when you start is that the other guys who work in the cemetery sort of christen you, by putting you inside a coffin and closing the lid, which is a very, very frightening experience. It doesn't sound like it, but once you get in there and they close the lid on you, you wonder if they'll just leave you in there. That was the initiation.'

But it seemed that working as a grave-digger calmed some of those teenage tantrums: 'It's like when you fall off a horse, you've got to get right back on, or you might not ride again because your fears can grow to be too intense. So I thought in my case the best way of beating my fear of death was to confront it, to get as close to it as possible. And I've never had any problems with it since.' Grave-digging was never going to be a long-term profession for Rod, and on more than one occasion, eldest brother Don was urged by their father to give Rod a roasting about knuckling down to a decent job.

By now, and by his own none-too-modest admission, Rod was 'getting pretty good on the guitar', and Don realised how much he had improved. So, with Don, he set off for Tin Pan Alley (Denmark Street), the street in London's West End where Rod fondly imagined all great guitarists of the future went for their instruments. The guitar Rod chose was a Gibson acoustic priced at £40, which was roughly £40 more than he had to spend. However, Don indulgently signed on the dotted line as guarantor of Rod's hire-purchase agreement – an act of generosity he was later to regret, when one of Rod's long adventures away from home caused him to forget to make the payments, and he was forced to pay up.

Rod learned very early in life that the music business could be hard and disappointing. He was just 16 when he tagged along with the Raiders for a recording session with eccentric independent producer Joe Meek. A former RAF radio technician, Meek had worked as an engineer on records by British singing stalwarts of the time such as Frankie Vaughan, Anne

Shelton and Petula Clark, before establishing his own RGM Sound, a tiny studio built above a shop in north London. From there he produced a string of hits including John Leyton's echo-laden 'Johnny Remember Me', and the swirling instrumental 'Telstar', a number one hit for the Tornadoes. Meek had happened to see the Raiders in a north London church hall, and had called them into his studio to record a horror-rock instrumental number entitled 'Night Of The Vampire'. During a tea-break, they asked Meek whether the young vocalist they had brought along could try a couple of numbers. Permission granted, Rod stepped up to the microphone and sang some Elvis Presley and Eddie Cochran songs. But the unpredictable Joe Meek, who was personally overseeing the session, brought it to an early close in typically dramatic fashion. After ten minutes of rasping youthfully around in a bid to get adjusted to his new colleagues, Rod was alarmed to experience Joe's considered opinion: Meek suddenly burst into the studio and blew a giant raspberry in Rod's direction. Meek, who was to commit suicide in a fit of depression in 1967, on the anniversary of Buddy Holly's death, ensured that Rod's first recording opportunity came to nothing.

As he became more heavily involved in music, new influences were having their effect on the impressionable youngster. Rod recalls: 'I was listening to Woody Guthrie and Ramblin' Jack Elliott, and turning into a leftist-Marxist type. You name it, I'd ban it. I skipped across Europe with just a guitar singing songs like "Cocaine All Around My Brain". It was a wonderful experience roaming around Europe. Dylan came out with his first album and that was a turning point. I knew every song from that album – "Fixin' to Die", "Man of Constant Sorrow" – a great album. From there on I decided I'd become a beatnik, hair right down the back, radical left-wing type. My mum and dad more or less kicked me out. I was generally smelly, but that was all part of being wonderfully rebellious. To be anti-social and rebellious you had to smell at the same time.'

Four decades on, it is hard to recall the heady idealism of the new wave of thought that swept the young of the early sixties. Jack Kerouac's *On the Road* philosophy was handed earnestly on from teenager to teenager: they hadn't necessarily read the book, but they still received the rootless message of the new freedom. The poetry of Allen Ginsberg was spouted by nodding duffel-coated devotees in smoky coffee bars. The word 'beatnik' entered the language, and battalions of rebels were launched in relentless search of a cause. The leading candidate was the threat of nuclear war. CND, the Campaign for Nuclear Disarmament, was formed under the leadership of intellectual leaders like Bertrand Russell and Marghanita Laski.

Those idealistic thinkers at the head of the Easter Ban the Bomb marches to Aldermaston were followed by waves of supporting youths. Among them in 1961, 1962 and 1963, protesting at the Atomic Weapons Research Establishment, was the slightly less than totally dedicated Rod Stewart. While others carried the banners, Rod was more concerned about looking good and looking out for girls, although he was genuinely scared and concerned, like many millions around the world, by the Cuban Missile Crisis. Taking his guitar along on the marches, Rod would join a dozen other guitar-carrying protesters on the front of a truck, all strumming the protest anthem 'We Shall Overcome'. One such appearance merited a photograph of Rod in the London *Evening Standard*, sporting a leather deerstalker hat with a leather jacket, white polo-neck jumper and faded denim jeans.

'It was the fashionable thing to do at the time. I did four marches,' recalls Rod. 'We did feel strongly about the bomb, but we had a lot of fun, too. There used to be an awful lot of hanky-panky going on. I remember I was going on a march with a girl, but before we went, I took her home and we had it away under the rug underneath the piano. Few people used to get any sleep on those marches – they turned into mass orgies. Not that I did too much marching. I had another guitar by then and I was in a band – we used to ride in a Land Rover.'

Although he jokes about the seriousness of his feelings, Rod was committed enough to the cause to get himself arrested on three separate occasions at sit-in protests in Trafalgar Square and Whitehall. Their passive resistance tactics had hundreds of CND members carried none too gently to the cells by the men of the Metropolitan Police. This was followed in Rod's case by a brief court appearance and a fine to be paid, inevitably, by Rod's father. The Stewarts may not have completely understood or even approved of what their youngest son was doing but, as with his model railways and his music, they indulged him.

On the annual march Rod, by then proficient on harmonica as well as guitar, recalls CND leader Bertrand Russell walking all the way ('poor old sod') without too strong a twinge of conscience. Rod was more interested in the appeal of available sex and plentiful supplies of alcohol, which made banning the bomb a not totally unpleasant experience.

Rod's memories of his sexual initiation are, perhaps not unsurprisingly, vague. On different occasions he has recalled the loss of his virginity as occurring under the family piano, and under a grubby blanket at the 1960 Beaulieu Jazz Festival with an older woman. He has remembered the latter coupling ending rather prematurely on his part, with consequent irritation on the part of his rather large instructress. 'I was very thin and she was huge, and she jumped on me and it was all over in 22 seconds,' he recalls. 'I wasn't a stud in those days.' The encounter with the woman, called Margaret – he never got to find out her other name – later provided some inspiration for Rod's classic hit 'Maggie May'.

That evening had got off to a somewhat difficult start, when Rod and his group of friends were refused entry to the festival on grounds of being too scruffy – something of an achievement at an outdoor jazz festival. A friendly farmer suggested they used an underground route via some old sewers, which had them happily emerging close to the beer tent.

However Rod's sexual education began, it is clear that once he became interested in matters carnal he was an eager pupil. Perhaps his first serious relationship was with a pretty ex-public-school girl called Suzannah Boffey, who was born in Surrey in March 1945, two months after Rod. Suzannah moved to London as an art student, and met Rod at a club off Shaftesbury Avenue in London's West End. They were both 17, and she says: 'He was my first proper boyfriend and I think I was his first proper girlfriend.' Suzannah was smitten enough with Rod to move to a bed-sit in Muswell Hill, just to be near him. Rod, who was known to everyone as Rod the Mod, Suzannah remembers, was still living at the family home in Highgate. On many an evening Rod would arrive with his guitar and strum away for Suzannah in front of the gas fire, or they would cuddle up and listen to Joan Baez's unmistakable soprano on the record player. Suzannah still has an old black-and-white photograph of her room with its circular mirror, pictures on the wall of top models of the day Jean Shrimpton and Celia Hammond, and a poster advertising the Richmond Jazz Festival.

Suzannah accompanied Rod on his early harmonica stints in London pubs, and together they hitched down to Brighton. But the relationship took a dramatic turn when she announced to Rod that she was pregnant with his baby. 'Looking back, I suppose it was inevitable that I became pregnant,' said Suzannah. 'We had been together all the time for months and we didn't use any contraception.'

Suzannah then went on to confront Rod's mother with the

news. According to Rod, his mother was underwhelmed by the information, and by no means about to force him to do what was then fashionably known as 'the decent thing'. Marriage was certainly not on Rod's schedule. He was not at all sure what he wanted to do with his life, but his plans most definitely did not include settling down and taking a wife at the age of 18, however attractive the obvious candidate for the role might be.

Perhaps the lowest point in this by now increasingly fractious affair came on the beach at Brighton, when Rod and his girl-friend were taking a weekend to try to resolve their situation. His bluntly bachelor attitude to their baby so enraged her that she picked up his guitar, which he had been idly strumming, and crashed the instrument down on some rocks.

A whip-round among Suzannah's friends failed to raise the £22 needed for an abortion and, according to Suzannah, Rod said she would have to have the baby adopted or they would break up.

The distraught girl did have the baby but she no longer had Rod, although he did go to the St Mary's wing of Whittington Hospital in Islington, north London, the night the child was born. With him was one of her closest friends, Chrissie Shrimpton, sister of Jean. In fact, while they waited for news of the birth, Chrissie told Rod about a promising young singer called Mick Jagger she was going out with, and who had a band called the Rolling Stones.

In an era when shame was still sometimes heaped on unmar-ried mothers, Suzannah pretended she was married to her baby Sarah's father and named him as Roderick Boffey, vocalist. Later she returned to the register office and had the birth certificate corrected.

Rod's daughter was adopted, and Rod later reflected that his tough stance on the baby was hard on the young mother, but in the long term best for them both. He was simply not ready for family life.

As they drifted further apart after this unhappy interlude, Rod also found himself moving through the beatnik phase, and towards the way he is popularly remembered. The metamorphosis into Rod the Mod was under way. Girls had certainly entered his life in a big way by this stage, and young Rod had many different ways of attracting the opposite sex. Surely the most bizarre – and least successful – was impersonating jet-setting airline staff, in the hope of lifting off a new romance. Rod recalled years later: 'Me and my mate used to dress up as airline pilots – the whole outfit, with the epaulettes, the hat, the little bag with all the maps in it – and wander around Heathrow trying to pull birds. It didn't work – the accent gave us away.'

One of the reasons why Rod was easing himself out of the beatnik movement was that he resented the way it was gradually being taken over by the less committed, the weekend beats, sneeringly dubbed the 'day-trippers' by full-time drop-outs. Day-trippers had respectable jobs, careers even, during the week and then reached for their joss sticks and duffel coats on Friday nights, whereas Rod's only formal employment at the time extended to the occasional foray into his father's shop to help out.

Rod now moved for a brief period out of the family home to the south coast. He was among a group of 20 beatniks dossing down in a derelict houseboat at Shoreham-by-Sea, Sussex. They had actually attempted a clean-up job on the sad craft, and a sympathetic observer might have described it as almost habitable. But the locals considered it, and the people who lived on board, to be an eyesore. Days were spent sitting around on Brighton beach in increasingly smelly duffel coats, strumming guitars, and in the evening Rod and the others would take it in turns to heat up some stew in a dustbin, albeit a new one bought specially for the purpose.

Again Rod fell foul of the forces of law and order. He recalled: 'All the greybeards in the area didn't like the idea of us all not working, so they got the police to drive us out with hoses of cold water. Then they towed the boat away and sank it so we wouldn't be able to go back, which was just as well really because the boat filled up with water every time the tide came in.'

Unfortunately, some of Rod's pals decided not to leave without a battle and scuffles broke out. A particularly reluctant evictee was a bearded individual known as John the Road. He happened to possess an historic firearm, a musket, which he fired off at the police. John the Road was probably in more danger from the gun than anyone else, but the police were not to know that. For a time all hell broke loose, and locals cheered as most of their unwelcome visitors were hosed into the drink. This incident made page-one news in both the *Daily Mirror* and the now-defunct *Daily Sketch*.

Rod did not last too long as a beatnik. Cord trousers, baggy sweaters and sandals were never going to be his uniform for long. He was too conscious of his looks – the bright and sharp Mod outfits that were coming into fashion were far more his natural style. In fact, clothes have always played an important part in his life. He frequently recalls what he was wearing along with significant moments in his life. For instance, he remembers 'I got my first leather overcoat the day President Kennedy was shot,' and 'I went on holiday to Bognor Regis when I was 15 and I had a little grey jacket that came to just above me backside.'

The rest of the Stewart family were delighted to see the back of the beatnik look. His mother decided to make it an irrevocable fashion change: 'Eventually I returned home with my tail between my legs. I was really smelly and I remember my mum burned all my bloody clothes, all my beatnik clothes. You know how long it takes to get our Levis perfect? I mean, I think I cried. And then me dad told me I had to get me hair cut.'

The posturing, almost effeminate, Mod style of dress could almost have been invented for Rod Stewart. The long hair was swiftly replaced by the forerunner of the spiky pineapple style that has become his trade mark. He borrowed his sisters' hair lacquer and became known for what was always called, in Cockney rhyming slang, a great 'Barnet' (from Barnet Fair – hair). Rod then threw himself enthusiastically into the Mod style: 'In 1963 I completely changed to a Mod, cut my hair off and loved smart clothes.' Having spent the previous two years trying to get him regularly into the bath, Elsie Stewart now discovered she could rarely get him out of the bathroom, as he preened himself and primped his hair in front of the mirror.

One of his first new outfits was a collarless leather Beatles jacket and a polo-neck sweater from the newly opened John Michael shop. This was followed by matelot shirts, washed-out denims and leather jackets in an attempt to give himself a French look.

'I used to have my hair like Dusty Springfield,' said Rod. 'It stood six inches above my head. Bottles of hair lacquer: it was like a rock when you touched it. We used to hold our hair on the Underground platforms so the bouffant wouldn't get blown down when the trains came through.'

The transformation from Rod the Beatnik to Rod the Mod was well under way. And, with his ever-indulgent parents to support him in his endeavours, Rod was now ready to make his mark on the world. His formal education had made little impression, but his musical education was about to begin. At the age of 17 Rod, like many teenagers, had become more than a little disillusioned with rock 'n' roll, and was looking for a different kind of music to latch on to.

After the initial excitement of the first wave of rock 'n' rollers, led by Bill Haley and Elvis Presley, pop music had degenerated into manufactured American teen idols like Frankie Avalon and

Fabian. Bill Haley possessed neither the songwriting ability nor the rebel-youth aura of Elvis, and was starting to repeat the hits of his *annus mirabilis*, 1955–56, when 'Rock Around The Clock' sold 25 million copies. Elvis had been largely silenced by going into the army, Buddy Holly had tragically met an untimely death in a plane crash, Jerry Lee Lewis had been disgraced through his marriage to a 13-year-old second cousin, and Little Richard was preparing to throw his bracelets and jewellery into the sea and return to the church. Suddenly, for teenagers who were dismissive of mainstream pop, the cool music to listen to was rhythm and blues and soul.

When the 17-year-old Rod went to see Booker T. and the MGs, Carla Thomas, Sam and Dave and Otis Redding in a soul package concert at Hammersmith Odeon in London, he became musically hooked for ever. Rod was enthralled by Otis. He was on stage for only half an hour but Rod hung on his every note, and when Otis sang 'These Arms Of Mine', Rod was moved to tears by Redding's soulful and emotive vocal delivery. Then, while working for the silk-screen printing firm the Framery in Kentish Town, Rod heard Sam Cooke singing two of his big hits, 'Chain Gang' and 'Cupid'. Along with Ray Charles, Cooke was the most important precursor of soul music, and Cooke's high, pure tenor voice and smooth delivery shook Rod to the core. Sam Cooke instantly became Rod's idol, and he decided that if he was going to be a singer, he would sing one key above his natural key – just like Sam. 'Anything Sam did, I would do,' Rod later admitted, 'apart from getting shot in a hotel room by a hooker' – a reference to Cooke's untimely death in a shooting incident in 1964, at the age of 33.

Hearing 'Chain Gang' prompted Rod to seek out and explore as many of Cooke's records as he could get his hands on, so he could study his technique. Today he still cites Cooke as his single biggest influence. To listen today to Cooke's record 'At the Copa', when he played the Copacabana, is to hear a blueprint for Rod Stewart's live performances. The Sam Cooke sway also brought about a sartorial, as well as a musical, change in Rod: 'That's when I jumped into a mohair suit.'

Some 30 years later, Rod would acknowledge, in biographical song, the debt of gratitude he owed to seeing Otis Redding in concert and hearing Sam Cooke's hits on the radio. His 'Muddy, Sam and Otis' track, which he was to write for his 1995 album *A Spanner in the Works*, chronicled what he has always regarded as memorable, life-changing moments.

CHAPTER TWO

Bright Lights, Big City

Cars and girls were my life. All I wanted was a Triumph Spitfire so I could park outside a pub and pull. Rod Stewart

A diverse group of musicians influenced the young Rod Stewart: Brummie blues singer Jimmy Powell gave him a start in his Five Dimensions; Long John Baldry saw the raw talent; Brian Auger provided some hard lessons in life on the road; and Jeff Beck found himself upstaged in his own band. But first there was Raymond 'Wizz' Jones.

Raymond had earned the nickname Wizz at school because he fancied himself as a bit of a magician. He welcomed the tag; it was far better than boring Raymond, he decided, and it all helped towards trying to establish an interesting identity out of his somewhat mundane, working-class roots in Croydon.

Like millions of youngsters in the USA and Britain in the fifties, Wizz was influenced by Bill Haley. Before he ever picked up a guitar, Wizz bought himself a black plastic jacket, painted Haley's lyrical catchphrase 'See you later Alligator' on the back, and went to see Bill Haley at the cinema – and got thrown out – every night of the week.

But he managed to see enough to know that he wanted to

play guitar, and when the Soho jazz scene gave way to skiffle and then embraced folk music, Wizz determined to be a part of it. He began busking around Soho, and one day he found the 17-year-old Rod Stewart beside him, joining in. Days later, he was sitting in a pub called Finch's in Goodge Street, idly strumming a few chords, when suddenly Rod appeared again. He whipped his harmonica out of his pocket and the two began playing together, before setting off in the general direction of Leicester Square, to busk in the streets.

Rod's enthusiasm for the harmonica had first been sparked by veteran American blues singer Sonny Boy Williamson, who used the instrument to such haunting effect on his 1963 tour of Britain. Then, that summer, the Beatles' first record 'Love Me Do' also featured prominent harmonica, and Bob Dylan would soon be blowing in the wind. The harmonica was becoming fashionable, and Rod found it easier to play the 'harp', as they then called it, than the guitar, especially after copying a young rival on the music scene, Mick Jagger. Rod later recalled: 'An important thing I learned at that time was how to play the harmonica properly. That was through watching Mick do it. I realised I had been sucking when I should have been blowing and vice versa.'

Buskers were still something of a novelty in London's West End, and Wizz and Rod certainly had curiosity value. It was not every day that you would find a scruffy Bohemian from Croydon and a snappily dressed Scot from Highgate singing in the middle of Leicester Square a skiffle and jug band standard called 'San Francisco Bay Blues', written by Jesse Fuller from Jonesboro, Georgia.

'We'd get an enormous crowd,' recalls Wizz, 'and we'd work it like a circus, with people looking out for the police. I often spent the night in the nick for busking and Rod must have done, too. You have to be quite extrovert to work the streets. I could turn that on, but in the beginning Rod was shy in front of an audience.' Wizz, at that time, was also a far more accomplished musician than Rod, to the extent that Rod once stormed off in a fit of petulance, simply because Wizz was playing so well he felt he wasn't good enough to keep up with him.

But Rod was eager to learn, and when one of his heroes, Derrol Adams, appeared at the Halfmoon, the famous music venue in Putney, Rod made sure he caught his performance, and made a point of carefully scrutinising every chord.

Wizz's great dream was to open a club in London, to emulate the blues club run at the Roundhouse by Cyril Davies and Alexis Korner. Eventually he found a room upstairs in a pub called the Porcupine, in Leicester Square, and one of Wizz's earliest recollections of Rod was an argument at the door about Rod's unwillingness to pay to get in. 'Then he stood at the back and heckled,' Wizz recalls.

It was Wizz who first showed Rod the have-guitar-will-travel nomadic life of a musician and invited him on 'raves', as Wizz called them, to Brighton. Rod, Wizz and their pals would all turn out of the Soho coffee bars and walk some three miles to Waterloo Station, where they would catch the milk train to Brighton and arrive at six in the morning, ready to hit the town. 'It was before the Mods and Rockers' fights,' Wizz stresses. 'We were more gentle. We just wanted to be noticed.'

After the Shoreham escapade, Rod had decided to ease himself out of the beatnik scene, and so he and Wizz headed for France, taking with them two ten-guinea Spanish guitars, fitted with the steel strings they could bend more easily to suit their bluesy style. They hitched to Dover, caught a ferry over the English Channel, and then thumbed a ride to Paris, where Wizz taught Rod the essentials of busking on foreign soil.

Over a period of 18 months, the pair went on several such trips. They would arrive in Paris, find a decent hotel, leave their passports with the concierge as security, then go off and busk. 'We could earn enough to live in a good hotel, have a couple of decent meals a day, and have enough to pay for taxis to get us from one pitch to another alongside the cinema queues,' Wizz proudly remembers. 'Sometimes we slept rough but generally it was a great life.'

Rod remembers those nights spent trying to sleep under bridges over the River Seine or under the Eiffel Tower as the harshest of his life. 'Towards the end of summer it was so windy and wet and uncomfortable sleeping on concrete,' he says. 'But looking back, it was all fun.'

A favourite busking area for Rod were the cafés of St-Germain-des-Prés on the left bank of the Seine. As he gratefully accepted the odd French franc for his entertainment, Rod can hardly have imagined that some years later he would be back frequenting the same cafés as a multimillionaire, with an adoring supermodel like Rachel Hunter on his arm.

'It was amazing,' Rod recounted in 1999, 'because I was there about four years ago, and I used to busk at St-Germain on the Left Bank with all those wonderful cafés, and I was sitting there with Rachel and this guy came along singing and strumming just like I used to, and he was singing "Tonight's The Night".' Did Rod put his hand in his pocket to reward the busker for strumming one of his great hits? 'Oh **** off!' came the laughing reply.

When other buskers followed the same Paris trail and the market became overcrowded, Rod made off for Spain, where he continued to busk but with less success. 'I went all over France and Spain on three pounds – not bad going,' Rod boasted. 'We could make 50 francs an hour in St Tropez.' When his money ran out in Spain, he took to sleeping under the arches of Barcelona's massive football stadium. Eventually, he was turfed out of the stadium by the Spanish police and, along with some other impecunious British nomads, was apprehended as a vagrant and taken down to the police station. Finally, the British Consulate was asked to repatriate Rod and he was flown home to London.

Back in Highgate and safe in the bosom of his family, he was able to have his first proper bath in weeks while his father, disgusted at the filthy state of the clothes that Rod had been wearing for so long, insisted the garments could easily have walked back home of their own accord.

Wizz, meanwhile, ploughed his folkie furrow and the busking duo gradually grew apart. Wizz was surprised when Rod turned up in the Hoochie Coochie Men two years later, and was truly amazed at how much Rod had learned. He says: 'Everyone copied each other. I learned all my licks from Davy Graham [a seminal early sixties folkie] and Rod used to watch and learn from me. I'd never realised he was going to be such a great singer. He didn't have that wonderful rasp in his voice then, that must have come from singing on the streets, where you really have to force your voice.'

At the time, partly because of his distinctive hairstyle, Rod was regarded as a bit of a joker by his fellow musicians-on-the-make. However, as Wizz now ruefully accedes: 'When he came up with those solo albums I was knocked out, because he had done what we had all been trying to do. Rod had been inspired by raw acoustic folk music and he had taken it, put it into a rock form, and come up with something new.'

Another singer to spot the untapped potential of the strange young man in Mod's clothing was an energetic if unsophisticated young blues singer from Birmingham called Jimmy Powell. With his throaty renditions of blues classics, Jimmy had built up a big reputation on the Midlands circuit with his band Jimmy Powell and the Detours, which then went on to become the Dimensions. He made something of a national impact when he hit the lower reaches of the charts in 1960, with the rasping 'Sugar Baby'. Jimmy had made enough trips down to London to sing on the same bills as better-known bands like Cyril Davies All Stars, to realise that the capital was the place to be.

London was just swinging into the sixties and music venues like the Crawdaddy, the Manor House, Johnny's Jazz Club, Eel Pie Island and the Marquee sprang up. 'It was a fantastic time for music,' says Jimmy. 'We didn't know then we were in on the start of a musical revolution. We just knew we were having a bloody good time. Every pub, every club needed music. If you were in a band you were in demand.' By 1963 Jimmy Powell and the Dimensions had won a regular Monday night booking at the Studio 51 club in Newport Street, London, owned by jazz trumpeter and bandleader Ken Colyer.

Rod was then just another would-be musician. He played the guitar not too badly, blew an enthusiastic harp, and sang in a voice that still had a long way to develop into the rasping tones that have become his trade mark. Rod joined in the many jam sessions and sang and played with different friends but he was not in a group. In between trips to the Continent he lived at home, and worked in his brother's business, painting signs and making picture frames for London shops. Jimmy Powell had decided that a harmonica player and occasional second singer would add yet another dimension to the Dimensions, and so he asked the youngster to join. It was not a happy experience.

The received wisdom on Rod Stewart's spell with his first professional group is that Rod eventually left because Jimmy Powell would not let him sing. Jimmy does not remember it quite that way.

'When I first saw Rod Stewart he was sitting in the corner playing a 12-string guitar during our interval. He was always a bit different. We all had long hair down our backs but he already had the puffed-up Mod style. When we got to know him and heard him sing I knew he had a good voice, but it was not the distinctive sound that it is today.' However, Powell decided it was good enough for his purposes.

'When I gave him the job I told him just to start playing some harmonica backing. Then I'd come play some harmonica and we'd have a bit of a war on stage. Then I told him to sing a couple of numbers and I'd come on and take over. He was hired as second singer. The idea was that after his numbers there'd be a big riff and it would be "Introducing Jimmy Powell ..." and I'd leap on and away we'd go.

'At first it worked great. We did very, very well. I remember we played Ken Collyer's jazz club in Newport Street. Ken booked us to do a blues night every Monday. It went ape-shit. We did an absolute stormer. Then he took on another band called the Rolling Stones to do Thursday nights and that went a stormer, and then he booked the Pretty Things to do Friday and that went a stormer.

'We all used to be mates and help each other out in those days. We all did the same circuit and then Georgie Fame came on the scene, and Geno and the Ram Jam Band and Jimmy James. London at that time was just fantastic.

'But Rod was always somebody who was never going to finish up as the second singer. He wanted to be *the* singer. Even from the start he would want to play all the best numbers. And he would snatch the band when I wasn't around and rehearse the best numbers with them. Then he would stick two or three more numbers on to the end of his spot, and I would be stuck there waiting like a lemon to come on, and he wouldn't come off.

'He would go on and do three or four or five more numbers. We would have rows but he didn't change. Rod was totally demanding, a very demanding person. He wanted everything he wanted doing when he wanted it. Of course, at that time he never got away with that because I was top of the band, and that was that.'

As time went on, though, Rod's spell with Jimmy Powell and the Dimensions became more and more fraught. Jimmy recognised Rod's undoubted talents as a singer, but he was not going to step down from his own band to ease Rod's path. In the end he didn't have to.

'In one paper years later Rod said he left Jimmy Powell because I wouldn't let him sing,' says Jimmy. 'But that was just his off-beat comment. I wouldn't let him sing all night because they were booking *me* and he didn't like that. He was very, very disruptive. He was so fucking disruptive. He just wanted to be the star of stage, screen and music hall. All the time.

'In the end he nicked my band. He wanted to go on his own. We were approached by the agency that was bringing over Chuck Berry. I didn't know about it at the time, but from what I can gather Rod and some of the lads got hold of the approach, cottoned on to it, spoke to this guy and they were offering megabucks to back this tour. Rod saw it as an opportunity to snaffle the band and get away from me and snatch it for himself, which he did. But he didn't last with the band that long after that. After the Chuck Berry tour, that was it, and it was a pretty disastrous tour. It was the time when Chuck was shouting abuse to people all over the country, and the thing closed down short of where it should have done.'

And so Jimmy Powell and the Dimensions dissolved into sorry disarray.

Before that stage, Powell claims to have had his difficulties with Rod, who frequently simply refused to do as he was told. On one occasion, Powell recalls that they turned up to play at a Rockers' venue called the 69 Club. Rod refused to go on. Powell insisted. They ended up having a stand-up row in the dressing room.

Jimmy Powell was, though, an early witness to the rapid development of both Rod's idiosyncratic clothes sense and his 'star quality'. He says: 'Rod was always different. There was always something about him. Even then he used to wear outrageous gear, and instead of underpants he used to wear ladies' knickers. Not because he was bent, but because he had to do something different.'

And, despite the acrimony of their final parting, Powell recognised Rod's talent: 'Rod was always different ... I knew he had something. He was a very determined lad. He would set his mind on something and go for it ... He was a fucking nightmare of a bloke to manage, but having said that he did have a skill and he did have a talent. I could see that.'

Decades later, mellowed by age, Jimmy Powell was able to look back on his days with Rod Stewart with a certain wry distance. As he put it: 'Rod Stewart was just one bad experience in a great life for me. I knew I'd never have his fame or his life, but I wouldn't want it. Music took me from a council house in the back streets of Birmingham to all sorts of amazing experiences.'

Not surprisingly, Rod remembers his time with the Dimensions slightly differently. 'I joined the Dimensions,' he says, 'before Jimmy Powell had joined. I was the bona fide harmonica player-cum-singer in me tweed trousers and leather jacket. It was never put down officially that it was Jimmy Powell's Dimensions. I remember every time we went along to try to get a recording contract everybody would frown on me for not being clean-cut. When I was singing with the Dimensions I was an amateur singer. I was not being paid too many pennies for doing so.'

Describing his time with the band to the music paper *New Musical Express*, Rod said: 'I was just the harmonica player and I did two numbers a night, the Beatles' "Love Me Do" and the Stones "Come On" – then I went home. But to me it was great being up there on stage. I used to dress up immaculately to do my two numbers. I don't actually ever remember picking up a wage [from Powell]. I think they thought: "Oh he's a silly bastard, likes being up on stage, don't give him any money.'"

Whatever the truth of the matter, it is generally regarded that Rod made his first appearance on record during his time with Jimmy Powell and the Five Dimensions, playing the harmonica on the 1964 hit 'My Boy Lollipop' by Jamaica's Millie Small, which reached number two in the British charts on 12 March. However, Jimmy Powell insists that this is just one of the many myths about Rod Stewart. Jimmy recalls: 'Everybody gives Rod the credit for playing but that is not strictly true. I did it. I played the harmonica with Millie because at that time I was recording for Chris Blackwell at Island Records [Millie's record label]. Rod was with my band at that time, but I played the harmonica.

'I guess that, because Rod was with me at the time and because he went on to become the known name, Chris forgot and thought it was maybe Rod Stewart, but it wasn't ... Chris just said come and play the harmonica one night and I did.'

Rod's first big break came in 1964, when he met blues singer Long John Baldry. Not too many blues singers come out of Haddon in Derbyshire, but Baldry was a young man who would have stood out in any crowd. He was a towering 6ft 7in tall and, with his fair hair and lanky, boyish features, he was a natural front-man for the wide range of groups he gigged with in the Soho pubs and coffee bars in the mid-fifties.

Baldry loved to sing the blues, and he started to build up a following from the moment he got up to sing with Alexis Korner and Cyril Davies at their folk/blues club, the Roundhouse. By 1961 Baldry had joined Korner's first permanent line-up, Blues Incorporated, who appeared regularly at the Crawdaddy Club in Ealing and at the Marquee, where they secured a residency leading a 'Blues Evening' on Tuesdays.

Towards the end of 1962 Davies left to form Cyril Davies All Stars, and when Baldry joined him in 1963, the group quickly became a major attraction on the London club scene. They produced two singles that year and appeared to be going places but, unknown to Baldry, Davies was desperately ill with leukaemia. It was his sudden death that was to pave the way for Rod Stewart.

The band's last gigs with Davies were at Eel Pie Island, a club situated on an island in the middle of the River Thames at Richmond, on the outskirts of London. On 7 January 1964, the contented crowd of R 'n' B followers who drifted away from the club after an All Stars gig included Rod, harmonica in pocket as usual, and at the time not attached to any band in particular. He made his way to Twickenham Station to catch the train to Waterloo, on his way home, and settled himself on a bench on the platform. The night was cold, damp and foggy, and as he waited for his train on the station bench underneath a dim gas light, Rod blew a few wailing notes from his harmonica into the icy night air.

Also waiting to catch a train home was Baldry, who had hurried away from the club. 'The platform was deserted, all sound quite deadened by the pea-soup fog,' Baldry remembers. 'Suddenly down the platform through the mist I heard this harmonica riff from "Smokestack Lightning". Sounds good, sounds pretty authentic, sounds just like Howlin' Wolf, I thought. It was coming from this figure wearing a Mod-style belted black leather coat, huddled up in a mass of scarves. Then this nose appeared. It was Rod.'

Baldry got chatting and learned that Rod had attended his show at Eel Pie Island, had enjoyed his performance, lived near him in Highgate and was interested in the blues.

Recalling that night, Rod says: 'I was coming back to London, and so was John. We were both supposed to be going in the same direction to London though we were on different platforms. John was on the right one because I was probably drunk.

Then he shouted: "Young man!" and came running over the bridge.'

Baldry, always looking for new talent, asked Rod if he'd like to come along to a jam session the following Wednesday, with a view possibly to joining Baldry's band. Rod said he'd love to. Until that moment the thought of earning his living full-time as a professional musician had never seriously crossed Rod's mind. 'If I hadn't been so drunk I would probably have turned the offer down flat,' he reflected.

'I was inviting him to come and play the harmonica,' says Baldry. 'I had no idea that he sang as well, but he suddenly said: "Do you mind if I sing a couple of songs?" He was a nervous wreck, but he went down so well that I offered him a job there and then.'

Before Rod set off for the jam session, Baldry was surprised to get a call from Rod's mother, asking him to make sure he didn't bring her son home late. Baldry was surprised at the request, as Rod was then approaching his 19th birthday and was well able to look after himself. However, Baldry was living in South Hill Park, south Hampstead, at the time, not far from where Rod's family lived, and so in fact it was no big deal for him to drop the prodigal son off on his way home. This was to become a regular event.

Baldry gained the impression that at the time Rod's parents were fairly set against him pursuing a singing career. He had been in and out of so many things in his teenage years, they must have been thinking, 'Oh God, what is he going to do now?' But after Rod had worked with Baldry for a while, they saw that he was happier than he had ever been in a nine to five job and that it was not just a frivolous way of life, so they began to come to terms with the idea. Rod had no difficulty in coming to terms with Baldry's offer to join the band for £35 a week. 'That was a lot of money in the sixties, and did I know how to spend it!' said Rod.

An early purchase was a Morris Minor Traveller which he used to take girlfriends out on dates. But Rod also showed a shrewd financial instinct when he spent £20, more than half a weekly Baldry pay packet, on an old oak Japanese lacquered chair which he bought from an antique shop on Chelsea's trendy King's Road.

Rod's impact on that first jam session with Baldry was less than memorable. 'He did "Bright Lights, Big City" and didn't go down too well,' Baldry remembers. But just days later, Cyril Davies died from a form of leukaemia at the age of 32.

His tragic death spelled the end of the All Stars and was a devastating blow for Baldry. It was another five months before he formed a new band called the Hoochie Coochie Men. The line-up was fluid, but Rod was enlisted as a permanent member on harmonica and back-up vocals.

At Rod's début at Manchester University, he was almost sick with nerves. He knew only one number, 'Night Time Is The Right Time', and he had had just the one rehearsal.

'Don't worry, just get up there and sing,' said Baldry and, as further encouragement, one of the band gave Rod a black bomber pill, promising him it would do wonders for his first-night nerves. Rod knew absolutely nothing about drugs and gulped down the pill.

It certainly had the desired effect. To the amazement of the university students, Rod leaped out on stage and somehow managed to make 'Night Time Is The Right Time' last a full 45 minutes, by singing the first two verses over and over again. 'I was up for about three days but I didn't half sing that number,' Rod later recalled of his chemically enhanced performance.

The audience didn't know whether to laugh or cry. There was a smattering of sympathetic applause, but Rod was so disheartened that he would happily have given up there and then. But Baldry admired Rod's spirit, and at subsequent rehearsals in

Soho cellars, he was pleasantly surprised to find he could successfully duet with Rod. Rod's place in the Hoochie Coochie Men was assured.

Baldry struck a deal with Rod that he would pay him ten per cent of everything the band earned. At that time the band could command between £30 and £40 a night, but by doubling and sometimes trebling their nightly gigs, Rod's wages began to mount up. It was hardly a fortune, Rod felt, but it was a tidy sum for singing a handful of songs a few nights a week. Better still, it all helped towards the £300 he was desperately trying to save up, to buy the bird-pulling sports car he had set his heart on. 'Cars and girls were my life. All I wanted was a Triumph Spitfire so I could park outside a pub and pull,' Rod admitted.

'Rod was a frugal person even back then,' Baldry remembers. 'Before he got involved with banks he put all his money into the Post Office and his only real expense was clothes. He didn't smoke and he didn't drink that much. If it was free he'd indulge, but I can only recall Rod being out of it drunk two or three times in all the time he worked for me.'

But when he felt the occasional need for Dutch courage to get up on stage, Rod would have no difficulty in knocking back three pints of Newcastle Brown then chasing it down with a Scotch. One night such over-imbibing took its toll and Rod left the stage mid-song, desperate to relieve himself, and raced upstairs to the lavatory. Alas he couldn't quite get there in time and grabbing a mug he peed into it. Alas for Rod, his intake had been such that the mug unfortunately overflowed, and when he rushed back downstairs to finish the song, the overflow was dribbling through the ceiling from the floorboards above. 'Long John went mad,' Rod remembers.

This mishap apart, Rod was mostly the very picture of self-restraint in his early gigging days but later, of course, when the Faces were on the road, it was a different matter.

From the outset it was clear that Baldry, with his already size-able following, was always going to be the lead vocalist. Rod did not begrudge Baldry taking centre stage because he had a healthy regard for Baldry's musical roots. Baldry had quickly turned Rod on to Muddy Waters, one of a select group of American artists whose work altered the landscape of popular music. His record-ings for Chicago-based Chess Records transformed his native delta blues into a music with widespread popular appeal interna-tionally, thereby laying a huge chunk of rock 'n' roll's foundation.

In particular a 1960 album called *Muddy Waters at Newport* had a profound influence on the then-emerging young white blues musicians, including Rod. Baldry seemed to have the only copy of the album in London, and Rod took it in turns with Mick Jagger and Keith Relf, singer with the Yardbirds, to borrow it. Rod retains a passionate reverence for Muddy Waters to this day. From Muddy Waters, Rod went on to listen to Jimmy Reed and John Lee Hooker. 'Blues came after being a folkie,' he says.

As Rod grew in confidence, Baldry generously allowed him more prominence at gigs. 'He was an impressive singer from the word go,' Baldry stresses. 'I was in awe of him as a singer even at that early age. Amazing. His voice was higher-pitched then, but there was a bit of Sam Cooke in there even in the early days. After a while he got fed up with just playing harmonica, and so he just sang and didn't even bother to bring the harmonica along any more. We used to do a lot of the Muddy Waters catalogue and Jimmy Witherspoon-type songs, and we duetted on quite a few numbers. But there was no rivalry between us, and Rod was very different from me. He had his hair back-combed up with spray, as if to see who could get the highest beehive. In many cases, club owners would bill us as Long John Baldry and the Hoochie Coochie Men with Rod "the Mod" Stewart. Lots of people used to say to me: "How can you let him take the spotlight, it's your show?" But I've never been greedy for the limelight.'

On stage, though, Rod would hide in corners or behind the amps. Sometimes, despite Baldry's chastisement, he would even sing with his back to the audience. According to Baldry, Rod was an extremely shy performer and an extremely shy individual, 'apart from when he was tracking down tarts – he wasn't so shy then'.

But even then there were distractions; Rod's old pal Rod Sopp was one. Sopp recalls fondly: 'Many times Rod and I would meet up in a pub, have a drink, then go off in my car. We always seemed to finish up forgetting the time, so Rod would be very late for the gig and Baldry would go mad.'

Baldry's long apprenticeship on the blues and R 'n' B scene ensured that the Hoochie Coochie Men got off to a reasonable start in London, and soon they secured a regular Thursday night residency at the Marquee in Oxford Street. A special thrill for Rod was the night they supported Sonny Boy Williamson in March 1964, to celebrate the Marquee's switch to new premises in Wardour Street. Later that year Rod would record Sonny Boy Williamson's 'Good Morning Little Schoolgirl'.

At one Baldry gig north of London at the Railway Hotel, Watford, there was a young lad in the crowd called Reg Dwight from Pinner who harboured hopes of a career in music himself. The future Elton John recalls: 'Rod came out and did two or three songs with the biggest hair and incredible outfit and stage presence, confidence and cockiness and then this great voice.'

Another to catch an early Rod Stewart performance on stage, this time at Eel Pie Island, was Jim Cregan, later to become not only one of Rod's greatest friends but co-writer and guitarist in Rod's live backing band in the eighties. During that early sighting of Rod, Cregan thought it was a bit strange to observe him singing three songs with a hankie up his sleeve.

Also in the audience at Eel Pie Island to see one of Rod's early appearances was a budding young keyboard player called Ian 'Mac' McLagan. But Mac was none too impressed with Rod's vocals. He thought he screamed rather than sang and the screams tended to be either very sharp or very flat. But he felt Rod had some kind of presence and considerable courage for getting up on stage in a three-button hand-me-down suit, a shirt with long pointed collars, a tightly knotted tie, trousers which stopped short of his ankles, and a bouffant hairdo. But the girls, Mac noted, seemed to go for Rod.

In fact, quite unknown to each other, Mac and Rod, later to team up in the Faces, were sharing more than just an interest in music that night at Eel Pie Island. A pretty girl called Linda was secretly dividing her time equally between them but, much to their chagrin, without dispensing any amorous favours to either of them beyond enthusiastic necking. So determined was she to thwart any wandering hands that she had safety-pinned her bra straps together. Rod and Mac only found out years later that they had shared similar frustration with Linda when, at a Faces rehearsal, Rod was talking about some girl called Linda he had gone out with. Slowly the penny dropped. Mac asked: 'Did she have a safety pin in her bra?' Rod said: 'Yeah, that's the one.' They eventually worked it out.

As word began to spread about the Hoochie Coochie Men, the band found themselves being booked seven nights a week, with as many as three gigs a night at weekends. They were especially popular in the north of England, which involved a lot of travelling. However, Rod's first taste of life on the road was hardly in the style to which he was later to become accustomed. The chauffeur-driven stretch limos with blacked-out windows and the private jets were still a world away. As one of the Hoochie Coochie Men, Rod had to travel in the back of a yellow ex-Bovril truck, which Baldry had bought to cart the group's gear around.

Baldry paid the sum of £40 for the truck, which looked like an old-fashioned removal van, and spent a few extra pounds having windows cut in the side to make it less gloomy for the occupants. He also had the interior lined with tongue-and-groove cladding, and old aircraft seats installed in the back. It offered little in the way of comfort, especially on the long winter hauls to and from the northern clubs, colleges and dance-halls.

As Rod lived in Highgate, north London, he was usually the last member of the band to be picked up as the Hoochie Coochie Men headed towards the M1 motorway. He would clamber into the van and settle down among the amps and speakers, occasionally getting up to move closer to its only form of heating, an old tubular open paraffin stove tied to the floor with ropes. 'It was a death trap,' Baldry concedes. 'Can you imagine what would have happened if we had had any kind of an accident?'

Rod and the rest of the band also had to come to terms with the terrifying antics at the wheel of their driver, Mad Harry. An eccentric former RAF fighter pilot, Mad Harry's other main duty was to announce the band on stage at each gig, while dressed in 1930s tails with his service medals pinned proudly to his chest, and to ask the crowd to show their appreciation at the end.

Mad Harry treated Baldry's beloved ex-Bovril truck as though it really was an aeroplane. He had the dashboard fitted out with altimeters and an array of other aircraft dials and instruments, and would climb behind the wheel wearing his leather flying helmet. When it was 'chocks away', he propelled the truck to the next gig at heart-stopping speed. His favourite manoeuvre on the way to Eel Pie Island was to career round a corner and nearly pull the truck over on its side into the Thames, a terrifying spin at the best of times, but bordering on a death wish with an oil-fuelled stove perched precariously in the back.

Baldry soon became disenchanted with that hair-raising trick and caught the train whenever possible. Pianist Ian Armit, a Scot who later moved to Switzerland, was so terrified that he could stand it no longer and went out and bought a car. But for Rod it was all a new and exciting adventure.

Much to Mad Harry's chagrin, the truck eventually died its death in Newcastle. Rod and the rest of the band were forced to make an ignominious arrival at their Newcastle University gig on the back of a tow truck.

As the months went by, Rod and Baldry forged a strong friendship that was to last throughout the sixties. They remain good friends to this day. Baldry's family also took a liking to Rod, especially his great-aunt Polly who was in her nineties and developed a great affection for him.

Rod's only major set-to with Baldry, in all the years they worked together, was born out of Rod's jealousy when Baldry was called in to appear as a guest star on a Beatles TV show called *Around the Beatles*. The show occupied a considerable amount of Baldry's time during the month of May 1964, and one night Baldry was unable to travel with the rest of the band to a gig in Portsmouth, on England's south coast, because he was required at the TV studios.

Instead, he decided to follow on later by train but arrived late, to find the band were already on and Rod having a tough job holding things together on his own. Baldry recalls: 'He got very annoyed and called me out from the stage, screaming something to the effect "I don't know why the fuck you bothered to show up." I got furious at him publicly insulting me like that. We had a big shouting match backstage afterwards.' Rod was duly sacked and dissolved into tears. He never thought for a moment that people got sacked in show business. However, they rapidly patched up their differences.

Indeed, Rod and Baldry became such good pals that some suspected they might be more than that, especially when the following graffiti was daubed on the walls of the gents' toilets at Eel

Pie Island: 'Next week: Ada Baldry and her Hoochie Coochie Ladies featuring Phyllis Stewart'. 'I don't know whether it was Ginger Baker who wrote it on the wall, but it was Ginger who coined the phrase,' says Baldry of the drummer who anchored the supergroup Cream. 'Ginger always referred to me as Ada.'

Rod and Baldry just laughed at the rumours but there was one night, however, when the two men found themselves sharing a bed in a Birmingham hotel after a late-night gig. The band arrived at the hotel in the early hours of the morning, only to discover the place appeared to be almost derelict. Exhausted and bleary-eyed they banged on the door, which was warily opened by an old woman who explained that there had clearly been a dreadful mix-up over the reservations, because the hotel was due to be demolished and work had already started.

The look of confusion on the faces of Rod and the other band members quickly gave way to desperation. At that hour there was no question of them being able to find alternative accommodation. Finally the woman took pity and agreed that they could come in and put their heads down for what was left of the night. At least there would be a roof over their heads.

Any hopes the band had that the remnant of the hotel would rate even one star in any accommodation guide quickly faded as they stepped inside. What was left of the premises was primitive in the extreme and pretty filthy. Rod and Baldry were shown into a room with bare floorboards and grimy walls, where the air was thick with dust. The room was empty except for a single bed in one corner.

The two singers glanced at each other, thought about tossing a coin for it, then agreed that as it was now past four in the morning and they were both in need of some shut-eye, the only reasonable solution was for them to share the bed. Wearily, they slipped between the covers, turned their backs on each other and closed their eyes.

A few minutes later, Baldry was all but asleep when he became conscious of something furry rubbing against his backside. What the hell was going on, he wondered. More to the point, what the hell was Rod up to? Rousing himself from his soporific state, Baldry sat bolt upright in bed and turned to face Rod, whom he found also sitting bolt upright with a similarly puzzled expression on his face. For a split second the two men looked accusingly at each other, then Baldry suddenly threw back the covers. There, nestling cosily between them and blinking up at the intrusion, was a huge fluffy cat.

The graffiti may have temporarily sown seeds of doubt in some minds about Rod's sexual preferences. Indeed, at one gig up north, when Rod's beehive hairdo was in its pomp, a girl in the audience shouted up at Rod: 'Are you a girl or a boy?' Rod's reply was: 'Come up here and I'll show you.' But Rod was always one for the girls, as Baldry consistently discovered, once he moved out of his Victorian mansion garden flat in Hampstead to a much more convenient home in central London. He was now to discover that his friendship regularly extended to letting Rod use his flat in which to entertain his ladies. (Rod was still living at home at the time.) The flat was in Reece Mews and ideally placed on two counts: it was close to the then highly fashionable nightclub the Cromwellian, which had become a popular haunt for pop stars, actresses and models, and it was also but a few steps from South Kensington tube station, from which an increasing number of mini-skirted dolly birds emerged clutching directions Rod had given them.

To accommodate them, Baldry obligingly took himself off to a pub or to see a movie, leaving Rod the run of the flat in which to explore the fruits of his burgeoning sex appeal. 'Rod was a great one for the girls,' Baldry remembers. 'He always had a tart in every port, as it were. And they weren't all blondes. I seem to recall quite a few black-haired witches as well. He was pretty active.' Many years later, after observing Rod's hectic love life via the newspapers in Vancouver where he based himself, Baldry added: 'He's just a randy old sod, and gets away with it every time.'

Old drinking pal Rod Sopp recalls: 'Rod was always very gentlemanly with girls. Even then, when he was in his teens, he would always open doors for females and pull chairs out for them.

'I don't think he and I ever pulled a pair of birds together except once when we got hold of a couple of grippers together in Belsize Park. We went to their bloody awful flat and there was a lot of grunting going on but he was missing out and so was I.'

Long John Baldry was good for Rod musically, in every way. 'He was very important in bringing blues to the British Isles,' says Rod, 'and without John's influence the Rolling Stones, the Yardbirds, so many of us may never have existed. So I take my hat off to him.'

On 19 June 1964, Rod Stewart's voice made it on to his very first recording, when he was featured on Sister Rosetta Tharpe's song 'Up Above My Head', which formed the B side of Baldry's single 'You'll Be Mine'.

It was a great moment for Rod to hear his voice on wax for the first time. But he was impatient for much bigger things that summer, as pop groups seemed to be mushrooming everywhere and gaining the kind of huge success he craved. That summer of 1964, Manfred Mann, the Spencer Davis Group, the Rolling Stones, the Beatles, the Kinks, Georgie Fame and the Blue Flames, Herman's Hermits, and the Animals all topped the charts – and all were British groups.

Baldry also included Rod on his album *Long John's Blues* of the same year, even if it was only singing the chorus with P. J. Proby on 'Got My Mojo Working'.

But while Rod was pleased to be featured on Baldry's records, he was naturally desperate for his own record deal. And that was proving elusive. 'Four or five record companies turned me down, saying my voice was too rough and gruff and I didn't look pretty enough,' revealed a disconsolate Rod.

But five years after being given a guitar by his dad, Rod at last landed a solo deal with Decca Records in 1964. Mike Vernon, a Decca staff producer, saw Rod performing at the Marquee and signed him to a solo recording deal. Rod was finally getting his chance at a time when Decca's other major signing of the time, the Rolling Stones, had just notched up their first number one hit, 'It's All Over Now'.

Rod had often seen the Stones playing to audiences of just 20 people with Jagger sitting on a stool to sing, and now he couldn't help but feel a pang of jealousy that the band were not only top of the charts, but causing their first fan riots on tour in Britain, with the girls going wild for the lead singer.

On 3 September 1964, an excited Rod arrived at Decca's studio in Broadhurst Gardens, west Hampstead (later to become the home of the English National Opera) to record several tracks from which one would be chosen to be released as his début single. Unfortunately in his enthusiasm Rod had mixed up the dates. When he eagerly presented himself at the studio, the receptionist icily informed him that he was precisely one week early. Cursing his mistake, Rod trudged home with instructions to return in seven days' time.

On 10 September 1964, even more unfortunately, he overslept. Studio time means money, and there were some anxious faces at Decca's number two studio when there was no sign of Rod at 11 a.m., the time the recording session was due to begin. When he still had not appeared after the best part of an hour, a call was put through to his parents' shop, where Rod's mother revealed that her Roddy was still in bed. When Rod came to the phone he was full of apologies, explaining that he had had a very late night. He was urged to jump in a cab and get down to the studio straight away. But Rod protested that he could not afford a taxi. 'Just get a taxi and we'll pay this end,' he was told.

Finally he arrived, the cabbie was paid, and it appeared that the day had been saved. Then Rod revealed that he had not learned the songs that had been orchestrated for him because he didn't like them. He felt they were too commercial. By now tempers were becoming somewhat frayed in the studio, and Rod was pointedly asked which songs the débutant would deign to record. When he said he had heard some numbers he liked on Sonny Boy Williamson's new LP, the question that naturally followed was: 'Have you got the music with you?'

Sheepishly, Rod had to admit that he did not have the music with him but he had seen a copy of the LP in a record shop, on his way to the studio. He volunteered to go and buy it so that the session musicians could listen to it, and pick up the chord progressions to reproduce for his recording. There was further embarrassment for Rod and more exasperation for his producers, when he then announced that he didn't have the necessary £2 on him to purchase the record. The sum was duly handed over so he could go and buy it. The LP was finally played into the studio over the speakers by the Decca sound engineers, and the musicians put together an arrangement to suit Rod's vocals. This was how Rod's first single, 'Good Morning Little Schoolgirl', arrived on vinyl. The B side was 'I'm Gonna Move To The Outskirts Of Town', from the same Sonny Boy Williamson LP.

The whole recording session cost the princely sum of £36.50: £35 for the musicians and £1.50 for drinks. Among the session musicians hired to provide the backing was John Paul Jones, later to find fame on bass with Led Zeppelin. To listen to the finished version today is to hear a somewhat muted Rod Stewart vocal, sounding as though his voice is echoing through a cupboard. The record does, however, contain some energetic piano backing.

Rod's version was issued on 16 October 1964, the very day the whole country was waking up to something very new. Harold Wilson won a general election by a whisker to become Britain's first Labour prime minister since Clement Attlee, after 13 years of Tory rule. Rod's record was promoted with a press release from Decca in which he was quoted thus: 'I'm not particularly bothered about my new record. Of course I hope it's going to sell and make me a lot of money, but I'm not pinning too much hope on it. I don't tear my hair out at nights and I don't make too many plans. I'd like a car – Austin Sprite – and I suppose if I really made a mint I might invest in a country mansion. I haven't thought about it that much. I sing the blues because they're something I know about. A white person can sing the blues with just as much conviction as a negro. All these negro singers singing about "walking down the railroad track" … they've never walked down a railroad track in their lives. Nor have I. You've got more to sing the blues about in the Archway Road, near my home, than on any railroad track I know.'

It was just as well that Rod professed not to be 'particularly bothered' about his début record. 'By the time I'd finished recording "Good Morning Little Schoolgirl", the Yardbirds had done the same song,' says Rod ruefully. 'Of course, mine went down the toilet and theirs became a Top Twenty hit.' Rod later admitted in the notes to his *Storyteller* anthology that his first record was 'fairly useless'.

But at least Rod had at last made a record, and that in itself was an achievement after so many disappointments. 'I was turned down by EMI and Decca when I went for auditions,' Rod pointed out, 'but Decca actually signed me in the end. I did some Sam Cooke stuff for them. Do you know what they said? "Your voice is far too rough."'

The public were not the only ones to be unimpressed by Rod's version of 'Good Morning Little Schoolgirl'. It was his only single for Decca. They already had a popular white blues singer by the name of Michael Phillip Jagger, who fronted the Rolling Stones, and were not in desperate need of another.

That first single did, however, precipitate two important events on Rod Stewart's bumpy road to rock-stardom: his first television appearance and the appointment of his first manager. The television appearance, on *Ready, Steady, Go!*, the ITV show that had just been launched to cash in on the beat boom, was not, perhaps, his finest hour. The programme, which showcased the latest pop acts performing their latest records while fans danced in the studio, had quickly become essential viewing for teenagers with its Friday evening promise: 'The weekend starts here!' Rod was so excited and nervous at the prospect of appearing on *Ready, Steady, Go!* that he tanked himself up in the pub beforehand, an unwise move since the programme's set required him to climb down a ladder and then walk towards the camera. The Dutch courage he had taken in the pub prompted Rod to stumble and fall down the ladder, although he did manage to make it to the camera. After the show that night, Rod ended up having a drink in the Intrepid Fox in Wardour Street, where he met for the first time a guitarist called Ron Wood, whom he recognised as being in a student band from West Drayton called the Birds. 'Hello face, how are you?' said Rod, cheerily introducing himself to the guitarist who had, of course, seen Rod around on the London music scene and who would link up with Rod in the Faces. That meeting was the start of a famously close and enduring friendship. 'I said "Hello face", because Ron's got a great face. The two of us have got huge hooters, loads of hair. We're almost identical, us two,' Rod says fondly. Woody's recollection of that first meeting is that Rod sported a black eye – 'probably from playing football,' says Rod.

Now two enterprising businessmen called John Rowlands and Geoff Wright had spotted Rod singing with the Hoochie

Coochie Men, recognised his solo potential and offered to manage him. Rod was concerned initially because he didn't want to offend Baldry or jeopardise his financial arrangement with the group. Baldry, who had his own management, raised no objections and so Rod decided to sign to the duo. However, as he was still under the age of 21, Rowlands and Wright were obliged to ask his parents' permission too. Once Bob and Elsie saw how keen Rod was on the idea, they quickly gave their blessing. They were only too grateful that their youngest son was showing a commitment to something.

But cannily Rod delayed putting his signature to any contract for two weeks until his elder brother Don, who was an accountant, had had the chance to scrutinise it. On checking the contract, Don and Rod shrewdly insisted that Wright and Rowlands should not receive any percentage of the money he was already earning, as a regular member of Baldry's band.

To celebrate their new partnership, the managers and their new signing repaired to the Kensington Palace Hotel for a slap-up dinner and champagne. After drinking to his rosy future, the man who was later to become famous as one of the world's most enthusiastic partygoers slumped quietly forward in his chair, fast asleep and dreaming of stardom.

Rod's soulmate in Baldry's band was keyboard player Ian Armit. Coming as he did from Kirkcaldy in Fife, Armit was bound to be popular in Rod's eyes, as he was of course a fellow Scot and, although Armit was older than Rod, they shared the same musical tastes. However, just as the Hoochie Coochie Men had established themselves, the band suddenly broke up. 'I was just told the band was finished,' Armit recalls. 'The way I heard it, Rod and John were told they had to break up the band because there was an idea for another band. That, of course, was Steampacket.'

At this point, Wright and Rowlands wanted to launch Rod as

a solo star with backing group. However, he was still none too sure of himself and so was very reluctant to become a leader. He felt much happier as just another group member. They did, however, persuade him to do one gig at the Marquee, backed by a group called Ad Lib. Rod did not enjoy the experience. In the winter of 1964, he also appeared regularly at the Marquee on Thursdays backed by Southampton outfit the Soul Agents, where the fee for the four of them was £12. But again Rod was unwilling to have the whole weight of an act resting on his shoulders. He still wanted to share the load and so Baldry's plans for a new band, Steampacket, suited him perfectly.

While working in Manchester, Baldry had been to a club called the Twisted Wheel, where he had immediately been impressed by a young organist named Brian Auger. Soon afterwards, Auger was summoned to a meeting with Baldry and his management. Jointly they came up with the idea of an innovative group that was to have three singers Baldry, Rod and a young girl called Julie Driscoll.

Auger, who in 1964 had been voted Best British Pianist in the *Melody Maker* Jazz Poll, at that time was being managed by the enterprising Giorgio Gomelsky, who ran the Crawdaddy Club at the Station Hotel, Richmond, where the Stones and the Yardbirds had first flourished. He also had 18-year-old Julie on his books and had given her a job as fan club secretary to the Yardbirds, while he sought the right moment to launch her. Julie had real talent but what she really needed was to get out with a band, and have the chance to perform in front of an audience.

'Here was the perfect time,' Auger recalls. 'So I suggested we had Julie. I said I could come on and do a couple of instrumentals, and then Julie could come on and sing a couple of numbers. Then Rod could come on while we played and sang back-up for Rod, and then finally we could bring on John and we could all back John. That way we could do all sorts of material – Tamla, blues, soul – like a travelling package show.

'At that time the word for someone who played up a storm was a "steamer", and because we had a package I came up with the name Steampacket.' The full line-up was Julie Driscoll, Long John Baldry and Rod Stewart on vocals, Brian Auger on key-boards, Rick Brown on bass, Mickey Waller on drums and Vic Briggs on guitar.

At the meeting it was made clear to Auger that he should run the band and take care of everything. He readily accepted. He also agreed to meet with the managers of all the various parties involved every Monday, for a post-mortem of the previous week's performances.

Steampacket made their début supporting the Rolling Stones at a concert at Exeter, and immediately became a major draw in the clubs and halls. They headed north and soon found they were playing to appreciative audiences of anything between 500 and 1,000 people, who had flocked to hear such an interesting spectrum of music.

Invariably Auger would kick off with a number by Jimmy McGriff or Jimmy Smith, both bluesy Hammond-playing organists who influenced a whole generation of R 'n' B musicians in the sixties, then on came Julie to sing Tamla Motown, Aretha Franklin and Nina Simone favourites, winding up with the Martha and the Vandellas classic 'Dancing in the Street'. Then it was Rod's turn to shine with Sam Cooke numbers like 'Another Saturday Night', the Drifters' favourite 'On Broadway', followed by a Howlin' Wolf or Muddy Waters blues. Finally Baldry took centre stage with his blues and gospel songs. Auger knew Baldry's pedigree and was well aware of Julie's budding vocal talent, but Rod surprised him, not just by the way he delivered on stage but by his flair and showmanship. Rod's previous shyness was disap-pearing fast.

Says Auger: 'When we arrived for a gig Rod would immediately get out of the truck and instead of grabbing a drum or an amp, he'd depart for the nearest mirror and back-comb his hair. He was very interested in image and dress. Then I noticed a lot of Roddies were turning up at the gigs. I remember specifically a Roddy standing in front of me, same haircut, same brown jacket, and I tapped the guy on the shoulder and said: "Come on, Rod, we're on now," and the guy turned round and it wasn't Rod. It was weird. Baldry had a lot of fans but Rod suddenly had his own visible band of supporters.' Rod's confidence had grown as an equal partner in the band. Now he was also beginning to realise the effect he could have on audiences.

Rod Stewart thought he knew his effect on women. However, Julie Driscoll intrigued him – she was out of his usual ken. On the way to gigs, he would sit in the back of the van and observe her as she either sat with her back straight practising yoga, or tried to teach herself French, with the help of a grammar book, which she peered at under the little reading lamp she had had especially installed in the van.

They had a mild flirtation but Rod was much more interested in Julie's best friend, Jenny Ryland. 'He seemed to go for long-haired blondes,' says Julie, 'and Jenny was blonde and pretty. She was lovely. All Rod's girls seem to look like Jenny. I think she was probably in love with Rod and they had a steady relationship for quite a while.' After the romance finished Jenny Ryland fell for and later married another highly distinctive solo singer, Steve Marriott of the Small Faces.

'I enjoyed working with Rod,' Julie recalls, 'except that we used to like the same kind of songs and he always got the first pickings. But what I liked was that he always seemed to sing with such passion and, given the space, he would always be on the move, jigging around, always on the go, always flamboyant. Our voices went well together and we duetted on things like "My Guy", the big Mary Wells hit.'

Their relationship was mostly a harmonious one, except on the night in the dressing room at the Klooks Kleek Club at the Railway Hotel in West End Lane, Hampstead, when Julie flew into a fury at Rod. The explosive row that followed is still etched in the memories of both Auger and Baldry.

Auger: 'It started by Rod making a nasty remark about Julie's legs. At that point she was a little heavy. She was a teenager and had some puppy fat she was immensely obsessed about, out of all proportion. There were all these guys lusting after Julie and she'd be running herself down. At a weak moment Rod attacked and scored a direct hit.

'He said something very nasty to Julie and she freaked out and it became a kind of screaming chaos. The balloon went up like you can never imagine. There was half an hour of hysterical shouting. Julie had a pint of beer and she threw it on the floor and it shattered and went all over Rod's shoes. She started to scream at Rod.'

Baldry takes up the story: 'Julie blew her top and thumped and punched Rod. She slapped him round the room and gave him a black eye. He was screaming "Get her off me!" He was screaming in terror.'

Auger, as MD of Steampacket, was relieved to find that this horrendous row was uncharacteristic, and that the band was largely a happy bunch. Any excesses were usually down to booze or birds or both, or the inadequacies of the clubs they played at such as Klooks Kleek, where it was not uncommon for performers to fall through the orange-box-and-plank stage.

At an all-nighter at the Twisted Wheel, Steampacket had completed their early set and Rod and the rest of the band then hit the bars for two hours before assembling for their second set.

All was fine on the second set until Rod finished off his spot and Auger started a slow blues to bring in Baldry.

Auger: 'When I came to the intro chord there was no John. So we went round again and the second time there was still no John. We went round a third time and John made it in. The line went: "Baby, baby, baby, what is wrong with me?" and in the pause for the chords to go through their cycle, guitarist Vic Briggs leaned over and said, loud enough for all of the audience to hear: "You're pissed, you c***." There was hysterical laughter.'

When a band had gone down well, club owners would invariably stump up a bottle of whisky to help them unwind back at their hotel over a game of cards – crazy eights or gin rummy. It was a regular occurrence with Steampacket and the band gratefully consumed all that was on offer and more. However, drinking bouts were carefully excluded from the agenda when Auger made his Monday morning reports.

Perhaps Steampacket's most memorable appearance was when they were booked to play at a party for one of the Guinness heirs, at a rambling English country estate near Leeds. Rod and the rest of the band knew this was to be no ordinary gig the moment their van swung through the gates and up the drive, and halted in front of a house of such splendour it took their breath away.

Rod, Baldry and Auger all dumped their gear in an upstairs room and then took up a flunkey's invitation to stroll over to the colourful marquee for a bite to eat. They were walking along the duck-boards carefully laid out to make a path across the rolling, scrupulously manicured emerald lawns, when they passed two expensively dressed ladies in long evening gowns and fur shoulder-wraps, dripping with jewellery. As they passed Baldry, who had recently made several appearances on *Ready, Steady, Go!*, one of them exclaimed in plummy, aristocratic vowels: 'Oh look, Agatha! It's that Big Jack Bradley!'

Rod and Auger were still smirking about this at Baldry's expense, when they entered the marquee to find the biggest running buffet they had ever seen in their lives. The tables were groaning with food and drink and they needed no invitation to get stuck in. Suitably replenished, Auger began overseeing the setting up of the band's equipment, but later looked round to find no sign of Rod or Baldry.

Auger: 'Rod had disappeared with some redhead with gigantic knockers and then John disappeared. Later I decided to start the set and Julie came on, but when I called for Rod he didn't appear. Frantically I signalled to our roadie, Eric Brooks, to go and find him. I said I thought he had gone upstairs. Rod had retired to some room opposite our dressing room.'

Some ten minutes later an agitated Eric reappeared.

Eric: 'He's not coming down.'

Auger: 'You must be joking!'

Eric: 'He's in this room with that bird. I banged on the door for ten minutes and told him he was on.'

Auger: 'What did he say?'

Eric: 'He told me to fuck off.'

Auger: 'Well get John, then, for Christ's sake!'

Eric duly disappeared to look for John and returned with an ashen face: 'Aug, John's had an accident.'

'Give me a break!' said Auger. 'How could he have had an accident here?'

Eric: 'Well, he had a few this afternoon and went to our dressing room and lay down on the bed, and some geezer came in and, without putting the light on, threw his suitcase on to the bed and it hit John in the balls. He can't come down.'

That was the end of it. Neither Rod nor Baldry appeared, although Auger does recall a rowdy Rod surfacing in time for the firework display, screaming at the top of his voice: 'On the blue, eighty-two!' while suave young men elegantly dressed in smoking jackets tut-tutted aloud. 'Who are these people? Who invited them?'

As Eric had consumed too much alcohol, to complete his dismal evening Auger was forced to drive the merry band back to London that Saturday night. At the Monday morning post-mortem the management greeted him with the news that they had received a telegram. It read: 'Due to the band's cavalier behaviour, the fee for Saturday's booking will not be forwarded.'

There is no doubt, however, that when Steampacket were fired up they were a fine band. Their live performances and several appearances on *Ready, Steady, Go!* were beginning to earn them a good reputation and, with soul music becoming big on the college circuit, the band generally went down well. But Auger, in particular, began to realise that they were never going to take off in a big way for one simple reason: there were too many managers involved. He and Julie had the same manager, Baldry had his manager, and Rod had his own representation. Inevitably there were arguments among the management, especially when it came to determining which company would release any Steampacket records. Rod was now signed to Immediate, Baldry to Pye, and Auger and Julie Driscoll to Columbia.

'Popular as it was, I knew the band was never going to go anywhere because it looked as though we were never going to get any records cut,' says Auger. 'Finally things went into auto-destruct.'

While still trying to pursue a solo career, Rod did in fact record some messy demos with Steampacket. EMI, who took Rod on from Decca, also tried to engineer that all-important solo breakthrough for him, but in vain. Two singles, 'The Day Will Come' and 'Shake', for which Brian Auger did some arrangements, were met with popular and critical indifference. Still there was no hint of the hits to come, and Rod later dismissed 'Shake' as a desperate attempt by himself to sound like Otis Redding.

At the end of an exhausting tour, Auger was feeling the pace. As well as looking after the band, he drove one of the two vans, which often meant him getting home two hours after everyone else, by the time he had dropped Rod off in Highgate, John in Kensington and Julie in Vauxhall, south London, before heading for his own home in Shepherd's Bush. He shouldered all the musical responsibilities and had the Monday morning meetings to contend with as well. 'We had a lot of fun but it got rather wearing in the end,' he says. 'Also, I thought Rod was fairly parsimonious in that at one point he left London for a ten-day tour of Scotland and England with one pound, and would constantly be at the bar saying: "Buy us a drink, will you?"'

As the summer of 1966 approached, Auger was desperately tired and in need of a break. But he was also conscious of the need for Steampacket to keep working, and so he begged Gomelsky to try to fix up the band with a summer season residency somewhere. That way, he figured, they would all stay put for a month or so instead of slogging round the country, a different venue each night. It would be like a working holiday.

Rod could hardly contain his excitement when Steampacket were subsequently offered a four-week engagement at the Papagayo Club at St Tropez, in the south of France. The very mention of St Tropez was enough to send his senses spinning in anticipation.

St Tropez had been a simple French fishing port until it provided the backdrop for *And God Created Woman*, the controversial movie that launched French sex kitten Brigitte Bardot to screen stardom. The opening scene has Brigitte rolling naked in the surf in her role as a freewheeling, highly sexed teenager who casually shares her amorous favours among her husband, her brother-in-law and a much older yachtsman.

When Brigitte later bought a holiday home in St Tropez, and was constantly photographed frolicking with her lovers or sun-bathing naked on her private beach, she unwittingly changed the town into a public playground for the rich and a resort famed for its nude and topless beaches. If St Tropez was the place where the famous Bardot body beautiful was acquiring an all-over tan, then St Tropez was the place for the budding jet set.

In the summer of 1966 the little harbour was overrun with expensive yachts and floating gin palaces, each one seemingly more grand than the next. As for the beaches, they sported rows of lithe, bronzed young girls stretched out on the sand, often wearing nothing more than a glistening film of sun-tan oil and a lazy smile. For Rod, the alluring prospect that lay ahead was of four weeks of strolling along these sun-kissed Mediterranean shores taking his pick of the bunch. But the fun-loving, pleasure-seeking girls who flocked to St Tropez that year never got to meet future superstar Rod Stewart; his midsummer's dream was rudely shattered when he was suddenly fired from Steampacket – and it was all down to money.

Although the St Tropez gigs promised to provide the band with a working holiday in an inviting location, there was one vital snag: the financial terms of the four-week engagement matched the swimsuits of the St Tropez beach girls – they were barely adequate.

A meeting was called at which Baldry, Auger and the three managers were present, where it was decided that, in view of the poor financial offer, one of the band would have to stay behind in England. As Steampacket could not function without its musicians and as Baldry was clearly the number one singer, it came down to a straight choice between Rod and Julie.

'I voted to take Julie,' says Auger. 'Julie was in my office and was managed by my manager. Also, we had a male singer in John. The myth has gone on that I fired Rod. I would love to have had the dubious distinction of having fired Rod Stewart. But I didn't. It wasn't a vote to get Rod out of the band.

'At that meeting I could have been overruled by John or by John's manager. John was the big name and whatever he had wanted would have gone. It was his band. I was simply one of the five people who didn't vote for Rod.'

The decision reduced both Rod and Julie to tears. Rod was devastated. Julie says: 'I didn't think it was fair and it upset me. I never really quite understood why it happened.'

Thirty-five years on, Baldry still feels a twinge of conscience about Rod's sacking. 'It was a sad business. Brian wasn't totally happy about the financial rewards he was getting, and persuaded me to be party to asking Rod to find other things to do. Rod was disappointed that I didn't stand up to Brian, and I look back on it and think it was a very wrong thing for me to have done. I should have stood up to Brian.'

Salt was rubbed into Rod's wounds when the rest of the band headed for the club on the Côte d'Azur. 'When we eventually got there,' says Auger, 'we walked in to find Brigitte Bardot standing at the bar.' Rod apparently got on his hands and knees and beat the carpet in frustration, when the news filtered through to him that he had missed out on a chance to meet the sultry screen siren in person.

Steampacket played four half-hour sets a night, seven nights a week for a month. The huge Papagayo disco really jumped to their music. But by then Auger was already planning to leave the band and form a new outfit bridging rock and jazz. When they came back from St Tropez the band fulfilled their existing commitments of a few gigs already booked, then split up. A recording contract was not a realistic possibility because of all the managers and record labels involved. Auger went on to form the Trinity, heavily aided by Julie Driscoll, and they had a big hit in the spring of 1968 with 'This Wheel's On Fire'. Baldry went on to form Bluesology with Elton John, and Rod grew a beard and joined Shotgun Express, which included drummer Mick Fleetwood. 'I knew his singing, just by reputation on the London scene,' says Fleetwood. 'This was a guy you would want in your band. He looked great, and sang like something from heaven. He'd got it all covered. He was a natural-born singer, a natural one of a kind, an image-*meister*, he was de luxe – and still is.' But another flop single called 'I Could Turn The World Around' failed to confirm Fleetwood's faith in Rod at the time, at least on record.

Auger suspects that Rod still believes, wrongly, that he fired him from Steampacket. More than ten years later, by which time Rod was a huge star, Auger found himself on the same bill as Rod at Maryland University. 'I left him an album and a note in the bandroom,' he says, 'but he never came to our bandroom, even though ours was just ten yards from his.'

Julie has no doubts that Rod blamed Auger. 'I used to bump into him occasionally and he'd always say: "Are you making any money yet or is Brian taking it all? You ought to be making more money." He'd give me a ticking off as though I shouldn't be so involved with just the music but I ought to make some money as well. But I never wanted to be rich.'

For Rod, his years with the Hoochie Coochie Men and Steampacket were all part of an invaluable learning process in all manner of ways. When Steampacket backed the Rolling Stones, opening their two shows at the London Palladium on 1 August 1965, all Rod's family turned out to see him walk out on to one of London's most famous stages. That night, Rod's mum Elsie went home knowing, for the first time, that her youngest child was going to be a star. Rod's sister Mary, who had bought a ticket to observe Rod from up in the Palladium gods – there were no complimentary tickets in those days – was convinced that her little brother was destined for great things.

It was at the Palladium that Rod saw mass fan-hysteria close up for the first time. He saw how a young Mick Jagger had teenage girls frenziedly fighting their way to the front of the stage at his sexual showmanship. Rod also learned a lot from Baldry. One piece of advice he took to heart was never to keep his legs together while singing. 'It sounds funny but it's absolutely true,' Rod agrees. 'It looks daft.'

Baldry observes: 'I still recognise little nuances in Rod as a performer on stage, on TV, or even on record. I know there are little bits of Baldry in there – the movements of the hands, the leg movements, the stumbling motions.'

But Baldry also learned a lesson from Rod: it helps to have luck on your side as well as talent. Baldry notes: 'Rod was very lucky – he always has been in his life. He wasn't hungry for stardom then in the way that Elton John was, for instance. Rod lucked out into many situations ... He didn't have to work at it. It just dropped in his lap. He just jumped straight out of the Steampacket situation into Shotgun Express with Beryl Marsden and Peter Green, which was basically the forerunner of Fleetwood Mac.'

Rod never bore Baldry a grudge for casting his vote against him and, after Baldry spent a couple of uncomfortable years on the cabaret circuit following his 1977 chart-topping ballad 'Let the Heartaches Begin', Rod helped produce a new album for him called *Everything Stops for Tea*, Baldry's attempt to get back to his musical roots.

'By then Rod was a very good acoustic guitar player in the Ramblin' Jack Elliott/Woody Guthrie mould, and he also played fairly decent five-string banjo. He duetted with me on a track called "Mother Ain't Dead", with him playing banjo and me on guitar.'

Former Hoochie Coochie man Ian Armit was also called in to play on the album, and was impressed at the musical authority

Rod had gained since they had last played together: 'As a record producer I thought he was very good. He had a really fine feel for the blues, a good ear, and he knew what he wanted. At one point Rod decided he wanted an electric harpsichord on "Mother Ain't Dead". I hadn't even heard of such a thing. The argument against it was that it would cost a fortune to rent and it would take hours of tuning in the studio. But Rod got his way.' And, according to Armit, Rod was right.

He was also fun to be with in the studio. 'He was the opposite of a hard taskmaster. There was a bar at the studios and we'd go out and have a quick one and then come back again. It was all very laid-back.' He also generously gave his old pal Armit a brief moment of glory when a sixty-second gap needed filling at the end of the album. Armit: 'Rod told me to put down something, anything, on the piano. So I did and they recorded it straight away. Then nobody could think of a title until Rod said: "I know. Let's call it Armit's Trousers." And that's how it ended up on the album.'

Baldry himself believes that a later LP of his, *It Ain't Easy*, had a strong influence on the album that was eventually to take Rod to superstardom. '*It Ain't Easy* was in many ways like a blueprint, a rehearsal for Rod's album *Every Picture Tells a Story* which was recorded a few months later. Most of the musicians we used were on Rod's record too. That album broke the mould for Rod. I had seen his songwriting talent coming from the folkie angle rather than the heavyweight, bashing, rock 'n' roll variety.'

But *Every Picture Tells a Story* was still a long way off, and Rod still had five more years of paying his dues.

CHAPTER THREE

Beck and Call

*I was a little bit despondent in the early sixties because
there were a lot of bands taking off like the Stones and
Yardbirds, and I used to go and watch them and I
thought there must be a place in there somewhere for
me, because I could sing as well as that geezer with the
big lips in the Rolling Stones.*   Rod Stewart

Rod's first taste of America and the big time came with the Jeff
Beck Group.

Jeff Beck had established enough of a reputation as a hot guitarist during his time with the Yardbirds to try and form his own
band. He recruited Ron 'Woody' Wood on bass and Rod as
singer. 'The original line-up,' Rod says, 'was going to be Viv
Prince, Jet Harris, Ronnie Wood and a couple of other people I'd
never heard of. It was a stupid band.

'We just rehearsed once over the top of a pub and I think Jeff
thought that this wasn't the best band in the world, so that was
knocked on the head. Then we had an Australian bass player
who was so bad we sent him back on the first flight to Australia.'

Rod finally made his début with Beck on stage at the
Finsbury Park Astoria on 3 March 1967, on a package tour
with the Small Faces and Roy Orbison, one of the most

distinctive singers of the sixties. As Rod recalls: 'We all walked on stage in our band uniform. We all had white jackets and Jeff had a different one on because he was the leader of the group. We got through one number and then the electric went off. Somebody had pulled the plug. We immediately blamed the Small Faces [who were headlining]. I always blamed Mac for doing it, or instructing someone to do it, because he thought we might steal the show. Beck decided this was the end of the show, he wasn't going to stand any more and walked off stage.

'I remember I wasn't too pleased because I looked down and saw I hadn't done my flies up. We'd been on stage for one and half minutes and the curtain came down and nearly knocked Woody over, because it was so hefty. I caught him and he knocked it into me and sort of did a dance off the stage. We still had to find someone to take the blame. In the end we made the drummer take the blame.' The unfortunate drummer was sacked. 'It was a real shame actually,' Rod commented, 'because his old man had bought him a brand new drum kit for the tour and he was sacked the first day. Very sad.'

The Jeff Beck Group was remarkable for its turnover of drummers. They certainly had more drummers than hit records, as no fewer that six stickmen were employed in the outfit's short life, including Viv Prince, Aynsley Dunbar, Roger Cook, Mickey Waller and Tony Newman. The sixth, Rod Coombes, was sacked after he simply froze and was unable to play properly at the first gig the band ever did, at Finsbury Park in March 1967. In Rod's view, Waller was the most memorable drummer, if only because he was so careful with his money that even Rod thought he was mean. Sightings of Waller buying a drink were allegedly as rare as those of Halley's Comet. When he did buy Rod a drink the singer celebrated not by drinking up but by encasing his glass in cling film, and keeping it upright in his car with a little note on the side that read: 'This is the first drink that Mickey Waller ever bought me.'

The débâcle at Finsbury Park was rightly roasted in the music press. 'The group were obviously under-rehearsed,' reported *Melody Maker*, 'and in the first house on the opening night Jeff walked offstage when the power failed. Rod Stewart attempted to salvage what remained of the act. In the second house they played badly and created a very poor impression.'

It was all enough for the band to abandon the tour to spend some time knocking themselves into musical shape. And it marked a new low point for Rod; he despondently wondered if he was ever going to make it. While contemporaries like the Yardbirds, the Rolling Stones and the Small Faces soared towards fame and stardom, he lurched from embarrassment to disaster.

Even when Beck notched up a Top Twenty hit with the foot-stomping sing-along party song 'Hi Ho Silver Lining' in 1967, Rod, who had had nothing to do with it, was musically appalled: 'For a guitar player like that to come out with a thing like "Hi Ho Silver Lining" was a crime.'

The band were treading water until they went to America for an eight-week tour in May 1968. It was Rod's first trip to the States and he was totally in awe of New York, so much so that on the opening night at the Fillmore East, Rod was consumed by a severe bout of stage fright. In England he had rarely sung in front of more than 800 people. Now he was having to go out and perform in front of a full house of 3,000 rock music fans who had principally come to see the Grateful Dead, topping the bill. He was terrified that the audience had come to the gig not expecting a white boy to step on to the stage singing the blues.

First on were a band called Seventh Sons who were so abysmal they were pulled off in the middle of their set, amid a chorus of deafening boos from the audience. Once the rumpus had subsided, the house lights were dimmed once more and on walked Beck, followed by Woody and Mickey Waller, with Rod barely visible at the back. Beck plugged in his guitar and stormed into the six-note intro to 'Ain't Superstitious', but nothing came from Rod's throat at all. He had suddenly developed a terrible bout of stage fright, fearful that black people in the audience would see through him, regarding him merely as a 'white imitator' – a white man having the audacity to come over to America to sing black music.

As he battled with his nerves, the rest of the lads played on to cover up for him, while Rod ran behind the amps to where he and Woody had stashed a small flask of brandy in a pouch for just such an emergency. Frantically he pulled open the pouch, took a slug from the flask and again tried, unsuccessfully, to coax some notes from his mouth, while Beck valiantly continued to cover for his absence. He stayed hidden behind the amps till the end of the number – a hark-back to his early Long John Baldry days. 'The audience were amazed,' Beck commented. 'They thought I was a ventriloquist.'

Fortunately, Beck's snarling guitar had such an impact on the audience that by the time 'Ain't Superstitious' had finished, they were on their feet cheering, and only then did Rod dare poke his bouffant-styled head above the amps and gingerly walk to the front of the stage. By the end of the set, the audience were so appreciative that they won two encores and were stamping their feet for a third, when the band finally walked triumphantly off stage. After that, the Grateful Dead proved an anticlimax.

One of the first things Rod did when he got to New York was to seek out the famous Apollo theatre, where so many of the great black artists he worshipped regularly performed. At first he had great difficulty persuading any taxi driver to take him there. They took one look at the young Brit with his fluffed-up hair, and told him it might not be advisable to venture into Harlem.

But Rod did eventually get to see the Apollo, and he would

have pinched himself then if someone had told him that some 17 years later, he would be one of only four white singers to be invited to perform at a special concert billed as Motown Returns to the Apollo, to mark the reopening of the famous music venue. In 1985 he would proudly take the stage at that concert to sing Otis Redding's 'Dock of the Bay', on a bill which included, among others, the Temptations, Diana Ross, Stevie Wonder, Wilson Pickett, Smokey Robinson, Little Richard and the Four Tops.

From the outset there was inevitable rivalry between Beck and Rod. It was the Jeff Beck Group, of course, but, much to Rod's amusement, some fans and even record company executives would come up to him and say: 'Great show, Jeff.' They automatically assumed that the band was named after the singer. Beck was distinctly unamused.

There was no doubt, however, as to who was top dog offstage. Beck stayed at the Hilton in New York, while Rod and Woody had to share a room at the considerably less luxurious Gorham Hotel. Woody remembers that on occasions they were so desperate they stole eggs from the automat. But they took comfort from the fact that the Gorham, rather than the Hilton, was definitely the place to be if you were looking for fun, because other rock stars like supergroup Cream and Jimi Hendrix also chose to stay there.

The wheel came full circle in 1985, though, when Rod was a superstar. In spite of their differences, Rod retained enormous respect for Beck's musical abilities and invited him on tour. Beck was to have his own spot on the show. He was elated and, during a Thames river boat party, he revealed his plans to his good friend Keith Altham, one of the most respected public relations men in the rock business. Altham's comment was: 'You must be mad!' and promptly bet Beck £100 he would not last 12 dates on the tour. 'You're on,' said Beck.

By a quirk of fate, Altham received a call a month later from Rod's manager, Arnold Stiefel, asking him to come over and do some PR for Rod. Altham duly met Stiefel and agreed to take on some PR duties. His next step was to take a party of British journalists over to America to join Rod's tour. When they arrived, Altham decided immediately to seek out his old mate Jeff backstage at the gig in Philadelphia.

He recalls: 'I went backstage and passed a number one dressing room which was about the size of a suite in the Waldorf Hotel. It was wall to wall with flowers. It looked like a cross between a crematorium and an Interflora shop. Inside there were buckets of champagne everywhere and food piled up on the table.

'The next dressing room was the band's – half the size of Rod's with not so many flowers here, and only one bottle of champagne.

'Next was the crew's – no flowers and just a bottle of Southern Comfort.

'Right at the end of the corridor was a door with Jeff Beck's name on it.

'I said, "Hello, Jeff." He looked up and without saying a word he proceeded to write me out a cheque for £100.' The roles had been reversed. Rod was now the unquestionable star. After seven shows Beck disappeared.

But back in 1968 the eight weeks Rod spent on tour with Beck put him on the road to stardom. As the tour gathered momentum, the Jeff Beck Group, who had blown the Grateful Dead off the stage, proceeded to do the same with Three Dog Night and Vanilla Fudge. Rod comments: 'I thought it was a foot in the door because I was playing with great musicians and playing something that meant something – we were updating Chicago blues. Jeff in some ways moulded my voice, because I had to learn in some way to fill in the holes that he left. There was only one guitar, bass, drums and piano, so there were plenty of holes for me to sing in. With Jeff being such a wonderful guitar player and so fluid we bounced off each other. It was the ideal combination: great music, great style, great visual. We had it all.

'But before that I really thought, aw gee, no luck. I'd been at it a long time, playing clubs all over Britain for about five or six years, and I thought it was becoming ridiculous. I was 24, 25 and wasn't getting anywhere. I was a little bit despondent in the early sixties because there were a lot of bands taking off like the Stones and Yardbirds, and I used to go and watch them and I thought there must be a place in there somewhere for me, because I could sing as well as that geezer with the big lips in the Rolling Stones.' With Beck, Rod learned to fit his voice in with a guitar and the tour was a genuine success. Rod also contributed three songs for Beck's next album, *Truth*, which was put together, recorded and mixed in a matter of days. 'Woody and I used to write our songs in Ronnie's mum's council house,' Rod remembers. 'We used to sit round with two bars of the heating on with Mrs Wood coming in and saying: "Don't waste the electricity, turn that other bar off!"' The emphasis on Beck's follow-up LP *Beck-Ola*, however, was largely instrumental with a heavy metal flavour.

Luck again played a major role in Rod's career when the Jeff Beck Group were down to play at Woodstock, the great American outdoor peace-and-love, hippie rock festival of August 1969. But Beck decided to pull out. Woodstock became one of pop music's great landmark events and there is no doubt that had the Beck band played, with Rod and Woody in their supporting roles, they would have been launched internationally as that set-up and Rod's career would have taken a completely different course. 'Woody and I have often talked about that,' Rod said later, with the benefit of hindsight. 'We think that was the best thing Jeff Beck ever did for us – not doing Woodstock.' Instead, Rod's road to recognition came through the impact he made on

Beck's album *Truth*. It was enough for Lou Reizner of Mercury Records to approach Rod about a solo recording deal.

As head of Mercury, Reizner had helped to launch David Bowie to stardom with the release of *Space Oddity*. He had been impressed with Rod from the moment he first saw him singing with the Jeff Beck Group, at the Shrine Auditorium in Los Angeles. Reizner happened to be staying at the same hotel as Rod, the Hyatt House Continental. They got chatting after the gig and Reizner raised the possibility of Rod recording a solo album. They agreed to talk again back in London.

At the time the one thing Rod wanted most in the world was a Marcos build-it-yourself car kit. But it would cost £1,000 and Rod simply didn't have that kind of money. So, as a bait to persuade Rod to sign for Mercury, Reizner gave him the money for the Marcos and Rod duly signed the contract on 8 October 1968. A bird-pulling Marcos was certainly a giant step-up from his first car, the Morris Minor Traveller.

'I was a very reluctant solo artiste, and signed a deal with Mercury Records simply because they gave me £1,000 and I wanted to buy a car,' Rod says. 'So if I hadn't driven I may never have been a solo performer and would have stuck with the Faces when I joined them.'

His first solo album, *An Old Raincoat Won't Ever Let You Down*, was duly released on 13 February 1970. Made up mainly of folk-oriented songs like 'Dirty Old Town', a cover version of a Stones number, plus four of Rod's own compositions, Rod admits he wasn't expecting great sales at all, although he loved the album. The record failed in the UK but in the USA it reached number 139 in the charts. 'One day I got a phone call from the record company telling me I'd sold 50,000 albums,' Rod recalls. 'I thought, 50,000 people like my voice. That's amazing!'

The album went on to double those sales in America and Mercury pressed for a follow-up, anxious to strike while the iron was hot. But Reizner found Rod in typically tough negotiating form. The singer was determined not to miss out on any of his money – he had kept the master tapes of *An Old Raincoat Won't Ever Let You Down* under his bed, until his cash came through. When it came to agreeing a deal for his second LP, *Gasoline Alley*, Rod drove an even harder bargain. He took Reizner's much-loved and carefully restored, pre-war Rolls-Royce as an advance against royalties. Rod had coveted the majestic car from the moment he first saw it. The record producer reflected sadly: 'I have regretted that ever since. I really loved that car.'

The Beck band may have been the catalyst for Reizner's signing Rod to a solo recording deal, but it also came about at a time when Rod's collaboration with Beck on records had started to turn irrevocably sour.

The seeds of discontent were sown when *Truth* was released with the album sleeve containing only the merest mention of the other members, in small print. On the next album, *Beck-Ola*, Rod had an input on seven of the ten tracks, and ensured his presence was noted by having himself listed on the album sleeve credits as Rod Stewart, vocalist extraordinaire.

When Beck later fired both Woody and Mickey Waller early in 1969, the group's disintegration was inevitable and led first to Woody, then Rod, looking to join another band. In many ways the end for Rod, in July 1969, was a relief. He was beginning to feel he could no longer take all the aggravation and unfriendliness that had developed. It had by now reached a stage where the members of the band were trying to avoid each other all the time. Rod told one interviewer: 'In the two and a half years I was with Beck, I never once looked him in the eye ... I always looked at his shirt or something like that.' But, if nothing else, singing with Beck had given Rod the chance to buy his first purchase of any value; he spent his first week's royalties from Beck on a sterling silver picture frame.

Rod's search for another band was to lead him to the Faces. The beginning of Rod's solo success coincided with his joining the Faces, but not before another flop single, 'Little Miss Understood', written by Manfred Mann's lead singer Mike D'Abo, had been released that same year, 1968, on Immediate. Old Harrovian D'Abo, who had written the beautiful 'Handbags and Gladrags', which Rod was to include on his first solo LP, kept asking Rod, at the time of recording: 'Can't you get rid of that frog in your throat?'

Rod's reply was: 'No, mate. That's the way I sing.'

CHAPTER FOUR

Facing the Music

We had five brilliant years together. No regrets what-
soever. It's only now I realise how good the Faces were.
We had no idea how good we were then. We really
didn't have the confidence to go out there and play. We
were the ultimate good-time band but we had no
option because we were drunk all the time.
Rod Stewart on the Faces

Whatever else he may be, John Peel is not a dancing man. And yet even today, the BBC disc jockey, who has long been acknowledged as Britain's guru of avant-garde rock music, still receives the odd letter from a fan reminding him of the night when he was spotted dancing deliriously on stage at Newcastle City Hall, with a bottle of Blue Nun in his hand.

The occasion was an appearance by Rod and the Faces on the night that Second Division football club Sunderland had done the seemingly impossible, and beaten mighty First Division Arsenal in the semi-final of the FA Cup in 1973.

'Quite simply,' says Peel, 'it was the best gig I have ever been to in my entire life. The whole place was in ecstasy. Rod and the boys were, inevitably, as they always were, an hour late coming on stage, but they were just tremendous. It was an incredible night.'

Peel, an early convert to the brash brand of rock that characterised the Faces, introduced them to a wider audience through his BBC radio shows. Of the several concert programmes they recorded for Peel, he says: 'I enjoyed their music so much I actually threw out someone who was heckling Rod – one of the few courageous acts of my life.

'When I'd first met the band I thought they were impossibly rowdy and vulgar people, and then it occurred to me that possibly they were having a much better time than I was. I liked the noise they made and their attitude to it. I was so sad when Rod became a big celeb.'

The Faces may have had a reputation as a hard-drinking, wild, fun-loving band whose party trick was to all fall down in a heap, but there are other rock aficionados besides Peel, such as writer John Pigeon, who believe that between 1972 and 1975 there was no one to touch them as a live band. They behaved like lunatics and pulled ridiculous faces, they were rowdy, they trashed hotels, they shared the same silly humour and sometimes the same women, but during that time they rarely failed to put on a good show. As Rod kept telling his pal Rod Sopp: 'I'm sure we can be bigger than the Rolling Stones.' He was very nearly right.

It has to be remembered that the Faces came along at a time when British pop music was going through a stagnant period. Rock venues were largely presenting a procession of deadly earnest musicians in voluminous jeans and T-shirts, who stood still and played lengthy, self-indulgent guitar solos. Introspective dirges were the order of the day. Even smiling was unfashionable for a time, so looking as though you were enjoying your music was unthinkable.

The Faces offered a complete contrast. Their clothes, their behaviour and their music were all loud. While other bands were performing on bare-board stages, the Faces were possibly the first group to go in for a complete look to the stage. They had mirrored panels laid down on the stage and gaffer-taped. On later tours they transported with them white vinyl flooring for the stage, which was meticulously scrubbed clean by roadies after every show. Style was important. Mac may have had a pint of beer perched on top of his piano but there were candelabras there as well, and he would produce a mustard-coloured duster every now and then and ostentatiously clean his keyboard.

Above all, a Faces gig was an invitation to a wild rock 'n' roll party and everybody was encouraged to join in – even in the singing. These days it's part of almost every performer's show to have at least one number where the audience can join in and sing along. But audiences at Faces gigs did not simply join in – they took over. On a number like 'Angel', for example, or 'Stay With Me', Rod would stop the band because the fans were simply too noisy, vociferously chanting the words of the song right back at him.

The Faces were nearly always late on stage, another trend now all too familiar to the long-suffering rock concert-goer, so that the crowds who flocked to see them were frequently overexcited, and often swelled way beyond capacity by late-comers who had joined the crush. When the band finally did appear they would be dressed up in handmade shirts and flashy satin suits, brandishing bottles of beer, Mateus rosé and even champagne, which they passed from the stage to be circulated among the audience. The idea was to get the audience as tanked up as they were.

The band members used to drink large measures of port and brandy, usually on an empty stomach. That way the alcohol hit home quicker. 'We never used to eat,' says Rod, 'just have a light breakfast and no lunch, so when you have the first one of the day it'll really get you going. The Faces attitude was: we were drunk on stage last night, so let's get even more drunk tonight. It was the ultimate heavy-drinking band. Not because we had a mission in life to be a load of boozers. We were scared and we didn't think we were very good.'

The moment Woody's guitar savagely snarled the first chords to launch a Faces gig was the signal for bedlam to break out, around the front of the stage. There was an unmistakable scent of danger in the air, of not knowing quite what was going to happen. Coupled with this, too, was a sense that everything could rapidly fall apart – which only added to the tension.

But it never quite did, despite the pitfalls the group dug for themselves. They organised for a bar to be set up at the side of the stage, with some of the roadies dressed in white shirts and black waistcoats, serving drinks. When Kenney went into a drum solo the audience were amazed and amused to see the rest of the band all hit the bar. Kenney was well aware that the reason he'd been given a drum solo was to allow his colleagues the chance to fortify themselves further with alcohol. He didn't mind that, but he did mind if the supping went into overtime – which it frequently did. On one occasion, the unfortunate Kenney was left flailing away with his sticks for fully 15 minutes, the look on his face becoming increasingly desperate and his drumming increasingly frantic, as he waited for the return of Rod, Woody and Mac from refreshing their throats. Invariably their return would herald more confusion and mayhem with Rod giving Mac a piggy-back on stage, Mac falling off into his piano, and Rod then lifting the diminutive Ronnie Lane bodily up to the microphone to resume the vocals.

The singalong, football terrace-style finale to a Faces gig would end with Rod feeding the fan fervour by kicking plastic footballs, thoughtfully provided by the record company's promotions man, from the stage into the audience. It prompted one critic to comment that being on tour with the Faces was like New Year's Eve every night. 'And that sums it up,' says Rod.

The Faces had a ball while producing wonderfully ragged, but delightfully uncontrived music. And yet when they first started out, they were so insecure and unsure as to whether they'd put on a decent show, that it was not uncommon for Ronnie Lane to edge to the front of the stage and humbly ask the audience: 'What d'ya think of us? Were we any good?' Deafening applause gave the answer.

'When we had a good night and we were all connected together and were all taking the same substance, or drinking the same drink and were on the same wavelength, there was nothing to touch us,' says Mac.

The Faces also enjoyed that priceless – and saleable – quality of appealing to both sexes. They appealed most definitely to young girls but their boyfriends liked the band too. They thought the Faces were 'good lads' and Rod was 'one of the boys'. The band's blatant pursuit of booze, birds, football, flash cars and having a good time struck a common chord with teenage boys. On the, admittedly rare, occasions when they troubled to listen to the words of the Faces songs, they found them chock-full of male chauvinism.

The females who featured in Faces songs were generally randy, causing the men emotional grief, or a right nuisance because they got in the way of the men having themselves a good time.

And, in songs like 'Stay With Me', written by Rod and Woody, it was patently clear what was expected from females who wanted to ride along on the Faces merry-go-round. The lyrics blatantly spelled out the message that a girl could stay the night for sex, but she should know that it was pointless her talking about love in the morning. If she did, she would be unceremoniously booted out of the door. Among the hordes of groupies who regularly lined up along the hotel corridors hoping to get close to the Faces after a gig, there were nevertheless dozens who were only too happy to accept the 'Stay With Me' agenda just to get close to the band. 'We all lived the story of that song,' says Mac. Rod agrees: 'The lyrics were just shagging lyrics – and there was quite a lot of shagging going on.'

Crucially, the Faces captured Rod Stewart at a time when his ambition, energy, showmanship and creativity were becoming unstoppable. For much of his career as the Faces lead singer, Rod was a double attraction, for he was simultaneously pursuing a much more lucrative solo recording career – a situation which inevitably led to jealousy, bitterness, and a break-up with repercussions that have lasted to this day. However, to start with, it was seen as a bonus.

But Rod Stewart might never have got his big chance if Steve Marriott had not left the Small Faces. An east London outfit who epitomised the Mod culture, with their centre-parting hairstyles and Carnaby Street clothes, within ten weeks of their formation the Small Faces had notched up their first hit with 'Whatcha Gonna Do About It', in September 1965. Named for their slight height and desire to be, in Mod parlance, a ' face', they went on to enjoy five Top Ten hits between February 1966 and April 1968, with numbers like 'Itchycoo Park', 'Sha La La La Lee' and 'All or Nothing', a classic example of 'blue-eyed soul' which even knocked the Beatles off the top of the British charts.

But Marriott was rapidly tiring of being screamed at by hysterical young girls. A former child actor who had gone on to play parts in films and on TV, he felt that he would have more to offer if he sought new rock pastures, and so left to form a new band called Humble Pie.

When lead vocalist and guitarist Marriott left, the remnants of the Small Faces were like a ship without a rudder. But Ian 'Mac' McLagan, who played piano and organ, drummer Kenney Jones, who had worked in a musical instrument shop, and bassist

Ronnie Lane, who had started work in a fairground, all wanted somehow to carry on. They felt their nucleus was strong enough to go on to other things.

They continued to rehearse unsatisfactorily as a three-piece. Soon afterwards, though, they were joined on lead guitar by old friend Ronnie Wood, who had just been fired as bassist from Jeff Beck's group. Woody, in turn, encouraged Rod to come along to listen to them going through a few numbers at rehearsal rooms in Bermondsey, lent to them by the Rolling Stones. Rod agreed, but first he wanted to hear for himself what he might be letting himself in for. He stood unseen at the top of the stairs listening to the combined efforts of Woody, Mac, Kenney and Ronnie Lane. What he heard were mainly instrumentals, so he knew how much they needed him before he breezed through the door. But for the first few minutes he simply sat and eyed them all.

'Woody had said turn up at eight, an hour after they'd all got there, and to stand at the top of the stairs and see what I thought,' Rod recalls. 'So that's exactly what I did. They played all these great riffs, all these great songs and no one was singing. So I wandered down the stairs and joined in.'

Mac remembers: 'We were jamming on a blues when Rod joined in singing and all of a sudden we sounded like a band. But I didn't want Rod in. Not another bloody lead singer, I thought to myself. I had been kinda relieved when Steve had left because he was very domineering. I was against the idea of having another lead vocalist, because I figured there would be an ego to go with it – and I was right. Also, I'd seen Rod sing with Beck and he'd sungbehind the amps. He would just stand there singing with a frown on his face. He could sing very well but I felt he just didn't have the stage presentation.'

One aspect of Rod that Mac did approve of, however, and also envied, was his extraordinary rooster-style hair. 'He always had a great Barnet. Woody did too. Woody used to cut his own and put coffee, butter, anything on it to keep it sticking up. Rod always had hairdressers.'

Ronnie Lane also had grave reservations about Rod. Ronnie harboured his own ambitions to be the lead singer, but recognised his own vocal limitations. He realised that if they were to become a group to be reckoned with and pick up where Steve Marriott left off, then they needed a strong front man. Rod, with his husky voice and his spiky-haired Mod looks, was certainly different, and could possibly fit the bill.

It was Kenney Jones who stayed up most of the night convincing Ronnie and Mac that the right thing to do was to give Rod a chance. They eventually agreed and Kenney formally asked Rod to join the band over a drink at the Spaniards Inn, near Hampstead Heath. Rod needed no second invitation and together they drove off to a rehearsal to tell the others. 'I just bit my tongue,' says Mac. 'I thought it would have to do.'

Mac had other reservations about Rod. 'We'd go out for a drink socially or we'd walk into a pub, and Rod would invariably be a gentleman and open the door for you. We soon worked out why.

'We'd go in and be first to the bar and if you're first, you pay. Rod was very shrewd with his money, very tight. Sometimes we'd drive to a pub in five cars, and there would be a lot of checking the car locks so as not to be first to the bar.'

The seven-sided 50 new pence coin had just been issued in Britain, Australian media magnate Rupert Murdoch was about to clinch the purchase of the *Sun* newspaper in London, and the BBC had just transmitted the first in a new 'nutty, zany and oddball' TV series called *Monty Python's Flying Circus*, when Rod's appointment as lead singer was officially announced in the music press, on 18 October 1969. Because he towered over Mac and Ronnie, it was decided to drop the title Small Faces and for the group to become simply the Faces.

They quickly gained a manager, Billy Gaff, and a recording contract thanks to a series of introductions, each involving Jimmy Horowitz, a musician who had played in Baldry's band Bluesology, and was now writing songs and producing records as well.

Horowitz was friends with Gaff, an Irish Jew who had a reputation as a tough businessman, as well as a man with a thorough knowledge of the music scene. While a student in London, Gaff had been involved in booking bands for the powerful Robert Stigwood Organisation, and had gone on to become road manager of the Eric Clapton/Jack Bruce/Ginger Baker supergroup Cream. Crucially, Gaff had seen Rod on stage during his time with Long John Baldry and the Hoochie Coochie Men and had been impressed. He had in fact been introduced personally to Rod in the Cooks Ferry Inn at Edmonton, where an embarrassed Rod was sporting a bright red face, having overcooked himself under a sun lamp. Together, Horowitz and Gaff shared a small, gloomy basement apartment in Warwick Way near Victoria Station, and became business partners when they formed a management-publishing-record company, Gaff Management.

The partners worked desperately hard. Initially, as they could not afford to take clients out to dinner, Horowitz even learned to cook so they could entertain them at home in their flat's long, ugly hall which they converted into a dining room, when the occasion demanded. Later, when Horowitz got married and moved out, they bought a long lease on offices at 90 Wardour Street. Appropriately, they were opposite the famous rock venue · the Marquee.

Here they threw themselves so hard into their work that Horowitz would regularly double up as an accountant in the office, from eleven until five, and then go off and make albums in the evening. On several recording sessions Horowitz was using

Kenney Jones as a backing musician, and one night they walked round to the Speakeasy, a trendy club frequented by rock stars, where Horowitz introduced Kenney to Gaff. Kenney in turn introduced Gaff to Rod and the Faces. They were impressed by Gaff's directness and quick mind from the start. They needed someone they could trust to watch their corner in all the increasingly complex deals that were now beginning to come their way. Gaff measured up. He was roughly their age and he spoke their language, rather than the bewildering business-speak of accountants and record company executives. And so, Rod's association with Wright and Rowland, having by now come to an end, Gaff became the Faces manager.

'He managed Rod and the Faces for five per cent and no contract,' says Horowitz. 'Then with a recording contract he upped it to ten per cent and then when Rod left the Faces he upped it to fifteen per cent. Most of the time Billy was managing Rod, he did a wonderful job. He was very protective of Rod and wouldn't let anyone screw around with him. He was very protective about Rod's work and his art.'

With Gaff as manager, all the Faces needed now was a recording contract. Both the Beatles' company Apple and the Who's company Track turned them down. Without Steve Marriott as frontman the band would not be the same was the explanation. It was also pointed out that Rod Stewart had not set the world alight, and he'd been trying to do so for five years. But Horowitz eventually paved the way. 'I also introduced Billy to Ian Samwell who was kind of the house hippie at Warner Brothers,' continues Horowitz. 'Warner Brothers didn't have much of an A and R department then, so they hired Samwell who was one of those happening people, a finger-on-the-pulse kind of a guy. He was very enamoured of Rod and the Faces and that's how a deal was signed with Warner Brothers.'

The recording contract was signed on 1 November, just

weeks after Rod had officially joined. It was achieved on the strength of six demo discs from the band, which Warner Brothers thought showed sufficient promise for them to pay the Faces a £30,000 advance. The deal allowed Rod to continue to make solo records for Mercury – and enabled him to buy a flashy Marcos Volvo car.

The band's first appearance, in June 1969, was a try-out under the name Quiet Melon at a Cambridge University ball, with barely adequate equipment. The band were paid £100 and were allowed to tuck in for free to the roast beef, champagne and strawberries, and jugs of beer which was the night's fare for the undergraduate revellers. 'It was a general piss-up,' remarked Mac, 'and we went on without any rehearsal.'

Ronnie, Kenney and Mac's initial misgivings about Rod having completely disappeared by this stage, they, Rod and Woody set about giving a whole new definition to the word rehearsal. For them it was a chance to get together and get drunk. 'That was the beginning of an era of serious, serious drinking,' says Kenney Jones. They would all meet at the King's Arms near the rehearsal room for a liquid lunch, and stay there drinking shorts till closing time, before running through a few numbers in the afternoon. Then it was all back to the pub again.

John Pigeon, who was then acting roadie on one of the Faces tours, later witnessed one such rehearsal at Wood Green, at the start of a British tour. 'They turned up late and they did a stupid version of "Crazy Horses" by the Osmonds – pretending to be the Osmonds – and that was about the extent of the rehearsal. They wrote out a set list and that was it! Then I was sent down to Marks and Spencer to see if I could change a $100 note and they all went off to the pub.

'We all then went up to Dundee and the night before the first show there I made the mistake of opening my hotel door to a knock, and various members of the crew came in with fire extinguishers and all my bedding went out of the window.'

Rod has always explained away the band's boozing habits as a reaction to fear. 'When we started nobody wanted to listen to us,' he said. 'Nobody had taken us very seriously and so we decided to go round to the pub beforehand. Call it Dutch courage, if you want. That's what it was down to – we were just lacking in confidence. It wasn't a conscious thing. We weren't trying to be different from every other band. That's just the way it came out. The booze came about because we didn't think we were any good. Me and Woody had been fired by Beck and the three Small Faces were out of work because the singer had left. So we went round the pub and we had one thing in common, and that was boozing and a sense of humour.'

By February of 1970, the Faces with Rod as lead singer had released their début album, *First Step*, to which Rod contributed three songs, with one each from Mac, Woody and Ronnie. It managed to reach number 45 in the LP charts but disappeared after just one week. The same month saw the release of Rod's first solo album, *An Old Raincoat Won't Ever Let You Down*, which failed to register at all in the British charts. In America, however, where it was released as *The Rod Stewart Album*, and where he was now rather better known as a result of his tour with Jeff Beck, it caused a lot of interest for its wide range of musical styles.

For many, the stand-out track was the Mike D'Abo composition, 'Handbags and Gladrags', on which Rod sang with all the anguished bluesy feel he could muster, to what was predominantly a piano accompaniment. Rod had always liked D'Abo's song and D'Abo was taken aback when, at short notice, Rod daringly called for some oboists and flautists to be brought in for the recording. D'Abo stayed up till four in the morning working out the woodwind arrangement. The result was a record which became one of Rod's best-loved down the years.

This was the track chosen for release as a single, but yet again Rod failed to make a dent in the charts. The album also included a gutsy but misguided attempt at covering the Jagger/Richards number 'Street Fightin' Man'. The traditional southern mountain American folk song 'Man of Constant Sorrow' and 'Dirty Old Town', Ewan McColl's lovely folk song about Salford, provided echoes of Rod's folkie roots.

In addition, there were four of Rod's own compositions. Melodically the best of the four was 'I Wouldn't Ever Change A Thing', in which the lyrics have Rod seemingly recalling his beatnik days, when he would sit for hours drinking and talking with friends about how they would put the world to rights.

The lyrics of 'Cindy's Lament' had Rod bewailing the fact that he has a girlfriend whose family do not approve of him romancing their daughter. But Rod has the last laugh, by wondering in the final lines how they would feel if they knew she had already spent the night with him. The title track, 'An Old Raincoat Will Never Let You Down', and 'Blind Prayer' also pick up on the theme of rejection.

It was during the making of this album that Rod began writing songs for the first time, and he was able to evolve a method of composing which has continued down the years. He would have an idea, sometimes only just a glimmer, and convey it to guitarists Woody and Martin Quittenton in the studio, who would develop it before laying down a basic track. Then he would take the tapes home and work out the lyrics.

Rod had originally been offered the chance to make *An Old Raincoat Won't Ever Let You Down* while he was singing with the Jeff Beck Group, but he had turned it down, not wishing to offend Beck. By producing the album as well, Rod conceded he had jumped in at the deep end, but insisted that the only success he had ever had was by ignoring the advice of record companies and other producers. He even got his own way over a bizarre little detail he wanted on the album sleeve. Around this time, for some strange reason, Rod liked to use the word 'thin' as a trendy adjective and he had it printed in the bottom left-hand corner of the LP sleeve.

As for the songs on the album, he said: 'I thought, something desperate's got to be done, so I told people what sort of sound I wanted, then I'd bring home the tape without the vocals on it and write words to fit the sounds. It was a strange way of going about things but it worked.'

Rod has since described his first solo album as 'naïve'. Nevertheless, it started to put him on the map in America. And that's where the Faces, too, had to look for a first glimpse of recognition.

British rock fans were initially aghast at the band's sloppy stage antics, their raw approach and their nonchalant attitude to their plentiful mistakes. 'There was a general smile whenever we played a dodgy note,' Rod concedes. Audiences were also bemused at the band's tendency to all fall down in an undignified heap, giggling to themselves, while they tried to carry on playing. 'People would ask: "Why are you shouting, why are you falling over, why are you taking your trousers down?"' says Woody. As for Rod, who on earth was this strutting peacock? Who did he think he was, running around all over the stage, jumping up on the drum riser and hurling the microphone stand up into the air? To British rock fans waiting to see their idols, the singer with the support group must have seemed like a demented drum major on speed. Rod was able to hurl the mike stand around because it was specially made of lightweight aluminium, just for that purpose, rather than much heavier metal.

But in America, and for some reason Detroit in particular, it was a totally different story. The Beatles were just about to go to court to dissolve their partnership, and President Nixon was on the verge of sending US combat troops into Cambodia, when the Faces made their North American début at the Varsity Arena, Toronto, Canada, on 25 March, 1970, where they were third on the bill to Canned Heat and the MC5.

But as the 28-date concert tour of America gathered pace, the sheer energy with which Rod conducted the continual party atmosphere was just what the American kids were in need of.

They had been dealt a surfeit of self-proclaimed fret kings, conjuring up ever more pained expressions, as their fingers stretched for ever higher notes on the upper reaches of the guitar neck. What Rod gave them was unashamed, no-nonsense, down-to-earth rock music and they welcomed him with open arms. A great night out was just what the American youth were looking for, to offset gloomy TV news revealing that President Nixon had authorised even more intensive pounding of the Ho Chi Minh trail in eastern Laos, as the Vietnam War raged on.

At first Rod was wracked with the usual nerves before every concert. He had more responsibility now than when he was with Beck's band and it frightened him. But once he took the stage, helped by the warm response he received, the worries melted away and the adrenalin flowed. As the tour progressed he visibly grew in confidence with every appearance, and the Stewart stage trademarks began to evolve.

While other vocalists stood right up to the microphone, Rod would stand leaning two or three feet away from the mike, put his head back, and project his voice with awesome power and clarity. He was never still for long, darting from one side of the stage to the other or strutting in time to the beat. Then suddenly he would strike a mid-stride pose, pick up the mike stand and straddle it across one thigh like a naughty girl he was about to spank. The crowd went wild. Always there was that distinctive husky vocal, but Rod swore to God that there was many a gig where he strutted from one side of the stage to the other, and realised members of the Faces weren't playing in the same time.

Even in a country as vast as the US, it does not take long for word to spread, and the message on the teenage pop grapevine was that the Faces were not just hot, they were really cooking. Suddenly they became a huge draw. The tour gathered irresistible momentum and, when it had finished, the American promoters quickly took the opportunity to book them again. If Britain was not yet ready for them, America was only too willing to welcome the Faces back. They returned to the US in the autumn for a further 28 dates, mostly headlining, and starting at a college in Vermont on 1 October, by which time Rod's second solo album, *Gasoline Alley*, was starting to make waves, charting at number 62 in the UK and number 27 in the US.

Gasoline Alley was again a mixed musical bag of songs. Woody provided the melody and Rod the lyrics for the title track, but the album was largely very different from what the Faces were producing, even though Rod was using them as backing musicians. There was a strong selection of ballads and acoustic guitar work, and Rod demonstrated again a quality that was to hold him consistently in good stead: a shrewd selection of other writers' songs which he felt suited his voice. For the *Gasoline Alley* LP he chose to record the Elton John/Bernie Taupin number 'Country Comfort', Dylan's 'Only a Hobo' and Bobby and Shirley Womack's 'It's All Over Now'. There was also a creditable version of 'Cut Across Shorty' by one of Rod's early idols, Eddie Cochran – even though there was a line missed out from the song. Rod later blamed Woody for the mistake, saying he forgot one change when they were laying down the track. The album received critical acclaim in America and spurred still more interest in the Faces.

When they reached Detroit, the Faces blew Savoy Brown, whom they were supporting, off the stage, and Rod was able to look down in triumph for the first time at an audience where girls were going crazy for him. Several showed Rod their appreciation by dancing topless, brazenly jiggling their breasts in front of him in time to the music. In their exuberance they had peeled off their T-shirts, unhooked their bras and hurled them at Rod's feet.

It was in Detroit that Rod was thrilled to meet up with David Ruffin who sang 'My Girl' and all the Temptations hits. Thereafter David would come on and sing '(I Know) I'm Losing You' with Rod when the Faces were in Detroit. Rod retains to this day a prized photo of himself almost climbing into David's mouth to see if his vocal chords were bigger, or even the same colour, as his own.

In New Jersey there was almost a riot when the concert promoter informed the Faces that as the show was overrunning, they would not be called upon to play. Rod sorted out that little problem by leading the Faces on stage where, suitably fortified by liberal amounts of alcohol, as usual, they proceeded forcibly to relieve Savoy Brown of their instruments and started playing. That caused another near riot. In Chicago, Rod almost literally managed to bring the roof down when he hurled the microphone stand through the ceiling of a club.

After generating such excitement among American audiences, it was difficult for Rod and the band to return to England where, unable to capitalise on the success of the Small Faces, interest in them was still barely lukewarm. A November release of the Faces second single, 'Had Me A Real Good Time', earned them an appearance on the BBC's popular weekly television chart show *Top of the Pops*, but it failed to register.

They jumped from playing to 20,000 frenzied fans in huge American arenas like the Los Angeles Forum, to performing in English pubs for 100 people or, as on one occasion, at Dudley Zoo, below the bill to T. Rex and Edgar Broughton. The comparison was brought home when Broughton openly dubbed the band that America was taking to its heart as 'a bunch of drunken

East End yobs'. That disparaging assessment didn't stop the BBC inviting these 'yobs' to record Christmas carols, for the Boxing Day edition of John Peel's *Top Gear* radio show, on which Rod sang 'Away In A Manger' accompanied by just a piano.

John Peel, of course, had quickly and knowledgeably latched on to the excitement generated at Faces concerts and loved Rod's sense of fun. Rod particularly endeared himself to Peel when he invited Rod and his steady girlfriend Dee Harrington to his wedding, where Rod spent most of the proceedings chatting amiably away to an eccentric Welsh aunt of the DJ's. Soon Peel and his wife were following the band around, including a trip over to Rotterdam where the band were booked on a TV programme. Afterwards they all repaired to a restaurant, where Rod and the rest of the band started a food fight and generally misbehaved in their usual over-exuberant fashion. Peel was perturbed to be told later that the restaurant was the HQ of an unsavoury Dutch underworld gang, and that they were extremely fortunate to have escaped with their kneecaps intact.

Happily for Peel, the Faces seemed to reserve some of their best live performances for his radio concert broadcasts, although no show approached without him fretting about whether they would all turn up to meet the strict 8 p.m. on-air deadline. To Peel's horror they were frequently to be found at 8.15 p.m. still knocking back drinks, sitting in the pub round the corner from the Paris Studio in London's West End where the shows were recorded. The audience, who mostly were not big Faces fans, but consisted of people who had written in for a ticket simply to be part of a BBC live radio show audience, were bemused, and worse, by such laxity on the part of the performers they had struggled through London's evening rush hour to see.

One of the authors attended one of these shows which descended into some disarray when the band took to the stage, played a couple of numbers, then put down their instruments and seemed not to want to play at all, while a joker in the audience yelled out: 'Sing "White Cliffs Of Dover" for us, Rod!'

When he went for a drink with Rod, John Peel was not the first to discover the singer had short arms and long pockets. Not only did Rod consistently dodge buying his round but when, in exasperation, the thirsty Peel got up and announced he was getting another drink, Rod would ask Peel to get him a Scotch egg or a sandwich as well. Peel remembers with a chuckle that when his wife's birthday fell on the day the Faces were recording a show for him, Rod purchased a particularly unappetising bottle of cheap wine from the Captain's Cabin, close to the Paris Studio, and presented it to her with a note that read: 'To Pig [which was her nickname] love from Rod.' Peel likes to say he keeps it as some sort of memorial – just about the only existing evidence that Rod has ever bought anyone a drink.

Only the hotels in America reserved a less than enthusiastic welcome for Rod and the Faces, and with every good reason. On their travels the band perfected a new sport: trashing hotels. 'We didn't trash hotels because we had an album coming out and wanted to get in the *Sun* or the *Mirror*,' Rod explains. 'We did it because we had bad treatment from the hotels, got drunk and let off a lot of steam. It wasn't preconceived, just generally off the top of our heads. We'd let off steam and smash a room up. In those days we just got a warning. We were always in a state of drunkenness or sobering up.'

The band discovered that 'rearranging' or, in some cases, demolishing hotel rooms proved the perfect antidote to the hours of boredom, loneliness, exhaustion, frustration and isolation they were now coming to experience on the road as they crisscrossed the States. Besides, the Faces were a party band. It was always in America's Midwest that the boredom seemed to precipitate the greatest party mayhem. Parties meant booze and girls, and with the Faces there were always large quantities of both freely available. All they needed was somewhere to party and the obvious place was back at the hotel. 'We'd take the whole audience back to the Howard Johnson motel or wherever we were staying,' says Woody. 'We'd just tell them where it was and have a pool party.'

'In those days we were often staying in Holiday Inns,' Mac recalls. 'We weren't going home, we were going back to the same room, no matter what city we were in – so basic and so mind-numbing it was like listening to muzak. So we had to break out of it. We had all this energy after a show and there we were back in this miserable-looking hotel, every night, in a town we didn't know and where we knew nobody. So we partied, and we trashed a lot of hotels.

'We'd knock on Billy Gaff's door and we'd invite thirty peo-ple into his room. Billy would open the door and he'd have his business papers out, his briefcases open, and he'd be on the phone. But none of us would give a damn. We'd pile in there, take our clothes off, and fall over, and we'd be feeling up girls' tits and there would be this maelstrom of faces and legs and bodies, and all of a sudden I'd come across Rod and he'd be pulling stu-pid faces and making silly noises, and everyone would join in, although they didn't know why they were doing it.

'Rod was the real instigator of all that. We were all raving loonies and crazy. It was endless crazy chicks all the time – the corridors would be full of them. Pretty girls would be lined up in the corridor, waiting to be brought into the rooms one at a time. Some of the girls were just fans of the music. They weren't there for sex or drugs, but hopefully they had friends who were. We were there for two things: music and fucking. My marriage didn't stop me shagging anyone I fancied. The girls were real keen and willing and so was I.'

The pranks were mostly played on people for whom the band

had some affection – which was why Billy Gaff came in for more than his fair share. 'He always looked like the world was about to fall in on him,' says Mac, 'and we were the world, and we did.'

Gaff's room was frequently attacked while he was asleep, after spare keys had been purloined from the hotel reception. Then, rounding up complete strangers, Rod, Woody and Mac would burst into Gaff's room, shouting at the tops of their voices, tip him out of bed on to the floor, then turn the bed over on top of him. While Gaff was being unceremoniously debagged, other members of the invading party hurled furniture and the TV set out of the windows into the swimming pool below and disconnected the lights, while still more havoc was being created in the bathroom with the flooding of the basin and bathtub.

Then they would all rush out of the room as noisily and as suddenly as they had arrived, leaving a naked Gaff gingerly to squelch his way round a darkened room that was ominously filling up with water. On other occasions, the band would simply debag Gaff and then mercilessly push him out into the corridor, into the heaving mêlée of fans.

'It was a nightmare,' admits Gaff. 'Horrendous. Rod was the instigator of everything. Whenever there was trouble Rod was at the forefront of it. But when anybody got arrested, he was nowhere to be seen.'

As the band's notoriety spread, hotels became ever more wary, less accommodating and ever more anxious to squeeze money out of them. In Sweden one hotel dared to charge them $100 for a cheese sandwich. In retribution, the band summoned a roadie who proceeded to saw through all the chair legs. A regular Faces response to bad treatment or dissatisfaction with their rooms was to take out all the furniture, and rearrange it as a room in the hotel corridor or, if they were particularly riled, on the hotel lawn. There they would sit reading newspapers as though it was the most natural room setting in the world.

As a variation, the band would completely strip a room of furniture, curtains, paintings, lights, the lot, and pile it all into the elevators. Rod enjoyed it best of all when this was a prank played on a member of the touring party who had picked up a girl after a heavy night's drinking, and was about to take her off to bed. He was tickled pink at the thought of his merry pal letting himself into his room, and saying to his prospective bed-mate for the night: 'Make yourself at home, darling' only to find the room completely empty when he switched on the light.

It was lucky the Faces were earning big bucks because the bill for the damage was always considerable, and it always had to be paid. 'The money I paid out for hotel damage was quite dramatic,' admits Gaff. It was even more dramatic when hotels cottoned on that they could make additional charges for lost room rental, while the damage was put right.

The catalogue of outrageous misbehaviour reached its peak of destruction in Tucson, Arizona, where the band happened to arrive at their hotel on a public holiday to find the bar temporarily closed. At that time the Faces considered there was no greater torture possible than to be denied a drink. There was only one way to vent their anger: take it out on the hotel. But first they were determined to get drunk somehow, and when a paltry two cans of beer were produced, they proceeded to employ a technique they had perfected for just such dry occasions.

All that was required was a 12oz can of beer, one-shot glasses for everyone and synchronised watches. As the second-hand hit 12, each member of the Faces filled his glass up to the line – just one ounce – and put the bottle down. Then they waited 60 seconds before knocking back the glass. They refilled and waited another 60 seconds before repeating the process.

'We did that regularly every minute on the button,' recalls Mac. 'If you can get through two cans that way and not end up rolling on the floor, it's a miracle. Everyone started giggling and it was crazy because we were used to huge amounts of drink, and even though we hadn't finished the second can we were rolling drunk.'

Suitably tanked up, they were now all set to extract violent revenge on the hotel, and the first target was to be an enchanting railway that ran all the way around the hotel grounds. It was a miniature railway large enough to take children on joy-rides, and certainly not designed to accommodate inebriated fully grown adults. The Faces thought it looked fun and soon had the train in motion. It rumbled along the tracks to the point where they had engineered an unscheduled derailment, which caused the engine to jump from the rails and thunder down a hill, a trail of carriages snaking crazily behind it, before ending its journey in a shattering pile-up. Mac relates: 'I was very drunk but I do remember we then wrecked several rooms. Billy's room was on the second floor and we threw all his furniture out of the window and set it all up again in the grassy area. We had everything working including the television set and the lamp by the bed! Billy was screaming at this point.'

Somewhat appropriately, Mac's high spirits were heightened even further by a telephone call he put through to England to the beautiful Kim Moon. Kim was the ex-wife of Keith Moon whose crazed destruction of cars, hotels and airports had earned him the nickname Moon the Loon and the title of pop's undisputed King of Havoc.

Mac, whom Kim went on to marry, recalls: 'I phoned Kim from my room and asked her to come over and she said she would. I felt good I'd had such a great telephone conversation with her, so we wrecked several rooms.

'At six the next morning I was awoken by the sound of a helicopter and then there was a bang on the door. I said: "Fuck off, whoever you are!" Back came the reply: "Open the door or I'll shoot!" It was the cops. We paid for the damage.

'Rod loved all that and next time we were due in Tucson we couldn't get into any hotel, of course. Not Tucson, I thought to myself. Helicopters, police, shooters. Where were we going to stay? But Rod got round this – we checked in as Fleetwood Mac. And what was the first thing we did when we got there? That's right, we derailed the train again.'

February of 1971 saw the Faces back in the US, in Jersey City, starting their third tour, and the band's second album, *Long Player*, was released the following month to excited reviews; it charted at number 29.

The extraordinary comparison between Britain's and America's views of Rod and the Faces can be summed up by the night Rod invited his old pal Rod Sopp round to his house to look at some home movies. 'He showed me this film *Los Angeles Welcomes Rod Stewart and the Faces*,' Sopp says, 'and there was an advertisement on it for Coke or Pepsi, and Rod said he wanted to do one of those. I said: "Whaaaat?" and he said: "Oh yeah. Joni Mitchell's done one and I've sold more records than her." I had no idea. I didn't realise they were doing as well as they were – they were still playing the Greyhound, Croydon, for £100 in their hands.'

The Faces were reminded of just how well Rod was doing when they stepped off the plane at Heathrow after an American tour, to find the Marcos car Mercury had promised Rod waiting for him parked at the kerb. Before long Rod also had a yellow Lamborghini Countach. But as the Faces began to see the financial rewards for their efforts, they too began to splash out and Mac bought himself a seven-gear British racing green TR6, with overdrive in second, third and fourth gears. One evening when Rod pulled up for rehearsals in his 'yellow knob on wheels', as Mac disparagingly described it, Mac challenged him to a race down a one-way street. The road had two lanes, but after about 100 yards it abruptly narrowed and then became one lane, as it snaked into a long arched tunnel which ran underneath a railway line. It would be a test of courage and nerve for Rod and Mac as well as horsepower and driving skill. With a roar of engines they were off, and Mac derived considerable satisfaction from nosing his car in front of Rod's and speeding into the tunnel ahead of him, even if did mean a scraping of Rod's wheel arch as he accelerated away.

As so often happens, what America likes today, Britain likes tomorrow. Faces fever was starting to build back home as winter was nudging the spring of 1971. The remarkable Rod Stewart explosion, marked by the LP *Every Picture Tells a Story*, was now but a few months away.

The detonator was 'Maggie May', a fine song and a classic example of Rod's unique gift for rocking a ballad. Rod wrote it with guitarist Martin Quittenton who had worked on Rod's first two solo albums, as a musician but not as a composer.

Martin had been playing in a band called Steamhammer, and Rod first spotted his talents when Mickey Waller persuaded him to go and listen to the band at the 100 Club, in Oxford Street.

Rod was then in the process of choosing musicians to back him on his first solo album, and Martin's classical training immediately appealed to him. Martin hailed from Sussex and was in many ways the complete opposite of Rod. He was a gentle, spiritual soul, and wasn't interested in fast cars and fast blondes; he had an uncomplicated approach to life. 'Rod rather liked my simplicity and non-hard-nosed attitude,' Martin recalls. 'We offset each other and he knew there was no side to me and he could relax with me.' Rod also admired his musical creativity, stating: 'He's got such beautiful chords in his head.'

When recording dates were set for *Every Picture Tells a Story*, Rod invited Martin to come up and stay at his house in Highgate, and played the perfect host. From the moment Martin was shown into the third bedroom, Rod thereafter referred to it as 'Martin's room'. Martin was touched to find that Rod had thoughtfully provided in his room a music stand in case he wanted to practise.

'One night we were in Rod's sitting room, I was on the settee and Rod was sitting in a chair, and he just asked me if I had any ideas for any songs,' Martin recalls. 'We started messing around with a few chords and up came "Maggie May". I thought up the 12-string guitar introduction to the song while I was on the tube, on the way to the studio, and I borrowed Rod's 12-string to play it when I got there.

'When "Maggie May" became a big hit I couldn't, at the time, see what the fuss was about. It took me a long while to realise it was actually a very good popular song.'

But for the record to become an international hit it needed two waves of the magic wand from Lady Luck, whom Long John Baldry believes is seated so firmly on Rod's shoulder.

Firstly, 'Maggie May' was so nearly omitted from the album altogether. Rod played the song to a friend who ventured the opinion that it had nothing to offer melodically. Fortunately for Rod, this crushing sentiment was delivered too late for the song to be excluded from the LP – quite simply there were no other tracks available. 'Maggie May', by its sheer existence, was in.

When it came to selecting a single from the album, the vote came down in favour of 'Reason to Believe', Rod's version of a gentle ballad by American singer/songwriter Tim Hardin, and 'Maggie May' was chosen as the B side. However, a disc jockey in Cleveland, Ohio, turned the record over and played 'Maggie May' as the A side. Six weeks later, on 2 October 1971, 'Maggie May' was a number one smash in America.

Rod had to wait only a further seven days before 'Maggie May' also stood at the top of the British singles charts. By then, *Every Picture Tells a Story* was also the number one LP on both sides of the Atlantic. It was an unprecedented feat in the history of pop music. Not even Elvis Presley or the Beatles had managed to achieve top-selling singles and LPs in both Britain and America simultaneously. The success of the LP was astonishing, holding off classic albums like Simon and Garfunkel's *Bridge over Troubled Water* and Carole King's *Tapestry*. Both Rod's single and the album remained top of the charts in Britain for six weeks. For Rod, it was his finest moment. Very, very few artists have co-written songs, sung them and produced an album, and done so with such spectacular success.

When Rod heard the good news that 'Maggie May' had knocked 'Hey Girl Don't Bother Me' by the Tams off the top of the charts in Britain, he took his family down to the pub for some wild celebrations. Rod's father, a popular figure round Highgate way, was especially excited. 'My dad would walk down the street with his cigar and people would say: "Your son's at number one, Mr Stewart," and he'd say: "He certainly is!" He was very proud.'

The entire family were aware that Rod's phenomenal success had made him a millionaire. But for co-writer Martin Quittenton it was a different story. Jobbing musician Martin had gone back to his Sussex roots and had taken a part-time job, in a music shop, for a few pounds a week to make ends meet. 'When "Maggie May" hit number one I was going to work on a number 31 bus,' he remembers, 'and as we were going round a round-about I heard the record coming from a jukebox, through the open doors of a pub opposite Worthing Pier. Soon afterwards I was told it was top of the charts.'

Down at the BBC's TV studios in west London there was mounting excitement at *Top of the Pops*, when it looked as though Rod was about to hit number one, thus completing the Anglo-American double. But with the Faces by now enjoying a well-founded notoriety as a wild, boozing band, their appearance on the programme was also greeted with no little trepidation.

There were edicts issued that the band simply must behave while on the BBC's premises, and desperate prayers were offered in the offices of the bosses in the BBC's light entertainment department that Rod and the Faces would not arrive awash with alcohol.

Naturally, Rod and the band had a drink or four but they arrived in good humour, and their search for fun at the BBC centred more on their two other main pleasures: football and girls. John Peel, who was to figure controversially in the show that evening, remembers a violent game of football ensuing in the corridors of the BBC's Television Centre, with the Wolverhampton pop group Slade as willing and determined opponents.

There was also an attempt to burrow into the dressing room of Pan's People, the troupe of nubile, liquid-limbed *Top of the Pops* dancers, at the precise moment the girls were expected to be slipping into their stockings and suspenders. But it was a failure, foiled by the difficulty of locating the exact room in such a rabbit warren of offices.

Then, a very different problem arose. Rod and the Faces wanted their old mentor John Peel to join them on the *Top of the Pops* studio set, and have him pretend to play the brief mandolin solo that features so distinctively at the end of 'Maggie May'. They felt it would be a nice gesture to the man who had done so much to 'break' the band in Britain. The unions rang the alarm bells at this suggestion, but after a discussion it was decided that it was permissible, as long as Peel did not actually pluck or strum the mandolin or produce any musical note from the instrument. He was allowed merely to look as though he was doing so. 'I had to swear a terrible oath that I wouldn't play,' Peel recalls, 'but even so they tried to keep me out of shot.'

The resulting showing on *Top of the Pops* on 13 October 1971 was a curious compromise, with Peel perched on a stool half-hidden behind Mac's keyboards, while the cameras tried to make out as if he was not really there at all.

Rod chose a deep red velvet suit to wear on the show, but at the historic moment that rock's new monarch should have been regally looking down at the rest of the pop field, from his lofty transatlantic number one perch, Rod somehow contrived an extraordinary fall from grace when he went walkabout in the middle of the instrumental break. 'On the first take he got so carried away he actually fell off the back of the stage,' Peel remembers. 'There was shrieking and shouting and he had to climb back up and start again.'

The final version had Woody going walkabout this time, jumping off the back of the stage and messing around with a football. The clip ended with the Faces maintaining their football fervour by kicking a ball around among themselves, while Peel mimed deadpan to the sound of the mandolin. It was all good fun and for Robin Nash, the producer of *Top of the Pops*, it was a relief that at least all the members of the Faces had turned up. Nash had yet to experience with some horror the night Ronnie Lane decided he wouldn't be able to make it to the studio to back Rod singing 'Angel', so he sent a cardboard cut-out of himself instead.

'Maggie May' stayed at number one for five weeks, meriting five consecutive appearances on *Top of the Pops*. On one of these programmes the band cheekily appeared miming each other's instruments, with Ronnie Lane sitting in on drums, Ian McLagan on guitar, Kenney Jones on bass, and Ron Wood at the organ. 'Maggie May' remained Rod's signature tune until 'Da Ya Think I'm Sexy?' temporarily superseded it some eight years later.

The success of 'Maggie May' as a single undoubtedly helped to keep *Every Picture Tells a Story* at the top of the LP charts. But one good song does not turn an album into a multi-million seller around the world. 'Maggie May', which also topped the charts in Canada, Australia and New Zealand, was only one of many outstanding tracks on an LP that was the culmination of Rod Stewart's efforts so far as singer, songwriter and producer. It was a wonderful mixed bag of musical styles – even if Rod discovered some coughing and spluttering on the tapes when he came to remix them years later!

By common consensus there are three – and arguably four – classic tracks on the album, notably Rod's own composition 'Mandolin Wind'. This is a stunning ballad about a frontier settler declaring his love for the woman who has stayed with him, while the buffalo died around them, during a freezing winter. Rod sprang a double surprise on this track. It was amazing that he managed to conjure up such startling imagery from the colonial-style house in Ellington Street, Muswell Hill, which was by then his new home in north London. And he made every pop producer sit up and applaud his audacity for projecting the sound of the mandolin in such dominant fashion. 'I always thought the mandolin was such a romantic-sounding instrument,' he says.

'I found the mandolin guy on "Every Picture Tells A Story" and "Maggie May" in a restaurant in London, and the fiddle player, too. They were both playing stock romantic songs from the 1930s. In the studio I'd just whistle the parts for them to play.'

Musically, the title track, 'Every Picture Tells A Story', is a mess: unbalanced and shoddily thrown together. But it is the vocals that pull the song out of trouble and, with Rod calling in his old friend John Baldry, plus Maggie Bell, to urge the harmonies along with infectious enthusiasm and energy, it all somehow ends up as a storming rock number. Considering Rod was then only 26, he demonstrated a remarkable breadth of vision as a record producer on Tim Hardin's 'Reason To Believe'.

Hardin's own recording of the song had been simple in the extreme, relying mainly on finger-picking guitar and barely audible piano. For his own version, Rod took the song crisply up-tempo, cleverly used a blend of organ and piano to flesh out the musical arrangement, introduced a soaring fiddle break in the middle, then sang his heart out over the top of it all to make sure the gorgeous melody was fully delivered.

'Tomorrow Is Such A Long Time' continued Rod's preference for covering the less obvious compositions by great songwriters. This one was Bob Dylan's, but Rod stamped his own vocal character all over it with double-tracked harmonies. '(I Know) I'm Losing You' was Rod's nod of appreciation to the Temptations.

On side two he also bravely included a rousing rendition of Arthur Crudup's 'That's All Right', which Elvis Presley had virtually made his own, some 15 years earlier. He followed that up with the traditional anthem 'Amazing Grace', sung just to a slide guitar. Recorded, incredibly, in just three weeks, *Every Picture Tells a Story* was, in every sense, an album for everybody.

Martin Quittenton believes there were two other important factors that made the album such a success. 'At that time there was a very good chemistry among all of us in the studio,' he says. 'That's why things didn't take very long to record. A couple of takes and that was it. Also, as a producer, Rod was very shrewd and tended to keep a slight edge to everything, a certain roughness and home-made quality. For instance, Mickey had the most basic borrowed drum kit – he used to turn up with just his snare, a bass drum, and sometimes a high hat, the most humble of equipment. But that roughness and home-made quality of course got completely erased on Rod's later recordings, by the American type of production.'

Every Picture Tells a Story was greeted with great critical acclaim, notably from John Mendelsohn in *Rolling Stone* magazine. He commented that Rod was the single most glamorous rock figure rolling, and that there was no better backing band than the one Rod assembled for his solo recordings. He added: 'His are just about the finest lyrics currently being written, lyrics constructed solidly of strong, straightforward images that convey intense emotions. He is eloquent, literate, and moving – a superb writer.' *Rolling Stone* named Rod Rock Star of the Year and there were glowing accolades from much of the music press.

The album became a multi-million seller worldwide and prompted Gordon Mills, then manager of Tom Jones, to offer Rod a cool £1 million for a year's work. Although Rod turned it down to stay with the Faces, the band itself inevitably had mixed feelings about *Every Picture Tells a Story*'s success. On the one hand, it meant that they were able to sell out their concerts at Madison Square Garden in New York two months in advance. But the Faces also had to swallow the fact that shortly after they had released only their second single, in 1971, Rod the solo star was being presented with five gold discs at a reception at the Amsterdam Hilton Hotel, to mark the phenomenal sales of *Every Picture Tells a Story* in Germany, France, Scandinavia and the Benelux countries. These were trophies to add to a gold disc for US sales.

The hard-working Billy Gaff was now able to secure the very best deals for his hugely successful client, Rod Stewart. But there were times when he wished his famous artiste was not quite such a rascal – particularly with women.

On one legendary occasion, Gaff was sitting in a vast board-room in Holland, about to clinch for Rod one of the biggest record deals ever. Gathered around the table were record company executives, lawyers, accountants and financial advisers, all waiting for superstar Rod to fly in from New York to put his signature to the money-spinning contract lying on the mahogany table.

Idle drumming of fingers on the table's finely polished surface eventually gave way to mutterings of impatience, and finally harsh words of exasperation as hours went by and still there was no sign of Rod. Gaff held his breath and his nerve and assured them his client was on his way. His relief was almost tangible as the man to whom the record company was committing its millions eventually sauntered in. But Rod wasn't alone. Tottering in on kitten heels and revealing acres of thigh in a tiny micro-skirt, arms draped around Rod's neck, was a bosomy model, very obviously braless in her virtually see-through, tight-fitting cheesecloth blouse. As Rod proffered his apologies for his tardiness, the girl clung adoringly to him, ran her fingernails up and down Rod's back and fondled his backside. She clearly had a different, more basic, and pressing agenda in mind for Rod other than watching him put pen to some documents.

Taking a glance around the room at the assembled businessmen, Rod asked if they could all hang on for a minute, whereupon he disappeared with his clinging companion into an adjoining office. Rod's prospective paymasters then proceeded to sit around the table looking at one another for an hour, shaking their heads, while Rod attended to the urgent needs of his ladyfriend next door. Gaff remembers Rod eventually emerging with a big grin on his face, dusting himself down and signing the papers, before grabbing the hand of his by now glowing female companion, to head for the airport and back to New York.

While it was Rod's coffers that were now overflowing, it was nevertheless a sweet moment for both him and the Faces when, three weeks after his multi-gold discs presentation, they appeared together at Madison Square Garden on 26 November, to face an ecstatic audience. They took the stage to a deafening welcome after four trumpeters played a fanfare followed by the entrance of two dancing bears, a Mickey Mouse and a Donald Duck. Rod, resplendent in a pink satin suit, cheekily reminded the audience: 'Don't forget, we're the same group that played Ungano's 18 months ago!' – a reference to a small west-side club in New York which had since closed down, and a marker as to how far he and the Faces had come in such a short space of time.

Such a meteoric rise to fame and riches was rather lost on Rod's mum Elsie. When Rod asked her what she wanted from him that Christmas, he had in mind a gift of some diamonds or an expensive watch. But after a lot of thought Elsie announced she'd like a new bread bin and a little bottle of perfume. Rod roared with laughter.

From the moment he hit the big time, Rod was always exceptionally generous to his family. He bought his parents a new house in Woodley Road, Muswell Hill. He even put a Rolls-Royce at his dad's disposal, but Bob was too humble to use it often. And when his sister Peggy was diagnosed with multiple sclerosis at the age of 23 and was forced to spend much of her time in a wheelchair, Rod had a special house built for her that would accommodate her wheelchair.

For Rod, the unparalleled success of *Every Picture Tells a Story*, not least in the UK, was a relief. At last he had the recognition where he craved it most – in Britain – and it was a complete vindication of all the hard work that had gone before. But most pleasing to Rod was the fact that the faith he had placed in himself to arrange, produce and write much of the album had paid off handsomely.

'I never get tired of listening to *Every Picture Tells a Story*,' Rod said recently, 'especially when I think how sloppily it was recorded. The whole album was put together in three or four days. We had a drummer, Mickey Waller, who didn't have a drum kit. He'd go in the studio and borrow somebody else's drum kit. The drum kit on "Maggie May" was half of Free's, half of Status Quo's. If you listen to "Maggie May" there's no crash cymbals because he didn't use any. And Mickey always brought his dog into the studio.' Incredibly, 'Maggie May's backing track was completed in two takes and Rod took just two to add the vocals.

The album turned Rod into a superstar and it was the start of a golden period for him on record: his next five albums all topped the British LP charts.

In the summer of 1972 advance sales for *Never a Dull Moment*, the follow-up to *Every Picture Tells a Story*, topped one million in America alone and went high into the British LP charts within a week of its release, on 21 July. But whereas *Every Picture Tells a Story* had been made in a matter of weeks, Rod spent four months putting *Never a Dull Moment* together. Success inevitably meant that Rod's recordings were bound to become more sophisticated.

The new album yielded another chart-topping single, 'You Wear It Well', also co-written with Martin Quittenton. It was somewhat derivative of 'Maggie May', but the fans did not seem to mind. 'The day "You Wear It Well" went to number one, I was on a Cornish beach being told to clear off by some Cornish people,' Martin told the authors with a wry smile. 'The record was on their transistor radio and I said to them: "Do you know, I wrote that song," and they looked at me as if I was bloody nuts. I was a bit bolshie in those days.'

On the album there were three new Stewart/Wood compositions, and three more examples of Rod's impeccable choice in covering other people's songs. These included a storming version of Sam Cooke's 'Twistin' The Night Away' and a rendering of Jimi Hendrix's 'Angel', in which Rod brought out and emphasised the melody, which had been largely overlooked by Hendrix.

Rod personally felt the highlight of the album to be 'I'd Rather Go Blind', a soulful version of an old Etta James blues song which had been a minor hit for singer Christine Perfect and Chicken Shack. Deliberately choosing to record the song because he had never heard it sung by a man, Rod knocked it off in one take.

Never a Dull Moment quickly shot to the top of the LP charts, and was helped on its way by Rod and the Faces using much of the album as the cornerstone of their live repertoire. Although it was a Rod Stewart album, it was the closest to where the Faces were on stage at that time.

But despite the worldwide acclaim Rod was enjoying, the phenomenal record sales he was generating and the wealth he was accumulating beyond his wildest dreams, there were times when Rod would happily have traded it all in for a chance to line up at Hampden Park in a Scottish jersey, alongside his soccer idol Denis Law.

'I'll never forget,' says John Pigeon, 'the night I was standing at the side of the stage when the Faces were playing Manchester. Rod was just waiting to go on and he dug me in the ribs and said: "Guess what I saw this afternoon? Denis Law's knob!" He was elated. He had obviously been in Law's team dressing room.

'I played football with Rod in north London when he was a big star. He's a good player, not one of those stars who dresses up in a football kit and everyone passes the ball to him. Rod was in the thick of it, and you knew that all those hard lads scrapping it out with him in midfield would happily have broken his legs. But he wouldn't hide or tell them to go easy on him because he had a tour to do. He played hard and gained everyone's respect. It was a brave thing to do and I always admired him for that.'

On another occasion, Rod's love of soccer came close to costing him his life. He arrived in Argentina to watch Scotland in the 1978 World Cup to be met off the plane by anxious record company executives, warning him of the dangers of bandits. Rod was advised, that to minimise the risks, he would be taken only to the most expensive restaurants which were deemed to be perfectly safe. He did not have long to wait to discover they were horribly wrong. 'We had only sat down for about five minutes,' he recalls, 'and in they came with guns shooting. They told everybody to put their hands on the table while they went around stealing every-one's watches.

'Then somebody in the back, one of the chefs, rang an emergency button that called the police. He got shot stone-dead right in front of our eyes. Then the police came storming through about three minutes later and shouted to all of us to get down under the tables.

'I was pushed under the table with two great big security guards on top of me. The two bandits were shot dead, lying in the gutter.'

The gravity of the situation was comically defused when the restaurateur asked Rod to pay the bill: 'You must be kidding,' he protested. 'I'm not paying the bill. The restaurant has just got held up and I was nearly killed.'

It was a disastrous World Cup for Rod. His beloved Scotland were eliminated in the first stages of the finals.

If football managed, literally, to keep Rod's feet very much on the ground, the mass adulation he was receiving still apparently failed to scotch an insecurity inside him, that close friends have pin-pointed as one of his character traits.

One night at a gig in Los Angeles Bobby Womack and Mick Jagger dropped by and called in at the band's dressing room. Suddenly it dawned on everyone that here in the same room were three singers who had all recorded Womack's classic song 'It's All Over Now'. The opportunity was too good to miss.

'We started jamming on it,' recalls Mac, 'and Rod walked out. He couldn't handle the competition. He was very insecure and always envied Mick. He was so pissed off when Woody joined the Stones because that was his Keith Richard.'

As Britt Ekland later revealed, Rod was jealous of Mick and there was, in any case, a running rivalry between the Faces and the Stones as they followed each other from venue to venue across the US. Mick enjoyed stirring things up with sarcastic comments to Woody about Rod wearing the same sort of gear on stage that Mick himself had been wearing the year before.

And when Mick turned up to see the Faces at Roosevelt Stadium, New Jersey, he went so far as to stand behind an amp pulling funny faces at Rod and shouting out to Woody: 'Look at the LV' (short for lead vocalist). If he had but known it, Mick would have made great play of the fact that the Faces sometimes warmed up backstage by listening to the Stones' pulsating live album *Get Yer Ya-Ya's Out!*.

Mac noted still more peculiar behaviour from Rod when David Ruffin from the Temptations first dropped by to see the band. 'Ruffin was humbling himself sitting outside Rod's room and Rod wouldn't acknowledge him,' Mac recalls. 'He was very rude to people he idolised. He'd play nothing but Temptations records, he'd put his head back and sing like David Ruffin, but he couldn't handle meeting him.' Eventually, of course, they did become friends.

What cannot be denied was that Rod's solo success gave the Faces a tremendous boost, both as a live attraction and as a spur to record sales. The Faces, with Rod on lead vocal of course, followed 'Maggie May' into the charts for the first time, reaching number six with Rod and Woody's composition 'Stay with Me', a song that became a favourite anthem at every Faces gig.

And the band's album *A Nod Is as Good as a Wink to a Blind Horse* chased *Every Picture Tells a Story* so hard that it ended up at number two in the LP charts. 'That's really when we came good,'

Rod says. 'The Faces as a band never surpassed *A Nod Is as Good as a Wink*. Incredible album.' Few would disagree.

Now they travelled in specially chartered jets and chauffeur-driven limousines. And so what if they trashed a few hotel rooms along the way? They could afford to pay for the damage as they were now commanding up to $50,000 per show. Everywhere they went Rod and the Faces were a sell-out.

The standing joke the entire time the Faces were together was to greet any problem, especially a lack of booze, with 'Right, I'm leaving the band.' So Mac took no notice when Ronnie Lane sidled up to him in the dressing room in Chicago in May 1973 and said just that. Every one of them had heard it – and said it – over and over again. But this time Ronnie kept repeating it all the while until the band took the stage.

Mac recalls: 'In the middle of a number he came up to me doing the Ronnie Lane glide and he looked at me and said: "Fuck off!" I got up from the piano and I kicked him so fucking hard he didn't know what had hit him.'

Ronnie Lane walked off. However, this time he was serious. According to Mac: 'Ronnie wanted to get Rod out of the group. He saw there was a power struggle and he thought if he said he was leaving that we would agree to throw Rod out, and make him leader of the group. But he was wrong. The answer was: Fuck off, Ronnie!'

As Mac recalls: 'It wasn't the only time I kicked Ronnie. In 1976, when Rod had announced he was going solo, we decided to reform the Small Faces and we spent two days in Joe Brown's studio, recording some tracks and writing together. Ronnie got very cantankerous. He'd drink Mateus but he wasn't a good drinker like the rest of us and he'd throw up a helluva lot, hopefully out of windows, but sometimes in cars. And if he drank brandy he'd fall down.

'This time he had a couple of brandies and he got very nasty, very bitter and very angry to the point where I physically kicked him up the arse and out of the studio, and told him to fuck off and not come back. I didn't speak to him then for some years and of course it turned out that around that time he realised he had MS. He was very down and upset with life, angry and bitter because he couldn't see the future. It was very sad that we kicked him out but he never told us.'

With Ronnie's departure in June 1973, fittingly at the Edmonton Sundown, the Faces were never the same again and Rod knew it and privately admitted it. 'For me Lanie was the Faces,' he said frequently. 'Once he left, it took the ass out of it for me.'

Mac agrees: 'None of us was the greatest musician but Ronnie was one of the finest bass players in that his approach was very fresh and melodic. Technically, he wasn't the greatest bass player, but he had some great ideas and he stuck to them and didn't overdevelop them. That was the basis of the band: Ronnie and Kenney rock solid. Ronnie wrote a lot, too, and so the balance shifted when he left. Basically, things changed because Rod then did not have a foil so it became in his mind Rod Stewart and the Faces.

'Also, the strength of the band and what people loved about us was the comedy, the silliness, the drunken behaviour and the good fun that came from having a bunch of different personalities. When Ronnie left we missed his personality.'

The balance of power had shifted. Rod was now first among equals. He had more clout and there was one less voice to say, 'Let's not do that.'

Examination of the Faces albums shows that Rod and Woody wrote the rabble-rousing songs, while the extremely poignant ballads that formed just as important a part of the band's repertoire were written by Ronnie Lane. Moreover, of all the band members, Ronnie was the most aware of just how much life had changed in a few short years. He had become thoroughly disillusioned with the life of limos, private jets and hotels and having to dress up on stage every night. If that was what the others wanted, then they were welcome to it, he decided, and headed off to recapture a simpler life.

Ronnie's replacement was Japanese bass player Tetsu Yamauchi who was a genial character but spoke hardly any English, understood less, and largely did as he was told.

Further divisions appeared in the band when Rod brought in Jimmy Horowitz with a 12-piece string section for the final tour. Mac was furious and felt strings were simply not what the Faces music was all about. Often the string section comprised different musicians every night, which meant Horowitz continually had to rehearse them, and the more there were, the more chance there was that they would be out of tune. For amplification they had pick-ups they were not used to. Mac was delighted when invariably one of the musicians would get fed up and pull off the pick-up which meant every one would get blown out. Mac took openly to ridiculing the string section when they came on.

Rod also brought in guitarist Jesse Ed Davis because he wanted a bit more power. So instead of it simply being the five Faces, the band now comprised a Japanese bass player, who had difficulty communicating and was going through emotional problems, plus an assortment of outside musicians.

The divisions boiled down to Rod, Kenney, the strings, Jimmy Horowitz and the managers on one side and Woody, Mac and Tetsu on the other. The two factions even ended up staying in separate hotels.

Another clear problem for the Faces was that the band had no records to put out. In America, a double live album, *Coast to Coast/Overtures and Beginners* was released, but it was so far below par that it severely damaged the Faces' reputation.

It wasn't only on tour that the cracks were beginning to

widen. The tension was all too apparent when the Faces went into the studio to record a new LP called *Ooh La La*, released in April 1973.

'Rod didn't come into the studio for two weeks,' Mac recalls bitterly. 'Un-fucking-believable! We had all written songs and put a lot into it and for two weeks he wasn't even there. So we did all the tracks and when he came down to the studio we hoped he would like them. But it was a case of: fuck it if he doesn't, because we've put in all the hard work. There was one song, "Ooh La La", Rod said he didn't like – didn't like the way it was done, and it was in the wrong key for him. I said: "Well, where the fuck were you? What key do you want it in?" He said he didn't know, he wasn't really interested.

'Eventually we got a key out of him and he went away and took the tapes with him to work at the words. So we cut it again with Ronnie doing the guide vocal, and Rod came down again and said he didn't like it. So Woody then put a guide vocal on it and it sounded great and that's the way it stayed. We recorded it three times.

'Rod had two deals, two careers, and every night he went on stage he was promoting both sets of records. We were promoting his solo albums so he should have been promoting ours.'

Jimmy Horowitz has a different view. 'One of the problems was that the Faces were undisciplined – Rod wasn't. They would book a session at a studio to cut a Faces album at six o'dock and Kenney Jones would be there with his kit at five-thirty, ready to play, and shortly after that Rod would turn up. Then Ronnie Lane would come in, and then they'd start looking for Woody and Mac, and they'd turn up about ten by which time Rod would say: "Fuck this, there's a football match on at eleven tonight and I'm going home for that." And he'd go and tell the guys to get on with it and that he'd come in and do the vocals when they'd cut the track.

'I know that Rod was very frustrated at trying to cut records with the Faces, and they always complained that he saved his best songs for his solo albums. But it wasn't so much that as the fact that he had more say in his own albums. He didn't like spending hours and hours in the recording studios. He liked to get in, get it done and go home. Also, if you listen to Rod's albums and compare them with what he was doing on the albums with the Faces, Rod's were so much more imaginative and interesting.'

The rift between Rod and the rest of the band became a chasm when, in an interview in the British music weekly *Melody Maker*, Rod described the new *Ooh La La* album as 'a bloody mess'. The rest of the Faces were understandably incensed.

As Mac remembers: 'The day the album came out we had a lot of press to do, all of us, but before we did any he had slagged the album off. There was no reason to do that. It was just bloody-minded. He had everything to gain from it being a success. He wrote some songs on it and we would be playing them every night.' In retrospect, *Ooh La La* had much to offer, notably the punchy rock number 'Borstal Boys' and Ronnie Lane's tuneful title track. But at the time Rod was not the only one to voice his criticism of the album.

Such was the popularity of the band in 1973 that, despite Rod's outburst about *Ooh La La*, the album got to number one, and a song taken from it called 'Cindy Incidentally' reached number two in the singles chart. The following year, *Overture and Beginners*, the sad attempt to capture on vinyl the excitement the Faces generated live, even got to number three in the album charts, despite heavy criticism.

Ooh La La proved to be the final Faces studio album and the band was to discover, to its cost, over the next two and a half years, that it was simply not enough just to be regarded as 'the best' on stage. They needed new material – and the new material was Rod's solo material. Inevitably, the Faces were left behind hanging on to Rod's flying coat tails.

On stage there was still no doubting the pulling power of the Faces. Their British tour of 1974 grossed over £100,000, the year's top-earning tour. But the betting was that the majority of fans were there primarily to see Rod. The following year, 1975, they toured the US together twice but they all knew this was the end. By now Woody had been 'on loan' to the Rolling Stones for their American tour.

Woody had been asked to step in temporarily to replace Mick Taylor when he quit the Stones in December 1974. The rest of the Faces resented Woody for it and suspected, rightly, that he was set to join them full-time. 'Jagger swore to me that he was never going to nick Woody from the Faces,' said Rod. 'I said: "You lying bastard, of course you will." And of course he did.'

Rod was disappointed that his old friend saw his future away from the Faces. The band also resented the fact that they were increasingly being billed as 'Rod Stewart and the Faces'. 'We were always on an even split in the Faces: albums, gigs, every-thing – even when Billy Gaff eventually billed us as Rod and the Faces,'says Mac. 'But I knew that was the end. I mean, it was never Mick Jagger and the Rolling Stones, was it?'

The answer to that argument is that Mick Jagger never had chart-topping solo hits and albums while he was with the Stones. Interestingly, Rod often went out of his way to restore billing parity at Faces gigs. Embarrassed at finding the marquee billing to be 'Rod Stewart and the Faces', Rod personally phoned pro-moters requesting his name be removed. But it cannot have escaped Rod that the other Faces were increasingly trailing along behind him, while he was flying to heights they were never going to reach. The fact was that the Faces had had just one Top Twenty hit in America, 'Stay With Me', which reached number 17 in 1972. For his part, Rod was becoming increasingly distant from the others, and was having to field questions every day about whether he was leaving the Faces and going out on his own. He also had a new girlfriend, Britt Ekland, and his own personal publicist and assistant, Tony Toon, who was doing a fine job of keeping Rod's name firmly in the headlines. More importantly, Rod had recorded his new solo album *Atlantic Crossing* in America, without the Faces. 'It changed Rod a bit,' Kenney reflects, 'because he had bagged himself a film star, Britt Ekland, and now he had his own dressing room. That's when things went wrong. When Rod moved to the States there was this transatlantic breakdown in communication.'

Atlantic Crossing was released in the summer of 1975 and became a Top Ten hit in the US. When top record company executive Mike Gill flew to America to present Rod with a platinum album, all the other Faces were there for the presentation. 'You could cut the atmosphere with a knife,' says Gill. 'I thought, this is the end.'

Yet, even though the band was clearly disintegrating and there was mistrust and hatred all round, Rod, Mac, Woody and Kenney never quite lost their sense of humour. The posters which proclaimed 'Faces 1975 Fall Tour' were regularly altered by the group to 'Faces 1975 Downfall Tour'.

Minneapolis was the last Faces' date in November 1975 and the following month, on 19 December, it was reported that Rod was quitting the group. 'I have only just made up my mind,' ran Rod's official announcement, 'but I'm definitely quitting this time.'

Tony Toon added on behalf of his superstar master: 'Rod no longer feels he can work in a situation where the group's lead guitarist, Ron Wood, seems to be permanently on loan to the Rolling Stones.' Although the rest of the band must have seen it coming, they were still furious with Rod – especially Mac. 'The way he did it was such a shock,' he says. 'I was naïve to it all. I do forgive but I don't forget. The first I knew of it was when I read it on the front page of the *Daily Mirror*. Typical Rod, the reason he had done it that way was that he had tried to one-up Woody. He had got wind that Woody was going to join the Stones and he one-upped him.' Ian McLagan did not speak to Rod Stewart again for another three years, and did not see him for another ten, even though for some of that time they lived just a mile apart in Malibu, when Rod was married to Alana Hamilton. The ice would finally be broken when Rod, by now living with Kelly Emberg, invited Mac to his birthday party. When the two men met, Rod acted as if nothing had happened.

Following Rod's announcement, the formal departure of Woody to join the Rolling Stones on a permanent basis signalled the death knell for the Faces. Without Woody, Mac and Kenney knew there was no point in trying to go on.

In all the chaos and confusion of the split, Mac's brand-new Hammond organ disappeared. He did not set eyes on it again until the Faces' reunion at Wembley in 1986, when he learned that it had been on permanent loan to Rod Stewart's band. That too began and ended in rancour.

Rod was touring Britain that year and Mac, who since the split had tried to re-form the Small Faces and was now making a living as a session musician, was particularly keen on a reunion. So he wrote to Rod and the other ex-Faces saying they could make a lot of money from a short tour, but that they should make an album together first. 'I even photostatted a dollar bill on the end of the letter so I could get the point across that money could be made. I got a reply from Woody but I never got one from Rod,' says Mac, conveniently overlooking the fact that Rod – now truly a superstar – had least to gain from such a venture.

Finally, it was agreed that the Faces would reunite for a handful of numbers at the end of Rod's Wembley gig on 5 July 1986, with Bill Wyman on bass; Ronnie Lane was also on stage, but in a wheelchair.

'That night we played and did four numbers and the crowd were going crazy wanting more,' says Mac. 'So I said: "Come on, let's do 'Sweet Little Rock 'n' Roller'," and he said: "No, I've done it with my band." So I said: "Yeah, that's what I mean. Now let's play it as rock." We went out there and slaughtered it. I felt better after that.

'Now when I see Rod at his birthday parties it's just as though we're doing a gig tomorrow. We have a drink and pull faces.

'The Faces were never given any credit until after we had broken up. A sloppy show was part of our deal. But eventually it got ridiculous. It was: "Look at my bum, I'm Rod Stewart!"'

The Faces ethos was very simple: have a good time and become the biggest rock band in the world. They certainly succeeded in the first ambition and for a time came very close to clinching the second. In 1975 it was announced that the Faces had achieved the largest gross of any British tour in 1974, bringing in more than £100,000 in 24 concerts. As the cash for their concert tours came rolling in, the Faces presented Billy Gaff with a special gift one Christmas. It was a doll specially made to resemble Billy and on the base of it was printed the words 'Have you got the readies, Bill?' – a question Rod was apt to ask the manager after every show the band performed at every concert venue throughout the world. Rod always liked to see the money – once he even asked to see in notes all £500,000 due to him.

The Faces were also the second highest concert draw of the seventies after the Stones, and commanded a fee of $250,000 for one LA concert on 30 August 1975, on their last US tour. 'We'd never admit it, but we were just a poor man's Stones when we started out,' Rod confessed years later.

There was a powerful chemistry between the members of the band at their best. Rod's rasping voice was provided with the perfect platform thanks to Ronnie Wood's quality guitar work, Ronnie Lane's melodic bass style, Ian McLagan's inventive keyboard-playing and the reliable rhythms of drummer Kenney Jones.

As they crossed the world leaving a trail of wrecked hotel rooms in their wake, the Faces were on an almost permanent high. Before the wrangling, it was, for Rod, the ideal set-up. He did not have the sole responsibility of being the named lead vocalist, yet he could grab a steadily increasing share of the limelight.

With the strong personality of Ronnie Lane to balance Rod's influence, the Faces were remarkably able to enjoy a hedonistic lifestyle of boozing, womanising and good-humoured bad behaviour and still produce some stunning concerts. When the atmosphere soured, Lane left and Wood began guesting with the Rolling Stones: the good times were over.

'We'd gone the distance,' says Rod. 'We had five brilliant years together. No regrets whatsoever. It's only now I realise how good the Faces were. We had no idea how good we were. We really didn't have the confidence to go out there and play. We were the ultimate good-time band but we had no option because we were drunk all the time. The booze came about because we didn't think we were any good. Me and Woody had been fired by Beck and the three Small Faces were out of work because the singer had left. So we went round the pub and we had one thing in common, and that was boozing and a sense of humour.'

Years later Rod reflected on the Faces: 'I couldn't stand the records. I almost got into fisticuffs about it. That was a fun period, but as far as being in a band where I learned to sing better, that was in the Jeff Beck Group.

'We were all really close mates. I don't think you get many bands nowadays who are real close soul buddies like we were. I never did convince them that I always wanted to be a band member and that's all I wanted to be. If I had been a member of the Faces for the rest of my life I would have been happy.'

After Woody had left to join the Stones, all the members of the Faces did get to meet up with Woody again when the Stones were touring the US. They all congregated in Los Angeles and felt it was only fair that Woody should be the one to throw a party for old times' sake. The party was convened in Woody's stylishly mirrored room at the luxurious Beverly Wilshire Hotel where he was staying. Old habits die hard, and the mirrors ended up smashed to smithereens.

CHAPTER FIVE

DEE TIME

We had a fantastic three years and there was a lot of love between us for a long time. But I learned that you can have everything you could possibly want and yet still be unhappy. Dee Harrington

While Rod was building his solo career, he had settled into a steady relationship with a lovely, classy blonde girl called Sarah. Although she lived with Rod at his home in Winchmore Hill, Sarah stayed largely in the background as her boyfriend's fame started to spread.

Friends like Rod Sopp and Martin Quittenton remember Sarah with affection. 'She was a very nice girl,' Martin recalls. 'A lot of people were very sad when he did not stay with her permanently.'

Sarah meant enough to Rod for Mickey Waller to find him in tears because he was missing her so much, while they were on tour together in the Beck band in America. But the pressures of touring and being away from home so much led to a parting of the ways – and to Dee Harrington.

The very last thing Deirdre Ann Harrington expected to be was belle of the ball, the night she tagged along with her best friend Patsy Noble and Patsy's boyfriend Jack Oliver to a party being thrown for Rod Stewart and the Faces, in Los Angeles.

It was 29 July 1974 and Dee, as everyone called her, was in the sprawling city of the angels on America's west coast to enjoy the holiday of her young life. Bored with the London scene and her job as PA to the manager of a small record company in Westbourne Grove, near the Portobello Road, Dee had decided to head for LA with Patsy almost on a whim. Jack Oliver was moving from London to California to work for the Beatles' company, Apple, and at a farewell party thrown for Jack at London's trendy Speakeasy club, Jack had blithely suggested: 'Why don't you two come over?' Dee and Patsy looked at one another, giggled, and said: 'Yes, why not?'

The following day, to ensure that they would not change their minds, the two girls each put down a deposit for a flight to the USA. They had three months in which to scrape together the remainder or risk losing their deposits. To save a bit extra, Dee gave up renting a flat in London and moved back in with her parents in Bourne, Lincolnshire.

As the jet thundered along the runway and headed out over the Atlantic, Dee felt she was literally casting her fate to the wind. She was just 21 years old and this was to be a great round-the-world holiday adventure. Los Angeles, she decided, would just be a temporary stop-over. She would find work there and then save up her money to go on to Japan.

Like almost every new arrival in Los Angeles, Dee was wide-eyed at the way everything around her looked straight out of the movies. She almost had to pinch herself. Was she really here in the sunny California that she had heard the Beach Boys sing about so often on the radio while she was growing up? Her sense of awe was complete when she discovered that Jack Oliver's house, where she and Patsy would be staying, was in Hollywood Hills, right underneath the famous Hollywood sign.

To help out at Jack's house, Dee took on the cooking duties and Patsy the cleaning chores. But their first desperate attempts to find more permanent work ended in failure, as they did not have the necessary documents and work permits. They were both beautiful girls, but even their efforts to cash in on their looks and become bunny-girls at the Playboy Club proved unsuccessful.

Instead, they ended up with jobs promoting shrimp chips in supermarkets, Dee in dreary suburban Crenshaw and Patsy in upmarket Marina Del Rey. But one day was enough. They both returned to Jack's house in the evening complaining their feet were killing them. The next day they phoned up to spin the line that they had had a car accident and wouldn't be returning to work.

What Patsy really wanted to be was a model. On one occasion, Dee went with her to the house of a photographer called Brian Hennessey. As Dee sat waiting for her friend outside his studio, idly thumbing through the Jobs Vacant section of the *Los Angeles Times*, Brian suddenly appeared and looked long and hard at her. By now Dee sported a healthy tan and her lustrous hair was golden from the Californian sun. She was tall, slim, with spectacularly long legs and she was fresh-faced with a wide, sexy mouth.

Brian liked what he saw and immediately asked Dee if she was interested in posing for some photographs. 'What sort of photographs?' she enquired nervously. Dee had taken a course at the Lucie Clayton Modelling Agency and Training School in London, and had modelled briefly before deciding that modelling was boring. When Brian went on to explain that *Playboy* had commissioned him to take photos for centrefolds, she said, 'No, thank you' very firmly until he mentioned that she could expect $3,000 a photo.

Without any work in prospect for Dee, that sort of money

was an attractive proposition. 'I'd never taken my clothes off before,' she says, 'but at that time, 1971, you didn't have to take very much off for glamour photos. You showed your breasts and that was about the lot, so I wasn't worried.'

As her money was rapidly running out and Brian seemed a nice enough guy who could be trusted, Dee agreed to some test shots where she would pose topless, but nothing more revealing. Brian duly picked her up in his car early one morning and together they drove down to the ocean, where Dee slipped off her bikini top and frolicked in the sand for the camera. Back at the house in Hollywood Hills, Jack announced that he had a friend coming to stay. He was called Kenney Jones and he was the drummer with the Faces pop group who, after the great reception they had received in the US earlier in the year, were currently embarked upon their fourth tour of America.

When Kenney told Dee how much he was missing his wife, she generously cheered him up by cooking him a plate of good old English roast. In return for their hospitality, he invited Jack, Patsy and Dee to a promotional party being thrown for the Faces that same night, at a disco called Bumbles. 'I'll put your names on the door,' he promised the girls.

Unknown to Dee at that time, just about every teenage bikini-clad blonde along the beaches of California would have given her best surfboard for an invitation to such a party. Rod's album *Every Picture Tells a Story* had just been released and was on its way to number one in the charts. Rod and the Faces were three weeks into their fourth US tour. They had taken America by storm, and from the moment they had arrived in Los Angeles they had been besieged by devoutly enthusiastic, beautifully tanned girls seeking divine revelation in their beds.

But as Dee thought about what to wear for the party, finally opting for a simple little blue and white dress and white clogs for her feet, she was neither looking for romance nor expecting to be the centre of attention at such a glitzy occasion. She was just thrilled to be going to Bumbles, which was *the* club in Los Angeles at the time.

Safely inside the disco, Dee sipped a drink and sat by the fireplace relaxing until Rod, resplendently attired in a white velvet suit, and the Faces swept in with a noisy flourish, followed by a massive entourage of retainers. Soon, they drifted over to talk to Dee and Patsy, whereupon Kenney provided the introductions.

As the party progressed, Dee shyly watched with a mixture of amazement and fascination, as a string of girls, with bodies that stretched the seams of their outfits to the limit, threw themselves unashamedly at Rod, whispering all manner of promises in his ear. But, she noted, he didn't seem to take a particular interest in any of them. 'Hordes of women arrived, all done up with glittery stuff on,' she remembers, 'and Rod seemed to peel women off him. Then he asked me to dance.'

Rod's invitation to Dee to dance with him was prompted by the first notes of soul queen Aretha Franklin's haunting version of Ben E. King's classic 'Spanish Harlem', echoing from the disco speakers.

A pair of clogs was hardly ideal footwear to trip the light fantastic with America's current number one male sex symbol, but Dee happily took to the floor with Rod. Envious female eyes sparkled from all directions, as the gauche young British girl accepted the invitation that they had all yearned for. When they got chatting, Dee found Rod both friendly and amusing. Rod found Dee to be refreshingly natural and unaffected, delightfully feminine compared with the girls who had been trying to paw him all night. And she was undeniably beautiful. This was something special indeed.

Horowitz, who had had plenty of opportunity over the years

to observe the Stewart libido in action, recalls his protégé's more usual chat-up technique, if it can be called that: 'He'd be in a place like the Dome or maybe Tramp, and he'd sit there having a beer or maybe a Bacardi and some leggy blonde would walk in. If it was a girl he didn't know, he'd maybe have Tony Toon do his dirty work and send him over to investigate and set things up. But as often as not he'd go over and introduce himself – with a nose like that it was hard to be anonymous. Next thing you know, he'd be chatting them up, the Rolls-Royce would be summoned, and off they would go.'

With Dee, though, it was different. Big star Rod might have been, but she found him straightforward and down-to-earth. 'I liked him straight away,' she says. 'There was an immediate attraction. He had a good sense of humour, was instantly likeable, and he was just like a regular guy.'

And Rod was not going to forget in a hurry that first time he slipped his arm around Dee's slim waist and held her close. In an unashamedly romantic gesture, he later bought two copies of Aretha Franklin's 'Spanish Harlem' and gave one to Dee and kept one for himself, as a reminder of that first dance they had shared together.

When Rod pulled a little toy Lamborghini from his pocket, saying he owned the real thing and that he had had a Marcos before that, Dee made out she knew what they were and looked suitably impressed. 'But,' she admits, 'I hadn't a clue.'

After the party, Rod and Dee wandered for miles talking about music, London, football and what she was doing in LA. They were so completely wrapped up in their conversation, that they quite forgot that walking around at night in Los Angeles is not the kind of hobby to pursue, if you value your chances of waking up in this world the next morning.

Fortunately, it was a police patrol car that spotted them before any muggers or maniacs. Rod and Dee simply protested that they were British and that they were nearly home anyway. The cops drove on shaking their heads. 'Crazy English,' they muttered.

A taxi took them back to Rod's hotel where they talked and talked in his room until four in the morning. Rod complained of a headache and wanted Dee to stay but, as the well-brought-up daughter of an RAF squadron leader, she was not about to make love to someone she had just met. Unwilling to risk the journey back home on her own, and with Rod convincing her he was none too well, Dee worked out a compromise and decided to stay the night. They both got into bed and went to sleep.

According to Dee, they made love for the first time the next morning, and when they got dressed Rod put on her white knickers as a symbol of their closeness. Dee was to reveal to the world, much later on, that Rod wore women's knickers all the time because he liked their softness against his skin. That day Dee went back to Jack's to pick up her bikini and met Rod, as arranged, round the pool of the Beverly Hills Hotel. He invited her to his concert that night at Long Beach, but first they would go shopping. The limo was summoned to take them to Sunset Boulevard, where Dee was astounded to find that a public sighting of Rod was enough to cause a huge traffic jam.

'I'd never seen anything like it,' she recalls. 'All these people started standing up in their cars shouting: "See you tonight at Long Beach, Rod!" It was incredible. Then when we got out and went shopping, we walked and the limo slowly followed us. It was like in the films. I could hardly believe it.'

That night at Long Beach Arena, Dee watched in awe from the wings as Rod and the Faces brought 18,000 youngsters to their feet in an adulatory frenzy, the girls screaming hysterically at Rod's every move. But there was something about the back-stage atmosphere that unnerved her: 'I was worried by all the security with guns,' she remembers, 'and the way people behaved backstage shocked me. They were all trying to get close to Rod. He was so popular. After he'd left the stage I followed this mass of people thinking this must lead to where Rod was. I came to a corridor and his room was at the end. I could see him but I was behind 20 other people all in a mad rush trying to get in.

'Then, after Rod and the band had changed, there were sandwiches and drinks in another room, and for the first time I was left having people I didn't know talk to me, and they were very strange. Who they were and how they got there I just don't know.'

The next week was a whirlwind for Dee as she and Rod became inseparable lovers. She went to San Francisco with him to watch another concert, where she saw still more hysteria every time her new boyfriend so much as moved a muscle. At the post-gig party she was horrified to find a man having an epileptic fit right in front of her. He began convulsing before pitching forward and knocking over a lamp as he crashed, twitching like a marionette, to the floor, causing the electric socket to buzz alarmingly. 'Of course, there were hundreds of people doing nothing. I ran off to get a spoon,' says Dee. 'All I could remember was that you had to put a spoon in their mouth to stop them choking. It was all so upsetting.'

Swept along on the manic rock 'n' roll tidal wave that was Rod Stewart and the Faces, Dee tried to sort out her emotions when they returned to Los Angeles. She knew she really liked Rod and that he made her feel special. 'It was quite a physical thing between us, but I don't know whether I was falling in love with him,' she says. 'I think I was just wondering: what is all this? But I also remember thinking how my mum would be pleased. She thought I'd marry an American and never come back.'

With Rod's American tour about to finish and his return to England imminent, Dee had some fast thinking to do. Now she had met Rod, did she really want to go on to Japan? Was Rod just a holiday fling or was he something more to her? Did she want to stay in Los Angeles? Even more pressing, did she want to appear half-naked in *Playboy* magazine? She says: 'When we got back to LA, Rod got Brian Hennessey to come round and show him the shots of me topless on a projector and tried to destroy them all. Rod had a love-hate view of the photos. He kind of liked them and yet he didn't. So, much to my relief, I didn't continue with the photos.'

Dee chose to stay on in LA while Rod went home. But soon he was on the phone to her to ask if she was coming back. 'I don't know what to say,' she told him.

Shortly afterwards, in August, Dee's money ran out and Rod was delighted when she told him on the phone that she was returning to England. They agreed to meet in a pub in Lancaster Gate. Dee was sitting waiting for him when Rod walked in and whisked her off to the Serpentine bar, to meet a couple of his friends, before taking her on to a trendy restaurant in Kensington Church Street. As Dee toyed nervously with the vegetable-shaped salt and pepper pots on their table and gazed at Rod, they both knew that California had been no quick fling. They both came from north London and they could have met up at any time. Yet, for some reason, fate had decreed they travel thousands of miles to find each other. As they looked across the table their minds were made up. 'That was it,' says Dee. 'I moved in with him.'

When she was asked to go back to her old job in Westbourne Grove, Dee readily agreed. She was determined to maintain some sort of independence. In the mornings she would slip out of bed as Rod lay back on the pillows, watching her dress.

'How can you get up and leave me every morning?' Rod moaned.

'It's easy!' Dee teased him.

'I went off to work and he couldn't bear it,' she says.

Before he met Dee, Rod had lived for a time with Sarah in her mother's flat in Wilton Crescent, and later, in her house in Notting Hill Gate. But he had also used some of his early income to buy a small house in Highgate, near the family home. 'I had a car outside that was worth more than the house I was living in,' he recalls with a laugh. 'I paid £6,000 for the house and the car, a Lamborghini Miura, was £8,000. I used to wake up every night and look out of the window to make sure no one had nicked it.'

The house was just five minutes' walk from his mum and dad's and Rod described it as: 'A detached house, like the colonial houses in the States with a veranda at the front.' Baldry was to rent this when Rod moved up the housing ladder to a more spacious, £30,000 home in Stanmore, a few miles to the north.

Now Rod was living at the Broad Walk, Winchmore Hill, in north London. It was a four-bedroomed mock Tudor house with two sitting rooms, one fitted with a thick pile white carpet and beautiful oak panelling, the other with parquet flooring lined with exquisite leather-bound first and second edition books. There was also room for Rod to build a Great Western Railway branch-line station that comprised yards of track and carriages he had made himself.

Outside were manicured lawns and rose bushes. Dee thought it was a lovely home but Rod, who was now reaping the rewards of his recording successes, soon put it up for sale and began searching for a new home, with the help of a man called Perry Presse who specialised in finding property for the rich men of rock.

Perry would ring up with details of houses that might be suitable, and Rod and Dee would pick him up in Rod's big old Rolls-Royce and go off to view them. 'But they never seemed suitable for Rod,' Dee recalls. 'He obviously had it in his mind that he wanted a place with a bit more splendour, because his accountant had told him to spend £100,000 on a house. But he couldn't find a house for £100,000!' The advice to Rod to plunge a large sum of his money into property made financial sense. In those days the wealthy often mortgaged themselves to the hilt because the interest on payments could be set against tax.

One day on the way back from the coast, Perry happened to mention that he knew of a house that had just come on to the market that might suit them, although he was not representing it. He told Rod they would pass it on their way back to London, so Rod said he would like to stop and look at it.

Rod was at the wheel as the Rolls glided round a big roundabout near Windsor and Perry pointed out a lodge house and a pair of wrought-iron gates, flanked on either side by two vast white pillars. They drove through the gates and up a drive surrounded by rhododendron bushes. Eventually, they drew up in front of Cranbourne Court, a magnificent Georgian mansion which took even Rod's breath away. 'Yes, I'd like to see that tomorrow, Perry,' said Rod as he turned the Rolls around and drove slowly back down the drive.

Rod and Dee were back the next day. Rod loved the house the minute the owner, Lord Bethell, showed them inside. Dee had her reservations as she looked round. It was so big, she thought. The house had 32 rooms in all, including eight bathrooms, and boasted several exquisite Adam fireplaces. It was set in 17 acres of grounds, and Dee smiled to herself as her rock-star lover and the Lord in Waiting to the Queen strolled the grounds together. She wondered if Lord Bethell knew who Rod was. 'He probably thought: who is this peculiar-looking person?' says Dee.

Rod bought Cranbourne Court for £89,000, a princely sum in 1971, but it was a characteristically canny buy: when a valuation was carried out, the fireplaces alone were deemed to be worth £22,000. Dee and Rod were interested to discover that the American comedian Bob Hope had once lived at Cranbourne Court, and Rod, in particular, was delighted to learn that the movie star Sophia Loren used to visit the house to buy items when it was owned by an antiques dealer. He liked the idea of the Italian screen siren gliding elegantly across his sitting room.

Rod and Dee would be able to move in at the end of the year and so, over the next three months, they set about collecting furniture for their new home, cramming it into their Winchmore Hill home ready to be taken to Windsor. Dee was impressed by Rod's shrewd good taste on their shopping expeditions, and the fact that he knew in his mind exactly what he wanted.

That autumn Rod and the Faces were due back in the US for yet another tour, their fifth. Dee flew to New York with Ronnie Wood's wife Krissie, arriving a day ahead of the band, who were due to play their first gig ever at Madison Square Garden. Dee wanted her reunion with Rod to be so perfect that she checked out every single room in the Sherry Netherlands Hotel, before choosing a fabulous wood-panelled suite she felt sure Rod would like.

The following evening, 24 November, was Thanksgiving Day. Rod arrived and promptly asked Dee to marry him. It was just three months since he had first set eyes on her. 'It wasn't the trendy thing to get married then,' she recalls. 'People lived together, or "lived in sin", as they used to call it. It was far more exciting to live in sin, but I said yes because we were having a great time, we had a fantastic relationship, I thought he was a fabulous man and we were together as much as we could be. But it was a bit of a shock.'

At that point 'Maggie May' was number one in both America and Britain, and *Every Picture Tells a Story* was still top of the album charts on both sides of the Atlantic. Not even the Beatles or Elvis Presley had achieved that. Rod was the biggest rock star in the world. Not for the first time since she and Rod had fallen in love, Dee thought to herself: why me?

'I was 22 and I never thought I'd get married at 22,' she says. 'I turned down the offer of a ring – I didn't want one. But we were engaged.'

The engagement quickly became public knowledge, with the inevitable headlines, and they talked of getting married on New Year's Day. Instead, though, when the moment came, they decided to throw a big party at Cranbourne Court on New Year's Eve, and move into the mansion properly the following day. House-proud Rod figured it would be simpler to have all the guests let their hair down while there was no furniture in the place. And so the happy couple spent their first night together in the mansion sleeping on a mattress.

When the removal van turned up to deliver the furniture they had so lovingly gathered for their new home, Dee was shocked to find that it took up a mere corner of one of the huge rooms. But Rod was overjoyed at the sheer spaciousness and grandeur of Cranbourne Court. When he showed his sister Mary into the hallway of his fabulous new home on her first visit, he excitedly threw himself on the floor and shouted with pride: 'It's mine, all mine!'

There was so much to be done in the house that Dee finally decided to give up her job and devote her energies to it, for splendid as Cranbourne Court was, it was clear that money would need to be spent on it if it was to be restored to its original glory. Rod's brother Bobby was brought in to oversee the redecoration, and, over the next two years, Rod spent a fortune transforming the old house into a mansion fit for a prince of pop. By the time it was finished it was a remarkable mixture of brazen opulence, exceptional good taste, exquisite elegance and typical Rod.

To give visitors a warm welcome, a large Stewart tartan curtain was draped on the inside of the front door, and a scarlet carpet was laid over the huge original black and white chequered stone tiles in the vast hall. After a two-year search, Rod and Dee found a magnificent crystal chandelier to hang from the hall ceiling. Two brass pillar-style lamps, both fully five feet high, stood sentinel at the foot of the sweeping, white-banistered staircase. On each of two landings above was an eighteenth-century statue of a bare-breasted maiden, recently acquired from Sion Lodge.

Dee chose a tartan carpet for the snooker room, with curtains to match, and, for added tartan effect, the square mouldings on the blue-painted ceiling were picked out in a startling red. Above the ornate stone fireplace Rod hung a pub mirror which proclaimed the legend: 'Stewart's, Scottish distillers of finest whisky.' On the walls were framed photographs of his Scottish footballing heroes in action, notably Denis Law, and his gold discs.

The dining room was painted blue and three Tiffany-style lamps, brought from Los Angeles, hung low over the specially made dining table. Surrounding it were eight peacock-tailed dining chairs.

In the music room the shelves groaned under the weight of LPs, books and Rod's hi-fi. A dozen guitars and banjos hung from hooks on the wall and a baby grand piano was installed. When the tuner arrived, he turned out to be blind. Thereafter, since neither Rod nor Dee could play very well, Rod invariably whispered to Dee: 'Get him to stay and play.' The blind man would then be slipped a generous tip so that Rod and Dee could listen to his wonderful piano-playing throughout the house.

A new wing was added to make way for a space-age kitchen that included a central circular work unit, with a breakfast bar made from solid cedar wood, long, yellow cylindrical hanging lights, and a large yellow mushroom-shaped dome equipped with extractor fans and more lighting.

Perhaps the most tasteful room in the house was the formal sitting room with its Chinese silk screens, antique furniture and Persian carpets. Leading off it was the much more informal TV room which had a fluffy white carpet and yellow walls covered in French advertising posters. There were deep maroon velvet sofas and a distinctive armchair. Only an environmentally unfriendly coffee table spoilt the room, the legs and struts being made from antler horns. The most ostentatious room, however, had to be the conservatory, a circular folly, its yellow walls stacked high with a collection of glass cases containing stuffed birds, foxes and other animals.

Upstairs, Rod and Dee chose as their bedroom a large bay-windowed room at the back of the house which looked out over a lawn to the classical formal gardens beyond. Above their king-sized bed Rod hung a large Scottish flag – yellow with a red lion. Another Scottish flag was draped over the bed-head and a third dominated one of the walls.

Two further rooms upstairs were turned over to Rod's model train layout, somewhat expanded since his teenage days. He even had a hole cut through the connecting wall at waist height, so that the trains could chuff from one room to the other, along a track mounted on a specially constructed stand. Rod spent hours painstakingly sanding, building, gluing and painting various additions to the layout. Expeditions to a shop in Holborn to pick up a packet of plastic animals or models of men digging on the line were one of his great joys.

When he was satisfied that the layout was more or less complete, Rod had an official opening of the line and cracked open a bottle of champagne to toast its success. The pride Rod took in his model railway, however, obviously did not rub off on Dee's

cat, Pussy Galore. One morning, Rod made an unsavoury discovery in a pile of sand he had lovingly colour-sprayed to look
like railway scenery: to his fury, Pussy Galore had left a very
messy, malodorous calling card.

While the interior of Cranbourne Court was taking shape, no
less attention was being paid to the gardens. The York stone
pathway encircling the house was taken up and carefully relaid,
and outside additions included fountains, paths, lawns, sundials,
rose gardens and rainbow-coloured flower-beds. Dee, who had
spent some of her youth in a country town in Lincolnshire, particularly enjoyed strolling along a wonderful azalea walkway.

A further £40,000 went on turning the outdoor swimming
pool at the side of the house into an indoor pool. Rod instructed
the builders to build round and over the existing pool, in keeping with the style of the main house. The extension also housed
a sauna and solarium, and there was a big red spiral staircase that
led up towards the staff wing and the corridors that ran the
length of the house. When it was all finished Rod could hardly
wait for his first dip, and watched with mounting excitement as
it slowly filled with 32,000 gallons of water from a solitary tap.
But suddenly two walls of the pool collapsed as the plaster gave
way. All 32,000 gallons of water had to be drained away again to
make way for repairs.

With a housekeeper, an extremely bulky chauffeur called
Cyril and brother Bobby living at Cranbourne Court, as well as
Rod's two collies, Mary Poppins and Sally, Dee was never going
to be completely alone when Rod was away on tour. But when he
first went away she missed him so much she went out and
bought a horse, a bird, a dog and the infamous Pussy Galore, all
in one day.

The bird was an ornate lorikeet Dee had purchased on a
shopping expedition to Harrods. She knew she had to buy him
when she spotted him hanging upside down on his perch and he

opened an eye and said: 'I saw you first.' From another shop she ordered a large cage to be built for the bird, but when she went to pick it up it proved to be too big to go through the door. Obligingly, the shop took the door off its hinges.

Dee named the bird Electric Birdy because he made a noise with his beak that sounded like electricity. 'He really liked me,' she says, 'and put up with Rod. If he screamed a lot, Rod used to lock him in the walk-in safe. He used to sit on the back of the huge teapot we had and Rod used to try and get him to go in and close the lid – he was only playing, of course.'

Dee's domesticity was complete when Rod had the field fenced off and a stable-block built. She bought three horses in all: a palomino colt called Cheval, a thoroughbred mare called Cara Mia and a mare she bought for Rod called Spotty. Unknown to Dee, Spotty was already in foal and later produced Little Spotty. While Rod played with his train set, Dee was content to go riding in Windsor Park. Rod rode occasionally but decided his Lamborghini was a quicker and more comfortable way of getting from A to B. And soon his love of cars also stretched to owning a Mercedes 600 with back-seat TV and two Excaliburs, as well as the Rolls and the Lamborghini.

If Rod was away Dee busied herself with looking for things for the house. When chauffeur Cyril drove Dee to Harrods in the Rolls or the Mercedes, she often wondered what people must have thought of her as he held open the car door for her and she would step out in jeans, purple boots from Biba and wearing no makeup, her hair barely combed.

When Cyril was driving her, Dee liked to sit regally in the back and tease him. 'You know, Cyril,' she used to taunt, 'if I was going to employ a chauffeur I'd have this young, really well-dressed, incredibly handsome chauffeur.' But Rod, she knew, would never have allowed that.

According to Dee, Rod enjoyed all this domesticity. He loved eating at home and having friends down to the house for a meal. And so, gradually, some sort of loose routine entered their lives, with Dee getting up every morning to go into the kitchen to make the tea and return with the post and papers. Letters from cranks are an occupational hazard of being a rock star and Rod received his share. 'When we first moved in there used to be this very mad German woman who wrote dreadful letters saying Rod was going to die,' Dee recalls.

For security a ten-foot fence was erected all the way round the house with barbed wire at the top, and Rod bought Dee an Alsatian she named after Carlo Ponti, the husband of Sophia Loren, whom she so admired. But still the fans somehow managed to get in. One night Dee was awoken by a crashing noise and assumed it was just Rod and his pal Rod Sopp, returning the worse for wear from a pub crawl. She was so sure it was the two Rods that she even turned on the outside lights for them, only to discover it was two fans so desperate to see Rod that had they had broken in.

On lazy Sunday afternoons, Rod and Dee liked to sit watching television or roasting crumpets on the crackling log fires. Invariably they would see young girls running across the back garden. It was the weekend and some of them had travelled miles for a glimpse of their idol, so Rod and Dee would go out and chat with them, sign autographs and send them home happy.

On the subject of one of the favourite topics of conversation among Stewart-watchers, Dee says: 'How can anyone say he was mean when we went on holiday to Mombasa, flew to Puerto Banus to stay on his boat, and we both had his and hers Rolls-Royces and Lamborghinis and a six-door Mercedes? But we were just as happy going down to the pub, as we often did, in our slippers and with the dogs.'

Some of Rod's friends did notice a change in Rod, however, after he acquired Cranbourne Court. Says Martin Quittenton:

'It was possessions and antiques and huge great rooms and it was very difficult to feel natural. I rolled up in a Renault 4 – not that I couldn't afford a bigger car, I wanted a Renault 4 – and there would be a Lamborghini outside. Suddenly it was a different life.

'When Rod wanted to talk to me some faceless person from the office would phone up, a different voice every time, saying Rod says can you do this and can you do that. So I said to him once: "Why don't you phone me any more?" He looked uncomfortable and didn't actually answer. It was fixers in the office and everyone doing things for him, and so the personal relationship between Rod and others was bound to change.'

Quittenton also remarks shrewdly: 'As for the acquisitiveness, if you are not sure about people, perhaps you have possessions instead because they can't be taken away from you.'

Meanwhile, as the live-in lover of the world's most celebrated pop star, Dee Harrington was inevitably coming in for a good deal of bitchy envy. Eventually the wives of the other members of the Faces came to realise that Dee was a thoroughly decent young woman.

But it took months for them to accept her. A new girlfriend on the scene appeared to be a danger signal. If Rod had fallen for another woman, they worried, it might give their men similar ideas. Naturally they also didn't like the fact that Rod was getting so much more attention, lived in a much bigger house, and eventually earned so much more money from his parallel solo career than their other halves. The menfolk in Rod's entourage, on the other hand, thought Dee was lovely in every way. She was thoroughly likeable, there was a natural warmth about her, she didn't do drugs and, in the mad mêlée backstage at Faces gigs, security men and roadies always made a point of keeping a protective eye out for her, to make sure she was looked after.

Dee was at first horrified by the shameless way the groupies offered their sexual favours. They were so obvious, so brazen, and so shamelessly determined. But in a way she found it oddly flattering to think that here were all these girls fighting to make it with Rod, and yet she was the one in his bed at nights. She was relieved to discover that when groupies somehow tricked their way past security to their hotel room, one call to the management would have them rapidly ejected.

Initially she chose to be with Rod as much as possible, before realising it was important not to suffocate him. To begin with she went on tour with Rod in America, but accompanied him less often when it became clear that the Faces preferred the general rule: No Wives. The exception was one memorable gig at the Roundhouse in London, where all the wives showed up and sat on chairs at the side of the stage, just a few feet from where the band were playing. First one moved her chair nearer the band, then another followed, and then a third decided she wasn't going to be outdone so she moved nearer, too. In the end they all shuffled on to the stage on their chairs, in full view of the audience, and much to the annoyance of the roadies.

When Dee did not accompany Rod to gigs she decided she would simply accept that groupies were always going to be part of the rock scene, and that it was best to blot them from her mind.

To please Rod, Dee dressed in very sexy, skimpy rock-chick outfits: tight little fashionable hot pants, shorts, or mini-skirts, tiny tops and figure-hugging halternecks. She had the perfect feminine frame for them and Rod liked her to make the most of it. Dee could look sensational. 'He always liked long legs and short skirts,' Dee says. 'Rod liked me wearing as little as possible and no makeup. But I was young and inexperienced and when we went out I looked at people like Mick Jagger's wife, Bianca, and thought how glamorous they were. So I'd go back home and try to make myself up and Rod would say: "Take that crap off your face." I always thought I looked a bit dreary except when I wore the huge, fantastic colourful feather boa he bought me. It was sequinned and glistening and when I'd wear it over little suede shorts and a tiny top, you couldn't really see I had any clothes on at all.'

Dee found Rod to be a passionate and ardent lover. 'He's instantly likeable and – I think he does this in all his relationships – he makes you feel very special,' she reflected.

There would be long nights when they would cosy up together and make love to Rod's favourite albums, like Otis Redding's first master-work, *Otis Blue*. Another Rod favourite in the bedroom was Bobby Womack's *Facts of Life*, a stirring collection of soul ballads by a singer Rod had long admired. 'This is a very good shagging record,' Rod asserted in typically forthright manner, years later.

Dee also learned Rod was capable of moments of great tenderness. He repeatedly told Dee he loved her and was rarely afraid to show his feelings. Jealous troublemakers would try and label Rod mean because he hadn't bought her a gold Cadillac or a diamond tiara. But Dee would not have wanted them anyway – the roses he personally picked for her from the garden when she was ill meant so much more to her. So, too, did his romantic admission that he had recorded Jimi Hendrix's 'Angel' just for her.

However, although there was evidently a lot of love between Rod and Dee, the papers were full of rumours that he was seeing other girls. One morning she and Rod were having breakfast in bed and perusing the morning tabloids, when Dee saw a picture of Rod in a gossip column with Princess Miriam of Johore. A frosty two hours followed while Rod tried to explain himself. Often the stories were pure fabrication but, while Dee had to put up with all the press rumours of Rod's affairs, Rod could not contain a jealous streak if Dee appeared to be flirting. She was an attractive girl and received more than her share of male attention. One night at Tramp, London's exclusive Jermyn Street club frequented by the rich and famous, Rod and Dee were enjoying a night out with the Manchester United football team. While Rod was deep in conversation with his idol Denis Law, Dee, who was looking her stunning best that night and in a vivacious mood, proceeded to dance with various members of the team. That was fine by Rod.

Then Ryan O'Neal, the handsome Hollywood actor whose libidinous exploits with beautiful women were reputed to run a close second to Warren Beatty's, started to show an interest in Dee.

Twice-divorced O'Neal – first from actress Joanna Moore and then from his TV co-star from *Peyton Place* Leigh Taylor-Young – had cut a wide romantic swathe through Hollywood with the diverse likes of Joan Collins, Barbra Streisand, Ursula Andress, Anouk Aimée, Bianca Jagger and Farrah Fawcett of *Charlie's Angels* fame. He was a good-looking man with a heart-throb reputation, thanks to the romantic movie weepie *Love Story*, and now he wandered over to ask Dee to dance and she accepted. Suddenly Rod's mood changed. 'That was it,' says Dee. 'He bought a pint of beer and came over and threw it all over me. I didn't know what had hit me. I stood up and got hold of his hair and shook him and pounded him. I was crying, hysterical – and drenched.'

As they bustled their way up the stairs, they were greeted by another one of Dee's admirers, the designer from Granny Takes a Trip who made all the Faces' stage clothes. Rod's response to his friendly 'Hi!' was a punch in the stomach. Outside Tramp, Rod showed an extraordinary insecurity when he said of Ryan to a distressed Dee: 'He won't treat you like I do' – a remark which, after the drenching and fracas, Dee could have taken in several ways. Dee assumed Rod meant that he was better for her than Ryan O'Neal. Dee was utterly bemused. All she had done was dance twice with – albeit handsome – Ryan, but to her Rod was acting as if she had left him and waltzed off to a new life with Ryan.

Rod was later mortified that he had behaved so badly in front of Denis Law. His idolatry of the Scotland and Manchester United striker was such that when Law visited Rod and Dee at Cranbourne Court, Rod ordered Dee faithfully to record for posterity every moment of their kick-about in the garden. To this day, Rod regards as one of his most treasured possessions the Scottish cap given to him by Denis Law in 1974, when Scotland qualified for the World Cup finals in Germany.

But while Dee was happy to indulge Rod's footballing fantasies or look after his domestic arrangements, it was not enough. She wanted to be something more than just an appendage to a famous pop star or the woman at home. She talked it over with Rod, taking care to explain to him that she was not dissatisfied with him or with her lot. She simply wanted to *do* something. She felt lost in the shadow of Rod's rocketing career and she started to want to find herself.

'Right from the beginning,' she remembers, 'he had that old-fashioned thing of me being the woman at home. But that wasn't enough for me, although I realise how it must have come over to Rod, as though I was saying it didn't matter if he was number one in the charts, had more money than anyone else, and the biggest house around – I still wasn't happy.

'I didn't want children or to get married. I didn't want to go out clubbing or behave like Bianca Jagger and be seen out. I must have looked like this miserable, confused female who didn't want to participate and yet Rod wanted to live the rock star's life. He had to because, although I didn't realise it at the time, he was an industry. He had to have a woman who was very glamorous and it was all to do with living this rock-star image and keeping those record sales and concert tickets going.

'Before, Rod was just himself with a job and it was great. There was a balance. But then he became enveloped in this great rock star's image. He'd hang out with the Gary Glitters, go to Tramp all the time and be seen, and women wanted to be seen with him. I got the backlash because the newspapers would phone up and ask me if I knew whether Rod was having an affair with Susan Ford, President Ford's daughter, or some other girl. It got so that any girl who spoke to him or sat at the same table as him was assumed to be going to bed with him. I'm sure he was in bed with quite a few of them. But I don't know whether any of these other girls meant anything to him. They never survived very long. I always used to say to the papers: "Well, I'm glad I'm not having a ding-dong with him because I'd never see him – because he's always at home with me!"'

As well as the fanatical teenage groupies fighting to get to Rod, there were now a bevy of beautiful girls from the showbiz world gravitating towards the band's concerts and parties. The band's propensity for partying and having fun was infectious, and Rod and the Faces were soon enjoying the company of gorgeous models like Kathy Simmonds, sexy 007 Bond girls like Julie Ege, established actresses like Susan George, not to mention ambitious starlets, glamorous pin-ups and party girls.

Beautiful, sexy, lovingly loyal and delightfully feminine as Dee Harrington was in her own right, Rod's wandering eye found many a tempting target as he surveyed the girls drawn like a magnet to the élite rock echelons he was now bestriding.

Among the most attractive and vivacious beauties temptingly crossing his path around this time was Bebe Buell, a ravishing American model on the books of the prestigious Eileen Ford agency in New York. Physically, Bebe fitted the mould of a Rod Stewart girl: she was tall, with spectacularly long legs, a rich mane of wild tumbling hair, and a curvy body which she took little persuading to display naked to the world as a *Playboy* centrefold. But, as Bebe was to reflect ruefully many years later, although becoming a *Playboy* centrefold was to give her a great image sexually, it was like throwing down a challenge to every rock star to conquer her physically. Posing provocatively nude for *Playboy* was like waving a red flag inciting all the rock bulls to take a run at her. Rod was just one of them.

But, as one of Rod's circle told the authors after witnessing an early Rod–Bebe encounter, Bebe wasn't exactly running away. Bebe had to admit that when she first got close to Rod, she found he reeked of rock star, smelled so good and registered an exciting sexual energy. As a woman used to men hitting on her and wanting her sexually, Bebe recognised that she had equally registered with Rod: 'Rod fancied me, big time.'

In time they would have an affair, but the snag for Rod initially was not only that Bebe already had a steady rock-star lover, Todd Rundgren, but Todd had also got to hear all about Rod Stewart's appetite for women, especially long-legged models.

Bizarrely, Bebe had arrived in the middle of Rod's superstar rock scene from the unlikely launch pad of St Mary's Residence, a women-only lodgings in New York run under strict rules by nuns. There, the virginal Bebe from Virginia had been settled by her model agency to encourage good behaviour and early nights. But soon Bebe was blatantly lying to the nuns in order to sneak out after dark, dressed to kill, to take a bus down Second Avenue to hang out at a downtown club she'd heard was enticingly decadent, called Max's Kansas City. Bebe's childhood idol had been Marianne Faithful and, greedy to experience a similarly stimulating life among rock stars in New York City, Bebe discovered Max's was all she hoped for, and more.

On her first visit there, Bebe met artist Andy Warhol and a wannabe singer by the name of Debbie Harry (later to find fame, of course, as the face and voice of the band Blondie) who was then working at Max's as a waitress. Bebe's striking appearance quickly earned her an entrée into the club's exclusive red-lit, smoky back room reserved for the trendy, hip and beautiful people. Bathing in the room's sinful atmosphere were Warhol acolytes, poets, painters, writers, fledgling actresses like Patti D'Arbanville, fashion models, photographers and rock stars like Lou Reed, John Cale, Alice Cooper and Iggy Pop.

Bebe also met and started dating Pennsylvanian rocker Todd Rundgren who, apart from his work as a well-respected writer, singer, and record producer for bands like Bad Finger and Grand Funk Railroad, was renowned in rock circles for something else, something which made him the envy of his rock rivals. 'He's famous for his huge penis,' is the unequivocal, forthright personal tribute Bebe accords in her rock memoirs to the man who became her first love.

Initially Todd was both intrigued and astonished to discover that such a beautiful model girl as Bebe had managed still to be a virgin at the age of 18. Todd was impatient to alter that status once they had started dating, and spent several unfulfilled nights with Bebe before going away on tour. Eventually he called her and flew her down to join him in Miami, Florida. 'Then we had mad sex,' states Bebe. 'He was the first man I'd ever had sex with, and it was extraordinary.'

After this consummation at the appropriately named Playboy Plaza Hotel, Bebe reports that she and Todd subsequently enjoyed a great sex life together, often in a drug-fuelled state on Todd's circular water bed. But having introduced her to the pleasures of the flesh, Todd began to dislike the thought of Bebe broadening her sexual experience with another man, especially with Rod Stewart, a rocker by all accounts as randy as himself.

Through Todd, Bebe had begun meeting all the singers and musicians she had idolised in her teens, including Mick Jagger and Rod, and Todd could not fail to notice how many of them openly salivated over his beautiful girlfriend, especially Rod. In Rod, the womanising Todd recognised traits akin to his own, which jealously prompted him to give Bebe, as she clearly recalls, the big Rod Stewart warning lecture. It was similar to the lecture Todd had felt compelled to deliver to Bebe when he sensed her sex appeal had registered over-strongly with two other famous Lotharios, Mick Jagger and Warren Beatty. Now he included Rod in the same dangerman bracket when he told Bebe: 'Watch out for these guys. They'll just try to have sex with you.'

It was not long afterwards that Bebe flew into London for a modelling assignment and was barely off the plane, before she was whisked off to the nightclub Tramp by Ronnie Wood where they happened to meet up with . . . Rod Stewart, no less. Rod was with a group of friends including David Bowie's wife Angie. Eventually they all repaired to Ronnie's sumptuous home The Wick, on Richmond Hill, where there was quite a gathering of British rock luminaries including Mick Jagger, Keith Richards and Eric Clapton.

By now exhausted after her flight, Bebe was in no mood to party, even if she was in the company of British rock's élite. She simply wanted to sleep and went upstairs to slip thankfully between the sheets of a luxurious double bed. Bebe swears she wasn't dreaming when she recounts how first Woody came into her room asking for a cuddle, which she briefly granted without anything particularly physical developing, before asking him to leave, followed later by Mick Jagger.

Her version of events is that Mick made it plain he wanted more than just a cuddle but she insisted it was sleep she craved, not sexual comfort, and Jagger eventually reluctantly sloped off. She says she was again about to fall asleep when there was a knock on the door and she heard a third male rock chancer say: 'Hello, dear, can I come in for a cuddle?' It was the husky voice of Dangerman Rod whom Todd had alerted her about, asking if he could join Bebe in bed. Knowing full well that Rod then had a devoted girlfriend in Dee Harrington and remembering Todd's warning, Bebe irritably snapped: 'Go home to Dee!' Gratefully she heard a crestfallen Rod's footsteps beating a retreat from her door. Ironically, Dee would eventually meet Bebe at a strange party where, she recalls, Bebe sat cross-legged, somewhat reverently, at her feet.

Bebe's and Rod's paths were to cross frequently over the next few years and, at a vulnerable moment in her life and at a bruised yet convenient moment in his, Rod called her up and Bebe found Rod's 'beautiful sexual energy' too much to resist.

Dee Harrington always calmly accepted that her rock-star lover was bound to be attracted to other women and was a constant target for persistent females, but she insisted that she didn't care if she and Rod weren't married, as long as they were together. 'I think he knows I'm the right one for him,' she said, 'and that when he does get fed up I'll get him feeling better again. Whatever anyone says, I'm the one he comes home to, aren't I?'

Eventually, though, Rod's constant womanising was bound to bring about a crisis in his relationship with Dee, however much she tried to turn a blind eye to his philandering. After one blazing row too many, Dee moved out of Cranbourne Court and went to live at Rod's Highgate town house. Rod had bought the house in 1972 to be near to his parents, but he rarely stayed there because neighbours complained about the noise when he and Dee held parties for his footballing pals. It was to be the first of many such departures. For a couple of weeks, Dee worked as a bunny-girl at London's Playboy club in Park Lane, and Rod hated the idea of other men feasting their eyes at close quarters on Dee's stunning minimally dressed figure in her bunny-girl outfit. During the six weeks Dee and Rod were apart, though, another classy blonde entered Rod's life: actress and model Joanna Lumley.

Rod met the stylish daughter of a high-ranking army officer at a football presentation evening. Joanna, now of course an international TV favourite as champagne-swigging Patsy in the comedy hit *Absolutely Fabulous*, was then still some years away from her TV breakthrough role of Purdey in *The New Avengers*. Back then, Joanna was grateful for even small TV roles, one line in a Bond film or promotional work, and she was there to present Liverpool and Scotland soccer star Kenny Dalglish with a trophy. Rod had been brought in, because of his well-known enthusiasm for the game, to give Queen's Park Rangers an award as most entertaining team of the year.

There was instant chemistry between Joanna and Rod. The intelligent, middle-class model-turned-actress from the charmingly sleepy Kent village of Rolvenden, liked the cheeky, streetwise rock star, even though that first evening she had to share his attentions with Denis Law and company. But Rod felt just a little intimidated by Joanna. She was most certainly not one of those girls you just wandered up to and began a relationship with with his then oft-used and somewhat unimaginative chat-up line: 'Allo, luv, wanna drink?'

So Rod spent the evening uncharacteristically tongue-tied and left without obtaining the lady's telephone number. The next day, he enlisted the help of Tony Toon's predecessor as publicist, a diminutive but determined lady called Sally Croft. According to Sally, the conversation went as follows:

Rod: 'Sally, do you know Joanna Lumley?'

Sally: 'Not really.'

Rod: 'Well, I was with her yesterday and I would like her to come out to dinner. Do you know where to find her? Can you find out where she is and talk to her?'

Sally: 'Yes, I can find her and ask her for you, Rod. But

Joanna is educated. She is not like one of your usual type of girls. So you are not to try to leap into bed with her on the first date, are you?'

Rod: 'Nah.'

Sally: 'If you queer it on the first night you won't see her again.'

The obliging Sally telephoned La Lumley to tell her the famous Rod Stewart requested the pleasure of her company at dinner.

'How very sweet of him,' said Joanna, and happily agreed to the date.

Sally organised the meeting and it went ahead. The following day she rang Joanna to find out how it had gone and to ask if Rod had behaved himself. The actress swooned an 'Oh, yes!' Sally asked if she had gone back to Rod's house and Joanna said: 'Yes.' Says Sally: 'I didn't dare ask any more.'

She could see that Rod and Joanna had really fallen for each other in a big way. Rod was very fond of Joanna's son, Jamie, and admired the actress's independence in bringing up the boy alone and always refusing to name the father. For her part, Joanna was entranced by Rod's beautiful Windsor home. She gasped visibly at the rambling rose gardens and the tennis courts, at the huge staircase sweeping up to a spacious room lined from top to bottom with cupboards stacked with clothes.

Rod shrugged at her reaction, saying, 'I liked it better when I slept on a mattress and hung all me clothes round the walls.'

After flying to Malaga for a few days to lounge on Rod's yacht, they were talking about marriage. Sally says: 'Joanna moved in for about a week, but I don't think she was used to sleeping with that huge flag above her head. It didn't last very long. I think he found Jo too clinging. When he was losing interest in her he made me and Cyril come out to dinner with him and Jo.

'Jo had a hairdo like the one she eventually had in *The New Avengers*. She had dark hair then. She said: "How do you like my hair, Roddy?"

'"It's awful," replied Rod, "I don't like it at all." So we had this row over dinner. It was very tense. To cap it all, Rod ordered drinks just for the men and I snorted, "We drink too, you know." He was being so rude. I knew that there was another girl on his mind – obviously she was waiting for him somewhere else. Cyril got as pissed as hell and going home he nearly had us all killed going the wrong way up a one-way street in the Rolls. But then Rod found someone else and that was the end of that.'

Afterwards, Sally recalls having an agitated Joanna on the phone at two o'clock in the morning, saying: 'Darling, what has happened to Rod? He said he would collect me at 11 o'clock and I'm still waiting. Could you phone him for me, darling? Please phone him.'

In a spirit of sisterly camaraderie, Sally would phone Rod the next day to be greeted by: 'Oh God, I got caught up with some tart somewhere.' Knowing Rod, she would then phone Joanna, explain how unreliable he was and advise her not to take it all too seriously. The romance inevitably foundered: 'Rod was a bastard to her, he was always arranging to meet and then never turning up. I like Jo but she was out of Rod's class. I advised her to get rid of Rod, and she agreed to dump him. She suddenly said: "Yes, nobody treats me like that," and she dumped him.'

Rod had genuine regrets about the end of the fling with Joanna: 'It lasted about two months. She was a smashing bird and I was very fond of her. She was dead classy and I was dead common and we got on like a house on fire.'

For her part, Joanna says that she still has a soft spot for Rod, although, 'He did not take up that much space in my life any more than I did in his life. It was blown up by the press into quite a giant thing but it was really a very short-term encounter.

'I did like him a lot. It was a fascinating world to drift into. Everyone comes alive at night-time, frequenting recording studios and clubs, then like owls they go to sleep during the daytime. It was weird.

'I watched how Rod dealt with the fame. It was quite interesting. I could see that if he behaved quite normally then he was left alone, but if he arrived in dark glasses and jumped out of a big car then people started to flock round him. You can almost turn it on by having security men saying: "Stand aside, please!" when no one is taking any notice. Jolly interesting.'

Meanwhile, Sally Croft was doing her bit to ensure that Rod Stewart did get mobbed wherever he went in Britain. Her experience and guidance helped him steer a positive path through the perils of the star-hungry tabloids. Their relationship gradually developed into indulgent aunt and spoilt nephew rather than public relations person and celebrity. But even for the resourceful Sally Croft it was not an easy job.

Her first visit to Cranbourne Court to discuss terms was not promising. Carlo the Alsatian kept prowling round terrifying the tiny PR lady; among the other distractions was Cyril the chauffeur who hungrily ate his way through what looked like a dozen servings of mixed grill from an enormous plate. Dee tried to calm the dog at the top of her voice, while Rod shouted at Cyril, who kept snarling: 'I've been up all night so I'm entitled to this.' It was difficult to decide who was shouting louder: Rod at Cyril or Dee at Carlo.

Rod made coffee, escorted the startled Sally into the garden and said bluntly: 'When can you start?' But Sally was flustered and insisted they met for lunch at London's stylish media restaurant, San Lorenzo, to discuss their working relationship in more detail. Sally arrived first. When Rod eventually turned up she was a little surprised to see that he had scarcely dressed for the occasion. However, she knew enough about the music business to know that rock stars make their own rules. Rod slumped opposite and said: 'Allo, luv.'

Sally recalls: 'He was as rough as anything. But he was a star. He still wasn't that well known in Britain but you could tell he was going to be a big name for a long time. He just had this amazing presence and he really wanted to succeed.'

The negotiations settled on a weekly salary for Sally of £20, by no means a generous remuneration even three decades ago. But Sally says: 'I had a job to get him to agree to even £20. And then he insisted the fee was to include all my expenses. "That's the lot," he said. "You're not going to charge me for anything else are you?"' In return for this, Rod wanted Sally to make sure that his name was never out of the papers.

Rod had selected liver and bacon from the menu and, when it arrived, he further startled his new employee by picking up the liver and carefully wiping it with his serviette, before putting it on his side plate. He repeated the process with his bacon. Sally watched open-mouthed. 'Rod, we are in San Lorenzo,' she spluttered. 'It's the gravy,' replied Rod, oblivious to her social alarm. 'I can't stand gravy.'

When she got under way with her new client, Sally soon found that her £20 a week had to cover a very great deal: 'I had to trail out to Windsor with journalists all the time, and pay my own way there and back. Rod would phone me up and ask me to bring this book or that book down with me. I would bring them but I never got paid. I always felt he was very mean, so mean. He never had any drinks in the house. He would never put his hand in his pocket to buy a bottle of anything.

'So, when I took journalists down we would all go down to the pub and the first thing he would say would be: "Sal, can you pay for this? I've got no money." I was out of pocket all the time. But he was so charming he got away with it. He would just grin at me and joke: "I've got short arms and long pockets, dear." He never used to carry any money. In restaurants I always had to pay, I never saw him write a cheque.'

It was around this time that a legendary story first surfaced about Rod being so appalled at a £200 bill which appeared to be heading his way, after a boozy night out with pals at a London nightclub, that he made an escape by squeezing through a tiny window in the Gents. In the process the trousers of his smart silk suit were torn and he was apparently later spotted scuttling down Jermyn Street, with the ripped seat of his pants flapping in the night breeze.

It was certainly an interesting environment in which to work for Sally. She would frequently travel out from London for a pre-arranged interview appointment only to find Rod still in bed. It was among her duties then to bully him out of bed and into the shower before meeting the representative of the press.

One morning, Sally arrived with a journalist to find suitcases parked around the front door. She asked Rod if he was going away only to be told bluntly: 'No, it's Dee. She's leaving.' Not that Rod was ever lonely during Dee's periodic departures. There were many shapely visitors.

Sally Croft recalls: 'There was a pretty little girl I met at the London Weekend Television studios. She was waiting there watching Rod and she looked so pleased with herself. When I asked her why, she said: "You've no idea what's going to happen to me tonight." I said: "What's going to happen to you tonight, dear?" She said: "I'm going to sleep with Rod Stewart." "Oh God," I said. "Well, don't count on sleeping with him tomorrow night as well, dear." She just simpered: "It's going to be wonderful."

'Rod had an amazing effect on women. He oozes charm. If he wanted a girl he could be so charming he was irresistible.'

Beautiful girls may have come and gone, but Rod had many long-standing male friends, among them Elton John, who spent hours listening to snatches of Rod's new songs and advising on musical ideas. Sally recalls: 'Rod used to send for Elton whenever he was doing a record because Elton was wonderful at saying which notes were wrong or a bit off. He and Rod were very close friends.'

Sally's last memory of Rod Stewart is of rushing to catch him at Heathrow Airport in order to extract her final wages from him in 1972. Says Sally: 'He hadn't paid me for six months so it was quite a lot of money. I knew he was going to America and I was determined to get the money before he left the country because I knew once he got to America I would never get paid. His manager Billy Gaff told me the time of the plane so I just turned up. I was desperate for the money. I said: "Rod, darling, I've come to say goodbye and here's my bill and can you give me your cheque before you get on the plane." And I got it.'

But, in spite of his dalliances and his reluctance to dip into his many millions, Sally Croft remained one of Rod Stewart's greatest admirers. 'Underneath it all, Rod is a really nice person. He just had this roving eye. I don't think he ever stayed with a girl long enough then to get to know her but he didn't mean any harm. Nothing bothered him. He was like a feather that just floated along through life.

'Football was about the only thing he ever got excited about. You just couldn't dislike him, however mad he made you.'

Rod's old friend Rod Sopp rejects suggestions that Rod was mean. 'In those days I earned around £10 a week as an insurance clerk. I couldn't afford to go to Tramp, so if we went there it was down to Rod. But in the pub it would be: "It's your go."'

Mostly Dee displayed admirable cool when directly confronted by rivals for Rod's affections, like the time she was in bed with Rod when Joanna Lumley called and asked: 'Is Rod there?' Dee loudly repeated the question mockingly mimicking Joanna's breathily plummy tones, as she passed the phone to Rod. Then she continued equally loudly so Joanna could hear: 'Come on Rod, are we going shopping? Or are you going to spend all day talking to her?' But there were other times when her patience was so sorely tested by females calling for her Rod that she pulled the telephone out of its socket.

On the occasions when Dee left Rod and went back to stay with her parents or when they had a row and weren't speaking to each other, it was always the unfortunate Mickey Waller whom Rod would enlist to try and patch things up between them and woo her back. Mickey disliked being the go-between but grudgingly agreed to play peacemaker. The pattern was nearly always the same. Dee would get a call at work from Mickey that invariably began: 'If Rod was to call you up, do you think you would speak to him? And if you spoke to him and he asked to meet up, would you?' Dee was so delightfully sweet-natured that eventually she would be won round.

Rod and Dee were back together again by Christmas 1974. It was the last they were to spend together but it was a memorable one. They invited 25 people to lunch, including Elton John who arrived in a kilt, bringing with him a present for Rod. Every picture tells a story and Elton's gift to his mate was – a Rembrandt, the etching *The Adoration of the Shepherd*, now worth an estimated £50,000. Elton later went on TV and said Rod's gift to him in return was an ice bucket, which added to Rod's reputation for being mean. But in fact he gave Elton a TV-side drinks cabinet which lit up and cost Rod the then not inconsiderable sum of £600.

Rod and Dee also threw a New Year's Eve party for 150 people and, as a surprise for Rod, Dee organised a kilted piper to stride through the grounds piping in the New Year. The party went on all night and at eight the next morning Dee, still looking exquisitely beautiful in her Victorian bustle dress, went out to feed the horses before she and Rod fell into bed exhausted.

The last person to leave, she remembers, was Ronnie Wood's mother. As she was leaving, Rod turned to Dee and thanked her profusely. 'Thank you so much,' he told her. 'It's been so fantastic and it wouldn't have been anything without all that you did.' Dee glowed with happiness.

Early in 1975, the Faces flew off for a two-month tour of the States while Dee chose to stay behind at Cranbourne Court. From the start she had been shocked at the heaving backstage chaos that followed the band's appearances. 'I remember the parties,' she says, 'and Rod was always trying to get people to help stop this barrage of people coming at him. I'd rush off and get someone to get him free. But Rod had to talk to record company people and do his bit, but not with me.'

Early one morning on that 1975 American tour, Rod phoned and asked Dee to fly out to Los Angeles to be with him. She said she would rather stay at home; she had planned to have the house spring-cleaned before he came back and wanted to oversee the cleaning. Fifteen minutes later, he phoned again and asked her once more to come out and join him. This time she did not dither further and the next day she was on a plane out to LA, where she was met at the airport by one of Rod's entourage, with a Mercedes he said Rod had hired especially for her.

Dee was in high spirits as she drove up to the Beverly Hills Hotel where she and Rod had first become lovers. They had a joyful reunion. However, it soon turned sour when Dee stripped off to take a bath and Rod spotted a scratch on her back. It was caused by Dee sleeping in her jewellery a couple of nights before, but Rod would have none of it and continuously accused Dee of having an affair.

A fierce row ensued. After it had subsided, Dee was almost relieved when Rod said he had a 'business meeting' to go to. It would mean she could have some rest after her tiring flight. But the time difference in LA played havoc with her body clock and when friends called by and invited her out to dinner, Dee felt awake enough to agree to go. Afterwards, she decided on the spur of the moment to drop in at the Troubadour club where she and Rod had enjoyed themselves years before. As she drove along Santa Monica Boulevard and pulled up outside, Dee suddenly saw Rod helping a blonde out of a limousine and disappear into the club. Dee's first thought was that it must be Krissie Wood and she gave them a toot on her car horn. When they appeared not to hear, Dee parked her car and innocently followed them inside. When she caught up with them in the bar, she saw the terrible truth: Rod was with a blonde whom she instantly recognised as the movie actress Britt Ekland. There was a deathly silence as the truth dawned. Then, after a few heated words, Dee turned on her heels and strode out.

Back at the hotel, Dee started to pack. She was seething that Rod had begged her to fly all the way out to LA and that he had then humiliated her like that. The next morning, she was at the airport ready to fly home to England. 'It wasn't Britt Ekland. I'd just reached a point where I didn't want any more. I had to go, and it was like I'd been given this opportunity to get out.

'Tony Toon was sent in the car to get me back. He was crying in the car: "Please don't go." I told him that this time I knew his job was to stop me getting on that plane but that he wasn't going to succeed.'

Despite Toon's pleadings, Dee's mind was made up and she checked in and boarded the plane, heaving a sigh of relief as she settled into her first-class seat. 'Then, after all that, the plane was delayed for four hours and the person in front of me threw up all over the first-class cabin,' she says. 'Other people demanded to get off but I sat there thinking: I shouldn't be on this plane. I started to worry, then panic, that the delay was dragging me back. But then I thought: how can I go back to that? That nightmare! If you choose to live with a rock star you have to be prepared to put up with a lot. I didn't know what I was going to have to put up with.'

When the plane finally roared down the runway and nosed through the Los Angeles smog into the bright sunlight, Dee knew she had just flown out of Rod's life and there was no going back. Her love affair with Rod Stewart had begun and ended in Los Angeles. One by one, she noted, the wives of the Faces had gone: 'Sue and Ronnie Lane, Sandie and Ian McLagan, Jan and Kenney Jones, Krissie and Ronnie Wood – one by one they had all departed. I wasn't Rod's wife, but now it was my turn to go, too. We had a fantastic three years and there was a lot of love between us for a long time. But I'd learned that you can have everything you could possibly want and yet still be unhappy.

'I wanted to grow as a person and Rod really didn't ever like me doing anything. He used to say: "You can't go out to work or everybody will say: Look at that man in that big house and he sends his wife out to work." He was going to become a tax exile and it seemed like a natural breaking point had come along. He needed to go off and have some sort of glamorous woman to be with.'

After the split Dee maintained her dignity but later couldn't resist a snipe at Britt: 'Who can deny that she is a beautiful girl? But I have been told she has got big feet.' Commendably, at a time when palimony lawsuits were becoming commonplace and abandoned girlfriends were suing famous exes for vast sums of money, Dee walked away from Rod with nothing. She wanted it that way. She had never been grasping or money-oriented, and she was sensible enough to know the best way to start a new life away from Rod was without having to feel beholden to him in the slightest.

It's a measure of Dee's balanced approach to her three-year rock with Rod that, 30 years on, she is content that the best thing she has taken away from their relationship is simply a jaw-dropping line she can occasionally trot out at dinner parties, when she sees fit. If the mood takes her, when anyone famous becomes the dinner-table topic of conversation and fellow diners talk about celebrities they have met, Dee can slay them all. Forks on the way to mouths are guaranteed to freeze in mid-air when Dee announces: 'I met Mick Jagger ... when I was in bed with Rod Stewart.'

'Absolutely true,' laughs Dee. 'I was staying with Rod in a suite at the Beverly Wilshire Hotel in Los Angeles and Ronnie and Krissie Wood were sharing the suite opposite. One day when Rod and I were in bed together, the door opened and in came Mick Jagger who started kicking the bed, telling us to get up.'

When Rod's new album *Atlantic Crossing* was released in the summer of 1975, the tracks included Rod's own composition 'I Still Love You' and the poignant Danny Whitten song 'I Don't Want to Talk about It'. He later conceded: 'I have to admit that Dee had to put up with an awful lot.'

Thirty years after they first met, Dee is still a strikingly beautiful woman, a mother of a 13-year-old boy, and now a highly respected figure in the rock music business. The walls of her west London home are lined with gold and silver discs for her efforts in guiding the pop duo Climie Fisher to international success. Ironically, Rod recorded 'My Heart Can't Tell You No' written by her protégé Simon Climie, and took it to number four in the US charts in 1989.

Dee and Simon subsequently formed a music publishing and production company with huge success, and Simon has emerged as a top record producer for artists like Eric Clapton and B. B. King.

Dee's and Rod's paths very occasionally still cross. At one music awards function in London she bumped into Rod and asked him what he was doing there. 'I'm here to pick up a lifetime wanker award!' laughed Rod. 'Surely not!' said Dee, slowly dragging the words out with heavy sarcasm.

Dee Harrington has the last word on her time with Rod: 'Apparently I haven't been completely forgiven for revealing to the press that he wore ladies' underwear.'

CHAPTER SIX

ATLANTIC CROSSING

I changed everything in 1975. I changed my bird, my house, where I live. I think it's good for everyone to do that now and then – a change of atmosphere, a change of environment. You can't keep on with the same person or the same music all your life. Rod Stewart

A move to Los Angeles was always on the cards once Rod had hit the jackpot. He was earning big money but too much of it was being eroded by crippling British taxes. 'I was advised to go and live in America for obvious reasons,' he said. 'I left Britain because I was paying 83 per cent of everything I was earning to the taxman. Giving away 83 per cent of your income is not fair. I was in a position to be able to move – a lot of people can't – and I fell in love with the place.'

Giving away a maximum 45 per cent to the taxman in America would be painful enough, but America had taken Rod to its heart and he thought he would be comfortable there. Another serious consideration for Rod was how long his success would continue, in such a fickle world as the music business. 'I thought, God, it might be all over next year, I've got to put some money in the bank,' he reasoned.

But there was considerable soul-searching before Rod finally decided the US had to be his best option.

He remembers spending an evening with his great pal Elton John who kept calling him a traitor, and playing him Elgar's jingoistic *Land of Hope and Glory* and *The Last Night of the Proms* on his record player. 'How can you possibly leave?' asked Elton, reminding him of all the football he was going to miss. 'He was right. It was a struggle with the football and everything,' says Rod, who spent his first two months in Los Angeles feeling thoroughly homesick. Frequently he found himself going 20 miles out of his way just to get a pint of English beer and an English newspaper.

The move to America coincided with a switch in record labels. Up until *Atlantic Crossing*, Rod Stewart's solo efforts had been recorded with Mercury. But in a series of complicated legal moves, Rod now effectively switched to Warner Brothers.

He had fulfilled his obligations to Mercury by recording, in 1974, his fifth solo LP, *Smiler*, an insipid album that lacked much of the verve of his previous records. The album contained mainly cover versions and included, as usual, a Dylan number, 'Girl From The North Country', Chuck Berry's 'Sweet Little Rock 'n' Roller', Sam Cooke's 'Bring It On Home to Me' and an instrumental version of 'I've Grown Accustomed to Her Face'. Elton John played piano on his own composition, 'Let Me Be Your Car'. The best track was another Stewart/Quittenton number, 'Farewell'. The oddest moment was a dog barking at the front of 'Sweet Little Rock 'n' Roller'. It was Mickey Waller's pet which, as usual, he'd brought to the studio.

During the Faces' final tour, Rod took record producer Tom Dowd along to a gig and, as Dowd confided to John Pigeon later, what he saw was something quite fantastic. The rapport that Rod and the band had with the audience was extraordinary. However, it was not something that would translate readily on to vinyl. So when Joe Smith, then head of Warner Brothers, called up Dowd and asked him to work on Rod's next album, *Atlantic Crossing*,

Dowd discussed with Rod at great length the type of songs he wanted to do and whether he would like the Faces to be involved. Dowd was a legendary producer who had worked with many of pop music's leading luminaries including Otis Redding, Dusty Springfield, Eric Clapton and Aretha Franklin, so when he expressed the view to Rod that the Faces were a limiting factor, he was speaking from a position of authority. He went on to suggest they flew to Alabama, to introduce Rod to the much-vaunted Muscle Shoals Rhythm Section.

When they went into the studio and the introductions were made, Rod visibly paled and, taking Dowd by the arm, walked him straight back out of the door. 'That can't be the Muscle Shoals Rhythm Section,' he protested. 'They're all white.' Dowd assured him that it was. Rod was so certain such a soulful rhythm section would be black that still he refused to believe it until Dowd asked the musicians to play for him, while Rod stood and listened from outside the door.

Finally convinced, Rod went into the studio, and, among the tracks he cut there at 10.30 in the morning, was 'Sailing', which was to become a monster hit for him in September of 1975. Again, Rod had a slice of luck. Bob Crewe, who used to write and produce the old Four Seasons' records, happened to be at the studio when Rod was recording the song, and Dowd told him he needed some background vocals to make it sound like a large choir. Crewe immediately volunteered to sing on the track, and rounded up a dozen of his friends to give the song the haunting anthem quality that Dowd was seeking.

Rod intended 'Sailing' to be an anthem for the terraces, and so it proved. Once Rod and his father were at Wembley for an England-Scotland soccer international and at half-time Rod popped off to get a drink. When he came back Rod was disturbed to find his dad crying. He asked him what was wrong and the reply came: 'You should have heard it. The whole of Wembley was singing "Sailing".' The tears were tears of pride.

The soaring 'Sailing', written by Gavin Sutherland who, with his brother Ian, led one of the better British pub-rock bands, Quiver, had a long run in the British charts in 1975, including four weeks at number one. The following year it re-entered the charts, this time reaching number three, thanks to BBC TV choosing the song as their theme tune for a documentary series about the aircraft-carrier HMS *Ark Royal*. The television success of 'Sailing', second time around, effectively brought Rod to the attention of a whole new range of people who might otherwise have taken little interest in him.

To launch *Atlantic Crossing*, Rod, by now ensconced in California, flew with Britt Ekland to Dublin, where he threw a lavish press party at the Gresham Hotel. Britt, who with Rod had been booked into the sumptuous Elizabeth Taylor Suite, set the tone for the event by pronouncing that she and Rod had replaced Elizabeth Taylor and Richard Burton as the world's most charismatic couple. 'We are probably the most beautiful couple in the world,' she said. On the media junket was John Pigeon who remembers that a very good time was had by all – so much so that the whole point of the exercise was almost lost. The aim, obviously, was for everyone to listen to Rod's new album, but someone had thoughtlessly neglected to ensure there was a record player available to play it on. When someone ventured that perhaps there was a tape of the LP available, it took an hour to find the tape, then another hour to find a plug for the tape recorder, and after one track the tape recorder stopped working. Eventually an aide was dispatched and came back with the most basic of record players. 'So there we were in Ireland,' recalls Pigeon, 'for an album costing thousands of pounds made with the best session musicians in the best studios with one of the best producers in the world, and we were listening to it on this incredibly shoddy piece of equipment. And most of the people were drunk.'

Generously, Rod also had his pal Rod Sopp, his parents and other friends flown over to Dublin to share in the fun. Sopp remembers Rod and his parents enjoying a loud singsong in the hotel lobby. Once the junket was over, he took Sopp over to Paris where they shared a room for a couple of days. They also went shopping and Sopp was pleased to find that, despite the wealth and fame, Rod had lost none of his old humour. 'We went to look at some antiques,' says Sopp, 'and I remember Rod telling a French woman: "Four grand? I could buy a new one for that!"'

In fact, the Rod Stewart sense of humour has always been very British and down-to-earth. On another occasion, Rod was staying in a hotel in Australia, when he was politely instructed to be on his best behaviour in his suite as the next occupant to follow him in was to be the Queen. According to Sopp, he then proceeded to unfold some of the toilet paper and write on about the eighth sheet in, which he figured was bound to be pulled by Her Majesty, a note which read: 'What are you doing sitting here when you should be writing a speech?'

Atlantic Crossing was very different from anything Rod had done before and represented a stark contrast to his records with the Faces. The homespun quality of Rod's previous solo efforts had been replaced by immaculate production, a polished sound that was technically perfect. For the first time there was no Dylan track and the album was divided into a fast side, which included four new songs from Rod, and a slow side, which attracted most of the attention.

Apart from 'Sailing', there was 'I Don't Want To Talk About It', a plaintive ballad which became a great favourite with fans at Rod's concerts, where they knew every word and sang along with him in their thousands. The mandolin was again much in evidence on Rod's self-penned 'I Still Love You'.

Absent from a Rod Stewart solo album for the first time were Woody and Mickey Waller. There was no contribution for the first time, either, from Martin Quittenton, although Rod had asked him to join him in the US to work on the album and to tour with the Faces. Martin turned the offer down. He could not see himself fitting in with what went on after the music: heavy drinking and wrecking hotel rooms held no attraction for him whatsoever.

Martin believes Rod's pride was hurt when he turned him down. 'I haven't spoken to Rod since he went off to the US,' says Martin. 'He had an album to do out there and he wanted the people he knew around him. But because I didn't go to America he took it as a snub. Perhaps it was pride that he couldn't just snap his fingers and I'd jump. I was the one that didn't. I was the one person, perhaps, that he didn't have to put on a show with and I was the one that didn't come.'

Four years after their parting, Martin had a breakdown, went into hospital and subsequently married the nurse who brought him back to health. They made their home in Wales, working for wildlife and planting numerous trees on their 15 acres. His only source of income became the royalties from 'Maggie May', 'You Wear It Well' and other songs he wrote with Rod that generate between £5,000 and £10,000 a year. 'Rod was very fair with me down to the last letter,' he says, 'but I do wake up at night sometimes wondering what I will do when the royalties stop.'

When Martin was strong enough after coming out of hospital, he went into a studio in Putney and recorded three new songs with Mickey Waller. He had the tapes sent to Rod with a letter explaining what he had gone through in the intervening years, and asked Rod what he thought of his new songs. 'That was in 1981,' he said, 'but I never did hear anything.'

Although some critics tried to make out that Rod had lost his soul on *Atlantic Crossing*, the fans did not agree. The album quickly went to number one and stayed in the British LP charts for a staggering 88 weeks.

Rod was still a Face when *Atlantic Crossing* was released, and that year they toured together in America to promote the album. It was an unhappy tour in every way, culminating in an appearance in Los Angeles in front of 55,000 fans at Anaheim Stadium, where they played a thoroughly ragged set because the truck carrying most of their equipment had failed to arrive on time, having broken down on the freeway. Rod and the boys were all for calling off the gig, but this was LA, the record company stronghold, and they could hardly disappoint all those thousands of fans waiting to see them. There would have been a riot. As Warner Brothers boss Joe Smith said: 'You can't let the fans down. They've paid up to ten bucks to get in to see you. What will they think if you don't appear? It will be a thousand times worse out there.'

Mac's brand-new, cut-down white Hammond organ was the only piece of equipment that had arrived and an SOS went out for the rest. 'We went on very late and played very badly,' Mac recalls. 'Each one of us was feeling insecure because everything was different from how it usually was.'

The makeshift amps and mikes continually broke down until Rod, having done his utmost to rouse the audience, realised he was fighting a losing battle with the equipment, and angrily hammered the stage with a mike that was refusing to show any sign of life. Mac recalls: 'Rod came over and said, "Fuck this, let's get off." We'd done a short set, maybe an hour, when Rod announced the equipment was rented and he was sorry about the show.'

The performance ended in near farce when Woody, believing Mac's organ was also rented, leaped on top of it and was about to vent his frustration by stomping heavily all over it when Mac blurted out: 'No, Woody! It's mine!'

While Rod was by now living with Britt Ekland in Los Angeles, Billy Gaff and Jimmy Horowitz had taken up residence in nearby Doheny Drive, in west Hollywood. It was round the corner from a popular haunt called the Roxy and, since California law decreed no bars were to open between two and six in the morning, Horowitz became accustomed to a knock on the door at 2.15 a.m. that revealed Rod and friends, cheerily demanding that he open up his own drink supply.

'We had a tiny wet bar area with a piano. There were long periods when Rod would turn up every night at the house with his mates and they'd sit around, drink and play the piano. Then, at five in the morning, Rod would summon Toon to bring the car round and they'd all totter off.' Rod had Britt but, as ever, he still enjoyed a night out with the boys. Rod also discovered that Horowitz could cook a very fine curry. It was not easy to find a good curry in LA, but Horowitz had taken a special course and threw tandoori parties at his home, to which Rod was regularly invited.

Horowitz remembers: 'Rod used to come and have a meal with us. But, if he was coming to dinner with the management, he expected us to put out the Mouton. One night when he was due for dinner, I went to a big wine store and bought as a joke a bottle of Chilean Cabernet Sauvignon that was on special offer for $1.99, and decanted it into a silver case.

'I also had some very good wine put by in case it was really awful and there were any problems with the artiste. But it turned out to be a wonderful wine. For $1.99 this was a real buy, a great wine. Afterwards, I told Rod about the joke, that it was a very cheap wine and that we had merely decanted it. He said: "Yes, it's not a bad wine, is it?" I told him I was going to go back to the wine store the next day to buy some more.

'So I went back to the store and said I wanted to buy a case of the Chilean wine that was on offer. They told me they had sold out. "How can you be?" I said. "I only came in here yesterday." They said: "Yes, but your friend Rod Stewart came in and bought the lot." He probably went home and had all his friends come by and was serving it in his crystal decanter and telling them it was Mouton or something. He would think that really neat to be able to get away with not having to buy a $10 bottle of wine but buy one for $1.99.

'It was not that he was cheap. He loved the idea of being able to save money and yet he was very generous with big things. He kept upping Billy Gaff's percentage and we're talking about a lot of money here: hundreds of thousands of dollars. But then he'd really try and stick him on a bottle of wine and think that was really funny. Or he'd say: "Let's go out for dinner, Gaff," and he'd choose an expensive restaurant and get there and say: "Oh, I didn't bring any money with me." Sometimes he'd get Tony Toon, who called Rod "her", to call up either me or Billy and say: "Oh, hello Miss Horowitz. The artiste wants to go to the Dome tonight so I've booked the table for eight o'clock. She expects you to take her." He thought he hadn't been wined and dined enough that month for his percentage.

'If a record company was taking him out he would look through the wine menu to see what the most expensive bottle was. I remember I was with him in Holland around the time of the Polygram merger, and we went out to dinner where he ordered the most expensive bottle available. He was not a great wine buff but he thought it really funny to find a $200 bottle of wine.'

If Tony Toon always referred to Rod as 'her', Elton John preferred to call him 'Phyllis', because of the famous piece of graffiti at Eel Pie Island. According to Horowitz, Rod called Elton 'Sharon' and then John Reid, Elton's then manager, became 'Beryl' and Gaff became 'Bridie'. He says: 'I think that's how Rod got a reputation that he was gay or something. But it's plainly not true.'

In 1976, Rod followed up *Atlantic Crossing* with another massive-selling album, *A Night on the Town*, which also produced three hit singles in America and Britain. The first, 'Tonight's the Night (Gonna be Alright)', stayed at number one in America for seven weeks – but not without controversy.

'Tonight's the Night' is a song about the seduction of a virgin, which some American radio stations felt was too sexually explicit for mainstream consumption, especially the line 'Spread your wings and let me come inside'. When programme controllers banned it from the airwaves they were besieged by angry fans demanding to hear it. In Britain, the absurd situation arose whereby 'Tonight's the Night' was played by Radio One, the BBC's main pop station, but was banned from BBC TV's *Top of the Pops*. It was deemed unsuitable for a family audience, they said. All the heated public discussion about the merits of the song, however, did no harm to record sales.

There was further controversy when 'The Killing Of Georgie (Part I and II')' was released as the third single. This was Rod's brilliant, sensitive song about the murder of a young black homosexual boy he knew. Inevitably, it produced a mixed reaction from both the gay and heterosexual communities, and prompted absurd discussion as to whether Rod was really gay.

In between these two hotly discussed hits came 'The First Cut Is The Deepest', Rod's version of a Cat Stevens song which happily contained nothing to offend anybody. According to Rod's *Storyteller* notes, when they went into the Muscle Shoals studio to record the song, it transpired that he was the only person there who appeared to be familiar with it. A frantic call had to be put through to Los Angeles for the record to be bought and then played down the phone, while seven musicians crowded around the receiver to listen to it.

A female singer called P. P. Arnold had achieved a minor hit with 'The First Cut Is The Deepest' in 1967, but once again Rod showed perfect judgement in picking a song that he felt had been largely overlooked, and which suited his voice admirably. In Britain, Rod's version was issued as the B side of his 1977 chart-topper 'I Don't Want To Talk About It'.

By now Rod was itching to get back on the road after an 18-month lay-off. Although he often found recording a long and frustrating process, he enjoyed getting up in front of his fans. Clearly, he would need a new band and one which would feel comfortable with his earlier material, as well as the very different songs that had proved such winners on *Atlantic Crossing* and *A Night on the Town*. After the sour experiences of the final years of the Faces, Rod was determined to choose his new companions with extreme care.

His choice boiled down to six men: Carmine Appice, a drummer he had known from his Beck days, guitarists Jim Cregan, Gary Grainger and Billy Peek, Phil Chen on bass and John Jarvis on piano. It says much for Rod's judgement that the musicians he picked became either long-standing friends or prolific songwriting partners or both. Fourteen years on, Rod asked Cregan to be an usher at his wedding to Rachel Hunter.

Rod found Billy Peek while watching television in Denver at two in the morning. He spotted him on the television screen backing Chuck Berry, and immediately picked up the phone to call Tom Dowd in Miami, failing to take into account the time difference and that it would then be five o'clock in the morning in Miami. He also forgot that Miami TV stations do not necessarily screen simultaneously the same shows as those in Denver.

Rod's call woke Dowd up. When he drowsily picked up the phone, Dowd heard Rod excitedly telling him he had just seen a red-hot guitarist on the television and that he was just right to play on the new album. 'What TV show?' enquired Dowd. Rod didn't know, nor did he know the name of Berry's guitarist.

The following day, Dowd was left trying to find out the name of a guitarist he had never seen who had been on television in Colorado the night before, in a programme that might have been made years before! It turned out that Peek was from St Louis and had been with Berry for seven years. He was duly tracked down.

Jim Cregan, who hailed originally from Dorset, had been in bands such as Blossom Toes and Family before making his mark with Steve Harley and Cockney Rebel, for whom he delivered the stunning acoustic guitar break on the band's 1975 chart-topper 'Make Me Smile (Come Up And See Me)'. Rod had already chosen the nucleus of his line-up by the time he saw Cregan with Cockney Rebel in Los Angeles, and asked him to join him.

'It was very difficult for me to leave Cockney Rebel,' Cregan points out. 'I liked Steve Harley and working in that band, and we were doing very well at that time. It was not much of a gamble going to work for Rod Stewart but it was still a gamble. Mick Jagger's solo career had foundered and Rod's could have foundered without the Faces. They were such a well-loved band that we might have been looked upon as a nasty little load of upstarts. It turned out not to be that way.'

Cregan fitted in so well and became such a close friend of Rod's that he happily toured with him over a period of 12 years. 'If you are asked to take four of your mates and go round the world first class or in your own Lear jet, have a lot of money in your pocket, have girls follow you wherever you go, and all you've got to do is play rock 'n' roll for two hours each night, you'd say YES, PLEASE!' Cregan explains.

Rod called up Phil Chen, who had previously worked with Jimmy James and the Vagabonds, while Chen was in Jamaica working with the legendary Doors, who had recently reformed after the death of Jim Morrison. 'To me Rod was the best singer, the Springsteen of that time,' says Chen. 'I loved all his soul stuff and so I was keen to join.'

John Jarvis had played on Rod's album *A Night on the Town,* and Gary Grainger had been with a group called Strider, who had once toured with the Faces, so they were, like Carmine Appice, both already known quantities.

Significantly, Rod's new band included three guitarists, a line-up he had long wanted to employ, who were also capable of providing strong vocal harmonies. In direct contrast to the halcyon days of the Faces, rehearsals did not mean three hours of lubricating the throat with alcohol at the nearest watering hole. When they started, they rehearsed for four solid months. In addition, there were not to be just sound checks before a gig. At Rod's instigation, they all got together for a little 20-minute jam session each night just before they went on stage to get the adrenalin going, like a kick-about before a football match.

As Jim Cregan says: 'It was great. You feel that you've done the first three numbers before you actually get on stage: you've got a sweat going, everybody is in a good mood and when you do hit the stage everybody is on fire.'

The band were relieved to find that, although the music was fully rehearsed, there was nothing choreographed about the performance. Rod was not mealy-mouthed about letting the band share the limelight on stage. 'We were never considered to be his backing group,' Cregan stresses. 'We were his band, his mates and we were allowed pretty much a free rein. The only thing he asked was for us to keep out of the way when he swung the microphone stand, otherwise we'd lose a few teeth!'

Unlike the Faces, Rod's new band had not started off on an equal footing with Rod. They were competent musicians, but since Rod had hand-picked them personally, he was clearly boss from the outset, and therefore knew he was unlikely to encounter the ego problems of the Faces that had led to their natural disintegration. The thorough professionalism Rod had witnessed on the making of *Atlantic Crossing,* and the general businesslike approach of Americans, had instilled a new discipline in him that he determined to carry through on tour.

The Rod Stewart Band's first gig was in Norway on 1 November 1976. Rod was understandably nervous. Despite his huge solo recording success, how would the fans react to Rod Stewart without the Faces? How would he perform without looking round and seeing the familiar grins of Woody, Mac and Kenny? But the roar that engulfed him when he took the stage in loose-fitting red satin trousers, white satin shirt and matching jacket quickly allayed any fears he might have felt.

When they all moved on to London and a concert at the vast aircraft-hangar-sized Olympia venue, Rod was given a fantastic scarf-waving welcome from the fans, as he ripped through favourites old and new and ended with 'Stay With Me' as an encore, which he sang triumphantly from on top of the piano. Moving on to Scotland, the end of the tour was blighted first by Rod losing his voice, and then by the police raiding the band's hotel searching for drugs. Several musicians and a secretary were charged with and convicted of possession of cannabis. But Rod's dynamic performances, Cregan's dazzling guitar work and the pace and power of the shows set the pattern for Rod's tours for years to come.

Plainly, Rod had lost none of his ability to work an audience. In Amsterdam, the fans lit cigarette-lighters and matches, and waved them in time to the beat as they sang along word for word to 'I Don't Want To Talk About It'. 'They sang so loud we couldn't hear ourselves,' recalls Cregan. 'I looked up and saw that Rod had started crying. I couldn't look at him because I was starting to cry as well. The whole band were turning away from each other, all getting choked up. It was having this whole audience communicating so powerfully they could move a band to tears.

'I had that experience only once ever again, at a great big open-air stadium in Berlin. The seats were very steeply banked, and everyone lit candles which appeared to go so far up that you couldn't see where they stopped and the stars began. You had the impression that the stars came right down to the stage. We all had the shivers.'

That unique ability to understand precisely what an audience wants, and to use that empathy to best effect puts Rod up with the greats, in the opinion of Jimmy Horowitz: 'Rod's among the Top Twenty all-time great rock 'n' roll artists, in my view. His solo albums are great rock 'n' roll classics and he's done the best shows I've ever seen. The Faces were a great band and he was a wonderful frontman for them. He really knew how to put on a show. He's a great, great showman and as he got more confident he got better and better.

'He basically liked the stage to be as simple as possible. He was the first star I noticed who insisted on "flying" all the PA. He had special riggers so that nothing was left on the stage except the back line of the amps. Much of the time they were covered by a curtain, so it looked as though it was just a stage with musicians on it. There was nothing in front of him – even his own monitors were flown.' With nothing on the stage it meant that Rod could run wherever he wanted and see every part of the audience. It was so simple, at a time when everyone else was doing light shows, lasers and explosions. His whole aim was to go out and sing.

'At hard-bitten places like the Garden in New York or the Nassau Coliseum he'd have everybody singing along. On "Tonight's The Night" there's the line "upstairs before the night's too old". The whole crowd would be singing along and he'd stop the band for that one line, while he grinned and jerked a fist and forearm into the air! He was like a rock 'n' roll version of Max Miller.'

Phil Chen, who played alongside Rod for five years, before parting in not the happiest of circumstances, agrees: 'To me, he's one of the greatest because he was so full of energy. He was a fantastic, incredible performer. He'd really go for it. He was a true artist and really lived his music. I didn't realise how much soul he had.'

Rod had experienced enough sloppiness and lack of discipline with the Faces to last him a lifetime. With remarkable dedication, he secretly began taking voice lessons in his early thirties from a cantor in Los Angeles, who taught him better breathing, how to control his voice and how to do vocal warm-ups and exercises. He did not enjoy doing them but, with the aid of a tape, he religiously put himself through a range of exercises half an hour before he was due to sing, to loosen up his face, lips, tongue and throat.

Part of Jim Cregan's job was to know in which key to set Rod's songs; mistakes had occurred in the past where tracks would be cut in the key they had been written in, only to find that they were too high for Rod when it came to the chorus. 'I had to know exactly what his best notes were and the highest note that he could possibly hit,' says Cregan. 'Suddenly he was hitting C sharp which was two notes higher and one day he actually hit D, which is unbelievable. Your voice is not supposed to get bigger as you get older, it's actually supposed to get smaller. But he found he had another three notes that he didn't have before. He said it was all down to his teacher. Rod's voice is wonderful. I would say he is the best white male vocalist in the world.

'He has been gifted with this voice whereby no matter what he sings it sounds soulful, even "Mary Had A Little Lamb". I've heard him sing really silly songs when we've been on a pub-crawl, and when he puts his mind to it he can make anything sound good. It's a wonderful quality; it's a gift he finds surprising. But he is a lot more confident about it and now he recognises it's a natural gift he can enjoy it more.

'As a performer, there is a lovely side of self-deprecation even when he is wiggling his bum at the audience. He doesn't really think it's sexy. It's far more from amusement than for deliberate sexual provocation. Rod knows he is attractive to women but he's not sure of himself to the point where he puts out a belief. Watching him from a few feet away he always seemed to have a smile on his face.'

On tour, Chen noted that Rod was a different man when Britt was not with him. 'Rod was always after the girls,' he says. 'But when Britt was there he just kept looking at the menu without ordering. He was more relaxed when Britt was not around. He has an amazing effect on girls. They went crazy and just wanted to touch him. In New Zealand we played to one per cent of the country and they really went bonkers.'

According to Chen, his spell with Rod came to an end when the band was scattered in different places. Rod thought about getting everyone together to perform just one or two songs for a *Billboard* award, but 'Everybody was fed up of travelling backwards and forwards,' says Chen. 'Rod's roadie called and said Rod had decided not to do the show and he'll get back to you. I never heard from Rod again, which was a little disappointing when you've worked closely with someone for five years. I called back and he was having a massage and the next time he was playing tennis and all these other flaky excuses. I knew what was happening. I wasn't stupid. Still, I got a lot of credibility playing with Rod. It did me good.'

When Rod embarked on a marathon world tour in 1980–81, Chen was not the only one missing from the line-up. Rod rejigged the group and out went Carmine Appice and Billy Peek, as well. New additions such as Kevin Savigar, who had studied classical piano for two years, and Robin Le Mesurier, who had once been guitarist with the Wombles, injected fresh musical ideas into the band which bore fruit both on Rod's new records and at his live performances.

It was the same successful pattern for Rod. He had once again surrounded himself with hand-picked musicians who had multiple qualities, besides syncopation and an ability to play totally and utterly together. They were creative enough to spark off Rod's talent; they could convincingly deliver the musical goods on stage and in the studio; and they could fit in with and contribute to the camaraderie so essential to a band on long, gruelling tours.

An examination of Rod's albums reveals just how vital a part members of the band played, not just as musicians, but as co-writers with Rod. Gary Grainger has a co-writing credit on four of the tracks on *Footloose and Fancy Free*, including 'I Was Only Joking', which is one of Rod's own personal favourites, and 'Hot Legs'. Grainger has four more on *Blondes Have More Fun*, including 'Ain't Love a Bitch'. Savigar contributed to no less than five tracks on *Every Beat of My Heart*, two on *Camouflage*, and one on *Body Wishes*. Cregan has four credits on *Body Wishes* and Le Mesurier two, including the instantly catchy 'Sweet Surrender'. But it was drummer Carmine Appice who shares the co-writer's credit with Rod on the song that was to change Rod's career, in a way that he could scarcely have imagined possible. The song was 'Da Ya Think I'm Sexy?' from the 1978 album *Blondes Have More Fun*. It was a phenomenal worldwide hit which topped the charts in no less than 11 countries, including the US and Britain, and proved to be one of the fastest-selling singles in Warner Brothers' history. But more than that, it changed for millions of people their perception of Rod Stewart.

'Da Ya Think I'm Sexy?' was a startling departure from what most people believed to be Rod's musical roots; this was a bouncy dance number which landed him right in the mainstream of the disco boom. Not only that, anyone who did not listen closely to the lyrics assumed from the title that this was Rod Stewart, the rock star famed for squiring sexy long-legged blondes, at his most vain, arrogant, narcissistic, boastful worst. It was not just the critics who loathed it. Fellow rock musicians like Ron Wood, his old Faces' guitarist and long-time friend, were appalled. Woody had always rated Rod's lovely soulful voice and it grated on him to hear Rod's descent into disco, when he was capable of much earthier music. 'I'm just glad I wasn't there when he was doing "Sexy". They knew what he could do, and that he wasn't doing it,' he commented.

When Woody visited Rod in his Hollywood splendour he was also sad that he seemed to have forgotten his roots. When Woody tapped cigarette ash on to Rod's carpet, Rod ticked him off and told him not to do it again. 'You what?' said Woody, deliberately tapping more ash from his fag.

Rod's camp, strutting interpretation of 'Da Ya Think I'm Sexy?', in skin-tight leopard-skin pants, only made the critics fill their pens to the hilt with even more vitriol. Rod's record producer, Trevor Horn, simply thought Rod's leopard-skin strut was funny and that it was obvious he wasn't being serious. For Trevor, the incredible international success was his finest hour to date as a record producer.

But Rod's most loyal fans hated the posing. Even Mary, Rod's loyal sister, admitted she loathed the sight of Rod in those outfits, but then she was always urging him to take the stage in a smart blue suit. Rod's humiliation was complete when Kenny Everett, the British radio DJ turned TV star, mounted a hilarious and memorable mickey-take of Rod gyrating in leopard-skin pants on his hugely popular TV show.

The irony was that Rod had recorded 'Da Ya Think I'm Sexy?' as a means of jumping on the same bandwagon as the Rolling Stones, with their bouncy dance hit 'Miss You'. The Stones had not been tarred with a disco sell-out for 'Miss You', and Rod and his chief guitarist Jim Cregan wanted to record something with the same flavour. The further irony was that 'Da Ya Think I'm

Sexy?' turned out to be the biggest-selling single Rod had ever had, and a gigantic international hit, while at the same time temporarily tipping Rod's career off course.

In Rod's often humorous song notes to his *Storyteller* anthology he is deadly serious when he says: 'If I ever wrote a song which put a fly in the ointment or a spanner in the works, it's this one. It was frightening, stirring up so much love and hate at the same time: most of the public loved it; all the critics hated it. I can understand both positions.' He also went on to set the record straight about the popular misconception that the song was sung in the first person, by pointing out that he was but a narrator telling a story about a couple, and that the song began: 'She sits alone, waitin' for suggestions. He's so nervous, avoiding all her questions.' Unfortunately for Rod, the singalong chorus seemed to have Rod asking the question: 'Do you think *I'm* sexy?'

Another twist was added to the 'Da Ya Think I'm Sexy?' story, when a Brazilian songwriter claimed Rod had stolen part of the song from his composition 'Taj Mahal', a tribute to the American blues singer who had named himself after the famous Indian monument. But UNICEF did not complain when Rod donated all royalties to them at a Song for UNICEF concert.

That one record sparked an extraordinary backlash against Rod Stewart and raised a number of questions, not least questions he needed to ask of himself, as to whether he still had a passion for music. '*Footloose and Fancy Free* was a good album,' Rod reflected, when assessing his career, 'but *Blondes Have More Fun* with Alana on the back cover, I don't know what I was doing. It sold six and a half million copies and not a decent track on it. I think my fans were embarrassed by it. After "Da Ya Think I'm Sexy?", for a couple of years I almost lost interest in music altogether. I was just going out drinking and shagging. I believed everything I read about myself. Do Ya Think I'm Sexy? Well, maybe I really am. I just got carried away with the image.'

Rod's devotees, who admired him for his distinctive voice and vivid songs, wanted to know why he now seemed more interested in playing the camp, preening poser waggling his bottom at them in tight Spandex pants. Rod wore ladies' knickers so you couldn't see them through his pants, and it was not uncommon for roadies to be dispatched to stores to buy them for him. It was a deliberate ploy to try and 'show off the toolbag', Rod later sheepishly admitted.

What had happened to the soulful singer, the R 'n' B fanatic? Where now was the north London boy who was always one of the lads? Why had the rascal of rock fallen so blatantly for the opulent, millionaire lifestyle of magnificent houses, flashy cars and leggy blondes? He had gone Hollywood, hadn't he? Such questions were all the more pertinent for the fact that the Sex Pistols were at this time breaking big with their anarchic brand of street-level, poor-boys' rock and were disdainfully holding up two fingers at fame and pop's rich older heroes like Rod Stewart.

The answer, of course, was that Rod was only human after all, which was the perfectly reasonable justification he put forward when persistently pressed on the point. What, he argued, was he supposed to do when a glamorous woman made a play for him? Run away?

Indeed, if those were the arguments railed against him, then he had 'sold out' some time ago: he had been perfectly consistent in his taste for beautiful blondes since his teenage years; he had been more than ordinarily rich since the success of 'Maggie May'; and, musically speaking, it was *Atlantic Crossing*, with its smooth, transatlantic feel, that had marked the greatest departure from the 'old' Rod Stewart. But the fickleness of press reaction is just one of the prices you pay for being an international megastar.

Says Horowitz in Rod's defence: 'Rod's a very, very wealthy man and you can't make that money and not change. It's impossible when you get that rich. People say: "I'll never change, I'll just be the same humble guy." But he was not that humble to start with.

'I think he's handled the success pretty well. He deserves it because he's worked at it. For all his failings, he has always taken his work very seriously, worked hard and always given tremendous value for money on his records and performances. He has never short-changed the public. He has always been conscious of his obligation and that people pay hard-earned money at the door. And he has always been very nice to fans. I've never seen him refuse an autograph or be rude to a fan – as long as they aren't rude to him.'

One tragic fan who experienced at first hand the rarely publicised caring side of Rod Stewart, was Londoner Colin Jones, who was badly injured when he fell 30 feet from a balcony at a Rod Stewart concert in 1983. The young trainee accountant spent four months in a coma and suffered terrible brain damage. Although Colin, who was 23 at the time, won compensation of £625,000, which helped to provide some of the round-the-clock care he needed, his life was wrecked by the appalling accident.

Rod took a particular interest in Colin's plight, visiting his home to offer heartfelt messages of support. He even gave Colin the treasured gold disc he received for his first hit single, 'Maggie May'. At the time, Rod said: 'I understand just what Colin's family is going through. It's amazing how much this awful injury must have hit not only Colin's life but his mum and dad's lives, too. That's why I had to come and see him. I wanted to give him something personal. The gold disc means a lot to me. I am sure he will look after it.'

In the same way that the wild behaviour and heavy drinking of the Faces have tended to obscure the fact that they were a tremendous rock band, Rod's reputation as a man with a seemingly insatiable appetite for fast cars and sexy blondes, partly

The early years: Rod aged 3.

A youthful Rod aged 12.

Rod's mother, Mrs. Elsie Stewart.

Rod on his very first TV appearance in *Ready, Steady, Go!* in 1964.

First taste of fame in the Jeff Beck Group 1967: left to right are Rod, Aynsley Dunbar, Ron Wood, and Jeff Beck.

Bouffant-haired Rod with Long John Baldry, Julie Driscoll and Brian Auger in Steampacket, 1965.

he Faces in the early 1970s: Ron Wood, Kenny Jones, Rod, Ronnie Lane and Ian IcLagan.

imiliar Faces and lifelong friends: Rod on stage in 1973 with guitarist Ronnie Wood, w a Rolling Stone.

Rod and actress Joanna Lumley were briefly an absolutely fabulous couple in the early 1970s.

Dee Harrington set the mould for blonde, leggy girlfriends, 1972.

They called each other Poopy and Soddy, but Britt Ekland and Rod were the most glamorous couple in rock, 1976.

Rod opens his heart up to Britt Ekland ...

Hello sailors! Rod and Alana Hamilton on board the *Ark Royal* in 1978.

Rod with Alana, his first wife, on their wedding day, 1979.

amily man Rod with son Sean and
aughter Kimberley, 1989.

Rod bends over backwards to please his
fans on stage in 1979.

elly Emberg became mother to Rod's daughter Ruby, but never his wife, 1984.

Sometimes dubbed the Tartan Terror of Rock, Rod in full Scottish regalia at Ibrox Stadium, Glasgow, in 1983.

A goal achieved: Rod playing football on Wembley Stadium's famous turf, 1988.

Blondes have more fun: Elton 'Sharon' John in fluffy wig perches on the knee of Rod 'Phyllis' Stewart at Wembley Arena, 1991.

Rod leading second wife Rachel Hunter to the altar, 1990.

Rod with supermodel Rachel Hunter in happier days at the Cannes Film Festival, 1995.

ea for five: Rod, Rachel, Liam, Renee and Ruby on a family outing, 1995.

family holiday in St. Tropez with Rachel and their two children Liam and Renee, 1995.

Rod and Rachel before she found the bottle to seek a new life without him.

A winning song from Rod at the Brit Awards in 1993.

roud father Rod with his beautifully grown-up model daughter Kimberley, 2000.

You wear it well: Rod dressed in
formal attire on a visit to Royal
Ascot, 2002, with his favourite
filly, Penny Lancaster.

Anyone for tennis? Rod's current girlfriend Penny Lancaster courts attention at a celebrity tennis tournament in 2003.

On the ball: sporty Penny Lancaster teams up with soccer-mad Rod at a celebrity football match at Upton Park, London, 2003.

enny sitting cozily on Rod's lap at the
aunch of a London nightclub, 1999;
le spectacles give Rod an almost
ntellectual look.

Hot legs: Penny's mini-dress is a cut
above on a night out with Rod
in Monte Carlo, 2003. She later hit
the headlines with her raunchy dance
for Rod and her father at a Monte
Carlo nightclub.

Hand on heart: Rod's touching display of affection for Penny Lancaster at a charity ba
in Los Angeles, 2002.

perpetrated by his own formidable PR machine, threatened, in the eighties, to obscure his talent as songwriter, lyricist and performer.

'He's never really been recognised as a great lyricist,' says Horowitz. 'Nobody's ever really given him the credit for that. But, of course, he has the reputation of being a great rogerer of women. Rumour has it he is very good in bed.'

Jim Cregan concurs: 'Even among musicians his reputation as a songwriter is not really that high. I think if he was more like Elvis Costello and had a bit more of a chip on his shoulder, people would study his lyrics with more interest. But because his stage persona and his famous gallivantings around the world are so much more what people are interested in, the other part of him gets overlooked. But he is a great writer.'

When Arnold Stiefel took over managing Rod in 1983, they mapped out a long-range plan to restore Rod's credibility as a bona fide rock 'n' roll star, after the slide that had begun with 'Da Ya Think I'm Sexy?'. 'He had a terrible image problem,' Stiefel admitted. 'His image became this glitzy guy with Britt Ekland and beautiful blonde girls who wore fabulous things and drove fabulous cars. I told him that we had to take four to six years to sort of rebuild him, without ever admitting to the world that there was any rebuilding to be done.' Stiefel was among those who blamed 'Da Ya Think I'm Sexy?'. 'The Rod Stewart Da Ya Think I'm Sexy? tour was Rod Stewart stretched out in Spandex pants, and it made every guy think: "He's hotter than me,"' he said. 'It offended and eroded Rod's core male audience. So Rod and I talked about building a rebirth to recapture his audience, and find out what his audience was going to be for the next chunk of his career.'

The first step on the road to rehabilitation was a new LP, *Foolish Behaviour*, which, despite being two years in the making and spawning the hit single 'Passion', did not reach great heights.

But Rod's next album, *Tonight I'm Yours*, was a huge improvement and had Rod writing and singing from the gut once more. It produced a hit single, 'Young Turks', a fine song from Rod addressing the subject of teenage pregnancy, and excellent covers of Dylan's 'Just Like A Woman' and Ace's 'How Long'.

By 1988, the rehabilitation was successfully effected beyond anyone's expectations. A US tour originally scheduled for four months was extended to 13 months, grossing $50 million, and Rod's album *Out of Order* sold over two million copies in the States in the first few months of its release. Kevin Savigar and Jim Cregan again featured strongly on the writing credits: 'Forever Young' is credited to all three.

Rod was back on top and able to admit to his past mistakes. 'In those days I didn't really concentrate on singing,' he conceded. 'I was definitely more interested in showing off the anatomy than in trying to prove my vocal prowess.' The recovery was so complete that Rod felt comfortable enough about 'Da Ya Think I'm Sexy?' to include a beefed-up version of the song in his shows – and was pleased to find it went down extremely well with his audiences.

While the planning, the hard work and the discipline were paying off for Rod and his band, there was always time for play when they were on the road. The hotel destruction that had been par for the course on a Faces' tour was largely replaced by jolly japes, jokes, pranks and other relatively harmless mischief – although Rod had to fork out $1,000 after a hotel in Japan suffered a few substantial alterations that the management had not been requiring. In Australia, too, Phil Chen remembers, there was a piano on a hotel landing that various members of the touring party felt should be transferred to the lobby by the quickest possible route: straight through the banisters.

It seemed that the further away the band were from home, the more mischief they were likely to make. Sax player Jim

Zavala had Rod and the band in stitches in Osaka, when he gave a new definition to dressing for dinner. Japanese restaurants often have a gas burner set in the centre of each table with a grill over it, on which the food is cooked on the spot. As it can be a messy business, diners are provided with three-quarter-length bibs stretching from neck to knee. As the evening's alcohol intake began to take effect, Rod's merry band were treated to the sight of Zavala leaving the table and returning, wearing just his bib and nothing else underneath. Encouraged to dance on the table, Zavala leaped up on top of it, quite forgetting the gas grill in the middle. The cheers from his fellow diners changed to gasps, as Zavala's joyful semi-naked jig became a tap dance of excruciating pain as the hairs on his calves were burned to a cinder. Everyone agreed they had never seen barbecued legs quite like Zavala's.

It was in Osaka, too, on the 1981 tour, that tour publicist Tony Toon made an extraordinary unscheduled appearance centre stage, right in the middle of the gig. Toon had challenged another member of the touring party to a race around the hotel, but had slipped and injured his leg so badly that it had to be put in plaster. Gamely, he decided that nothing would keep him from his duties, so he turned up at the gig in a wheelchair which he parked in the wings.

Right in the middle of a drum solo, Toon suddenly found himself being wheeled on to the stage and abandoned in the spotlight, in front of thousands of bemused fans. None too familiar yet with the braking system and the methods of propelling a wheelchair, Toon frantically wrestled with the levers, causing a fair amount of wheeling before he managed to trundle sheepishly across the stage to the sanctuary of the wings once more.

In Tokyo, five members of the tour party somehow managed to lose Rod, Jim Cregan and tour manager Pete Buckland, when they were all setting out for a disco. Uncertain of the whereabouts of the disco, the latter trio decided there was only one thing to do: find a pub. Fortified by sake, they staggered out into the street some time later to search for the others. In such unfamiliar surroundings they were now worried that they might lose each other, so they decided their best method of progress was to hang on to each other and hokey-cokey their way along the streets, with crisp white napkins on their heads tied at four corners to act as identification tags, should they become detached from one another.

Such shining night headgear on the Tokyo streets soon led to their discovery by the other five, who promptly tagged on to the back of them, and together they performed a hokey-cokey of such sake-fuelled agility that they brought the Tokyo traffic to a standstill.

'Rod's always had a good sense of humour,' says Chen. 'One night he asked Carmine Appice to wear a tuxedo to a party and said we would all be wearing them. He got there and only the waiters were wearing tuxedos – we were in casual clothes.' Somehow drummers appear to be the more frequent victims. Chen remembers: 'With Mickey Waller – I think it was the second album at Olympic Studios in London – Rod on one number said: "That's a bit too loud. Let's move you out into the hallway." Then he moved him even further away, then into reception, and then he had him moved into the street. It was like four o'clock in the morning!'

Not all the highjinks were quite so harmless. In 1977 Rod was forced to apologise after a party in the first-class section of a British Airways jet got completely out of hand, during a flight from Los Angeles to London. Rod and his merry entourage were unfortunately not allocated a block of seats together. Instead they were dotted around the packed first-class cabin and, as the drinks started flowing, they spent much of their time leaping up from their seats to converse, and worse, with their pals. When one of the party went to sleep, he awoke to find Rod had smeared jam and mustard all over his face. He retaliated by filling Rod's shoes with honey when he went to the lavatory. By the time they all got off the plane at Heathrow, the first-class section was littered with food, bottles, cigarette ends and rubbish, seats had been damaged and smeared with jam, cushions ripped and music headphones torn out. Some passengers described the scene as resembling 'Step-toe's yard' – a reference to the filthy junk yard that was home to two rag-and-bone men in the hugely popular British TV sitcom *Steptoe and Son*. At the Heathrow luggage carousel, passengers waiting for their suitcases were startled to see an inebriated Rod reposing under some leather bags, while another member of his group approached Passport Control with cigarettes in his hair and honey and jam smeared all over his face. Rod did apparently manage to open one bleary eye in time to laugh his head off as his pal proffered his passport and two slices of bacon slid gently out. He almost had the full breakfast when he opened his wallet to find $2,000 in cash and two fried eggs. The whole incident brought Rod unwanted publicity, including a picture of him making his way through Heathrow looking pie-eyed and wearing a hat at a jaunty angle.

In post-Faces' years, Rod hand-picked his band for tours and encouraged them to be semi-badly behaved, as well as to play and write songs with and for him. The extremes of hotel devastation of the Faces' days had gone, but the groupies were as tenacious and as tempting as ever. In an effort to ensure some sort of limits, Rod and the touring party formed an organisation called the Sex Police, at the instigation of tour manager Pete Buckland. By now many members of the touring party had wives and children or steady loves back home, and the Sex Police went into action if one of them disappeared off to their room with a groupie. The transgressor would soon find a member of the Sex

Police knocking on his door, ordering the female out. The rule was that the knock on the door had to be answered immediately, whatever the state of undress of the occupants, even if they were *in flagrante delicto*, otherwise the Sex Police were entitled to kick the door down and the sexual transgressor would have to pay for the damage. At one point the Sex Police actually had their own uniforms, which they wore on their scouting missions around hotel rooms.

Whenever more than one big-name rock band is touring a country at the same time, there is bound to be rivalry, most of which is good-humoured, Occasionally, though, there is an edge to it, as in the time when Sting, who was just about to go on tour in America, took over the private jet that Rod had been using for his own tour. When he first got on the plane and took his seat, Sting was amazed to find a few choice remarks about him had been scrawled indelibly on a table.

However, the Sting tour party decided they would take revenge. Keith Altham, press representative for the cream of rock stars over 20 years, takes up the story: 'When they got to Los Angeles, they picked a night when they knew Rod would be at one of the Hollywood premises, billed as appearing there in person, and a sort of three-man hit squad with a driver bought black sweaters, black trousers and black balaclavas with eye-holes in them. Then they got a rented car, went down to the docks and bought 150 feet of heavy industrialised chain and some big heavy padlocks. They drove out to Rod's house, charged out of the car and secured the chain around his big electronic gates. It took Rod four and a half hours to get into his house that night. He was not amused.'

Rod was amused, however, by Elton John's comic capers. With their shared love of football, the two superstars have been friends – and friendly rivals – for 35 years. 'Elton used to be so funny with us,' says Cregan. 'The pranks would go on and on –

dreadful tricks!' In 1976, when Rod was appearing at Olympia in London on the back of his latest album, a huge banner outside the venue proclaimed the LP title *Blondes Have More Fun*. Elton had the banner taken down and replaced with another which read: 'Blondes have more fun but brunettes earn more money. Happy Christmas – Elton.' When Elton later turned up for his show, Elton's bannerhad been replaced by one which read: 'Blondes have more fun and brunettes have more hair transplants.'

Elton subsequently discovered that Rod's record company were hiring a barrage balloon to float high over London, proclaiming 'Blondes have more fun.' According to Elton, he tried to bribe someone to cut it loose from its moorings but was told that it would be too dangerous, in case it floated into any of the Heathrow airport flight paths. Elton got around the problem by forking out £200 for marksmen to shoot it down, and it eventually expired and flopped down on top of a double-decker bus.

Even when he ceased to tour with him, Cregan's friendship with Rod blossomed over the years, to the point where they would see each other two or three times a week when Rod was at home in Los Angeles. They also regularly speak to each other on the phone, write songs together and record together. In the mid-eighties, when Cregan was feeling extremely homesick for England, he started hosting Sunday lunch parties of roast leg of lamb and roast potatoes for Rod and a group of close English friends. Then it grew into an institution, with Rod and other members of the group taking it in turns to be host. Afterwards there is often a singsong around the piano, with Rod leading the way on anything from Muddy Waters and Otis Redding songs to a selection from *My Fair Lady*.

When Cregan got married in 1990, Rod was not only one of the ushers at the wedding but he also footed the bill for the reception for 100 guests, and allowed it to be held in the ballroom of his house. When Rod married Rachel Hunter a few months later, Cregan was an usher to Rod and offered his house for the reception, an offer warmly appreciated by Rod but in the end impractical, as there were so many guests.

But theirs is a friendship that was slow to blossom. 'Rod is a hard man to get to know,' Cregan concedes. 'It took me three years to get friends enough with him whereby I wouldn't feel uncomfortable in his company if nobody was saying anything. He is quite shy and he is rightly suspicious. Musicians would try to join the group just to give themselves a step-up, just to say: "Oh, I played with Rod Stewart."'

As long-term music associate as well as buddy, Cregan has had a unique insight into Rod the songwriter. He says: 'He wears very lightly the responsibility of going off and writing ten or 11 sets of lyrics, which is quite a big job. But I know the responsibility of it scares him so he puts it off and off until the tour is more and more imminent, and the record company is screaming and shouting "It's time to deliver, Rod." That is the motivation, that's when the talent comes shining through. He works really well under pressure.'

Rod's songwriting formula has barely changed from the days when he collaborated with Martin Quittenton and Ron Wood. 'Usually he gets the music and the melody together first with collaborators like myself or Kevin Savigar,' says Cregan who, being an ace guitarist himself, has a rather more disparaging view than some of Rod's abilities in that quarter. 'He is hopeless on the guitar. He can strum three, maybe five, chords: a little Woody Guthrie, a bit of Muddy Waters, a touch of Bob Dylan. He does not have the instrument in his hand when he is writing. He listens and if he has an idea he will sing it. It is a purer way to write because you are not cluttered with any mechanics, it's all in your head.

'But we always have to provide the music first and that gives him the canvas on which to do the lyrics. When he's got it how he wants it to be musically, he then addresses the lyrics and sits with his lyric books, scribbles down the words and his assistant types it up. But without some kind of musical backdrop he doesn't begin. His lyric books will eventually become auction material because he has one for each song, with all the notes it in. He has a couple of rows of them, nice leather-bound books, in his house.

'Although he may come up with a title while we're throwing the melody around, he has a title book with a list of two or three pages of titles that he hasn't used yet. Maybe he writes them on a bit of paper and sticks them in his pocket in a restaurant, you never actually notice him doing it. He has a fertile imagination but he is not like other lyricists who are always noting down phrases to use.

'Rod gets stories up through his pores. He doesn't read a lot of literature or poetry. He reads a lot, but it's mostly autobiographi-cal and not particularly heavy literature. He pretends sometimes to be very Jack the Lad and invulnerable, and that is the persona he has used to get him through his career. Yet the songs give an insight into his real, romantic self. The romantic in him is very often well disguised.

'He is not a quick writer. We wrote "Red Hot In Black" together and it took us five days. Once again, he wanted to use unusual images. Line one runs: "I met her in a little French café, legs like a young giraffe." Of course, the first problem was, what line would you find that rhymes with "giraffe"? We wanted to keep the line and in the end we cheated with: "She was sitting reading Baudelaire, not exactly working class."

'He takes his writing really seriously. I know because I've been around when he has been sitting down, wracking his brains to get just the right phrase and words that not only feel right but sound right. I remember sitting in a bar with Rod and his assistant Malcolm Cullimore. The three of us were trying to finish a song that had to be done that night. It was the last song on the record and if we didn't finish, the tour would have to be put back. Basically, we were sweating blood and bullets. We went into the studio and Rod started singing the song. When it came to the blank line, a line appeared and I don't know where from. Rod is a lucky boy.'

Cregan believes the best song he and Rod have written together is 'Never Give Up On A Dream' from *Tonight I'm Yours*, which was inspired by a newspaper report about Terry Fox, the cancer victim who ran across Canada. 'Rod turned up with the *Los Angeles Times* under his arm one day and said: "Have you seen about this bloke?" Rod was very touched by the idea and said we should write a song about the guy. We knocked it up in an afternoon. Then Rod got stuck with the lyrics – he said it began to sound as if he was preaching – so he got Bernie Taupin to come in and help out. We dedicated it to Terry Fox, and gave a whole big bunch of the royalties to cancer research.'

Rod's song-bag is littered with examples of lyrics first entering his head at strange moments. The chorus from 'You're In My Heart', for instance, came to him while he was standing outside a hotel in Toronto with record producer Tom Dowd. With no tape recorder immediately to hand, Rod sang it to Dowd, who faithfully wrote down the music there and then on the back of a cigarette packet.

Similarly, 'Gasoline Alley' came to Rod thanks to a chance remark by a young girl fan outside the Fillmore West, in San Francisco. They were chatting and the girl said she must get off home otherwise her mother would think she had been down Gasoline Alley. Rod generally has a tape recorder and a notebook by his bed, as several songs have come to him at night, notably 'Tonight's The Night'.

Cregan hazards a guess that one of Rod's own personal

favourites is 'I Was Only Joking'. It is an extraordinary baring of the Rod soul, which finishes with Rod admonishing himself for pouring his heart out in a song, and 'owning up for prosperity so the whole wide world can see'. That line gave everyone a shock when Rod came to sing it in the recording studio. 'He originally meant to say "owning up for posterity ..."' says Cregan. 'Somehow it was either written "prosperity" on his sheet that day, or he confused the two words in his head when he was singing, but it turned out to be one of his most honest lines. That really is revealing: I pour my heart out to you for cash! A Freudian slip!'

CHAPTER SEVEN

BRITT POP

If you screw another woman while you're with me, I'll
chop off your balls.   Britt Ekland

Britt Ekland, the woman who was to take Rod's life in a new
direction and reshape it over the next few years, had first found
instant international fame as the Swedish starlet who had swept
Peter Sellers, one of British cinema's greatest post-war stars, clean
off his feet.

A raw young Rod Stewart was just embarking on his first few
gigs with Long John Baldry, early in 1964, when Britt-Marie
Eklund was making headline news by becoming Sellers's young
bride after a whirlwind few weeks.

Acting impulsively upon a psychic vision by his astrologer
that someone with the initials B. E. would make him very
happy, Sellers wooed, won and wed Britt with extraordinary
haste.

Britt had flown into London to appear in a movie called *Guns
at Batasi*, and Sellers set out to charm her after seeing her photograph in a London evening newspaper. Believing this beautiful
B. E. to be the embodiment of happiness he was now so
eagerlyanticipating – conveniently overlooking the fact that
Blake Edwards was the director of his *Pink Panther* movies which

were to bring him such success – Sellers arrowed in on Britt like a heat-seeking missile.

Britt, who had gained an entrée into movies in her native Sweden on the strength of a more than passable resemblance to her teenage idol, the sultry French screen siren Brigitte Bardot, was then a young and unworldly 21.

Naturally, she was bewildered and quickly overwhelmed by the passionate pursuit mounted by Sellers who was nearly 40, much cherished in Britain as a member of BBC Radio's cult *Goon Show*, lauded as one of international cinema's finest clowns and a man who counted members of British royalty among his close friends.

When Sellers proposed marriage, Britt found herself accepting. On 19 February 1964, the day after Baldry and Rod had played a gig at the Gun in Croydon, Britt became Mrs Sellers and moved full time into her husband's opulent fifteenth-century house near Guildford, Surrey, with its stone floors, lattice windows, inglenooks and beamed ceilings.

During their four-year union, Britt had little choice but to grow up fast, married as she was to an outwardly exuberant, inwardly moody, tortured genius almost twice her age who was capable not only of extreme tenderness and overwhelming generosity, but also of insane jealously and reckless behaviour.

Britt eventually had to contend with traumatic rows, dreadful days of alarm over her husband's sudden heart attacks, and nights when an insecure Sellers would take her to bed, and stimulate his efforts towards trying to achieve the perfect orgasm by taking isobutyl nitrate.

As the young bride of such a renowned actor, Britt found herself suddenly thrust into the most glitzy of circles, which was why she was never intimidated by the aura of stardom surrounding Rod Stewart by the time they got together.

Indeed, Sellers moved in much more illustrious company

than Rod. He enjoyed a special relationship with the Queen's sister Princess Margaret, and the Stockholm starlet soon found herself taking tea and making small talk with the Queen at Windsor Castle, as well as opening the door of Sellers's stylish Mayfair apartment in London to welcome, as friends of her husband, such Hollywood movie luminaries as Steve McQueen, Goldie Hawn and Robert Wagner who dropped by.

By the time she met Rod, Britt had also gained an insight into the frenetic world of rock music. After divorce from Sellers, with whom she had a daughter, Victoria, Britt later fell in love with Lou Adler, a record producer who had discovered the chart-topping group Mamas and Papas and who owned a multi-million-pound record company. Britt bore him a son, Nicholai, and while living at Adler's Malibu beach house, she became thoroughly unfazed when the likes of Jack Nicholson or Mick Jagger came calling.

It was on stage at the Rainbow Theatre in north London that Britt first set eyes on Rod Stewart, at the charity première of the Who's rock opera *Tommy*, produced by her lover Adler. She later fleetingly met him at Mick Jagger's birthday party, where she teasingly patted down Rod's spiky hair and cheekily asked him whether it was real.

Not long afterwards, Britt was devastated by the break-up of her long-standing relationship with Adler. She was shattered to discover he had secretly been cheating on her with a glamorous young blonde model whom Britt had regarded as a friend. It was all too much for Britt who decided her affair with Lou was irrevocably over. She packed her bags and moved out.

Some six weeks later, on 5 March 1975, she was still smarting from the pain of their split when actress Joan Collins suggested a pick-me-up, by inviting Britt to join her and her then husband Ron Kass for a concert by the Faces at the Los Angeles Forum. Britt had no desire to go anywhere or see anyone and had to be cajoled by an insistent Joan into making the effort. As Lou Adler's live-in lover, Britt had regularly had access to the pick of concert tickets to see the cream of rock stars performing live gigs and, although she knew some of her girlfriends regarded Rod Stewart as hugely attractive, she was certainly not overly smitten by what she knew of him.

But when Rod strutted on stage in a green velvet suit and delivered his customary energetic performance, Britt had to admit to herself that there was something about his cocky stage presence that was very attractive, especially, she noted, the way he wiggled his hips and bottom as he sang. 'I looked into the spotlight and there was this incredible man, so sexy, so animal-like,' was Britt's recollection of her first sighting.

Afterwards, Britt joined Joan and Ron backstage to offer Rod their congratulations and thanks, and Joan invited Rod to join her party for dinner at the exclusive Hollywood restaurant Luau's. There, Britt was intrigued to discover, the private off-stage Rod Stewart was much shyer and quieter than the riotous concert performer. She said afterwards that Rod sat coyly in the restaurant like 'Little Boy Lost', saying hardly a word.

After the meal, they went on to a party at the home of singer-turned-film star Cher. As the evening progressed, the mutual attraction between the rock star and the beautiful blonde actress grew and grew, and Rod began imagining what it would be like to take such a glamorous film star like Britt to bed. Britt had little difficulty in reading Rod's thoughts and reflected afterwards: 'By the end of the night, I knew that I would have Rod, but I wasn't going to be a one-night groupie. My strategy would be entirely different with Rod than with any other of my lovers. There would be no harm in keeping him waiting, because I figured that Rod needed to respect a woman.'

This display of such predatory sexual self-confidence from Britt was something that her Swedish friends in her teens would never have guessed at. Britt had grown up knowing little about sex and with many inhibitions, partially caused by her podgy figure in her teens and somewhat protruding ears which cruelly earned her the nicknames of either Fatty or Dumbo. She also had two long front teeth, which were filed down after she married Peter Sellers. But now, at 32, the Britt Ekland who had made up her mind to 'have Rod' was physically in full bloom: a striking blonde beauty who was thoroughly confident in her sexuality.

For Rod, Britt would be a most glamorous partner, the type of glittering movie star a rock idol was expected to have on his arm. On screen, after several forgettable movies, Britt had achieved 'sex-bomb' status in the 1971 gangster film *Get Carter*, thanks to a brief but startling and controversial scene in which she lay partially naked on a bed, indulging in what amounted to phone sex with Michael Caine. She had also memorably performed a nude dance as a seductress in *The Wicker Man*, which has become a cult horror movie.

Britt's glamour-girl status was emphatically secured when, in the year prior to Britt's meeting Rod, the producers of the latest James Bond film, *The Man with the Golden Gun*, cast her in a major Bond girl role, as agent Mary Goodnight. Britt was then 30 years old, almost middle-aged by Bond girl standards, but she had always looked after herself and her body was in such lithe, athletic shape that the producers decided she should spend much of the film showing off her figure in a small bikini.

While movie fans all over the world agreed Britt was a worthy Bond girl, off screen Britt's natural sex appeal and vibrancy had attracted a stream of mostly famous admirers after she split up with Peter Sellers. Before she and Rod became lovers, her experiences with men included a fling with Hollywood golden boy Ryan O'Neal, and highly charged liaisons snatched with legendary Hollywood lover Warren Beatty when he strayed from Julie Christie.

Britt was fully aware of her physical impact upon men. Effortlessly she turned male heads, and she had a healthy sexual appetite, but with Rod she kept a rein on her emotions while offering him an ever more tantalising glimpse of amorous pleasures to come – but only when *she* so chose.

Initially Rod was utterly dazzled by Britt's natural blonde charms, and when she presented herself so tantalisingly on their early dates, Britt mindfully exuded sex appeal right down to the tips of her fingers which, Rod noticed, were painted glistening red.

Ever since Britt had been told in her teens that only au pair girls wore pearly-coloured nail varnish, she had taken the tip to heart. Before she stepped out on dates with Rod, Britt always took pains to paint her beautifully manicured fingernails a striking red. 'Men admire my long red nails. I'm told they look very sexual and the feeling of long nails drawn lightly across a man's back is always very sensual,' Britt liked to purr knowingly.

Her colourful hand signals were not lost on Rod on his early dates, as he savoured with increasing relish the prospect of making love to Britt, when she deemed the time was right. If Britt wanted to play a waiting game, then Rod wanted her enough to bide his time.

Britt and Rod met up several times without succumbing to the sexual electricity that increasingly crackled between them. But after only a few days they realised, following an intimate dinner together, that they were falling in love. Britt told Rod she loved him and Rod smiled that he felt just the same way. They happily decided that it was a miracle that two people who had only just met should fall so headlong for each other. Yet still they did not rush into bed.

Britt said soon afterwards: 'Rod was touring with his band and staying in a hotel. He didn't want to smuggle me in at night and out again in the morning. He didn't want our love-making to begin like a sordid fly-by-night affair.' Rod was displaying a sincerity and a sensitivity he rarely bothered with on lesser conquests, who were lucky to last a night.

For Britt, after relationships with older men – marriage to Peter Sellers and her long affair with Lou Adler – it was refreshing to be with someone who was more or less her own age. Britt was just 18 months older than Rod, but she had enough savvy and experience to stay out of Rod's confrontation with Dee Harrington in the Troubador. When Dee caught up with the man in her life, Britt at first thought she was just another groupie after an autograph. But when she heard Dee say in a voice shaking with anguish: 'I am going to take the next plane back to London, if you don't want me to stay here with you,' she wisely, and coolly, walked away.

It says a lot for Rod's ability to stay calm in a crisis that when he later joined Britt at their table, after finally parting from his girlfriend of five years, Britt noted: 'His composure was remarkably cool. There was not the slightest trace of anxiety.'

Britt knew that she was heading for a serious affair with her newly discovered rock star, when they went to a party at singer Joni Mitchell's house, a few days later. Bob Dylan and Paul McCartney began a jam session in one of the huge rooms and they invited Rod to join them. He refused, staying firmly by Britt's side. Afterwards he told friends: 'I don't think anyone has ever turned down the chance to jam with Bob Dylan, but I was so much in love with Britt.' The feeling was reciprocated. 'He was a very boyish person,' says Britt, 'very generous emotionally, and in an emotional way I was swept off my feet.'

The couple, who became Hollywood's most glamorous partnership, swept into an unstoppable physical affair. Years later, Britt was to document her feelings in those heady days at the beginning of their relationship in a book, *True Britt*, which angered Rod almost as much as her financial demands. She wrote: 'Rod admitted that he was in love with me that night; and I could not easily say I felt less about him. As always, I had fallen in love before anyone could even get out their stop-watch.

'From that moment on, we were inseparable, kissing and cuddling in our new-found passion. We were oblivious to the stares and embarrassment we caused. It mattered little that our first time in bed together yielded no greater reward than that of any other of my experiences. Perfection, however, was ultimately achieved. Very soon we were making love three or four times a day. We were like two interlocking pieces of jigsaw and we matched physically. We were both slender, small-boned and long-legged.'

Britt was much more than just another pretty face to Rod. After his long on-off affair with undemanding Dee, she was a strong-willed mature woman, a partner with a real mind of her own. And for Rod, the meeting coincided with a rootless, drifting period that followed his first flush of success. 'For a few years after I became successful and bought the big house in Windsor, all I used to do was go upstairs and play with my model railway,' he said later. 'Sometimes you lose a little bit of sanity and therefore lose the idea of the music you've got. I would be up there for weeks on end, wouldn't make any records, wouldn't write any songs . . . and that's wrong.'

Direction aplenty came from the engaging Miss Ekland. But it was by no means a one-way process. Britt learned from Rod's typically thoughtful band that he usually preferred big-boobed Amazons. Gallantly she offered to have a 'boob job' to enhance her 'miniature equipment' to please him. Rod declined. Britt said: 'He thought I was perfect as I stood. He liked my teenage-preserved figure and my long blonde hair. I think the little girl image was different for him and he liked it. He liked me always to dress in virginal white stockings, panties, petticoat, negligee and peel it all off like the leaves of an artichoke. And in bed I wore only Joy, his favourite perfume by Patou. We would make love in all sorts of crazy places.'

Once, just for the thrill of it, Rod and Britt made love on the back seat of Britt's Mercedes, which they chose to park in the long, unlit drive of the house belonging to their famous neighbour, actress Goldie Hawn. Britt was sure that Goldie would have been very understanding if she had found out.

Thus it was a feeling of deep bliss which attended Miss Britt Ekland as she stepped into a three-year love affair, which was certainly Rod Stewart's most serious relationship to date. Rod was similarly delighted with the new love. He said: 'With me she can be natural and let herself go a bit. She's like a child all over again. She giggles a lot, which is something she has never done before. I've brought all that out in her.' Then he tapped his forehead and said: 'She's good for me here; she stretches me mentally. I'm a changed man. I just don't fancy other birds any more. Britt's everything I want.'

When Britt travelled to England she was delighted to be welcomed by members of Rod's family, even if they did occasionally get her name wrong and call her Dee. She was entranced by Rod's luxurious Windsor home, with its elaborate model railway and its paddocks and manicured grounds. She was put off initially by Rod's father's awkwardness with women and his mother's sternness, but Mr and Mrs Stewart soon came to approve of the forceful, independently successful new girlfriend their son had found. Bob Stewart even awarded Britt his greatest personal accolade: he took her breakfast in bed.

The Stewart clan were extraordinarily tight and close-knit. Rod's father busied himself collecting the rents on various British properties the star had shrewdly invested in, and although Rod's mother was confined to a wheelchair with a weak back, she was still a force to be reckoned with. But at Christmas, in the small family home in Cambridge owned by Rod's elder brother Don, Britt found herself becoming a real part of the family.

The annual family reunion at the season of goodwill to all men is very important to the Stewarts. As they squashed together for the traditional turkey lunch, Britt felt more at home than in the most luxurious of international hotel suites. She was particularly moved when Rod's family also welcomed her children, Victoria and Nicholai. Rod and Britt cheerfully squeezed into a single bed so that they could stay for the celebrations.

Britt was different from most of Rod's previous girlfriends in other ways, too: she made it clear from the start that Rod Stewart's range of experience was now to be enlarged to encompass a totally new concept, fidelity.

Rod told Britt soon after they met that Dee knew he had other women, but that she didn't mind. Britt made it painfully clear that she did not feel quite the same: 'I looked at him straight between the eyes. "Then that's where I am very different!" I said. "I would mind a great deal. In fact, if you screw another woman while you're with me, I'll chop off your balls!"' – which left little room for misinterpretation.

Rod appreciated this strong and beautiful woman and her direct approach, and he certainly got the message. Asked very early in their relationship if he felt tempted to stray, he replied: 'Bloody 'ell. Don't talk about it. She'd go mad. She'd take a carving knife to me.'

Britt was as underwhelmed by certain aspects of the rock-star lifestyle as she was with the idea of Rod entertaining other lovers. Perhaps the least-appealing personality as far as she was concerned was the ubiquitous Tony Toon. Britt was amazed that Rod depended so heavily on the services of the publicist. She found his use of the slickest and cheapest gimmicks to provide a constant stream of stories for the papers, primarily the British tabloids, deeply unattractive.

Britt was appalled when Rod went along with the stunts Toon came up with to make headlines. Tony helped, for instance, to create the worldwide newspaper reaction when Rod allegedly stood up President Ford's daughter Susan on a date. Rod confided to Britt: 'It wasn't true. I didn't stand her up. I just couldn't get back to Washington from my tour in time to take her out,' but he did not mind Tony's rather more imaginative account of events being broadcast far and wide. 'I want the publicity,' said Rod. 'And Tony's only doing his job.'

For Tony Toon, the arrival of Britt Ekland was heaven-sent. She was beautiful, blonde and brimming with sex appeal, of course, but above all she was newsworthy. Thanks to Toon's deluge of tips and snippets of news about the new twosome, Stewart and Ekland for a time became the hottest celebrity couple on the circuit. 'We are the last of the great lovers,' Britt pronounced. 'Yes, I think we are a contemporary Burton and Taylor.' And she added: 'We make beautiful photographs.' They were quotes heaven-sent for their assiduous publicist to build on.

Britt wasn't totally averse to life at the centre of the glamorous new relationship. What she missed was some of the sort of glittering jewels that Burton provided for Taylor. 'What I lacked in diamonds – and it became transparently obvious that Rod wasn't going to give me any,' she said, ' – I compensated for by wearing the gaudiest of costumes to match those of my new pop hero.'

Yet still they weren't living together. Rod was keen to move the affair on to a more permanent basis but Britt was not in such a hurry. She had two young children to consider. She did not doubt that Rod's so frequently demonstrated expressions of love for her were stong enough, but could he really accept the kids as well? In fact, Rod genuinely loves children and regarded Britt's two as a bonus. He insisted to her: 'It's like starting out with a ready-made family and it will be good to have kids around the house. A home isn't a home without kids.'

At last, she agreed and, although marriage was certainly not upon the horizon, the couple made a pledge of loyalty to each other. Rod still held on to his houses in England but, in the summer of 1975, he and Britt decided to start house-hunting in some of the most exclusive suburbs of Los Angeles, for their US home. They eventually settled upon a stylish but neglected 20-room mansion in Carolwood Drive, one of the leafier locations in not quite Beverly but Holmby Hills. Rod paid three-quarters of a million dollars for the house and paid a further $100,000 into 'the Carolwood account', for Britt to begin renovations.

It was to be a massive job. Wild cats had formed a colony on the terrace and the house had to be fumigated to clear out a huge variety of bugs and insects. Then the real spending began. Britt and Rod found they shared an enthusiasm for art nouveau, and so soon all manner of stylish fitments and fittings were arriving at Carolwood Drive from all over the world – but at a price. The living room, which was the size of a basketball court, cost some $30,000 to equip with dignified wood panelling. Lamps, candelabras and other exotic furnishings arrived from Paris; paintings were purchased at Sotheby's in Los Angeles; crockery, linen and cutlery came from London, New York and Hong Kong. The two and a half acres of grounds were lovingly redesigned.

Some of the couple's shopping trips were featured on a BBC programme which portrayed Britt as pushy and somewhat full of herself. However, after the documentary was screened, Rod chivalrously defended his lady: 'We're desperately in love,' he said. 'Some people think that in the BBC TV documentary Britt came over as a bit of a bitch. But that was the editing of the film. I mean, you can take *Match of the Day* and make it look good or bloody awful. She's not a bitch. She's so bloody helpful. The boys in the band all love her. Whatever happens in the future, I'll never find a better woman.' For Rod, for the moment at any rate, this one was for real.

Rod's beloved cars – an AC Cobra, an Excalibur and a £26,000 Lamborghini Countach which had been flown out from Italy at a cost of £2,000 – competed for room in the garages with Britt's solitary Mercedes. The house even had a guest cottage in the garden for Tony Toon – but then, nothing is perfect. Britt did not mind that. She felt she had never been happier. This was five-star living at its most indulgent. Even when eating alone the glittering twosome donned full evening dress. Rod grumbled a little when he found Britt insisted they adhered to a strict timetable for meals with her children, Victoria, then 11, by her marriage to Peter Sellers, and Nicholai, two, from her relationship with Lou Adler. Rod was not keen on routine: 'She insists we all sit down to meals at the same time. I rebel against this regimentation. I hate it. But I put up with it.'

The couple were besotted with each other and their rapturous new life together. As Britt recalls: 'We made love at all hours of the night and day and we refused to be inconvenienced by guests. Barbecue meals round the pool were always popular, but we would not think twice about leaving our guests to chew on their spare ribs and their conjectures, while we sought the refuge of our bedroom to make love for maybe the second or third time of the day, trying to set fresh records on the previous day's accomplishments in bed. Our bedroom was a love nest in every sense of the phrase, with blue ribbons softening the brass hardware to convey the cosiness of a child's cot. Rod regarded every orgasm as a testimony of his love for me.'

Rod the romantic loved nothing more than to surprise his new love with a dramatic gesture. Once, while she was working in New York, he flew from Los Angeles to be with her and startled Britt by sneaking up behind her in a chemist's shop, and putting his hands over her eyes and saying 'Guess who?' At first she was terrified because she thought she was being mugged, but when she calmed down she appreciated the effort.

Although Britt tried to temper some of his more loony traits, she really did appreciate the lively Stewart sense of humour. She encouraged him to stop pulling funny faces every time someone pointed a camera in his direction, but she also said: 'There's a sense of schoolboy naughtiness about him. I can say what I want and be as silly as I want when I am with him.'

Rod has always been an accomplished mick-taker. When Britt remarked one evening that one of her films was on television that night, he retorted, deadpan: 'Is it a talkie?'

On another occasion, Rod leaped on Concorde to fly from New York to catch up with Britt filming in Paris. Warmly remembering his busking trips, Rod enthusiastically showed his lover all his teenage haunts as well as the more traditional attractions. They wandered the streets hand in hand and kissed on every corner of the city of romance. Later, they drove to the south of France in Rod's exotic Excalibur, exploring quiet, tucked-away villages and distant vineyards on their way. The sentimental journey included a stop for alfresco love-making beneath a stone bridge at sunset, the actress later dreamily recalled.

Theirs was most definitely a worldwide love affair. When Britt had to jet off to the Philippines for the filming of *High Velocity*, Rod came too. Of course, the press were also on their trail, but Rod was an old hand at shaking them off. When he and Britt ate out, Rod would always book their table in the name of Mr and Mrs Cockforth, which had the double effect of shaking off the pursuing press and ensuring smiles all round when they arrived.

They could scarcely have been closer. Britt recalled: 'We tried to explore as much of the Philippines as we could. We discovered, three hours' drive out of Manila, a rain forest where we could swim in the hot and cold mineral pools, and on one occasion Rod dived in wearing a spare pair of my bikini briefs because he had forgotten to bring his own trunks. Rod was never self-conscious about those kinds of things. Very often he chose to wear my cotton panties on stage. Not only were they more comfortable for him, but they were seamless and invisible beneath his skin-tight trousers.' Another addition to the ladies' knickers legend.

Gradually, the two careers were being brought closer together. Rod had to return early from the Philippines to Los Angeles to lay down the tracks of his single 'Sailing'. The song was always very special to Rod: even before it swept to number one in Britain, the sentimental side of his character found its haunting melody, composed by Gavin Sutherland, so moving it brought tears to his eyes. He thought it was one of the finest tracks he had heard.

When Britt returned to the US, the pair joined forces for Rod's promotional tour across America and on to Europe. A non-stop round of press conferences became something of an ordeal, especially for Rod. Reporters were much more interested in discussing the couple's domestic arrangements – 'When are you going to marry?' 'Will you have children?' – than they were in Rod's music. Britt handled the intrusive questions much better.

In Chicago, Rod exploded with anger and tore up a journalist's notes because he felt Britt answered the personal queries too frankly and too fully. 'When they ask about our private lives, tell them to get stuffed,' yelled Rod back in the hotel suite. 'It's none of their bloody business.' Britt did not agree and angrily retorted: 'How can you say that when you're throwing a press conference? Once you've asked them, they are entitled to ask any questions they like. If you don't want people to ask about our lives together, then you should never have agreed to the tour.'

Rod was incensed and the couple launched into their first major fight. In her book, Britt recalls: 'Rod grabbed my shoulders and started screaming: "You do as you're damn well told," adding a profusion of expletives. Whack! My face stung as his hand flew. I clenched my fist and sloshed him back as hard as I could. We were all over the bedroom, turning over table lamps and furniture. It was like a western bar-room brawl and suddenly my black and silver lace dress was ripped from my body. At that point, I burst into tears and collapsed on to the bed. Rod quivered with self-reproach and fell limply beside me, and began to cry himself.'

The intense public scrutiny was taking its toll. Rod was full of the most profuse apologies once he had calmed down. He even bought Britt an exclusive new Ted Lapidus gown to replace the one he had torn. As she drily records: 'For Rod, that was a gesture of overwhelming proportions. He paid nearly $400 for the dress and it took him some time to recover. The only other present he gave me through our entire relationship was a diamond bracelet.' If the relentless media interest in their relationship was one significant pressure threatening the couple's long-term happiness, then Rod's traditionally Scottish view on spending money was another.

Britt tried not to react to what she considered examples of penny-pinching meanness – she knew Rod had come from a family background where cash was always short – but her feeling of irritation at Rod's reluctance to be parted from his money gradually grew. Their telephone bills were a regular nightmare. Britt would write to query the bill to buy Rod time to pluck up the enthusiasm to settle the account, but it did not always work. Once, all three of their lines were cut off and only reconnected upon payment of an extra $240. Rod badgered Britt to buy her groceries at the cheapest store in town. He even told Tony Toon to warn her to cut down on spending. Britt paid Rod $100 a month for the upkeep of her two children, but she resented being criticised for spending money on wining and dining his frequently visiting friends, who always seemed so thirsty and hungry.

One of Britt's most marked influences on Rod's life was on his style of dress. They both enjoyed the thirties' films of Fred Astaire and Ginger Rogers, and Britt bought several antique dresses of the period. She took him to the Hollywood memorabilia store, Harold's Place, to find him an authentic thirties' straw boater. The hat was worn with great flair on the cover of Rod's 1976 album *A Night on the Town*. However, later Rod was bitterly to regret the headwear. Britt also introduced Rod to the idea of wearing a bit of make-up.

Yet, if a promotional tour with Rod was fraught with emotional problems for Britt, it was a picnic compared with life on the road with the Faces, still his band at the time. The entourage numbered some 30 people, most of them, in Britt's view, extremely odd. And the process of transporting musicians, equipment, technicians, lighting crew, managers, stars and all was a bewildering new experience for Britt. To her, hotel rooms were refuges in which to sleep or rest, or even to stay on holiday. She had not previously seen them as places to attack.

Perhaps her earliest introduction into the raw, unbridled animalism that is a rock group on tour occurred in beautiful Hawaii. It was August 1975 and Rod Stewart and the Faces were one-third of their way through a massive tour of 60 cities in three months. The band had played two highly successful concerts on the island and Rod and Britt were staying in the premier suite of the luxurious Kahala Hilton. Britt was busy packing while Rod and friends were enjoying a last beer on the beach.

As time drifted past the normal check-out hour of noon, the next occupants of the suite arrived in reception. Australian singer Helen Reddy and her manager and husband Jeff Wald were not impressed by the offer of alternative accommodation, while Mr Stewart and Miss Ekland made their exit.

The volatile Mr Wald decided to take matters into his own hands. Rapping on the door of his favourite suite, he confronted a bemused Britt. Britt recalls: 'When I answered the door a small abusive man started ordering me to get out of the suite. He just terrified me and I was so scared that I called the switchboard to have Rod paged.'

Rod and assorted roadies and Faces rushed back from the beach to deal with the situation in their own decisive way. Rod snarled a single-word instruction – 'Destroy!' – and the opulent hotel room was transformed into a war zone within seconds. Britt stood and stared open-mouthed with astonishment as the wiring in the television set was attacked, towels were stuffed down the toilets, followed by vigorous flushing, telephones were ripped from their sockets and Rod arranged for the bed to collapse. Woody applied one final, clever touch by unscrewing the mouthpiece on the telephone and taking out the microphone. It meant that if and when the incoming Mr Wald tried to call down for help, the operator wouldn't be able to hear anything and would hang up.

Meanwhile, downstairs, more trouble had started. Opinions differ as to who shoved whom first, but what appears to have occurred is a flyweight contest between Faces' keyboard player Ian McLagan and the now incensed Mr Wald. Unfortunately for him, Mr Wald fell against a wall and dislodged an indifferent reproduction of John Constable's ubiquitous *Haywain*, which cracked him smartly on the side of the head. A free and frank exchange of views followed, with several of the Faces expressing forceful opinions on what could happen to Mr Wald should he decide to continue the fracas. The hotel management called the police. Wald decided to have McLagan charged with assault. McLagan filed countercharges.

Gradually tempers cooled and Rod Stewart, satisfied with the alterations to the suite, commented: 'The next time they ask us to leave, maybe they'll be more courteous.' With that he led his party from the hotel. Billy Gaff handed a representative of the hotel's management some $2,000 and the incident was closed.

Britt was flabbergasted. She found the encounter even more extraordinary in retrospect, when she and Rod returned to the same hotel some months later, to be greeted by flowers and fruit in the suite and not a mention of the previous excitement.

Yet, as the tour progressed, Britt was to become even more bewildered. Rod Stewart had always appealed to a particularly attractive and inventive breed of groupie. Girls – often rich and beautiful girls – seemed to regard Rod as some sort of sexual Messiah, to be grabbed and squealed at whenever the opportunity arose. Anti-groupie security was tight, particularly when the lady in the star's life was in evidence, but one night in West Virginia a stunning and somewhat stunned blonde got to Rod and Britt's bedroom door. Britt remembers: 'I thought it was one of the guards and when I opened the door she almost brushed past me. Her eyes were glazed as she cried: "Where's Rod? I'm going to screw him."' Britt decided this was one function of room service she was going to refuse and angrily slammed the door on that particular female.

However, she could not shut groupies completely out of their life together. Endless telephone calls from girls telling her to get the hell out of Rod's life and threatening to give her cocaine with broken glass in it steadily disillusioned Britt Ekland about the glamour and fun of life on the road with a rock band. Yet more disturbing to her were the raunchy letters the young females would write to Rod. Some actually addressed their letters to Britt, with instructions for her to describe Rod's anatomy in detail: 'Draw it for us,' one letter urged.

Britt also had to cope with odd behaviour from other quarters. She was particularly puzzled by Rod's reaction to a request from Rolling Stones Mick Jagger and Keith Richards. When

Mick and Bianca dropped in to see Rod before a New York concert he was frosty and offhand. Soon afterwards, Rod made his triumphant return to London with his enormously successful series of concerts at Olympia; they became the hottest tickets in town. Even stars were buying them on the black market. Jagger and Richards asked for passes but Rod ruled they should be kept out. He even ordered extra security guards at all doors. This broke all rock business codes. Britt reckons that, for the first time in his life, Tony Toon was speechless. Britt decided that deep down her rock-singing lover was simply jealous of old rival Jagger, still widely acknowledged as the world's top rock star. But the clamp-down on security continued: at one point, security men even stopped Britt entering with Rod's own parents.

Rod and the Faces finally split just before Christmas 1975. Britt insists that she was not involved in the decision. The following year Rod surprised Britt by asking her to come into the recording studio, to add a sexy voice-over in French to the final line of 'Tonight's the Night', for his new album *A Night on the Town*. Initially she thought he wanted her to sing. She reacted honestly: 'I can't sing. I've got a lousy voice.' But Rod assured her she wouldn't have to sing, just talk to the music. Then he darkly hinted that if Britt did not join in he might ask the beautiful Stevie Nicks of Fleetwood Mac to do it. That convinced Britt to agree. How suitable a Swedish actress of 34 is for the part of a sobbing, young French virgin who is about to be deflowered is debatable, but in any case her anguished muttering of '*A mon dieu*' cannot have done much harm. Despite a ban by BBC TV's *Top of the Pops*, because of Rod's suggestive lyrics, 'Tonight's the Night' was yet another worldwide success and the album another bestseller.

'What I was saying,' said Britt afterwards, 'is: "Hold me tight. Put your arms round me. I'm a little frightened. I love you so much!"'

'No, she isn't,' interrupted Rod. 'She's saying: "Get your trousers off, Jock."'

Britt's recording début was not a financial success for her, however: 'I didn't get a dime from the multi-million-dollar royalties and I didn't ask for one. I did it all for love.' Britt did eventually get paid to record a single of her own, in 1979, after she and Rod had split up. Britt's record was called 'Do It To Me (Once More With Feeling)' and on the flip-side was a disco-style song 'Private Party', in which Britt breathily issued the invitation: 'Tonight's the night – do with me as you please.' The irony of the line, after contributing to Rod's 'Tonight's the Night', was evident to all who heard it. The record blatantly played on Britt's sex-symbol image: one picture-disc version of the single featured Britt in naked poses on each side of the vinyl. Despite this alluring marketing ploy, Britt's single failed to rival Rod's chart success.

No one could accuse Britt Ekland of holding out for cerebral movie roles, but she did want to work again. After a period of being the other half of a rock star, her agent persuaded her to take a role in *Slave*, a movie set, predictably enough, against the background of the slave trade, which was to be made on location in what was then known as Southern Rhodesia. She did not enjoy the separation from Rod and, because of the sanctions which then applied to Rhodesia, telephone calls were hard to connect. When she did manage to get through, she appealed to Rod to send her a romantic message. The response rattled through on the telex within hours. It read: 'Dear Britt. Here is the romantic message you wanted. Tired of wanking. Please come home, Soddy.'

Soddy was Britt's pet name for Rod, while he called Britt Poop or Poopy. It just suited him, she felt, because, well, he always was a bit of a sod.

Britt went on to make another action adventure, *King*

Solomon's Treasures, in Swaziland, before heading home with a present for Rod of a $1,200 lion's head and skin. 'It's like having another member of the family in our house,' said Rod. The dead creature was spread out on the carpet of the rented flat in Portland Place, in central London, that the couple took over briefly from Rudolf Nureyev.

The relationship seemed idyllic. All that was needed to complete the blissful picture, it appeared, was a glittering showbiz wedding and the patter of tiny feet. And for a time it looked likely that a happy ending had been written into the script of the Hollywood love story. But Britt already had two children by different fathers.

Thoroughly modern and fiercely independent as she was, she could not bring herself to consider having another child without a husband to stand by her. Rod understood and proposed as their jet flew towards Britt's homeland of Sweden. Soon the newspapers were full of quotes detailing Rod's plans to get married and have children with Britt.

But not all the publicity was so positive. Rod's glitzy lifestyle had long encouraged criticism, particularly in the trade press, that he was losing his roots and selling out to commercialism, with a consequently disastrous effect upon his music. Now he was accused of being completely overwhelmed by the influence of this famous film star who was endangering his whole career.

Rod reacted dramatically. He gave a press conference at which he insisted that Britt had no such influence, that he had no intention of marrying: 'She is not the right woman for me. I have no plans to marry her.'

Not surprisingly, the effect on their relationship was devastating. Britt broke down as she tackled Rod about the cruel words. He weakly tried to play down the remarks, saying that it was simply how he had felt that day. Tony Toon was instantly summoned to fix up a new interview, to give Rod the opportunity to deliver a complete retraction. 'I should not have said these foolish things,' he said. 'Britt is the only woman in the world for me and one day we will marry.'

Of course, he simply succeeded in refocusing the media spotlight on the love affair. In such a situation a story linking Rod with British actress Susan George was just what the newspapers needed. Britt and Rod met the shapely Susan at a Los Angeles dinner party, and as Britt chatted to Queen's Freddie Mercury, Rod talked with Susan George.

When Britt decided that it was time to go home she chose not to interrupt Rod's conversation, simply whispering in his ear that she was taking the car and leaving. Back at the house she began to wonder. As she put it: 'Maybe Rod fancied Susan, I fretted. She had big boobs and most of Rod's earlier women had big boobs. What if he slept with her?'

After two hours, Rod returned home and the lively discussion surrounding his tête-a-tête with Susan George developed into a fracas. Britt blacked her eye as she cracked her head on the bedpost, and Rod rushed to get some ice cubes to keep down the swelling. The evening was concluded by an emotional reconciliation. As Britt put it: 'We made love and the incident was doused.' Except not quite. The newspapers had to deliver their side of the story, which, somewhat more imaginatively, suggested that the dinner party had been enlivened by Britt hurling a glass of champagne over Rod and accusing him of an affair with Susan George.

Tony Toon was questioned over his role in this version of events but proclaimed his innocence. Susan George stated categorically: 'Any talk of a romance with Rod is a load of rubbish. I was merely talking to him about tax problems and he asked me to say hello to his mother when I got to England.' Rod's love life was always able, with the aid of a skilfully heated quote, to edge earthquakes off the front pages of the tabloids.

In February 1977, as Rod and Britt celebrated their third Valentine's Day together during Rod's tour of Australia, he paid generous public tribute at a press gathering to the strong-willed nature of his lover. 'Before I met Britt I was drifting. I was getting to the point of not caring. But she gave me back my self-confidence. Before, I never gave women the time of day. I was terrible to some of them, treating them with utter contempt.' And he added with words that were to come back to haunt him: 'But I could never do that to Britt – I would hate to see her hurt.'

There was yet more speculation about the strength of the romance after Britt was reported to have hired a locksmith to gain entry to the Portland Place flat, in the hope of finding Rod closeted with Susan George. Britt insisted she had paid a locksmith some £40 simply to get into their flat, after she had returned from Munich and Rod was in Scotland with the keys.

With Rod devoting more time to his music and his new band, Britt found herself thinking more and more about their relationship. When he found time to take a cruise on the QE2 with her they were blissfully happy together. They appeared for all the world like young honeymooners to other passengers. Rod even felt inspired to write two songs on board. He also found time to pace the decks late at night, musing on a favourite preoccupation of his: the *Titanic* disaster. In his black velvet cloak lined with red silk, he must have felt himself in tune with the doomed liner.

But although the cruise provided a cheery respite for the lovers, their relationship was itself heading towards a few treacherous icebergs. By June 1977, after the couple had been living together for two years, Britt was examining her future.

Her trusted agent Maggie Abbott counselled about continuing life in the goldfish bowl. She felt the affair was heading nowhere. At one time Britt's feelings for Rod were so strong that she would have instantly dismissed such advice. Instead, she decided that perhaps all they needed was a break from each other. She planned a trip home to Sweden to the picturesque seafront house in Smadalaro that had once belonged to her grandfather. When she told Rod she was taking the children and going away for a while, he agreed the holiday would do her good.

Rod was right. The hot Swedish summer was a peaceful and happy time for Britt, Nicholai and Victoria. When Rod rang she felt she was talking to a stranger. When she returned to Los Angeles at the end of July she found him looking exhausted. He was working hard in the studio, but he delighted Britt with the words of a new song he had written for her: 'You're in my heart, you're in my soul ... you'll be my breath till I grow old ... you're my lover, you're my best friend' was just what she wanted to hear.

But a meeting with old flame George Hamilton, the perma-tanned actor then married to a beautiful blonde actress by the name of Alana Hamilton, was to shatter that happy return. Britt had enjoyed a fling with the engaging Mr Hamilton in the south of France years before and the two were still friends.

Britt was at a Hollywood party given by film producer Alan Carr, and was busy apologising for Rod's absence when what George Hamilton said completely stunned her. 'Fancy Rod going out with Liz. I never thought you two would bust up,' he smiled. Britt's own smile vanished instantly from her lips. She froze at her old flame's words, and Britt's life was tossed up into the air. The expression on her face told Hamilton she knew nothing of Elizabeth Treadwell, the curvy Californian socialite who was enjoying a fling with the man she thought was confining his favours only to herself.

The recriminations were long and painful. Britt, never one to duck an issue, insisted Rod make his choice there and then. Reluctantly, she gave him a week to do it. He moved out of their Carolwood house and Britt was left alone with her pain. Sadly, she was told that Liz Treadwell was not the only one. Rod had been seen with a succession of other women.

The affair with Liz Treadwell, though, had added poignancy for Rod. It occurred while he was in the studio recording the album *Footloose and Fancy Free*, on which one of the tracks was '(If Loving You Is Wrong) I Don't Want To Be Right'. Rod admitted later: 'That really fitted into what was happening. I was seeing Liz Treadwell, but Britt didn't know. The whole track was done live in the studio. Liz was there and I'm singing: "If loving you is wrong, I don't want to be right …" You couldn't help but sing it with guts. That was the last track we recorded.'

The feelings Britt felt for Rod Stewart melted away like a snowball on Malibu beach. She swiftly acquired those essential Hollywood break-up accessories: a psychiatrist and a lawyer. She expensively examined her innermost thoughts at this terrible time in her life, and even more expensively issued Rod with a $12.5 million lawsuit. The following months were painful for both Rod and Britt.

Britt's version of events is that at first Billy Gaff came to plead Rod's case but she insisted on discussing the situation with Rod himself. They reconciled, they split apart. Her father jetted in to lend support. She lost 20 pounds in weight. They reconciled again and then more news of Rod with fresh affairs split them up again.

Britt herself had a fling with a young actor during the making of an undistinguished TV movie called *The Great Wallendas*, based on the lives of a famous circus family. Then she returned to Rod, but they were unable to conjure up their old magic. Britt blamed Rod: 'Rod was back into the whole groupie thing and he really thought that I would accept it all without so much as raising an eyebrow. One night he came home so drunk that Tony Toon had to drag him across the floor to the bed.'

Britt changed psychiatrists but she knew in her heart that she really had to change men. In desperation, she turned to ex-lover Lou Adler, who generously put a house at her disposal. With sadness in her heart, she moved out of Carolwood.

Britt records the miserable farewell: 'Rod lingered around the house that morning and he asked: "Are you really going?" I tried not to look at him for fear I would burst into tears. "There's no option, is there?" Rod did not answer. He took sanctuary in his room. There were no goodbyes.'

Both the size of the lawsuit and the intimate details of their life together revealed in Britt's book wounded Rod Stewart. Although the financial acrimony between the two was settled out of court, Britt's version was very much in the public eye. The cash demand was 'a big shock to me,' said Rod. 'I lost a lot of faith in women.'

Emotionally, Britt took the parting badly and tried everything to numb the pain. She had been very young when she had broken up with Peter Sellers, now it took longer for her to recover from the traumatic upheaval of breaking up with Rod. In her sadness Britt started pigging out and then throwing up. For a while she became anorexic and remembers that for six months she didn't once eat a proper meal. 'My emotional troubles threw my whole body out of tune,' she said.

Rod was anxious to get the Britt Ekland period out of his hair, epitomised in his mind by the picture of him sporting a boater on the cover of *A Night on the Town*. On a 1975 television documentary reflecting back on his life and music, Rod said: 'Nowadays I am just improving my persona. I wouldn't have changed anything apart from THAT album cover, where I was wearing a straw boater. I don't think that was me. That was a bad period of my life.'

Later he grumbled: 'I've lost all the songs about drinking piña coladas under a parasol. I was just listening to Ekland all the time, having stupid album covers done. The music was overlooked for a few years there.' Rod blamed Britt for his foray into fatuity during the mid-seventies, which he came to feel was his most negative period. 'The image was being built for me and I just let it happen until it ran away with itself. It was stupid, posing all the time. I deserved the criticism I got and I certainly did get some. We're all allowed to make mistakes, though, and I've come through the other end of the tunnel.'

As he told a press conference: 'A lot of the criticism was absolutely correct. I had left what I started out to do: to be a rock 'n' roll singer. I was in love and I did a lot of foolish things.' But was it all Britt's fault? 'Well, a great deal of it,' said Rod. 'Also, I closed myself off and didn't go out and listen to music the way I do now.'

Fans recall that the *A Night on the Town* boater really seemed to bother Rod. On the tour after the release of the LP, the official logo was a drawing of him putting his fist through the somewhat stagy headwear. The boater had seriously embarrassed the singer.

He said: 'It was Britt's idea to wear the straw boater on the cover while holding a glass of champagne, which is just not me. I think that album cover is the most embarrassing thing I've ever done in my life. So shortly afterwards, when I'd fallen out of love with Britt, I looked at it and said: "My God, Stewart, what have you done now, lad?" So that's why we came out with that tour logo.'

Rod refused to agree that he ever really 'went Hollywood'. He said later: 'The whole thing about "going Hollywood" has been blown out of all proportion. First, I live nowhere near Beverly Hills, I live in Holmby Hills, which is a Los Angeles address. And I don't go out with film stars the way I'm supposed to. OK, I live next door to Gregory Peck, but I just say hello to him and he's the only one I know. I don't go to ritzy parties. If I did I'd admit it.'

But Britt did have an enormous, positive influence on Rod.

'She was a great girl, and had a great rock 'n' roll spirit to her,' he reflects. Britt was perhaps the first really worldly woman with whom he had shared a long relationship. While Rod never felt fully at ease in the movie world, always preferring musicians to actors for playmates, Britt did open his eyes to many of the finer things in life, from French antiques to continental films.

And he might not have attended so many 'ritzy parties' if it weren't for Britt, but he was not exactly one for staying in anyway. Another ex-girlfriend described him as the 'least domestic person' she has ever known: 'All he wanted to do was go out.' Rod did hit the social scene when he was living in Hollywood but he has always hit every available social scene. Rod didn't regard it as going Hollywood, most of the time he was just going out.

It was shortly after Rod had split from Britt that he embarked on a three-month fling with Bebe Buell. Rod had got to hear that Bebe had finally split up from Todd Rundgren, the same Todd who some years before had warned her that Rod would only want one thing from her.

As was customary, Rod got Tony Toon to pave the way by asking him to call Bebe up in November 1977, to tell her Rod was inviting her to dinner. Bebe in turn told Toon that if Rod wanted to take her to dinner he'd have to call her himself. A few minutes later Rod was on the phone inviting Bebe to have dinner with him at his hotel, in the dining room. Believing she was heading for an intimate meal with a man she had known on and off for years, Bebe remembers dressing demurely, and being astounded when she arrived at the hotel to be greeted by a posse of British journalists and photographers shouting: 'Bebe, darling, look this way, smile,' as flashbulbs popped all around her.

The newspapers had a field day touting 'leggy model' Bebe as Rod's new girl which, in the wake of his split with Britt, gave Rod's image as a rock stud a timely boost. In her outrageously candid and bold recollections, about her life at the centre of the rock scene, Bebe says she found it upsetting that she had been used in this way. But, with her self-esteem at a low point having been dumped by Todd after living with him for five years, she embarked on an affair with Rod 'against my better judgement'. She explained: 'We liked each other sexually and had a real fondness for each other.'

Rod made her laugh, Bebe noted, and at a vulnerable time for her, he kept telling her how beautiful she was and not to neglect her modelling work. When Rod went off on an American tour, Bebe went with him for several concert dates and then towards the end of 1977, he flew her to England to spend some time with him. But it was a far from smooth relationship.

One night, while Bebe languished at Rod's home, Rod met up at a party with another American model, Marcy Hanson, whom he had flown in. Rod's two-timing was too much for Keith Moon, the wildly eccentric drummer with the Who, who had been a friend of Bebe's for several years. He loudly let Rod know in no uncertain terms what he thought of his behaviour.

Bebe knew nothing of the rumpus until, predictably, it hit the newspapers. But it was all soon forgotten and after spending New Year's Eve in the Caribbean, Bebe was back in London to celebrate Rod's birthday, early in January. Rod then flew off to Rio to continue his concert tour and called for Bebe to join him. But, once in Rio, Bebe says she quickly became prickly over Rod's flirting with other women, notably with a countess who frequently hitched up her dress to reveal her pubic hair snipped into a perfectly shaped triangle. After a flare-up with Rod, Bebe decided it was time to fly back to London where, in any case, she was due for a modelling assignment.

As she stepped off Concorde at Heathrow Airport, Bebe was astonished to be beseiged by dozens of reporters and photographers wanting to know how she felt about breaking up with Rod.

He had let it be known publicly that their affair was over, backed up by his publicist's stark confirmation: 'He's given her the boot.'

Unfortunately he had neglected to explain the situation to Bebe, and she was not amused. Nor were some of the young staff she had befriended at London's Portobello Road Hotel when she checked in. They set up a dartboard in the basement bar and attached a picture of Rod's face to it. Bebe started to feel a whole lot better as she and her pals took it in turns to throw darts at it.

Some 25 years on, Bebe insists in her frank reminiscences in *Rebel Heart* that she doesn't dislike Rod, and she has some nice things to say about him, not least that he's amusing, intelligent and witty. But, looking back, she considers going out with him to have been 'total insanity' on her part, her big mistake. It was, she swears, something she would never have done if she hadn't been hurting so much from her break-up with Todd. Bebe's stated view is: 'Rod Stewart is a dangerous person if you're a woman. If you go out with him even once it's plastered everywhere, and for some weird reason, he's always been able to use women to get attention.' She concluded: 'He's somebody I'd like to forget.'

CHAPTER EIGHT

BLONDES HAVE MORE FUN

*I remember telling my dad that I was getting married
and he said: 'What! But you're only 34! Wait another
ten years.' He was absolutely right. I was still a kid
inside.* Rod on breaking the news to his father that
he was to marry actress Alana Hamilton

Alana Hamilton appeared to have all the qualifications to be Rod
Stewart's ideal woman. She was blonde and beautiful, of course,
and, at 5 ft 11 in, with the requisite long and shapely legs, she
easily measured up to Rod's unwavering physical standards. But
Alana was much more than just another pretty face. She possessed a mind and a determination which was to have an
enormous impact on the life of Mr Rod Stewart.

Yet there was nothing in their first meeting at a Hollywood
party in March 1978 that predicted a marriage and children for
the rock world's most dedicated bachelor. They were introduced
at a star-studded party given by Rod's close friend, actor David
Jannsen, better known as the Fugitive, and his wife Dani, who were
doing some nifty matchmaking after Rod's break-up with Britt.

'It wasn't really an instant thing,' said Rod. 'At first I thought
she was just another blonde that I should bed, but it wasn't quite
as straightforward as that.'

The next day, when Rod instructed his faithful aide Tony Toon to ring and arrange a dinner date with the former wife of actor George Hamilton, the response was cool. 'What's wrong with Rod ringing me himself?' said Alana. 'I thought he was very cocky and sure of himself and I thought: who does he think he is anyway.'

Toon was startled to find that the lady was by no means bowled over by the suggestion that she meet the famous rock star for dinner. She wasn't even sure she could make it. But if she heard the invitation from Rod's own lips she just might. Not for the last time, Rod complied.

However, the statuesque Texan model and stylish lady about Hollywood was most certainly not inclined to become just another decorative bimbo, notched on the bedpost of the libidinous Mr Stewart. Although she was single when they first met, she had never considered the singer as a possible suitor. She told friends afterwards that Rod Stewart was the last person she would have thought of dating: 'Given a list of 100 men, his name would be last on the list. Besides, he has a funny-looking nose.'

In fact, her reaction to her first encounter with the famed Rod Stewart was even less promising: 'I didn't really like him,' she said. 'I had this sort of image of him. I thought he'd be cocky and that we'd never have anything in common.' But then she noted that Rod kept staring at her, and realised there could be more to the spiky-haired singer than a string of hit records and a wild reputation.

As it turned out, their first impressions were both wrong. Having agreed to meet for dinner, the alluring Alana refused to sleep with Rod – for all of 48 hours. Rod realised she was no run-of-the-mill one-night stand, and Alana was struck by the attractive and amusing man underneath the brash exterior. It was to be a relationship which dramatically changed both their lives.

But in those early months together they were just like any other pair of new lovers. Rod adored Alana's accent: 'She's from Texas. And I'd never had a girl from Texas ... I'm lying again, probably just a couple. Anyway, it took me a couple of days and many clever wordings before I got her between the sheets. I'm extremely happy I've found a nice lady at last.'

Alana Collins was born in the tiny Texan town of Nacogdoches, and was given her unusual name because her mother had a crush on Alan Ladd at the time. Alana stood out at school where most of the other girls had more usual names like Mary Lou or Billie Jo, and she hated her name because nobody could pronounce it. Even compared with Rod's down-to-earth origins, Alana's family were very poor. Her mother and father separated soon after she was born, and Alana was brought up by her granny and her uncle on their small farm in a rural outpost.

As a child she helped planting vegetables and feeding the chickens. She can remember existing for days on potato soup until Granny's pension cheque came in, and then the family would walk the three miles to the grocery store. They bought their food in huge sacks which her grandmother later used to fashion little dresses for Alana. Her mother worked in Houston and came back every few weeks. Alana used her height and her beauty and her remarkable self-belief to climb out of the poverty trap via success as a model. But she never regretted her harsh childhood.

Always very religious from an early age, Alana became a member of the Church of Religious Science and drew great strength from prayer: 'I've been going to church and praying for years. I'm very religious. I've prayed for almost everything I've wanted in life and most of the time I've gotten it.

'My religion teaches you that you control your life by your thoughts. You are master of your own fate. I believe in that totally.' But reports of her devotions were frequently garbled:

a source of considerable irritation. 'The way it was printed made it sound as if I was practising some kind of voodoo,' she said.

Rod loved Alana's vibrant energy and her sense of fun. He said she was the first girl he had found with the same sense of humour as him. David and Dani Jannsen had thought Rod and Alana would be perfect for each other and Rod agreed they had been right. But in their first whirlwind of mutual attraction they almost wore each other out. The two jet-setters were both 33 when they met and were initially consumed with a determination to compete with each other. They went out every single evening into the nightlife of Los Angeles, for six weeks, to show how life was one long entertainment and then, both exhausted, sat down and agreed to stay in.

Rod recalls: 'We said to each other, "Who are we trying to impress?" The answer was each other. That was really the turning point. Then we went through all those little tests. We knew we were great together in LA but we both knew that we might hate each other away from there, living in a hotel together. Dirty socks and all that. And we went through all that and it was still great. We knew that we were made for each other.'

Rod and Alana had much in common. They were both blond and neither had ever been jilted. Alana always insisted she had been the one to end her relationships and Rod said: 'I've never lost either. No one has ever left me. The trouble is, I love a girl with spunk who can stand up for herself. Alana's independence is what I like.'

The couple did not wish to move in together. Even eight months after they first got together, Rod was still in Carolwood Drive and Alana had her own home in Beverly Hills. Rod said: 'She has her own house and lives there. I stay at home. We made that decision at the beginning. We swap around. She sometimes stays over at my house, or I go over to hers. It's good that we don't live together. Britt and I made a big mistake about that. You should keep it separate and independent.'

One of Rod and Alana's favourite pastimes was to go shopping together. They found they had almost identical taste in clothes, although Rod did concede that some of their matching outfits were a shade bizarre. Alana said: 'Rod likes me looking slinky and sexy. He adores me in miniskirts and high thin heels.' For a woman still conscious of being called 'bird legs' at school, slipping into miniskirts just for Rod wasn't easy, especially as Alana seldom wore short skirts, believing her calves were too thin. 'I liked more feminine clothes: a party style with lace and frills,' she said. 'Basically, though, he likes me in anything as long as I don't look too oldladyish. And if I buy really raunchy jackets and coats I have to be careful, because he'll have them off me as quick as a flash and wear them himself!'

By the autumn of 1978, Rod was hard at work on the European legs of an ambitious world tour and concerned about his first British concerts for two years. He was anxious about the reception, keen to be seen as the old Rod, rather than what he knew had come to be known as the 'Hollywood' version. As the tour got under way, Rod confided: 'When I was with Britt I was pretending to be something I'm not. She brought out a posh, phoney side in me. I lost a lot of friends by going around with her. Now it's back to square one.' But someone must have liked him still: the British leg was sold out, he had a number one single, 'Da Ya Think I'm Sexy?', and an album at number three, *Blondes Have More Fun*.

When the tour began, in Manchester, Rod realised he need not have worried. The 12,000 tickets for the four shows sold out in just four hours, and the wave of adulation that swept from the audience to the stage, as the band struck the first few chords, almost overwhelmed him. He said afterwards: 'You don't know what it's like to have an audience respond like that. I was so moved that tears filled my eyes and I cried momentarily. I lost my voice and couldn't remember the words of a song I've been doing for years. When we did "Maggie May" and "Sailing" the fans were singing and we were playing. I don't know who was entertaining who most. They knew all the words. I felt so humble. My fans are the best in the world.'

Also on the road was Alana. Before she met Rod Stewart she had been to only one rock concert. After watching her new lover's remarkable live performances, she was, like so many people, hooked. And she was a voice of reason in the hectic male-dominated world of a travelling rock band. She insisted that Rod took his vitamin pills and cut down on his alcohol intake. Rod relished the attention. 'Marriage is closer than it has ever been,' he said. 'I really am in love with her. And she is not an ugly girl.'

The couple found time to pay their respects to the doomed aircraft-carrier *Ark Royal* in Plymouth docks, where she awaited her final voyage to the scrapyard. Rod was the first to admit that he owed her something for the huge success of "Sailing". 'She helped to build my reputation and I desperately wanted to visit her before she was scrapped,' he said. 'The song is still a show-stopper at my concerts and every time I sing it in the future, it will give me a very special feeling.'

When the Stewart family met Alana, they were somewhat taken aback by the forceful former model. Rod's father was even less impressed when he kept reading that the couple were 'trying for a baby'. 'You're not even married,' he yelled down the phone at his famous son. However, Alana quickly met with the approval of Rod's great mate Elton John, who generously spent £5,000 on three rings for her birthday.

Rod seems to have found his triumphant return to Britain inspirational in all sorts of ways. Because, just nine months after he opened his sell-out homeland success, Alana gave birth to their daughter Kimberley, in July 1979.

But on one subject at least, Alana agreed with Rod's father. She wanted his baby all right, but only if they were married first. They organised a very low-key wedding away from the prying cameras of the press, in Los Angeles, in April 1979. The ceremony was conducted by the Reverend Jackie Eastland, a minister in the Church of Religious Science. Rod was impressed by the Reverend Jackie's insights into their future, though less impressed when she was dubbed his 'personal psychic' by the British press. Rod credited the Reverend Jackie with predicting a medical problem for his friend Elton John, and began to share some of Alana's convictions.

Rod's father was shocked when Rod phoned him to tell him he was getting married. 'But you're only 34,' said Bob Stewart. 'You're much too young. Wait another ten years.' When his mother caught up with him she took him by the arm and whispered: 'Make sure you keep your trousers on in the future. Be a good boy.'

Rod bought Alana a beautiful art deco ring of diamonds set in onyx, which she decided was an impractical idea for a wedding ring, so, when Kimberley was born, Rod gave her another, a twist of emeralds and diamonds set in gold.

Two months before Kimberley's birth Rod was keen to point out that he had not been pushed into marriage simply by the pregnancy. He knew after a month with Alana that they would be together for life. He explained at the time: 'I never said that I'll try to be faithful now that I'm a married man. I did say: "For the first time in my life I will be faithful to one woman: my wife." I am really glad we got married. I have never been happier and for the first time in a long time I am leading a normal life. We keep on getting happier the more we get to know each other.'

The birth was a very emotional time for Rod: 'I was there when she was born. Now that was something else. An amazing experience. I didn't hold Alana's hand – she was far too busy shouting and getting on with it ... When she was actually born. Well, it's probably nearly as good as Scotland beating England. A once-in-a-lifetime thing. And thank God she hadn't got my hooter.'

When asked if Kimberley would be spoilt, Rod recalled his own indulged childhood: 'Well, I was spoilt rotten and I've turned out OK. No, she'll get anything she wants out of me. I haven't thought about her growing up yet but I like to think I'm fairly liberal. That may all change when she gets to 15 or so, of course.'

Rod and Alana calculated afterwards that their unborn baby kicked her way through 43 Rod Stewart concerts around the world, while still in the womb, and heard 43 renditions of 'Maggie May'. No wonder that by the time she was 16 months old her doting dad was giving the toddler piano lessons, and remarking on her amazing aptitude. Why, she even seemed happy to sit captivated by a video of one of dad's concerts. 'Without wishing to sound like a doting father – and I don't really care if I am a doting father – you just try and get a kid this young to sit still and watch TV for an hour,' he said. 'All these songs had registered with her. They were in her subconscious. It was absolutely amazing.'

Rod had one of his rare public flare-ups when he, Alana and baby Kimberley disembarked from the QE2 at Southampton on 1 October. He angrily refused to be photographed with his little daughter. Afterwards he snorted that he was not remotely ashamed of her: 'It's just that kids are not very pretty at that age, and we had already decided to wait a bit before she was photographed. Anyway I hate those dumb pictures of fathers holding babies and smiling like melons. They look so stupid.'

Rod and Alana were astonished when Kimberley was born a girl. All the tests had indicated that Alana was expecting a boy, and they had planned to call him Roderick Christian. Rod had even joked about flying Alana over to Scotland so the youngster would qualify to play soccer for his beloved national side. Fortunately, he did not bother.

When young Kimberley arrived, they were at first stumped for a name. After two days they came up with Kimberley from a book of names – no other significance. Her full name is Alana Kimberley.

'I don't feel tied down by being a father,' said Rod. 'I'm a happy man. I know sex and sexy things surround us wherever I go. I have always had a weakness for long-legged blondes, but since I'm married to the best, I'm not going to be interested any more in testing for any other fish in the sea. We have never been happier together than we are now.'

He was sincere when he said: 'It's a hundred times better than I ever thought possible, and I just look forward to it going on getting better. My reputation as a killer with women precedes me wherever I go, even now that I am a married man. But I plan on standing by the vows I made when I got married. I know my hellraising nights are over, as far as others are concerned. Now it is just Alana and me that raise the hell with each other.'

Alana was happy too, shrugging off reports of her husband's previous philandering: 'I could not care less about what he did in the past. I have never been jealous. Those things written about him by women he knew! I don't know what has happened to good taste in this world. It reaches the point where nothing is sacred.'

She could not comprehend the tales of Rod having boisterous fights with Britt. For her and Rod, she said, their lowest point was half an hour of sulking after they could not agree on a colour scheme for the house. Alana stated: 'I am fairly good-natured, and the only time Rod gets into a bad mood is when he's not working.'

Unlike Britt, she did not make the mistake of getting

involved in the musical side of his business: 'I can't carry a tune in a bucket. If I sang one of Rod's own songs he wouldn't be able to recognise it. At home, Rod makes up little songs on the spur of the moment, which he sings to the baby.'

Rod worked hard at his marriage with Alana. Friends report a real determination to make the relationship a success. However, one lingering irritation remained in his life in sunny Los Angeles: he missed Britain. He missed the seasons, the newspapers, the pubs, the pals and the football. But he got a blast of a sound that really reminded him of home when an old friend, comedian Jonathan Moore, gave an unscheduled bagpipe performance on Christmas morning in 1980. Rod woke to the familiar sound, threw open the bedroom windows, and roared with laughter when he realised Jonathan had sneaked into the grounds to serenade him.

In their early days, the Stewarts' life together was very simple. They went to few parties, entertained only occasionally, even though a magnificent ballroom was added to the house. Alana's only rival for Rod's affections was his beloved weekend football game with his Los Angeles Exiles side – an enthusiasm she most certainly did not share. However, they did exercise together at regular keep-fit classes. Although, as Alana put it at the time: 'Rod enjoys it, but it's torture for me. I only exercise because I feel I ought to.'

When she had finished breast-feeding and they got more organised at home, Alana tried to please her man in the kitchen as well as elsewhere. She bought English recipe books and attempted his favourite steak and kidney pie. But for Christmas she insisted on a traditional Texas-style dinner of roast chicken, black-eyed peas, sweet potatoes and banana pudding. No wonder Rod also used to work out on an exercise bicycle in the evening as well.

The years have always been kind to the singer. Although he

has enjoyed a drink, he also knows when to stop. 'I might go crazy for five or six nights in a row and then I'll say: "This is it," because I look in the mirror and there's a big spot coming on the end of me nose so I decide to stop. Or worse still, if me hair won't stand up, then I know that something is wrong!'

Rod's late-night drinking sessions were now supplemented by vegetable juices. 'Really, all you need is lung power,' said Rod. 'The most important thing is that I don't smoke.'

And so, Rod's determination to stay fit helped more than just his football. It also enabled his concert routines to reach remarkable athletic heights. The energy levels at Rod Stewart concerts were always higher than at those of his contemporaries. As they moved into their mid-thirties, the gap grew.

The buzz of live performing always required him to make an extra effort. The first few weeks of a tour would see Rod lose seven or eight pounds. Alana was much more of a country music fan than Rod. 'She tries to kid on but she don't really like rock 'n' roll,' said Rod. 'She likes watching me perform but she likes the slow songs, the romantic ones. I think that most women do. I like making the fast ones – fast and furious.'

Rod Stewart wasn't ever going to join the many casualties of the rock business. While the early deaths of stars like Keith Moon, Elvis Presley and Led Zeppelin's John Bonham all saddened Rod, his solid family background always set him apart from those rockers who move out of the fast lane only to overtake. After Bonham died, Rod said glumly: 'I had a sneaking feeling about Bonham, that he was pushing it just a bit too much and not being fit enough to carry it off.'

The shadow of Britt Ekland occasionally passed across Alana's ideal view of her new life. After Britt's autobiography came out with its frank, although largely positive, view of Rod Stewart, Alana threw up her hands in horror. 'I really do think,' she trilled, 'that this kiss-and-tell syndrome is disgusting. It's appalling. I mean, I swear to God that if I was starving in the streets and someone offered me a million pounds, I wouldn't write such a book. I just honestly don't understand how you can write intimate details about someone you once cared for.'

Alana was particularly angered by Britt's complaints about Rod's meanness with money, suggesting the multimillionaire was so careful with his money that he used to grumble about the grocery bills. Alana was aghast: 'When I moved in [to the same Carolwood Drive home Rod had shared with Britt] I went mad when I saw the grocery bills. I said: "Rod, this has got to stop," and he said: "Oh, is it expensive?" He didn't even know. Sure, he's conscientious about money, but I've never known a less stingy man. He gives me an unlimited budget. If he was mean with Britt, maybe it was because he didn't want to spend money on her. A lot of men are like that with their girlfriends. With their wives, it's a different story.'

Alana found it hard to be generous, however, when it came to Rod's previous life. She simply loathed people who assumed that Rod was nothing more than an insolent womaniser. All right, so he went out with a lot of women, she would say, but then he was a good-looking man, and all men like to sow their wild oats. Alana described all Rod's previous girlfriends as 'old sluts', and felt that Rod just wasn't ready to settle down until he met her. She believed that he was waiting until the right person came along and that he knew he would never marry Britt. Alana said: 'Today he believes in the sanctity of marriage as much as I do. I basically think that if a man is happy at home and in love with the person he is with, I don't think he wants to go and pop into bed with any little groupie who comes along.'

She and Rod certainly threw themselves into the family-building business with enthusiasm. Their second child, a son, to be called Sean Roderick, was born in September 1980, only a little over a year after Kimberley was born. Rod had just returned to California from the Bahamas, where he had been on a song-writing trip with Richard Harris, an old friend.

The next night, at their beach retreat just up the coast from Malibu, Alana's labour pains started. As her contractions increased, so did Rod's speed in his Lamborghini as he drove at up to 90 mph towards the hospital. Alana was screaming: 'I'm going to have it in the car!' and Rod had not a clue what to do. He might have watched Kimberley's birth, but he dreaded the thought of having to deliver his second child himself, particularly in the cramped passenger compartment of an Italian sports car designed for speed, rather than its potential adaptability into a maternity ward.

The next thing Rod heard above Alana's yells was the wailing siren of a police car. He skidded to a halt and, being British, leaped out and moved towards the policemen – definitely not the thing to do in gun-happy California. The cops both jumped out and shouted 'Freeze!' to the anxious rock star. Happily, the law officers were Rod Stewart fans, even though, as he observed afterwards, they must have been ten years younger than him.

The guns were quickly exchanged for autograph books. Then Rod explained the urgency of his problem, whereupon the Highway Patrol really came into their own. They swept Rod and Alana to the waiting ward at top speed. Just as well as it turned out, for young Sean Roderick arrived a mere 15 minutes after they did.

In fact, it was a difficult birth and Sean made his entrance into the world via a Caesarean operation, which prevented Rod witnessing the second marvel of his life. However, Rod is credited with the ultimate footballer's reaction to the birth of a son: 'I'm over the moon.' Later, he noted: 'Kimberley looks just like Alana but Sean is more like me, though. He's got a real big hooter there, a real Stewart hooter. I think when he's old enough I'll do what my dad did to me. He always put a tennis ball at my feet, you know. I'll try that tactic, but if he turns out to be a chess player who likes classical music, then I shall support him all the way. He's got a very intelligent look on his face, which worries me. I don't really think he's cut out to be a rock 'n' roller. That comes from his mother. She's got an IQ of 148. It doesn't come from me. I was a secondary modern school idiot.'

Sean was very welcome, but by no means planned. Rod and Alana did not intend to have a second baby so soon. As she put it: 'No one in their right mind wants to have two babies in nappies at the same time.' In under two years, Rod and Alana had gone from being avid partygoers, to parents of three children under five. They decided not to extend the family any more for a while. Alana said: 'I'd like to have a rest. I've spent the last two years being pregnant and it's hard work.' Soon after Sean was born, poor Alana caught glandular fever, followed by chronic fatigue syndrome.

Alana was convinced Rod would be an ideal father, when she saw how well he got on with her son Ashley, from her marriage to George Hamilton. Ashley was only three when Rod and Alana first fell in love, and initially he was jealous of the strange spiky-haired rival for his mother's affections. But Alana watched how Rod's zany sense of humour and dogged persistence gradually made a friend of the young child. By the time he was six, Ashley was putting on his own private rock 'n' roll concerts in his bedroom, singing along to Rod's song 'Hot Legs'. Only Rod was allowed to watch.

Razor wire topped the high wall surrounding Rod's Carolwood Drive mansion. Security is a fact of life in the swisher parts of Los Angeles. But Rod was most worried when the children were very young. The fans never bothered him and he would cheerfully chat at the gates and sign autographs, but he said: 'We've got some nutters who try to get over the fence. When you've got three kids you can't afford to take chances.'

Soon after Sean's birth, Rod left to start his next tour. Alana had to stay behind in the US for their longest separation since meeting: all of three weeks. There was the inevitable press speculation. Said Alana: 'We were both very lonely then. But I had just had the Caesarean with Sean and was still breast-feeding. I just couldn't have gone on tour. Unfortunately, now we've been together for a while, people are looking for cracks in our relationship. But I trust Rod. If you are going to get worried about what sort of women groupies can be, and that your husband has to go away, then you shouldn't marry someone in Rod's profession.'

All the same, Alana bridled a little at what she felt was a double standard: she understood Rod's need to go to a nightclub to unwind after a concert, but she knew that if she went to a club without him, Rod most certainly would not approve. 'A few years ago, I would have felt tied down,' she said, 'but now I find my children more interesting than anyone I could meet in a nightclub.'

Rod loved being a father from the very start and played for hours with both children. 'I don't know what I did with my life before I had children,' he said with a grin as he arrived in London, in November 1980, for another successful concert tour. His new album, *Foolish Behaviour*, included a song dedicated to his daughter, 'My Girl', as well as the thoughtful 'Oh God, I Wish I Was Home Tonight'. Although the tour was another towering sell-out success, it was a crucial time for Rod, after all the flak he had taken for 'selling out', so he was more nervous than he had been since his early days. About two hours before the show began he found himself shaking and, on the second night, he even forgot the words of 'Maggie May'. As the tour went on, though, he eased back into his familiar, confident style.

At the time, Rod considered *Foolish Behaviour* to be his finest work to date. Its subsequent success gave him a feeling of real personal satisfaction: 'We can't be at the top for ever, but if this was all taken away from me, just give me the wife, kids and guitar and I could do it all again. I know I could, it's in there.'

As he approached 36, Rod sensibly began to qualify his statements about his inability to imagine himself rock 'n' rolling into his forties. 'You know, it would have been very easy for McCartney to have retired five years ago, but there's this old die-hard thing in him that still has so much music to make. Well, it's the same with me. It's what I've done all my life, and I'm not about to give it up when I know deep down that the best music I've ever had is on this album.

'When it starts tapering off and I'm not pleasing myself any more – and there has got to be a turning point – that's when I'll change.'

He wrote all the tracks on the album and the flow of inspiration was never stronger. He even included a song about killing your wife. 'I know I'm going to get some stick over that,' said Rod.

After their three weeks apart, Alana flew into London and installed herself with the children and their nannies at the Dorchester Hotel, in central London, as a sort of tour base camp. Alana went along to some of the concerts, but, more often than not, she waited with the family back at the hotel for her husband to jet in on his days off from rushing around Europe.

Rod felt he was living a double life. He adored the children. He even changed their nappies once each so he could at least say he'd done it, and the sentimental side of his nature could not resist their babyish hugs and cute adoring faces. Yet, in a way, he was captive to a career that forced him to stay young. Rod was beginning to feel more mature. He loved Alana for her strength and even for her jealous, possessive qualities. Rod wanted to prove to the world and to himself that after five years of philandering, of playing the jet-setting super-stud pop star, he could settle into this new role of happy, family man. As he said at the time: 'It's very confusing. For the first time in my life, I find that I have two personalities and that I am split down the middle. Half of me is the family man and the other half is the 35-year-old who will not grow up. I know deep down that it is time that I grew up. After all, you can't be in rock for the rest of your life, but I am trapped in a business that refuses to let you grow up.'

His friends remember a quieter, more thoughtful Rod Stewart on tour. Rod insisted that he had come to realise that taking out an endless stream of different women was pretty unimportant, even if it had been enjoyable. The children had quite an effect on the singer: 'It's amazing when you go home and they put their arms around you or tug at your trousers and look at you with their open, honest faces. It's a remarkable experience to me. Now I have to prove to myself that I can stick with one woman. I've had years of running through one woman after another. Now I want to make a relationship work.'

Alana who had originally negotiated the $2 million purchase of the beach house, when she fell instantly in love with it while Rod was on tour. She sent him photographs of it and indicated how keen she was to buy it, and he gave her the go-ahead, without actually seeing it. Built on tall, sturdy wooden stilts to allow the ocean to lap underneath at high tide, the house boasted vast windows looking out to sea and comprised 11 bedrooms. Sitting out on the 20-foot-high deck, Rod composed some of his most memorable songs, for which he found the sun and the sea great inspiration. It was in this idyllic seaside setting that Rod and Alana threw wild parties, as well as using the house as a romantic retreat at weekends. Rod's bedroom was home for his huge brass four-poster bed surrounded by pretty floral curtains. He loved to tell visitors: 'That bed has had a few rough and tumbles in its time. I call it the midnight trampoline.'

The house was also a favourite weekend place for the three

children. They loved to leave the smog of Los Angeles, go down to the beach and have their famous parents to themselves. Years later, Rod said: 'Kimberley and Sean spent a lot of time at the beach house. I've got such fond memories of those two tiny things crawling around on the big rug in front of the fireplace. The kids loved the place. Sean used to call the ocean "Daddy's pool".' Rod's old rivalry with Mick Jagger was often in his mind when he compared lifestyles. Rod considered Jagger's relationship with Bianca to be very much an 'open marriage'. He and Alana, he maintained, had a much more traditional view of the marriage vows. And Jagger irritated Rod with some published criticisms of the Carolwood Drive house. Britt had helped Rod develop a love of antiques and he was very proud of his collection of lamps. When it came to beautiful objects that were likely to appreciate in value, Rod always insisted that he positively enjoyed spending some of his millions. He stated: 'I'd rather put my money into antiques than have it all in the bloody bank. I've got nothing in the bank. I just spend it on things that I enjoy seeing around me. I've got no time for people who pretend they haven't made any money out of this business.

'Jagger's one who tries to make out he's come in from the street. He had a go at me about my collection of lamps in an interview. They all come round here, drink my booze and then go away and knock me! Why pretend all your life? Why not be honest? I think people admire those who are honest. I am wealthy – relatively wealthy – and I enjoy it. People are so embarrassed about being successful. That's one of the things I love about Elton. He has made a lot of money; he is also quite prepared to share it with people. He is probably the kindest guy I've ever met in my life. I respect him for that; he's a marvellous man; I love him. I've got no time for pretenders.'

On the American leg of the tour Alana took time out to visit her tiny home town of Nacogdoches. Rod wanted to see where she came from, but the return visit was painful for Alana because to her the house seemed so small.

Of course, the publication of Britt's book, *True Britt*, at this time was a brutal blow to Rod. He claimed to have stolen a copy on the way through Heathrow towards a concert in Brussels, though aides quickly insisted that they had paid for the copy after Rod had picked it up. He snorted angrily at the suggestion that he had not liked Britt's children and at the patronising references to his family. And he firmly rejected the idea that he wanted to be the permanent centre of attention. As Rod remembered, it was Britt who went bananas if she was not featured in every photograph at every reception. But he laughed at Britt's description of the two of them having similarly shaped bodies and long legs. But he was genuinely hurt by the book because he had been hopelessly in love with the lady for a long time, and he recalled many marvellous moments together. He said: 'It's just sad to me that someone so close could write these things. But then, I wouldn't like to get hurt the way I hurt her.' An even more disturbing reminder of previous loves was the arrival on Rod's Los Angeles doorstep, in 1981, of 18-year-old Sarah Thubron, his illegitimate daughter from a teenage romance with an art student. It was hardly the happy reunion Sarah had hoped for. A newspaper had paid for her flight and she turned up with a photographer. Rod leaned heavily on Alana for support. He said afterwards: 'It was all so wrong, and it was so awkward with my other little daughter and my son sitting there, when this girl came in after all these years. It is a part of my life that has gone now. She can't expect to just step back into my life again. Perhaps she should never have been told. Perhaps that would have been the best thing for her.'

For Sarah, the meeting was even more upsetting. She had been adopted as a baby and brought up by Brigadier Gerald Thubron and his wife Eve, in a quiet country village in the south of England. She did not know who her father was until she was eighteen, when her grandmother told her that he was someone very famous. 'When I asked my adoptive parents, they told me my father was Rod Stewart. At first I did not believe it,' says Sarah.

She remembers her first meeting with her father as a complete disaster. 'And for that I blame Alana. Before I could see Rod I had to be vetted by Alana and his lawyer. The lawyer was all right but she thought I was a threat to her and her kids. I took an instant dislike. She was offhand and didn't even look nice. She was too tall. I got the impression that she wanted to make sure I was not after any of his money.

'When I finally got to see Rod it was all very embarrassing. There were lots of people around the recording studio. There was no emotion. At one point, I walked out in tears. I thought he would be fatherly and hug me like a father should. I felt more like a fan than a daughter. Alana did not want us to be on our own together. Bitchy is too strong a word to describe her, maybe she was just a little bit jealous. She told me I was something from his past and could not expect to walk into his life.'

Sarah's bitter disappointment at her first encounter with her natural father meant that she was to wait until Alana was off the scene, before contacting him again.

Gradually the rock 'n' roll lifestyle began to pall for Alana. When Rod got together with rock writer Robert Palmer, they burned the midnight oil talking about his music for once rather than 'Britt fucking Ekland', as he colourfully put it.

Palmer recalls one incident when Alana turned in early, soon after midnight, saying: 'You're not going to stay up all night are you, Rod?'

'Oh no, dear, we'll just listen to some music for an hour or two,' replied Rod, with as much innocence as he could summon.

'I want you to know that when we got back to Los Angeles

after our last encounter with you, Rod came down with the flu and was as sick as a dog,' said Alana drily to Robert.

'Good night, dear,' said Rod, bringing out a much-prized Jimmy Reed tape. Their session ended shortly after six a.m.

The spectre of the formidable Miss Ekland raised itself in person when Britt encountered the Stewarts at a London nightclub. Accounts differ, as they say, to exactly what happened. Alana recalls Britt brazenly coming up to Rod, sitting on his knee and kissing her former lover. She therefore decided that her predecessor needed cooling off, and poured champagne down the back of her dress to conclude the clinch. Britt describes the champagne incident as 'untrue, but very imaginative'.

On tour, Alana had a profound effect on Rod's behaviour: he was the model of good husbandly behaviour. However, as soon as she was off the scene, Rod, Jim Cregan, Kevin Savigar and company would indulge in just the sort of boys-night-out behaviour that Alana had thought had been left behind. The male rock bonding was something she found hard to come to terms with.

Jim Cregan and the others got the feeling that Alana wanted to keep Rod away from anybody and everybody, that she wanted only to team him up with her starry pals. He sensed Alana's dislike of the boys in the band and Rod's football team, and got the impression that Alana was only interested in Rod hanging out with Liza Minnelli and other big-time Hollywood stars. Rod's mates saw that he wasn't comfortable with this situation. Rod would tell them that he'd been out with some top Hollywood stars, but that when he wanted to get his football team round to the house Alana would object.

'There was an awful period,' said Cregan, 'when we'd start to make a record and the band would be in the rehearsal room at two, and Rod would show up at five or six and then stay only an hour and then bugger off to some Hollywood party. At the bottom of this was Alana, who I'd come to like and respect later on, but at the time she was a terrible nuisance. She wanted Rod to be extremely Hollywood and be at all the A-list parties, whether he wanted to or not, and I don't think he really wanted to.'

'Tora, Tora, Tora (Out With The Boys)', Rod's irresistible rocker from *Tonight I'm Yours*, celebrates the wild macho feeling that has always stayed close to his heart. It was a celebration of a Friday night out: boozing, punch-ups in the disco, trouble with the police and finally 'indecent exposure in the parking lot'.

'My wife hates that track,' Rod said. 'She asks me: "Why do you stay out drinking with the boys in the band until three in the morning, after you've been with 'em in the studio all day?" She's got a point there. I really enjoy her company, too, and I'm really working at the marriage. But I really think that if you're gonna make rock 'n' roll, you've got to live the lifestyle.'

Rod has always felt at his most relaxed talking about male subjects with male friends. Whether it is the finer details of an historic Scottish goal or the even finer details of a shapely passing female, he felt there were some conversations you simply cannot have with ladies present. Rod was sorry that Alana never quite understood that.

Rod also began to resent that Alana could never quite bring herself to accept his mates. He opened his house and his life to her more glitzy Beverly Hills celebrity acquaintances, but Alana was less willing to become friends with Rod's more ordinary down-to-earth musical or football-playing pals. Rod felt she wasn't very understanding about the simple things he wanted out of life: to be able to go out and play football and have a drink, without the clock being held over him.

Early in their relationship, Rod and Alana were totally besotted with each other; they would spend 24 hours a day together. But gradually Rod wanted to spend more and more time doing the thing he had always enjoyed: being one of the lads.

Alana felt threatened and insecure. Just a few months before

Rod was to leave her, Alana had silicone breast implants to increase her bust from 34A to 34B, possibly as a desperate attempt to try and save their relationship. After the three births and all the breast-feeding, Alana felt she needed a little uplift. She had always wished she was bustier and felt her body would be more in proportion if she filled out a bit. 'I also did it because I thought it was something that would please my husband,' she said.

Alana knew she was being possessive of Rod but she wanted life to stay the same as it had been when they first met. She became furious and ranted and raved at him when he spent all day every Sunday playing football. She felt it should be a day for her and the family.

She said afterwards: 'Suddenly I found myself with three children and a lot of responsibility. I was no longer the sort of fun, party girl Rod was used to. He didn't realise that once you've got children you have to raise them. I resented his drinking and playing football with the boys. Instead of sitting down and saying: "We love each other, let's work it out," we just wanted each other to bend to our will.'

The total communication they had enjoyed in their early days together also began to break down. Alana would sulk. Rod would go drinking with the boys. As Los Angeles legend goes, she sometimes tracked him down in bars, once angrily pouring a drink over his head, and another time telephoning the bar in which Rod had allegedly been telling friends he was putting on his tin hat and going back home into battle.

Forceful, opinionated Alana gradually grew tired of being confined to the role of housewife. In spite of Rod's millions and the endless opulence that surrounded her life, by the time young Sean was two she was itching to get back to work. It was important to Alana to earn some of her own money. She had started work at 14 behind the counter of a Texan Woolworths and she liked being financially independent. A former successful model, her switch into acting had just been getting under way with a role in an action movie called the *The Ravager*, starring Richard Harris, when she had been swept off her feet into motherhood, following the birth of Kimberley.

Alana's previous husband, George Hamilton, had always made it clear that he did not want a working wife. Rod minded less. Alana insisted, though: 'I would not leave my husband and children to go on location, so whatever I do will have to be close to home.' But she was rejected for several roles before landing a small part in the Goldie Hawn movie *Swinging Shift*, in which she played a gum-chewing girl from Texas who arrived in Hollywood, determined to make a name for herself. At least that was not difficult for her to imagine.

As well as wanting her own money, Rod increasingly found Alana determined to have her own way in arguments. She was never prepared to bite her tongue. However, she was always honest about her forthright approach to life: 'If I have a gripe I have to get it into the open,' she said. 'I'm a believer in being honest.' So when Rod broke with his long-serving manager Billy Gaff and his faithful headline-maker Tony Toon, Alana was not surprised to get the blame. A flurry of bad publicity followed, along with the graffiti attack on the walls of the Carolwood house, which announced 'Alana Piranha' to passing motorists. She shrugged and denied telling Rod to fire Gaff and Toon. She said that while Rod was surrounded by people telling him he was wonderful, she always told the truth. Rod had to get used to her honesty, she insisted.

She said at the time: 'I wish I could take the credit for Billy Gaff's departure, but I can't. I never get involved in Rod's business. I kept my mouth shut. I thought, I'm the wife, I'm not going to stick my two cents in. But if it happened again I would stick my two cents in. When Rod told me he was going to fire

Billy, I said: "Are you sure?" Billy wouldn't take any of Rod's calls. In the end, Rod sent him a telegram firing him.'

Rod insisted publicly that it was his decision to ease the old guard out of his entourage, and put Alana's manager Arnold Stiefel in charge of his own affairs. He was also angered by the graffiti. 'She is not a bloody piranha,' he said. Billy Gaff denied all knowledge of the giant insult on Rod's walls, but cheekily added that he was considering holding a party for all the people who might have done it – except he couldn't find a hotel big enough.

Despite Rod and Alana's best efforts to repel all boarders, however, by 1981 the marriage was already experiencing problems. They both desperately wanted it to work and prove all the cynics wrong, so they went to marriage guidance counsellors for advice. But the couple were coming more and more into conflict over the children. Rod kept hankering to return to live in Britain: at times he tired of the endless sunshine, saying that on the few occasions it did rain in southern California, he would rush out in the downpour until he was soaked. Nor did he want Sean and Kimberley to become totally American. Even Alana agreed that some Californian youngsters with their private phone lines and their foul language gave cause for alarm.

The couple's sincere efforts to make their relationship work were not helped, though, by the fact that Alana was clearly not at all popular with many of Rod's male friends. Jimmy Horowitz, Gaff's partner, recalls: 'I never got on very well with Alana. She was a very odd choice for Rod. She thought she was the queen of Beverly Hills. I think she liked Rod because he was one of the top ten big rock 'n' roll stars in the world, but she wasn't very comfortable with musicians.'

And Alana's humble upbringing never prevented her from insisting on absolutely the very best of service, usually at the top of her extremely loud voice. 'Rod is a pretty easygoing guy,' recalls Horowitz. 'As long as he can stick somebody for a bottle of wine, he's happy. Alana used to complain all the time, very loudly and very vocally, and make terrible scenes so a lot of hotels at the end wouldn't take their reservations.'

Alana's demands did not stop there. 'I remember flying back from New York to Los Angeles with them one time. I was at the airport with them,' remembers Horowitz. 'They had decided to go at the last minute and they were flying first class. Alana was really angry because first class in a 747 is split into two halves by the spiral staircase, and she wanted the four seats all together in the front sections, for her, Rod, one of the babies and the nanny. I couldn't get them, they were sold, but I managed to get them four seats behind. Alana was trying to get the people to move. There was one guy there she wanted to move who was executive vice-president of Chrysler or something, who didn't give a fuck about Rod Stewart or Alana. He had his seat and he was not going to move.

'She was causing all kinds of a ruckus. They had to call the supervisor. In the end it got sorted out. But some time later I saw the airline computer come up with Rod and Alana's name followed by the initials DP, which stand for Difficult Passenger.'

Difficult passenger was an understatement the night Alana refused to accompany Rod on a rare chance to ride on a red double-decker bus in Los Angeles. Horowitz recounts: 'They had done five nights at the Forum in Los Angeles. Rod likes to be one of the boys and instead of all going down in limos they went in a London bus. Alana didn't take too kindly to it. She had some big row with Rod and the band. She was going to go home in the limo but the limo had already left and they were on the bus. She said: "I'm not going back to Beverly Hills in this," and she stormed off the bus in the middle of Inglewood, the darker part of town. Apparently she was walking along in her sprayed-on trousers when the police picked her up and said: "Hey, you shouldn't be walking along here at night."'

Alana clashed with Billy Gaff and Jimmy Horowitz on more than one occasion. She liked to take charge of Rod's social life. Horowitz recalls: 'I wasn't even on this tour but there was going to be a big after-tour party which was going to be held in a private room at the Dome. So I got a call from Tony Toon saying would I like to come, and Billy – but on his own. Now Billy's the manager. The tour manager, Pete Buckland, wasn't invited. Most of the key people weren't invited. Me and my wife Carol and Billy were, but no partner. Alana was the one organising. I thought this was really bad.'

Horowitz's secretary at the time he was running Riva Records was called May Pang. In their busy office in New York they became used to some peculiar demands from the star and his wife in Los Angeles.

Alana's dependence on the advice of her psychic became particularly wearing. According to Horowitz: 'We had to give them the numbers of every flight they took, and then Alana had to see if the numbers were right and if they could fly on that flight.'

All hotel rooms also had to be checked out in advance to ensure the vibes were suitable for the strong-willed Mrs Stewart. Horowitz remembers trudging through one of New York's snowstorms with May Pang to run a rule over yet another hotel room: 'It was really miserable. We walked for miles to find this hotel to see if it was good enough for Alana. Suddenly the thought hit us: if this psychic is any good why doesn't she just take a look in her crystal ball and vet the rooms from California? That made us laugh a lot, but we didn't say that to Rod.'

But even worse for Horowitz was the night Alana had him thrown out of the house by armed guards, which perhaps helps to explain the strength of his antipathy towards the lady. 'I never really forgave her for that,' he said. 'I was in New York and Rod was having a really big party at home and Billy rang and said: "I'm in London, Rod wants someone from the company to be at the party, you'll have to go. Fly to Los Angeles for the party or Rod will be disappointed."

'So I flew in on a Saturday night and my crazy Jonathan, the guy who played the bagpipes on Rod's lawn, picked me up at the airport. He's a good friend of Rod's, so I said to him: "Why don't you come along to the party with me? Rod will love to see you." There's always a lot of security at these parties and I don't normally bring people, but it was just a party for Rod not a sit-down dinner. So we went in there and he wasn't on the list but we were ushered in. And then Alana saw Jonathan and me together. She knew he wasn't on the list so she ordered the armed guards over to throw us out. Rod said to me: "You can stay." I said: "Fuck off, Rod. I'm not staying. I flew 3,000 miles to come here out of courtesy." I was so annoyed. This was not like Rod. This was purely Alana. She didn't like Jonathan because he is not a big star in Beverly Hills. Everyone was so embarrassed. I was totally mortified.'

Appearances were always important to Alana, but even that razor-sharp mind did not always prevent her from sounding silly. In the depths of the winter she arrived in London sporting a fox-fur coat and announced: 'I don't believe in wearing animal furs, and I would never wear a seal fur or anything made from an endangered species.

'I feel guilty, but the trouble is that I catch cold easy and they told me the English winter had arrived, so I took it from its secret hideaway. I console myself that the fox was dead before I bought it.'

But Alana could not always get her own way. When she arrived at the St Peter's Basilica in Rome in a split leather miniskirt cut short to show off her long legs, the guards decided she was not suitably dressed and turned her away. 'We are on hallowed ground, madam, and you are not decorous,' she was told. For once Alana accepted the ruling with not too bad a grace: 'I didn't really think my skirt was that short, but I guess they have their codes. They were turning a lot of tourists away. Anyway, they were all very polite about it. We are moving on now. When I come back I'll make sure I wear a longer dress.'

Protocol upset Alana nearer to home when she and Rod were separated by nationality at a Hollywood dinner in honour of the Queen, in March 1983. With other British celebrities Rod was a top-table guest while Alana was forced to fume along with other non-Britons just out of the limelight. What no doubt rubbed salt into the wound was that Rod delighted in telling all concerned just how upset his wife was by the snub.

The summer of 1983 saw the rumours about the marriage fuelled to boiling point. Rod was working hard on yet another tour in Europe and Alana embarked on another film in the US. For little Sean and Kimberley, it must have been a mystifying life of nannies, first-class travel, top hotels and constant media attention. In June, they made a brief appearance on stage at London's Earls Court, during yet another sell-out concert by their father, and on the other side of the Atlantic, they visited Alana's relatives in a suburb of Palm Beach, Florida. Rod and Alana were unquestionably leading increasingly separate lives.

Rod hated being apart from the children and phoned them regularly. At first, little Kimberley refused to talk to her father because she was so angry that he had gone away. Eventually, though, when she came on the line, the rugged rocker and his beloved four-year-old sobbed transatlantically to each other.

By September 1983 Rod was being sighted in England with the traditional 'mystery blonde', although denials were formally issued from both London and Los Angeles. The biggest public nail in the coffin of the glittering marriage came from Rod's ever-loving ever-indulgent mother, Elsie. Asked about the chances of a split, she replied frankly to *Daily Express* showbiz editor Garth Pearce: 'I am not sad. I didn't want them to split up but I could never understand why he married her in the first place. After all the lovely girls he had seen and been with. Oh blast!

'Still, he's gone and done it now and that's it. There was always an atmosphere while Alana was around. She is not a sociable sort of girl who will sit down and chat with you. In fact, she doesn't say anything at all. Rod is completely different on his own. He relaxes and we can all get together properly, like we used to. My husband wished Rod had married a girl from Scotland. He'd have been a lot better off.'

Alana was shocked and hurt by Elsie's comments. She thought she had got on reasonably well with Rod's parents, and suggested that Elsie was suffering from a problem that faces mothers who cannot accept that their little boys are growing up, when they reach 38 years old. 'Maybe I'll feel exactly the same way when my children grow up and get married,' she said rather more charitably.

While Rod was still in England, Alana moved out of Carolwood Drive and down to the beach house at Malibu, taking the children with her, but said it was simply to get away from the heat. Then she moved back to Carolwood, but she did frankly admit: 'There have been some bad times. Sometimes things get us both down. I'm waiting for Rod to come home so we can talk this over. There are long separations and all the travelling and me with the kids. Sometimes I get very unhappy.'

On Saturday 10 September 1983, Rod went with Elton John to watch Watford play Notts County in an English soccer match. As the inevitable reporters badgered him for a comment on the state of his marriage, the usually cool celebrity snarled: 'Go away. I don't want to say anything.'

A final attempt at reconciliation at Christmas failed. And

after the parting came the recriminations. In January, reporters found Alana at a Hollywood party to celebrate the end of filming the TV movie *Masquerade*, in which she had a small guest role. Happily for the headline-seekers, she announced: 'I've had just enough beer to say what I think about Rod Stewart. As far as I'm concerned the marriage is over. If he wants to go out with a series of mindless, moronic young models rather than being with me and the children, I don't think I'm losing anything. I'm well aware of the other women in Rod's life, and if that's the way he wants to go then it's his loss. He's lost a wife and two kids. All I've lost is someone who can't grow up.'

Rod was publicly angry at Alana's allegations after the break-up, but inwardly very hurt. He knew that some of the things that she was saying were true. After his split with Britt, he had sounded off about his rejection of the Hollywood lifestyle, but his life with Alana had been dominated by Tinsel Town. He enjoyed his days out playing soccer with his mates and his nights out drinking with them, much more than being one half of a glittering showbiz couple. He had very much wanted his marriage to work, but Alana had simply wanted the sort of commitment that Rod could not bring himself to make.

CHAPTER NINE

A Talent As a Muse

I am a musician. I'm not just a sex machine. I know I've written some good songs which have made people happy. I would like to be remembered for that, not how many women I've bedded. Rod Stewart

Rod Stewart was on his knees, helping to cultivate a Pennsylvanian garden, when he realised he must have fallen in love again.

With the agony of his split from Alana fading month by month, Rod had spotted a 25-year-old model called Kelly Emberg on celluloid, at the preview of a forgettable film called *Portfolio*. Not altogether surprisingly, she had all the physical qualities Rod has always looked for in a woman. She was tall. She was blonde. And she was utterly beautiful.

Kelly had first made an impact on the modelling scene in 1978, and her exquisitely lovely face and perfect figure soon earned her regular exposure on the covers of magazines such as *Glamour*, *Vogue* and *Harpers Bazaar* throughout the eighties. She made her first impact on Rod when she was one of several beauties along with supermodels Paulina, Carol Alt and Julie Wolfe who were featured in *Portfolio*, a movie about the inside world of modelling and high fashion. The film included a music track

featuring hits by the Eurythmics, Joe Cocker, Tina Turner and
... Rod Stewart.

Once he had caught sight of Kelly, Rod demanded in typical
Rod fashion to get hold of Kelly's phone number. Having purloined it, in equally typical Rod fashion he was too shy to make
the first approach himself. Instead he commandeered a pal to
make the first call and together they cooked up a ruse. 'My mate
Arnold rang and said: "Rod saw you in the film and he wants to
write a song about you,"' the artful singer revealed. He added
with obvious delight: 'And she fell for it.'

With a touching naïvety, Kelly could hardly contain her
excitement at the thought that Rod Stewart wanted her as his
muse. 'Really? Does he really?' she gasped. The ploy was evidently working, and then it was pointed out to Kelly that Rod
would need to meet up and talk to her for just such a purpose.
Kelly agreed, but she was careful to point out that she already
had a boyfriend – 'skinny little squirt' was Rod's eventual assessment of his love rival.

Although she knew the song 'Maggie May', not a single Rod
Stewart album figured in Kelly's music collection. She wasn't
even too sure what he looked like, save for the general idea that
he was that singer with the stuck-up hair and long nose. Warily
Kelly went out and bought some of Rod's records, so she could
get a picture of the songwriter who professed to be so inspired by
her. But still there was an awful lot she didn't know about Rod,
two things in particular: 'I didn't know his reputation, or that he
was married with kids,' she says.

When they eventually met, Rod found Kelly to be even more
beautiful in the flesh than she appeared on screen, but it was
Kelly's easygoing, relaxed approach to life that won over the rock
star. Decades of being the groupies' target, and the focus of
determined attention by international beauties like Britt and
Alana, had helped to make Rod wary.

So, although the sparkle in Kelly's eye and the girlish giggle in her voice set the exhausted hormones sparking back into action, Rod was very cautious. Kelly very definitely found Rod attractive, but she was wary too. He was 15 years older than her and Kelly's friends warned her about Rod's reputation with women, and the danger of becoming just another notch on his bedpost.

Consequently Kelly played hard to get, which impressed Rod because it was something he was not used to. He needed all his charm to woo Kelly away from her boyfriend, and Rod discovered that she had an old-fashioned morality which he found endearing, and which won her his respect. This was one woman he would not try to rush into bed. 'We went out for a long time without having sex,' he admitted.

Kelly, a sweet young woman of 23 who always believed that love was for ever, recalled: 'I thought: "What an interesting guy." I saw his sensitive side . . . and fell in love with him, I guess.'

Rod was captivated enough by Kelly to keep his promise and write a song for her. The result was 'Infatuation' which was included on his *Camouflage* album. It was only when Kelly took him to her country home in Pennsylvania that Rod realised the strength of his feelings. He was hooked.

'I went to stay at her place in the country and ended on my knees in the pouring rain, digging holes and putting plants in. To my surprise, I found I thoroughly enjoyed it,' said Rod.

On his own admission Rod always needed a woman. In the early days of his relationship with Kelly, he said frankly: 'It's much too early to talk about the possibility of marrying Kelly, but I do want to get married again eventually. I always need a woman in my life. I'm lost without a woman. I'm totally dependent on a woman. And it's not just a sexual thing any more. It used to be, but not any more. I need someone who can be a friend as well.

'I don't want to end up at 50 as some lonely old bachelor. I want a home and a wife to go back to. And I also want more children. Armies of them.'

Inevitably, Rod's falling for Kelly left Alana disillusioned and bitter and signalled the final breakdown of his marriage to Alana, at the end of 1983. At that point Rod decided to move out of the Carolwood mansion and rent a small house in Hollywood Hills just off Sunset Boulevard. Taking time to lick his marital wounds, Rod found he was much more at peace with himself than he had been for several years.

He said: 'Now I'm separated, I live very simply in a small place. It's just two bedrooms, one little living room, a toilet and a pool, and it's great. I've had servants all around me for the last ten years and it was really starting to get on my nerves. Now I'm doing it all myself – even the housework – and I'm enjoying myself more than I have in quite a while. I used to live up there where the rich and famous live when I was married. Now I live with the regular people. I guess I've got back to the streets, or as near as I'm ever going to get back to the streets. Because when you literally come from the streets, you're not in too much bloody hurry to get back.'

Rod came to realise that he had long been seduced by a lifestyle of conspicuous consumption. While Alana was still driving the children around in his black Rolls-Royce Corniche, Rod trimmed down his collection of cars, and put a hold for a time on the shrewd buying of his beloved art nouveau treasures.

He did not regret the flamboyant displays of wealth, for a time at least; he just grew out of it. 'I think it's a period you go through,' said Rod. 'And I think that anyone who has earned the sort of money I've earned will sometimes do the same. You want to experience as much of life as you can, and some of that is having material possessions. But I've completely grown out of it now. I've sold the yacht, and I'm down to just two cars now, and I'm going to sell one of those because I never drive it. In the end you get everything in perspective, and all those things weren't making me happy. It took a long time for me to find out that big houses, fast cars et cetera are not necessarily the answer. And I think I've learned my lesson.'

Getting down to your last Porsche Carrera is not exactly life on the poverty line, but for Rod it was an important and significant change. Alana may not have succeeded in getting him to take his adult responsibilities seriously during their marriage, but the break-up had certainly had its effect. By the summer of 1984 the friends who expected Rod to return instantly to his old philandering ways were to be surprised.

As Rod and his band toured Canada, for instance, an intriguing and stunningly attractive pair of females tagged on to the party. The boys in the band could not decide who was the more attractive – the shapely 35-year-old mother or her slender 16-year-old daughter. And they were both demonstrably available to the star of the show. But even this tantalising twosome could not tempt Rod.

Rod knew that gorgeous girls were throwing themselves in his direction even harder than ever before, but he just did not want to know. 'It's ridiculous, the way the girls are behaving on this tour,' said Rod. 'It's worse than ever. The lines on the face must have helped. But nowadays it gives me great satisfaction to say: "No, thanks. I don't want to know."

'It's a bit of an internal struggle sometimes, and I might lie in bed alone wondering what I am missing. But when I wake up next morning I pat myself on the back and think, good boy.

'I love women. I have a great appreciation of them and I'm not denying that in the past I've made the most of my opportunities, but how many times do you need to prove over and over again that you can have whoever you want? When you do that all the time you only prove that you're lacking something in yourself. So I think I owe it to myself, as well as to my girlfriend Kelly, to say no.'

After Britt's much-resented rebuilding of his image and Alana's relentless social climbing, the easygoing Kelly was just what Rod wanted. 'Kelly is a very good influence on me,' said Rod. 'She doesn't want to dominate me, but at the same time she wants respect. She doesn't want me playing around. And I really don't want to any more. She can trust me. I'm not the same person I was. Despite what Alana says, I don't want to carry on doing what I was doing at 25. What I'm looking for now is one loyal person by my side. I'm at the stage where I want to prove to myself that I really do want just one woman. And Kelly is enabling me to do just that. She's got me.'

Kelly was, like Alana, from Texas, but when she and Rod met she was living in a luxury Manhattan apartment and was earning over $4,000 a day as a top New York model, so at least Rod knew she was not after his money.

'She's a slightly unsophisticated country girl at heart, which is lovely,' said Rod. 'After what I went through with Britt and Alana, it's nice to have someone who is the complete opposite in that respect. She is quite different from Alana in most ways. Alana could be a bit snooty and put people's backs up but Kelly is the kind of girl who wins everybody over.'

Kelly was certainly more of a hit with Rod's family than Alana. She joined the rowdy Stewart clan at the annual England v Scotland soccer match, and both his mother and father took to the unpretentious model who made their son try his hand at gardening.

But Rod still had formally to disentangle himself from wife Alana, who was still living with Sean and Kimberley in Carolwood Drive. It was going to be a complex business, not least due to the fact that he and Alana had signed a prenuptial agreement. For the first time in his colourful love life, Rod was facing the break-up of a marriage, with two children involved, and all the added legal complications that that entailed. Rod winced at the unpleasant publicity but accepted its inevitability. He always found breaking up, as the song says, so very hard to do. Rod could never face the lady in question and discuss a diplomatic departure. Every time he ended a relationship he inspired angry headlines.

As Rod said after the split with Alana: 'I think it's the way we break up that upsets me. I never face them and make a clean break. I'm a bit lily-livered when it comes to that. I just wait until I'm found out, which always happens in the end.'

Rod often regretted the way he left his lovers, if not the decision itself. He knew how much he had hurt Dee and Joanna and Britt and Alana, but he could not help it. He tried to explain: 'I'd like to change the way I handled some personal relationships. I wish I wasn't so cowardly when it comes to dealing with people, but it comes from shyness and from not wanting to hurt people. I have been rotten to women, but not intentionally. I never wanted to hurt any woman, or anybody. From the outside it may look as if I hate women but I don't. I need a woman by my side. I need a woman to bounce off. They give me so many things.'

Alana's public washing of their dirty linen annoyed Rod, and he was incensed by her version of their split. He angrily insisted that he had not simply abandoned his family to go running off after yet another model. He had met Kelly Emberg after he split with Alana.

Rod insisted that his marriage to Alana had been in trouble for a long time. 'I married the wrong person,' he said simply. 'We were miles apart, really. I think nine out of ten men have to be pushed into marriage and I was no different. I tried to worm my way out of it, but I don't regret it now. Look what I've got out of it: two wonderful kids.'

Looking back, Rod believes they should have remained just

lovers rather than becoming husband and wife. He reflects: 'I think between Alana and I there was a bit of a rush to judgement. Maybe we should have just romanced each other for a while. We were an extremely wild couple, the epitome of the partying couple. We had great fun together and it was one of those things whereby once we got married, it all changed. I'm not blaming it all on her. I take responsibility too.'

The biggest problem between Rod and Alana had been what Rod came to regard as his wife's snobbish attitude towards his friends. Almost a year after the break-up he observed: 'I accepted all her friends, the wealthy and famous in Beverly Hills, and welcomed them in my house with open arms. But she would never do the same for the boys in my band, the guys I play football with, and the ordinary people among my friends who don't happen to be rich and famous. There were many other things, but that was the biggest breakdown in our marriage.'

Rod was deeply upset by allegations that he did not care about his children. In fact, it was the complete opposite. As far as Kimberley was concerned, he later admitted, she was helplessly spoilt. 'I'm to blame. I've spoilt her, but she is my first one and she is beautiful.' Alana, Sean and Kimberley still lived in the Carolwood Drive house while Rod still lived up Sunset Boulevard, in his more humble rented house. Most days he would collect Sean and Kimberley from school, and take them home for splashing games in the pool.

Rod said: 'I pick them up from school, bring them to the house and make lunch for them myself. I really love my kids so much, and I spend as much time with them as possible. We make meals together, and I teach them how to slice up the cheese and bread and I even clean up after them. And now Sean has fallen in love with football, so he makes me put on my Scotland jersey and then we kick a ball around the yard. That's the wonderful thing about being a parent: there is so much to teach them and show them. And they really pick up fast. And when I'm away, I make sure I speak to them every day on the telephone.

'Alana hasn't bothered to mention that we were seeing marriage guidance counsellors for two years. They were very helpful in trying to rekindle the spark, but it was too late. I never thought it would be this traumatic for me, but it is. There's not an hour goes by when I don't think about it and worry about my kids and whether I'm letting them down.'

The public image, fostered deliberately for so long by Tony Toon, of Rod Stewart the ruthless seducer of an endless stream of blondes was one that Rod felt had got way out of control. 'I'm not the womaniser I am supposed to be,' he said. 'I might have gone off the rails a bit when I moved to Hollywood. I did neglect my music, but the music is still very important to me. I am a musician. I'm not just a sex machine. I know I've written some good songs which have made people happy. I would like to be remembered for that, not how many women I've bedded.'

And to Alana's accusations of alliances with 19-year-old bimbos, Rod retorted: 'It is her who is going out with every guy she wants to, and me who is sticking to one girl. Kelly is the only girl I've been out with since Alana and I split up. I'd love to have had all the girls I'm supposed to have had. The idea that I was always cheating on my wife while we were still together is rubbish. And Alana knows that.'

Rod was angry when Alana took Sean and Kimberley to a child psychologist because they were so 'disturbed' by the break-up. According to Rod: 'All that happened was that Kimberley had one or two bad dreams, and Sean got a bit naughty and starting saying "I hate you" when he wasn't allowed to have his own way. Most parents would regard it as quite normal, but in California people rush off to a child psychologist at £50 a session.'

Alana accused Rod of being a forgetful father, of meaning

well with the children but spending too little time with them. She described him as a lost soul, confused, lonely and very sad. 'Rod's trouble,' said Alana, 'is that he has never grown up . . . and he never will.'

But although their parting was public and painful, Rod and Alana were still united in their determination to protect the children. Rod insisted that, in spite of everything, he did not dislike Alana. 'I don't think you ever dislike someone you've really loved. And deep down, whatever she says about me, I think Alana still loves me. Without a doubt. She would never be so vindictive as to cut me off from the kids. She knows how important it is that they should have a father's influence.'

Rod knew that the end of his marriage to Alana also meant the end of his dreams of having Sean and Kimberley educated in England. He said: 'But I still hope they don't grow up to be Beverly Hills kids, never playing on the street, and never doing any of the things I did when I was growing up. I think it will be a pity if they miss out on that completely, but I'm afraid they probably will.'

Rod was so anxious to see as much as possible of his children that he planned to bring them along on part of his next tour. To head off Alana's objections, he went to his own child psychologist who advised that so long as the trip did not interfere with their schooling, it was good for the youngsters to be with their father.

Rod planned their excursion to fit in with their holidays. He said: 'Now it's just a matter of getting permission from the ex-wife.' He felt he and Alana had come through their most difficult time and said they were good friends. Rod admitted: 'But she's a bit overprotective with the kids, and she thinks there'll be thousands of women hanging around my hotel rooms. Of course, it won't be anything like that. I'd let the kids sleep in the same room as me. They can come in with their nanny and all their toys and set up Stewart camp.' Alana agreed and Rod was delighted to risk his hard-won reputation as one of rock's wildest hellraisers, by bringing along two wide-eyed youngsters on the road.

Rod always tried to put his family first, and although he had no plans to marry Kelly, she became perhaps the closest of all the ladies in his life to his mum and dad. Kelly helped Rod, for instance, to organise the 80th birthday party for his wheelchair-bound mother Elsie, in January 1986. More than 100 guests were invited to the Firs, a banqueting centre in Palmers Green, north London, when Rod decided to mark his mum's big day.

This was a far cry from the usual champagne and smoked salmon showbiz functions that usually confront Rod. No celebrities or hangers-on were invited, just family and close friends, dining on Hungarian pancakes, made with chopped egg, tomato and spinach, followed by roast beef and Yorkshire pudding. For dessert guests were served Coupe Jamaïque: pineapple with rum and raisin ice cream. There was sherry and Martini and red and white wine. The occasion was a real family success, climaxing in a Cockney knees-up to a four-piece band. Four years later there was another big Stewart family celebration when Rod's parents celebrated 60 years of married life. Rod conceded that he had got to know his mum and dad more in the last ten years than in the previous 35. Elsie had always been more outgoing than Bob Stewart but, as the years went by, Rod came more and more to respect his father's quiet, thoughtful and puritanical demeanour.

Rod relaxed in the bosom of his family, and Kelly enjoyed every minute. Kelly was also a hit with Rod's troubled eldest daughter, Sarah. Poor Sarah was so upset by the frosty reception she was given by the haughty Alana that she did not see her father again, until the marriage was over. Sarah recalled: 'There was no way that I could get together with him again while Alana was on the scene. But once she was gone I contacted him again.

He said he was pleased to hear from me and we met in a London hotel.

'Kelly Emberg was with him and she was really great. She accepted me straight away and she was really nice. We all went shopping and he bought some clothes. I suppose he would have bought me something if I had asked, but I didn't bother.'

Sarah saw her father again after she went to one of Rod's London concerts and the party afterwards, where she met Kimberley and Sean properly. 'I saw him quite a lot that year,' said Sarah. 'And he even bought me a birthday present – a bracelet and a box of chocolates – although I had to remind him the night before.'

As he moved into his forties, the legal wrangles over the divorce continued, but Rod took great care not to let them sour feeling between himself and Alana and the children. 'It's really nothing to do with Alana and me now. It's the lawyers who just can't agree,' he shrugged as he arrived in Britain, in May 1986, to rehearse for his first British concerts for three years. For the man who was supposed never to want to grow up, Rod was curiously at ease with middle age. Everything Joan Collins had done for the older woman, he could achieve for the older man, he thought. 'Anyway, I think we men do get better the older we get. Everyone keeps asking me about turning 40 as if suddenly I should have cobwebs covering me. I like middle age right now. It's like a silly novelty. My knees haven't started to click like Cliff Richard's. I've never felt so good in my life or looked so good, so I'm loving every minute of it. I'm probably the oldest swinger in town.'

It was never easy for Kelly. When she went with Rod to the Malibu beach house she was confronted by a note pinned to the main wardrobe. A bitter farewell message from Alana, it read: 'Attention all sluts. Hands off my clothes. Signed, the soon-to-be-ex-mistress of this house.'

Alana still used the house with the children and Kelly had to put up with pictures of happy family scenes, featuring Rod's wife beaming at her. Rod used to rush down before taking Kelly and remove some of the snaps, but Kelly still got upset at many of the memories involving Rod's previous love that the house held. It was, after all, Alana who had been the driving force behind the Stewart purchase of the $2 million beach house.

In spite of the difficult circumstances, even Alana conceded that Kelly got on well with Sean and Kimberley, and she was grateful to her for that. Alana recalled: 'At first it really hurt me that Rod was able to find someone so quickly, but then I realised it was just his pattern. He needed to find a woman immediately because he hates being alone. I'm not jealous of Kelly Emberg, because our break-up had nothing to do with her.

'It had to do with problems we should have worked on, and if it hadn't been her it would have been some other blonde. I haven't met her, not because I've tried to avoid her, but it just hasn't happened. I know she's sweet to my kids when she's around them and that's very important to me.'

Alana felt that the 15-year age difference between Rod and Kelly was important to him, but she did not think Rod was happy with Kelly. And when she heard of Rod's brief romance with English actress Kelly Le Brock, the strong-willed star of Gene Wilder's hit 1984 movie *The Woman in Red*, she was delighted: 'I was actually pleased when Rod had an affair with Kelly Le Brock and I thought they might end up together. She's much more the kind of girl I could see Rod with than Kelly Emberg.'

But while Rod and Kelly accepted that they had to take turns with Alana and the children at Malibu, the fabulous Carolwood home became the focus of Rod's complex divorce settlement with Alana. This was a marriage that had been a great deal easier to start than it was to finish. It was March 1987 before the agreement was finalised. Rod was to buy a luxury $5 million, 15-bedroomed home in the swish Los Angeles suburb of Brentwood for Alana and the children, and he was also to provide a generous cash sum and future regular payments. In return, he was to get the Carolwood Drive house back.

Although Alana had criticised the décor she had inherited from Britt, she was sorry to leave Carolwood. Living on the same street as Gregory Peck, Barbra Streisand and Burt Reynolds carried the sort of cachet that was important to Alana. It had been the scene of some of Hollywood's most glittering parties. And it was the first home Sean and Kimberley had ever had. She said: 'The children love the house because they were born here, it was their home and they'd never known anything else. They just didn't want to go. Sean's a real home bird and whenever he is away he can't wait to get back to his dog, his skateboard and his bike. But the more I talked about moving the more he and Kimberley came to accept it.'

The idea of making Kelly Emberg the second Mrs Rod Stewart certainly started to enter the singer's mind, and particularly Kelly's, in December 1987, when their daughter Ruby Rachel was born. But Rod was still very cautious of marriage after the painful split with Alana and their long, drawn-out divorce. Moreover, he had thrown his relationship with Kelly into crisis by squiring Hollywood blonde Regan Newman around various nightspots, while Kelly had been pregnant. According to Kelly, Regan had made a blatant play for Rod one night at the London nightclub Tramp, by approaching their table and dropping Rod a note in front of her. 'What actually hurt most was that he took the note in front of me and then acted on it,' Kelly was reported as saying.

When Rod started escorting Regan around town, it soon crept into the gossip columns and Kelly noticed that Rod was becoming cold towards her. As Kelly explains it: 'I was going crazy and I couldn't stand what was happening to the two of us. He was trying to hold on to me and have an affair with this woman at the same time. And that wasn't right.'

Soft-hearted Kelly eventually forgave Rod, just as she had when he had embarked on a fling with English actress Kelly Le Brock. She lost count of the times he got away with telling her he was sorry. But, with their baby to consider, Kelly persuaded Rod to make a real effort to make their relationship work. But his straying had sowed seeds of doubt in the minds of both of them, as to whether marriage was really the right course for them.

In 1988, after four months of gentle persuasion, Rod finally coaxed Kelly into following in Britt Ekland's shoes, by appearing with him on one of his records. This time it was 'Lost in You', a track on his new album, *Out of Order*, which made the Top Twenty and realised three more Top Twenty singles.

Kelly was against the idea from the start but, even though she finally consented, Rod had to pour her several glasses of wine so that she was nicely merry to overcome her nerves. It then took some considerable time for Kelly to stop giggling before she could record her line: 'I miss you too,' in answer to Rod's 'I miss you.'

Rod's line was heartfelt. Whenever modelling assignments took Kelly away from him he groaned: 'I have withdrawal symptoms. I miss her so much.' But he would always push the subject of marriage further forward into the future. 'I believe in marriage, because I come from a big family. I want to have more children – as many as I can – so that when I'm 80 I have lots of kids around me. I want to be able to commit myself to one person in marriage for the rest of my life. That's the hardest thing, when you get married you have to say: "Can I grow old with this person?" The one thing Alana and I didn't do was sit down and talk about what we wanted out of the marriage, which is what I would do if I got married again.'

When Ruby was a baby Kelly was forced to take some time off from modelling, and the three of them spent some of their happiest moments at the Malibu house. The rhythm of the ocean and the distance from busy Los Angeles helped to isolate them from the rest of the world.

Rod has always had a special feeling for the elegant beachside home. It housed much of his valuable collection of art nouveau lamps and furniture, which he started collecting even before he knew what they were. It was Britt Ekland who tutored the rock star in the elegant style and encouraged him to invest some of his massive income in art.

Rod might criticise Britt's discretion, but he has always been grateful to her for her advice on this score. 'She advised me well and it's probably the best investment I've ever made. My pieces are now worth a fortune.'

Collecting art nouveau had developed into one of Rod's real passions. He read up on it as much as he could and searched through tiny, hidden-away shops in one country after another. 'I could become quite a dealer now if I wanted to,' he was able to boast. 'I think what first attracted me to it was that in the early days you never found it in anyone's house. Later it became a cult thing. When I married Alana she became interested in it as well, and then Kelly really got into it. It's a very feminine style, with sensuous lines, and I think that's why so many women like it.'

No one could accuse Rod of exactly growing old gracefully, but as he eased into his mid-forties the rocker seemed to be at peace with the world. He spent two or three hours a day playing with his beloved model railways. Although he joked about his appearance – 'When I see myself in the mirror in the morning, it's a horrible sight' – he still kept up the football which helped him to stay fit, and consequently made him look years younger than his real age.

According to Rod: 'You can't thrash your body as much as

you could when you were younger. If I want to sing five times a week I have to get eight or nine hours of sleep each night. That cuts down a lot on my frivolity. Every other morning I have to get up and take the kids to school and I have to be up at 7 a.m. They don't want their father smelling of alcohol with bags under his eyes, so I cut back on it a lot.'

In 1988 Rod was fit enough to take part in a charity football match before the England-Scotland game at Wembley, and he achieved his lifelong ambition of scoring a goal at London's famous old stadium, watched by his proud father.

In 1988–89 America's well-respected *Forbes* magazine printed a list of the world's 40 highest-paid entertainers, and Rod was listed at 36, with earnings of $21 million.

And as the eighties came to a close, Rod put down the secret of his long success as a singer to 'more luck than anything. Attitude is the most important thing. I like a good time. If I want to go out and take my trousers down in public I will do that until I'm 80. I'm going to annoy all the rock critics and keep singing until I haven't a breath in my lungs.'

Rod's success as both singer and songwriter is beyond doubt. By 1990 the Rod Stewart song-bag totalled more than 100 and he was showing no signs of slowing down. The release of *Storyteller: The Complete Anthology 1964–1990* served as a reminder of Rod's achievements both as a gifted, prolific song-writer and as a singer whose records consistently made the charts. *Storyteller* also served to pin-point the sharp contrast between the folkie flavour of his early recordings, and the artfully produced, classy songs of the eighties.

But Rod's record sales in Europe were sluggish at the end of the eighties, and he was given a welcome and timely boost when he notched up yet another Top Ten hit in both the US and the UK, towards the end of 1989, with his exhilarating version of a Tom Waits composition, 'Downtown Train'.

Rod's UK record boss Rob Dickins, desperately searching for a suitable song to regalvanise Rod's popularity, had picked out the track for Rod but was far from sure he would go for it. When he took the Tom Waits recording to play to Rod at his Epping home, he pleaded with the singer to listen to it then say nothing. Then Dickins asked him to listen to it twice more, without comment in between. Dickins was relieved to find after the third spin of the record that Rod loved it. Rod felt he could extract and exploit the song's strong melody, which had been largely lost in the original Tom Waits version. Rod knew he had a hit on his hands when he sent his own 'Downtown Train' track to his sister Mary, and she told him she had cried while listening to it. 'Downtown Train', which was then hurriedly added on to the *Storyteller* anthology, was an important hit for Rod. 'It jolted everyone back to what Rod could do, and reminded everyone why they loved him in the first place,' says Dickins.

Exactly a year later Rod was up in the Top Five with a duet with Tina Turner on 'It Takes Two'. All dates for Rod's British tour in 1991 were quickly sold out, and further proof of his resurgent popularity was the instant chart entry at number 20, of the latest in a long line of hit singles, 'Rhythm Of My Heart'. The single peaked at number three and the new album, *Vagabond Heart*, which Rod dedicated to his father, reached number two in the album charts.

CHAPTER TEN

LOVE ON THE ROX

People think I was drawn to him by fame and money. But I had my own fame and money. What attracted me to him was his sense of humour. He's a naturally very funny guy. Adorable. He might have a naughty sense of humour, but deep down he's a real softy. Rachel Hunter

When Rachel Hunter was born in New Zealand, on 8 September 1968, Rod Stewart was 23 years old and was starting to attract an excited female following in the US, as lead singer with the Jeff Beck Group.

Rachel was just three when Rod was falling in love with Dee Harrington, and creating pop history by topping the charts in America and Britain with 'Maggie May'.

Rod was 45, more than twice Rachel's age, when they were introduced to each other at a nightclub in Los Angeles, in September 1990. Just one glance at Rachel was enough for Rod to know she was exactly his type. Standing before him was a creature of exceptional beauty, with a smile like a Pacific sunrise and legs so long they seemed unsure when to stop. The little girl whose parents had grown up listening to Rod Stewart records – 'Hot Legs' was one of her mum's favourites – had blossomed into a stunning young woman.

She was nearly six feet tall, with eyes like African violets and a splash of reddish-blonde hair that tumbled around her shoulders. There was a fresh-faced, girlish quality about Rachel's looks, but the endless flood of photographs of her posing in swimsuits and skimpy underwear revealed a ripe, young body that was undeniably all woman.

Rachel had embarked on a modelling career after her blossoming beauty was first spotted by a photographer, on a New Zealand beach, when she was just 14. She was about to embark on a secretarial course at the age of 16, but her potential as a model was enough for Lacey Ford to bring her over to New York to join her mother Eileen's world-famous model agency, Ford Models Inc. Rachel's impact was instant. 'I walked off the plane when I was 16 and I was straight on to the covers of *Vogue* and *Elle*,' she recalls.

Rachel swiftly proved popular with photographers, but the agency were struck not just by Rachel's looks but by her bubbly personality and her constant good humour. She rapidly became one of the most in-demand models on the agency's books, and by the time she met Rod, Rachel was a cover girl able to command £6,000 a day, and as such was enjoying minor celebrity status.

Before she took up with Rod, Rachel had had only one serious boyfriend, an American heavy metal guitarist called Kip Winger. Like many a teenage girl, Rachel had always wanted to meet a rock star and after she had seen the swarthy Kip on stage, she called his manager, gave him her number and intimated she would not be displeased if Kip felt like giving her a call.

Kip was no stranger to female adulation. He had enjoyed his fill of it as part of shock-rocker Alice Cooper's touring band, even though he had a clean-living reputation, for getting on the tour bus with a briefcase while the others clutched bottles of Jack Daniels.

After leaving Alice Cooper to seek solo success, Kip was

considered enough of a beefcake to qualify for a *Playgirl* maga-zine photo-shoot, for which he adopted a shaggy-haired, hairy-chested stance, wearing just a sheepish smile and a pair of ostensibly well-filled red posing briefs.

Ironically, many years before, Rod had been offered £8,000 to pose nude for *Playgirl*, and had turned it down.

Girls passing Kip their phone number was nothing new for the *Playgirl* pin-up. But with Rachel angling for a date, Kip checked out her physical credentials in photographs and was licking his lips by the time he picked up the phone to call her. He might have had an adoring fan club, but it was not every day that a shapely cover girl and supermodel like Rachel Hunter gave him the come-on. They duly arranged to meet at a Los Angles hotel where Rachel was on a modelling assignment and, according to Kip, the instant mutual attraction quickly exploded into a highly charged intimate 48 hours for the couple. 'Rachel said she'd only had one lover, but I think I taught her most of what there was to know that weekend,' Kip was later reported as saying. Within three months, they were living together.

While Rachel was embarking on her affair with Kip, Rod Stewart appeared to be edging ever closer to marriage with patient, sensible Kelly Emberg, but evidently with some misgiv-ings. On 27 January 1990, Rod was a guest of British chat-show host Michael Aspel and nervously told Aspel, in front of ten mil-lion TV viewers: 'Don't bring the subject round to marriage or I'm going home!'

Of course Aspel pursued the topic and Rod conceded: 'My mother and father have given up on me being married now. But my girlfriend certainly hasn't and I don't think there's any reason why she should. She wants to be secure and she wants the baby we've got [Ruby] to be a Stewart, and I can understand that.' But Rod then betrayed his mixed-up feelings when he put his head in his hands and sheepishly winced. 'Did I really say that? I did say what I just said, didn't I?' he asked incredulously. Then, recovering his composure, he admitted: 'I'm pretty close to marriage now, closer than I've ever been. I'm closer than Mick Jagger, put it that way.'

As it turned out, by the end of the year Rod was to marry, just weeks before his old rock rival Jagger tied the knot with his longtime girlfriend Jerry Hall. But to the surprise of almost everyone, Rod's bride was not Kelly but Rachel Hunter.

The long-suffering Kelly had finally reached the conclusion that Rod was never going to marry her and, fed up with his womanising, decided she would be better off without him. She had been contemplating a new life without Rod for a year, before she walked away. 'There had been affairs and there had been items in the tabloids about things he had been doing with other women,' she explained. 'He always had a reason and said people were just jealous of our relationship.'

But by now Kelly had turned 30 and was taking a long, hard look at her situation and weighing up the future. She admits she found it hard being in love with Rod, when she realised he was wrong for her. 'In the end he didn't know if he wanted to get married,' Kelly said, 'and if he didn't know after a baby and we'd been together seven years, then I felt we shouldn't. So that was basically why I left.'

Rod concluded: 'Kelly and I were very close to getting married. I just didn't quite do it. I needed that little push.'

Kelly was deeply upset, but realising her seven-year affair with Rod was finally and irretrievably over, she moved away quietly to set up home with Ruby Rachel at Manhattan Beach, a stylish residential area hugging the Pacific Ocean, right on the edge of Los Angeles. Her new house, she said, could fit inside the ballroom of Rod's Carolwood mansion.

Inevitably, Kelly's split from Rod made headlines all over the world. 'It was on the news that I was suing him for $25 million and I was shocked,' says Kelly. 'I was so upset, I couldn't believe my lawyer would do something like this. I had no idea what the complaint said in it. It wasn't something I wanted to do and I was appalled that even happened.'

Rod was genuinely hurt that Kelly Emberg had chosen to seek a new life away from him, although deep down he knew he could hardly blame her. But in the summer of 1990, at the age of 45, he suddenly found himself single again, and he was beginning to despair of ever finding the right woman he could wholly commit to.

For a rock star like Rod, a shortage of willing female bedmates was never going to be a problem. And when career commitments took him to France, soon after Kelly's departure, he freely indulged himself. He was to film a Pepsi commercial with Tina Turner in Cannes, where he checked into the luxurious Carlton Hotel. 'I was staying in Cannes and I was flying birds in from here, and flying birds in from Paris and I was so unhappy,' Rod told *The Times Magazine*. 'I was flying in shags and I thought, this is it, mate, you've got nothing else in your life, this is all you do. And then BASH! Two weeks later she came along.' *She* was Rachel Hunter.

While Rod had slipped back into the single life again, Rachel's affair with Kip was also coming to an end. During the intense early months of their relationship, they had talked about marriage, but Kip wasn't ready for the commitment and felt they were both too young. With their respective careers taking them in different directions, they parted without acrimony, with mostly happy memories and a realisation that their relationship had probably simply run its course.

Rachel's year with Kip, however, had been an eye-opener for her in every way. Kip, a trained ballet dancer with a sharp brain as well as brawn, claims he was utterly faithful to Rachel. But that did not prevent the New Zealand teenage model from witnessing the seamy side of rock excess, on tour with Kip's band. 'I remember there was this one girl on the crew bus who would give 40 [oral sex acts] a night,' she shuddered. 'She was really disgusting ... When I look back at those girls, what they had to do to get backstage – the sliminess and big boobs and blonde hair and pink lipstick – it's just so smutty.'

Around the time of her split from Kip, and six months before she met Rod, Rachel suffered a nervous breakdown. She was just 19, and four years of hard modelling work finally took its toll. 'I curled up in the foetal position and my mum was with me, and I had this total nervous breakdown,' she revealed in the *Mail on Sunday*. 'I was a kid. I'd been through so much and I felt so lonely and so overwhelmed with everything. I had worked for four years but I was still a kid.'

With the help of a therapist, Rachel got through her crisis and developed a new sense of purpose and a new zest for life. Resuming her modelling career, she was more in demand than ever. She followed up a lucrative Revlon contract with an eye-catching appearance in the prestigious *Sports Illustrated Swimwear Special* magazine. She was taken to the Lesser Antilles to be photographed for the special issue, and when the pictures were published her cachet as a celebrity model soared.

For her next assignment, Rachel was singled out to display her shapely figure for an advertisment for *Sports Illustrated* 's 'Super Shape-up' exercise video. And one of the millions of viewers who caught sight of Rachel's dazzling smile and perfect frame on the cable channel CNN, as she went through a promotional exercise routine, was Rod Stewart. He gazed approvingly at the TV every time Rachel appeared on the screen promising: 'You too can have a body like mine.'

Quite by chance the two found themselves in the same Los Angeles club, the Roxbury, on Sunset Strip, west Hollywood, soon afterwards, and Rod was not slow to move in on Rachel.

'He came up and put his face in front of mine and made some odd comment,' Rachel remembers. 'I started laughing and then he started imitating the exercise video. I suppose that was when the first sparks of romance started.'

Despite the 23-year age difference there was an instant chemistry between them. 'I don't know that it was love at first sight, but she was, and still is, a stunning woman.' says Rod.

Accompanying Rod on the night he met Rachel was long-standing friend Ricky Simpson, a millionaire hotelier. He has no doubts. 'It *was* love at first sight. He was absolutely besotted and I remember him telling me: "She's the most wonderful woman I've ever clapped eyes on." A couple of days later Rod had become so obsessed with Rachel that he kept watching her keep-fit video for hours on end.'

Within days Rod and Rachel had become lovers, and within weeks they were head over heels in love and talking about having children together. Rod was so bowled over by Rachel that when she had a modelling assignment in Palm Beach he flew to be by her side, for just a few precious hours. This romantic gesture was captured on Ricky Simpson's camera. A silver-framed photo of them cuddling on that night was Ricky's wedding present to the couple, a few months later.

As news broke of Rod's new affair, it appeared for all the world that Rachel was simply a newer, younger version of all the girls who had gone before. She was, it seemed, just another of Rod's leggy blonde model girls. But Rachel was different, and not just because her endless legs made her an inch or two taller than the famous new beau at her side.

Despite, or perhaps because of, her youth, Rod felt Rachel was somebody special. He could not fault her looks but there was also a spark of vitality, a sense of energy and fun about her that Rod found simply irresistible. Six months after finding herself in such a fragile emotional state, Rachel was simply swept off her feet by Rod's ardour. 'People think I was drawn to him by fame and money,' said Rachel. 'But I had my own fame and money. What attracted me to him was his sense of humour. He's a naturally very funny guy. Adorable. Soon I began to see how kind and considerate he is. He might have a naughty sense of humour but deep down he's a real softy.'

They had known each other little more than six weeks when Rod suddenly got down on one knee and asked her to marry him, while they shared a tuna sandwich together on a picnic in a Los Angeles park. Rachel swallowed hard, joyfully accepted, and Rod slipped a beautiful sapphire and diamond engagement ring from Van Cleef on her finger. 'He asked me to marry him and I said: "OK, let's do it." Three months later I was married.'

As soon as Rachel had accepted his proposal, Rod was excitedly on the phone to members of his family to tell them the good news. Of particular importance was a call to his 60-year-old brother, Don. 'Are you sitting down?' he asked when Don picked up the phone. 'I'm getting married and I want you to be best man.'

The family were naturally surprised that Rod and Rachel were to wed so soon. They knew Rod had split up from Kelly, but they were taken aback at this sudden new turn of events. Rod had absolutely no doubts. 'I realised,' he said, 'that this was the woman I wanted to spend the rest of my life with.'

Rachel was fully aware that she was marrying a man who was old enough to be her father. Indeed, her actual father, Wayne, an airline worker, was just a year older than Rod. But she said: 'Rod's a fine man and has made me so happy. He has taken me higher than I've ever been.'

Rachel's parents flew over to meet their future son-in-law with several misgivings. Rod's track record with blondes worried them both, particularly Wayne. Rod remembers: 'Her father said, "If he thinks he's going to get away with what he's got away with in the past, with my daughter, I'll come round and put one on him." My brother said, "If he thinks that, then he's got another think coming!"'

The whirlwind affair with Rachel coincided with a hectic period in Rod's career. He was in the middle of recording a new album in Los Angeles, and was planning a long and arduous world tour for the following year.

Now, suddenly, he was deeply in love and getting married as well. The pressure to continue recording meant that Rod had to hurry away to the studio, immediately after attending a wedding rehearsal at the chapel on Rodeo Drive.

It was never destined to be a conventional wedding right from the moment Rod and Rachel sent out 250 invitations to family and friends, asking them to the Presbyterian chapel in Beverly Hills, Los Angeles, on 15 December 1990, and a 'piss-up' afterwards at the Four Seasons Hotel. 'Are you sitting down?' said the invitation. 'Rachel Hunter and Rod Stewart invite you to be a guest at their wedding.'

Neither was it ever likely to be a strictly formal church ceremony, from the moment guests arrived to find themselves being led to their pews by 'blind' ushers in dark glasses with white canes: it was a Rod joke about the blind leading the blind. The bride added her own air of informality when Rachel swept up the aisle to join her husband-to-be at the altar, slipped an arm around his waist, then ran her hand over rock's most famous bottom and pinched it, in full view of the assembled congregation who broke into spontaneous applause.

Rachel had arrived some 35 minutes late and Rod, resplendent in a formal grey morning suit save for a stud in his collar rather than a tie, fidgeted nervously and was clearly relieved when she finally stood beaming at his side.

It was ten days before Christmas and the chapel had been seasonally decorated, the pews festooned with branches of

Christmas conifers and white ribbon. Among Rachel's eight attendants in mid-calf maroon dresses was Rod's daughter, 11-year-old Kimberley. The chapel rang to the singing from a children's choir and ended with a blessing, after Rod and Rachel lit candles at the altar. Kilted pipers greeted Rod and Rachel, as they left the chapel, with a stirring rendering of 'Scotland The Brave' and 'When The Saints Go Marching In'. Omitted from the ceremony was the request for the intervention of anyone who knew of any just cause or impediment why Rod and Rachel should not lawfully be joined together in matrimony (legal under Californian law), and Rachel opted to cherish her husband rather than obey him.

A double-decker London bus and three coaches, decorated with huge white bouquets, conveyed the majority of the guests the two miles to the reception at the Four Seasons Hotel. It was a reception that was never likely to bow to protocol: 'Sex on the beach required for entrance' announced the sign that greeted guests, and once inside they found a football had been produced and the groom and his son were proceeding to enjoy a kick-about on the plush, beige, patterned carpet.

At the wedding dinner guests were seated at tables named after football teams. The three-foot-tall wedding cake comprised a huge base, in the shape and colours of a Union Jack, and on top was another layer, shaped like the Houses of Parliament and Big Ben, with a giant kiwi perched on the roof, in celebration of the bride's country of origin.

Amid all the merriment, Rod briefly slipped away to a separate bar to talk football with members of his soccer team, the Exiles, some of whom had been 'blind' ushers.

Rod's wedding was certainly not a star-studded affair. Instead, the singer and his young bride preferred a real family-and-friends occasion. Rod thoughtfully included on the guest list John and Sheila Padget who ran the pub near his Epping home, and his faithful fan club organiser John Gray was also among his nearest and dearest. The mild-mannered statistician from the Department of Transport in London has dedicated most of his spare time, in recent years, to running Rod's international appreciation society and editing the excellent *Smiler* magazine, which has subscribers in some 37 countries worldwide.

'I was amazed to be asked,' says John. 'It was the trip of a lifetime. I was made so welcome by Rod and his family. And it was great to see people like Ian McLagan from the Faces and Long John Baldry. Rachel made a lovely bride. She was even more beautiful in real life than in photographs. Her father had been quoted in the newspapers, saying that Rod would have to look after her or he would have him to answer to. At the wedding, Rod's brother Don, who was best man, referred to that in his speech and said that he would have him to contend with as well.

'Rod just sat there beaming all the time. He really enjoyed himself. And when it came to his speech he certainly seemed delighted. He said: "I feel like a dog with two dicks."'

However, the marriage was but a few hours old when Rod encountered bizarre teething problems of his new bride's making. Rachel, in high spirits, gathered up the folds of her ivory calf-length wedding dress and hoisted them almost to her hip, before slumping back in a chair and high-kicking a leg at Rod, thereby revealing a tantalising expanse of her bare thigh, white stockings and suspenders, and a frilly white garter.

Rod feigned embarrassment, then sank to his knees in front of Rachel and seized the garter between his teeth. Roared on by the guests, he began to tug it down Rachel's shapely thigh, over her knee and down to her ankle, like a playful puppy pulling at a lead.

Finally, to tumultuous cheers, Rod tugged it over his giggling bride's white satin court shoes and rose to his feet, with a broad grin and the garter hanging from his mouth. He further savoured the achievement by waltzing Rachel round the room, with his prize still clamped triumphantly between his teeth. Mrs Rod Stewart the Second simply threw back her pretty blonde head and laughed heartily.

Those guests who had not met Rachel before found her entrancing. Rod's family were only just getting to know her and, although they could see how deeply in love Rod was with Rachel and that she appeared to adore him, there were some who had misgivings about the age gap. As the festivities at the reception gathered momentum, Rod's sister Mary observed the happy couple hugging and kissing, then leaned across the table to say quietly to other assembled Stewarts: 'That girl will break his heart one day.' It was a warning that was proved to be chillingly prophetic.

Kelly Emberg and daughter Ruby pointedly and tactfully stayed away from the wedding. Embarrassingly for all concerned, Rod and Rachel had found themselves sitting just a few tables away from Kelly a week before the wedding, when they all attended the opening of a new Beverly Hills nightspot owned by London club owner Peter Stringfellow. Kelly wore a brave smile – and a tiny, figure-hugging mini-dress with a deep, plunging neckline.

However, just as Rod was preparing for his £250,000 wedding, Kelly's lawyers served him with a massive palimony suit for almost that figure per year. Kelly claimed £240,000 as annual income to keep her and Ruby in the style they had previously enjoyed. And the suit was served on the day of his stag night.

She insisted: 'Rod is capable of paying for raising a child commensurate with a man of his means. Throughout our relationship Ruby and I were never deprived of anything we wanted.'

Kelly backed up her claims for £20,000 per month with a detailed list of expenses that included £1,205 per month for food, and £385 for Ruby's clothes. But she agreed that Rod had already paid for furniture and a nanny and allowed her to use credit cards for other items.

Happily for all concerned, the acrimony was ultimately resolved and Kelly subsequently became Rod's interior designer, in charge of prettying up his many homes. In the 1998 interview in the *Times Magazine*, Rod said of Kelly: 'She's the most beautiful woman, as honest as the day is long, and I sometimes wonder why she ever got mixed up with an arsehole like me. I broke her heart, you know. I was shagging around when she was pregnant – that's terrible, terrible, I hate myself for it.'

Sadly for Rod, his mother Elsie, suffering as she was from multiple sclerosis, felt unable to travel to Los Angeles to see her youngest son get married to Rachel. But it was the best possible Christmas present when he brought his new bride over to London to see her.

Also absent from the festivities were two of Rod's closest friends, Elton John and Ron Wood. Woody was recuperating from a car crash and Elton sent an apology and a £10 gift token from Boots the Chemists with a note, saying: 'Buy yourself something nice for the house – E. of Windsor.' Among the other gifts was a Scotland football shirt from former Scotland footballer Gordon Strachan, which Rachel immediately tried on over her wedding dress.

Spending their first Christmas together in England afforded Rachel an opportunity to become acquainted with Rod's fabulous home in Epping. Rod had bought Wood House on the exclusive Copped Hall estate in Epping Forest in 1986 for £1.2 million, outbidding King Constantine of Greece in the process. Built in Jacobean style in1898, Wood House had been used by Sir Winston Churchill as his campaign headquarters for elections in the days when he was a local MP. It was a home that Rachel in particular would come to love with its sweeping drive, rose gardens, tennis courts and stable blocks.

Rod's mansion in Carolwood Drive had been put on the market for £8 million. It had been home to Britt, Alana and Kelly, but now with the wisdom and energy of youth, Rachel persuaded Rod to lay to rest a few ghosts and help in the search for a new home for the newly-weds.

They saw in the New Year together at a party at a London hotel and then flew off to New Zealand to visit Rachel's mother Jeneen, at the family home in Brown's Bay, north of Auckland. Jeneen claims to be psychic and that she's guided in her work as an artist by a spiritual guardian. As she looked ahead, Jeneen saw babies, even twins, for Rod and Rachel. 'She foresees all sorts of things through the cards,' Rod reported. 'She said that career-wise I was going to tour in a different way. She saw before we got married, the babies, and saw twins coming the next time round.'

For Rachel, the New Year held the prospect of either trailing round after her husband on his massive world tour, or seeing very little of him. She decided to reschedule her modelling arrangements and go with him.

But before they departed there was time for Rod to appear on Michael Aspel's TV chat show again, to sing 'Rhythm Of My Heart', from the *Vagabond Heart* album, which would reach number two in the British album charts and number ten in America. During the course of their TV chat, Aspel referred to Rod's new bride as 'Helen', which had Rod tearing off a shoe and chucking it at the chat-show host in mock fury. The two authors were in the studio audience as was Rachel and, as they witnessed afterwards, Rod's new wife was particularly annoyed at what she saw as a cheap shot by Aspel. 'It was belittling,' she raged. 'I felt humiliated and angry. He knows my name. He behaved like a complete s***t. Rod was furious. He threw a shoe into the audience to make light of it, but he was seething. Aspel's lucky Rod didn't throw him into the audience.'

For Rod, 1991 was to be the year of the new start. In 1990 he had been deeply shaken by the death of his father, aged 86. Bob Stewart's passing in September had been deeply felt by all members of the family. Although it had not come as a surprise – Bob had not been in the best of health for some time – Rod in particular was profoundly shocked.

When his sister Mary telephoned the sad news that their father had passed away, Rod just couldn't take it in. He was so overcome with instant grief that he immediately put the phone back down again without saying a word, and fell into Rachel's arms weeping, leaving Mary still hanging on the other end of the line. 'What was strange,' says Rod, 'was that I met Rachel only a few weeks before my father died, and her birthday is on same day as he died, 8 September. I had a strange mixture of feelings. I was elated because I was so in love and devastated because I'd lost the greatest man in my life. Rachel was 20, I was 45, I'd met what I thought was going to be the love of my life, and my dad had gone.'

Sadly for Rod, he was never able to introduce to his dad the woman whom he was already convinced was going to be the great love of his life. He desperately wished he could have introduced him to Rachel, and that his dad could have witnessed that he had finally met the woman of his dreams. At least Rachel was able to offer Rod her moral support as he faced up to the funeral. Desperately sad though the occasion was for him, Rod was able to say that the occasion did his father justice. 'It was a magnificent funeral, the whole of Highgate stopped. Women just stood in the streets. He was a great man, a lovely man. I didn't really mourn his death until a year later, because I'd met Rachel and emotionally I was really confused.'

Although he clowned around and teased him, Rod remained respectful of his father and his views until the end. He knew his father was embarrassed by some of the more lurid reports of his not-very-private life, and that, in turn, irritated Rod. However, he never forgot the sacrifices his parents had made to give their youngest son the very best they could afford. And Rod's father of course was the full-blooded Scot he always aspired to be himself. Although he lived in London for most of his life, Bob Stewart never lost his rasping Scottish accent. Rod is a sometimes uncomfortable cross between a Cockney and a Scot; friends say he can never quite decide precisely which identity to choose.

Rod is intensely proud of his family. Indeed he once announced: 'We're directly related to the Royal Stuarts, you know. My dad's brother did all the studying just before he died. The spelling was changed by Mary Queen of Scots' mother, because there was no 'e' in the Celtic vocabulary.'

But in the cash- and celebrity-conscious society of the United States, Rod has become the sort of aristocrat the Americans understand best: a famous millionaire. 'I prefer the American class system,' says Rod. 'In England, so much is based on the way you speak; it's very false. You're not considered intelligent if you're a Cockney. I'm not saying we're all brain surgeons, but we have heads on our shoulders, us Cockneys.' But even making that point his confusion was evident, for he continued: 'There I go again. One minute it's my Scottish heritage and the next I'm a London Cockney.'

Close friends noticed signs of a new maturity following Rod's trip to London for his father's funeral. He had already met and fallen for Rachel before his father died, but the assurance with which he swept into a new marriage with his first full-scale church ceremony suggested he was no longer looking over his shoulder for paternal approval.

Rod was 46 in January 1991, but his physical fitness and air of youthful enthusiasm made him appear years younger. So, when he announced after the wedding that he was planning to start a family with his beautiful new bride, no one doubted his resolve.

While Rod's first British tour for five years was greeted by both critical acclaim and enthusiastic audiences, it wasn't all plain sailing. Rod's voice more than once gave cause for serious concern. Cancelled dates on the European leg of the year-long world tour were blamed on hay fever, throat infections, and the appalling British weather during the spring – there was even hail and snow at Rod's Wembley show.

A specialist reportedly diagnosed an allergy to pollen and dust, and after a brief rest Rod was able to resume the tour, but cut the show back by 40 minutes as a precaution. Then, on 20 July, Rod was visibly out of sorts when he appeared on stage in Hamburg, for a show that was televised live to 100 million viewers throughout Europe. He seemed to lack his usual energy and his voice was clearly lacking its customary power.

Yet by the time he returned to the US on 28 July to begin the American leg, Rod was able to look back with satisfaction on his biggest and most successful European tour.

The tour also helped 'The Motown Song', a second single taken from the *Vagabond Heart* album, to reach the Top Ten. It was a lively up-tempo number and its release was accompanied by an imaginative animated video, which cheekily cocked a snook at several of Rod's younger chart rivals. Among the victims were Sínead O'Connor, shown nicking her lathered head while shaving and reemerging with her pate sporting sticking plasters, Michael Jackson moonwalking backwards into a manhole, Madonna left gyrating in a cone bra and girdle, and Vanilla Ice disappearing under an avalanche of ice. Particularly satisfying for Rod on the *Vagabond Heart* album was the collaboration on 'The Motown Song' by his longtime vocal favourites, the Temptations. By the miracles of modern recording methods, however, Rod and the Temptations never met: they were in two different countries at the time of recording.

'Broken Arrow', a wonderful version of the searing love song by the Band's Robbie Robertson, was the third single to be released from *Vagabond Heart*, and was destined to give Rod a hat-trick of hits. The general success of the *Vagabond Heart* album was especially pleasing for Rod, as he dedicated it to the memory of his father and included on the sleeve-notes a heartfelt thank-you to his dad, for his foresight in having bought him a guitar for his 14th birthday instead of a model railway station. Rod added in his notes: 'Thanks for the Tartan pride, Dad' and included a passport-sized photograph of his father in a Scottish tam-o'-shanter.

While Rod was on the road, Rachel picked up her modelling career, yet took care never to be away from her husband for more than a few days at a time. And by October she was able to break the news to a joyful Rod that she was pregnant. He immediately whisked her off to a smart Manhattan restaurant where they celebrated until the small hours.

Rachel's baby was due in the spring of 1992, perfectly timed to coincide with the end of Rod's massive world tour. A new chapter in the life of Rod Stewart was about to begin.

CHAPTER ELEVEN

BABY BABY

I've been tamed. I've put my last banana in the fruit bowl.
Rod on his blissful life with Rachel Hunter

Rod's final, sell-out concerts of 1991 were on 18, 19 and 20 December at the Sports Palace in Mexico City, where he performed each night to a crowd of 20,000. Following this he allowed himself a well-earned three-week break to enable him to spend Christmas in England.

It was over a festive pint at his local in Epping that Rod confided to fan-club organiser John Gray, for his fan magazine *Smiler*, the true extent of the agonies he had gone through in the British high-pollen summer, particularly during the concert he had given in Sheffield.

'I was trying to compete with the pollen and it made my throat swell up,' he revealed. 'I had to take cortisone to make it go down again. I was supposed to take the pills on a full stomach with a glass of milk but I'd been taking them on an empty stomach. I was bleeding internally for an hour and a half while I was on stage. I shouldn't have gone on. It was the one time when I should have just said to everybody: "Go home!" Every time I closed my eyes I had to hang on to the mike stand because if I'd let go I would have fallen over. I was singing away and I kept thinking I was in my mum's kitchen. I was hallucinating which is apparently what you do when you bleed internally. I'm all for saying the show must go on at any cost but that was ridiculous. I was so disappointed.' Rod confessed he had found the whole experience so uncomfortable that he doubted whether he would tour England again during the summer months.

On 11 January he picked up the *Vagabond Heart* tour once more in the US, and was heartened to discover that American rock critics had clearly forgiven him for his Spandex trousers years. From more than 70 American gigs he had collected only one bad review, and even found himself hip enough to feature on the front cover of *Rolling Stone* magazine for the first time in 14 years.

While in Canada, he recorded Elton John's 'Your Song' as his contribution to a special tribute album to the songwriting talents of Elton's long-time friend and lyricist, Bernie Taupin. The album consisted of new versions of John–Taupin hits performed by a wide range of artists, including Eric Clapton and Tina Turner. Rod chose 'Your Song' because he professed he had always felt he could make a better job of it than the man himself. When it was released as a single, however, it managed to reach only number 41 in the British charts.

As the tour rolled on to Australia and New Zealand, Rachel was determined her pregnancy was not going to prevent her from accompanying her husband to as many of his concerts as possible. Not every young newly-wed and mother-to-be would choose to spend the first year of her marriage trailing all over the world after her rock-star husband. 'But if you have a relationship with a guy like Rod, then that's your life,' she explained.

At least Rachel could genuinely claim it was a new experience for her. With old flame Kip Winger she had witnessed groupies more than willing to cater for a rock musician's sexual needs away from home. But she was relieved to find that the fans' adulation for Rod at the concerts she so loyally attended rarely went beyond tossing bras and other items of underwear on to the stage.

Prior to this tour, Rachel had never seen Rod live on stage. She was present at Aberdeen when it started, and by Christmas she had seen no less than 122 of his 140 concerts. 'She's been amazing,' Rod said. 'She hasn't complained once.' Eventually Rachel would come to learn that, as Mrs Stewart, she would spend up to 18 months at a time on tour around the world. They would simply set up home on the road at whichever city the tour embraced, and try to make it as comfortable as possible. Inevitably such a gypsy existence, even allowing for quartering themselves at the smartest hotels, led to lost clothes and possessions. Rachel was particularly sad about a £5,000 diamond bracelet that went missing and was never found.

It was a mixture of luck and good planning that the last leg of the tour should be 'Down Under', where naturally Rachel felt very much at home. As with every tour, the itinerary requires meticulous planning and together Rod and Rachel had decided that their baby, whom they knew in advance to be a girl, would be born in London. Because of Rachel's advanced stage of pregnancy, the couple chose to cruise to England on the QE2 and Rod forked out £26,000 for the Queen Mary cabin suite, next to the captain's bridge, to ensure Rachel enjoyed every comfort.

On Monday, 3 June 1992, Rod's fifth child weighed in at the Portland Hospital at 8lb 3oz with the father very much present. 'It was like Scotland scoring a goal. You never quite get used to it,' was Rod's cheery comment when he emerged beaming from the hospital. He went on to drop a heavy hint that this was not the last time he expected to be a dad: 'There are plenty more tunes in the old fiddle yet,' he said.

The baby, who was born with long legs like her mother, was given the name Renee after one of Rod's favourite songs, 'Walk

Away Renee', which was first a minor hit for a group called the Left Bank in 1966, and then a major hit for the Motown group the Four Tops. After so long on the road Rod and Rachel were thankful to stay at home in Epping for a while, rather than having to check into yet another hotel room in yet another town every few days.

According to Rachel, Rod was the near-perfect dad. 'He is doing very well as a father, changing nappies and things,' she declared. 'He's pretty good around children and very at ease with it all.'

For his part Rod was equally fulsome in his praise for his wife. When quizzed about Rachel he even went so far as to say, for the first time in his life, that he would rather see his manhood cut off than be unfaithful to her: 'I've been tamed. I've put my last banana in the fruit bowl,' was one of his choicer quotes.

Visitors to the Epping estate noted that Rod seemed thoroughly content with his new domesticity, and there was no doubting the two great loves in his life: Rachel and Scotland's football team. Fluttering from the mansion's flagpole were the New Zealand and Scottish flags, while in the grand lodge there were seven framed wedding photos of the couple, plus one of Rachel in Scottish soccer star Gordon Strachan's shirt.

Rachel soon regained her figure and although clearly revelling in motherhood, she was also keen to get back to modelling. On the agenda was the Rachel Hunter calendar, which was to feature her in sexy swimwear and lingerie, and other lucrative assignments.

Unlike Kelly before her, Rachel was rarely shy of stepping out of Rod's shadow and demonstrating she was her own woman as well as the wife of a famous rock star. She appeared increasingly assured in interviews and on TV, where she was always quick to stress that she was not after Rod's money. The subject of the age difference between herself and Rod was inevitably raised frequently, but she dealt with it expertly: 'As a lover he outdoes men half his age,' she explained in one TV interview.

On returning to the US, Rod and Rachel set about finding a new home although, now she was a mother, Rachel began to echo Rod's often-expressed view that, ideally, Britain would be a better place in which to raise a family. That view was enhanced when Rod took son Sean to his private school one day, where he was less than impressed to see the kids nonchalantly sitting with their feet up on the desks, wearing baseball caps turned the wrong way round, and paying scant attention to their teacher. 'Los Angeles is not a great place to bring up children,' commented Rachel in a TV interview. 'It worries me. In America the school system is not very good and there are problems with gangs and drugs.'

At least in their sumptuous new home, a magnificent mansion in exclusive Beverly Park in Los Angeles, they enjoyed their own four-acre park, patrolled by armed security guards. Complete with swimming pool, sauna complex and a domed conservatory, Rod's new base was conveniently not much more than a goal kick away from his Exiles soccer pitch.

Towards the end of the year Rod was again riding high in the charts with 'Tom Traubert's Blues (Waltzing Matilda)'. He had been searching for an outstanding song from a whole batch being offered to him for recording and, after listening to several, asked to hear something really unusual. Up came 'Tom Traubert's Blues', a song by Tom Waits, whose 'Downtown Train' had previously provided Rod with such a massive hit. Rod was only halfway through listening to Waits's version when he knew he simply had to record it.

Astonishingly 'Tom Traubert's Blues', with its familiar 'Waltzing Matilda' chorus, went straight into the British singles charts at number eight, Rod's highest-ever chart entry position, apart from 'You're In My Heart', which had gone in at number seven in 1977. Once again, Rod had shown shrewd judgement when it came to covering other composers' material. At one point it looked as though 'Tom Traubert's Blues' would give him the UK Christmas number one, but after such a great start the record peaked at number six.

In Britain for Christmas as usual, Rod saw the opportunity for a short soccer tour of his beloved Scotland, with his LA Exiles team. But on 13 December at Firhill Park, Glasgow, in a charity match, he suffered an injury on the pitch that had tour promoters, record company executives and not least the former Brentford FC part-timer himself turning white with anxiety.

Rod, decked out in a snazzy green soccer strip with UK Tour 1992 printed on the breast pocket, played with his usual whole-hearted game even though the calibre of the Scottish Celebrity XI demanded respect. The opposition boasted several star pros but Rod was not about to start shirking tackles, and when Motherwell ace Davie Cooper expertly swerved past him he went in for the tackle and fell awkwardly. Gingerly he got to his feet, clutching his knee, and hobbled off the pitch, clearly in considerable pain although he refused immediate medical treatment. To add insult to the injury, Rod's Exiles went down 4–3.

Later Rod was horrified to hear from a doctor that he had severely torn his cartilage, and that he might as well forget about touring and live performances for some time. He was also told that he might never play football again. Interestingly, it was the thought that he might have to hang up his boots that hit Rod the hardest.

Such a gloomy on-the-spot assessment of the damage persuaded Rod to seek a second medical opinion back in the US, and it was there that he underwent a three-hour operation to have part of his cartilage cut out by surgeons, using the very latest technology.

'I'm so pleased I waited until I got back to LA,' he said. 'The

British doctors told me it was ligaments and I'd be out for years. Instead I was in and out in a day and will be playing again soon. So much for the experts!'

By February 1993 there was a 'new' Rod Stewart album on release that caused much controversy among Rod's most loyal fans. The reason was that the album, *Lead Vocalist*, contained no fewer than seven old tracks and only five new ones. It was asking a lot in the recession for Rod Stewart fans to fork out the full CD price for so many tracks that they already possessed. But, despite the grumbles, fork out they did and in Britain the album astonishingly went to number two in the charts.

At least the five new numbers showed an imaginative selection. They included a searing vocal performance from Rod on a reworking of the Rolling Stones composition 'Ruby Tuesday', and a lively version of the soul number 'Shotgun Wedding', which had first been a hit for Roy C back in 1966 and which Rod remembered from his days as a Mod. Both were issued as singles and reached numbers 11 and 21 respectively.

If *Lead Vocalist* was something of a let-down, Rod's next album turned out to be one of the most crucial of his career. Ever since the launch of the music channel MTV, Rod had been at the forefront of the music video revolution, and it was only natural that he should be approached to star in MTV's series of *Unplugged* programmes. One of the very best ideas to come out of MTV had been to invite rock superstars like Eric Clapton, Paul McCartney and Bruce Springsteen to abandon the high-decibel approach of a normal live gig, and to be filmed instead in a TV studio, presenting their best-loved music in a simple setting, without the aid of electrified instruments.

When Rod was asked to film an *Unplugged* set the idea immediately appealed to him. During the gruelling 18-month *Vagabond Heart* world tour, he had introduced a 30-minute acoustic 'sitdown' set as a way of varying the tempo of his concerts. It had proved both popular and effective and *Unplugged* was a logical extension. Rod was also quick to point out that one of the major influences on him when he was starting out was the way Bob Dylan employed lots of acoustic guitar in his early albums, like *Blonde on Blonde*.

On 5 February, at Universal Studios in Los Angeles, it was Rod's turn to see if, like Clapton and McCartney before him, he could still hold a small audience captive without huge stadia-style trappings and his renowned energetic stagecraft.

He arrived on stage in a blue suit and wearing glasses, the latter, he immediately explained, were to allow him to see the audience. Then he perched on a stool, rolled up his sleeves, and proceeded to deliver what he later described as 'some of the best vocals of my life'.

He kicked off with 'Hot Legs', but it was the early Rod Stewart hits which proved most effective in an acoustic setting, partly because that was the way they were originally written.

There were loud cheers from the audience when Rod introduced Ronnie Wood, who perched beside him and rolled off the opening chords of 'Cut Across Shorty', from the *Gasoline Alley* album of 1970. Prior to launching into a sensitive rendition of 'Reason To Believe', Rod warned the audience: 'We haven't done this all together since we recorded it 22 years ago. Most of the band weren't born.' Then he added with a chuckle: 'And my wife was only one!'

In the audience with eight-month-old Renee, Rachel briefly blushed when Rod introduced Van Morrison's 'Have I Told You Lately' by saying: 'This is a lovely song and I'd like to dedicate it to my wife.' Rod then proceeded to sing it with his eyes clamped tightly shut, his voice cracking with emotion. At one point he made a baby-cradling motion with his arms and then dissolved into tears. By the end of the song Rod was unashamedly dabbing his eyes with a towel. 'Usually it's only when Scotland score that

I get tearful,' he commented later. 'I was so wonderfully in love with Rachel I just broke down.'

Rachel was touched by such an open show of emotion as she watched her husband's tears on the TV monitors. Woody, who cheerfully shared a bottle of Bacardi with Rod during the evening, also realised Rod's tears made for great television.

Apart from 'Tom Traubert's Blues', the *Unplugged* set consisted mainly of Rod's earliest material including 'Handbags And Gladrags', 'Mandolin Wind', and a fresh and inventive version of 'Maggie May'.

It was not hard to spot how comfortable Rod seemed to be with Ronnie Wood on guitar alongside him. They swapped good-natured banter all the way through, and Rod could not resist a dig or two at Ronnie's membership of the Rolling Stones. 'Here's a song we used to do before you went and joined that other band,' he jibed. And when he introduced 'It's All Over Now' he fixed Ron with a grin and observed: 'You lot did a version of this, if my memory serves.'

Eventually the CD of *Unplugged ... and Seated* consisted of 15 tracks and offered a shade over 70 minutes of music. But significantly 'It's All Over Now' did not make it on to the *Unplugged* album. Nor did 'Sweet Little Rock 'n' Roller', although it did afford Rod the opportunity to explain to the audience why there was a dog to be heard barking on the original record. 'The drummer on the album [Mickey Waller] would always bring his dog to the studio,' said Rod.

Also missing from the CD was 'Gasoline Alley', although it did surface as the B side to 'Have I Told You Lately', the first single to be released from *Unplugged*. Besides Ron Wood, Rod called up long-time musical cohorts Jim Cregan on guitar and Kevin Savigar on keyboards, as well as a full string orchestra to help him through what he rightly viewed as one of the most important gigs of his life.

If Rod had any qualms about how his fans would react to *Unplugged ... and Seated*, he did not have long to wait. The album shot straight into the US Top 200 album chart at number two: the highest chart entry for any Rod Stewart album in America. It stayed at number two for five weeks but he could not dislodge Janet Jackson from the top spot. Even so, it was the highest position Rod had achieved in the US album charts since *Blondes Have More Fun* had hit the top in 1979.

In Britain *Unplugged* also reached number two in the album charts. Crucially, it was also critically well received. 'It's just Rod and a bunch of acoustic instruments and a set of mostly old favourites sung with touching vigour and swagger,' said the *Independent*. 'It reminds you of how good he was and tells you how good he really is.'

Days after he had filmed *Unplugged* in Los Angeles, Rod flew to London for another important but very different milestone in his career. It had been a long time coming, but on 16 February 1993, Rod Stewart finally won his first major British award. More than 21 years and 40 hits after 'Maggie May' first topped the charts, the British record industry at last got around to honouring him. They bestowed on him a Lifetime Achievement award; Rod had already won a coveted Living Legend award at America's Grammies in 1989.

The Brit Awards are the British equivalent of the American Grammy, and there was no disguising Rod's pleasure at becoming a recipient. He turned the event into a family occasion by inviting along sister Mary, brothers Don and Bobby, plus, of course, Rachel, to share his big moment at the star-studded ceremony in London.

Poignantly the organisers flew Long John Baldry over from his home in Vancouver to present the statuette to Rod, who was genuinely surprised but delighted at his former mentor's appearance.

Rod told the audience he had made three promises when he had first started out in the music business: to stay in a job for six months, to save up £300 to buy a sports car, and to pull as many birds as he could. 'All these things have come wonderfully true,' he reflected but, mindful of Rachel's presence in the audience, he quickly added the tribute that it was Rachel who had at last given him a deep and meaningful relationship.

There were many big-name bands at the ceremony, not least Simply Red, but it was Rod who was asked to top the bill. He closed the show by singing 'Ruby Tuesday', then rolled back the years by bringing on former Faces Ian McLagan, Kenney Jones and Ronnie Wood, for nostalgic renditions of 'Stay With Me' and 'Sweet Little Rock 'n' Roller'. True to the old Faces tradition the performance was somewhat ragged but certainly didn't lack for enthusiasm. Afterwards there was much face-pulling and looning in equally traditional Faces fashion.

That night only Ronnie Lane was missing from the original line-up. But he was not forgotten. Earlier in the year, over a reunion lunch, Mac, Woody and Rod had quietly decided to pay for hospital treatment in Texas, which Ronnie needed in his battle against multiple sclerosis.

Although Rod was in London for the Brit Awards it was his personal life, and particularly his continuing palimony battle with Kelly Emberg, that was capturing headlines.

In June 1992, Judge David Horowitz had ruled that Kelly's claim to be Rod's wife and share half his fortune was not valid because they had no contract. But he said she could still argue about the 'value of her services' to try to win a slice of his fortune.

Now a judge in Los Angeles Superior Court ruled that Rod must pay for their seven years together, but, under the terms of the agreement, neither party could reveal the settlement. There was speculation that Rod was ordered to pay Kelly £10 million after weeks of bartering between their respective lawyers. The pay-out was thought to be on top of the £7,500-a-month child support for Ruby.

At least the matter had been sorted out, and now Rod was free to concentrate on the release of *Unplugged ... and Seated* to the British press, at a small private cinema in London. The very fact that he was prepared to put in an appearance was proof positive of how important he regarded this new development in his career to be. He even persuaded Ronnie Wood to turn up too and together they sat in the front row, taking liberal sips from a bottle and passing jokey comments about themselves, as the MTV film rolled.

By 28 July Rod was embarked on a six-month A Night to Remember tour of the US, Canada and various German festivals, which consisted of nearly 80 dates, including two nights in Philadelphia, one of his favourite venues. He always maintained that the city provided the best crowd in America, and was a good yardstick for how he was faring.

The aim was to take the acoustic style of *Unplugged* to the fans, and many venues sold out tickets in record time. For several years, Rod had spoken of going on the road with a band and a small orchestra that would accurately reproduce the sound of his early records. But it was not until the 1988–89 tour that he felt confident enough in the concept to perform live, for the first time, 'Mandolin Wind' and 'Reason To Believe'.

Now he was ready to give it a real test, buoyed by the fact that 'Have I Told You Lately' from *Unplugged* had given him a Top Ten hit on both sides of the Atlantic. In Britain it entered the singles chart at number seven, which equalled the 1977 hit 'You're In My Heart' as Rod's highest-ever new entry. It peaked at number five in both Britain and the US.

'I think an evening of Rod Stewart with an *Unplugged* feel is just what a lot of people my age and older would like,' he explained. 'A lot of them don't want to come out and see shows because they don't want to get pushed and shoved around. It will be nice for them to come out and see a show where there is not going to be a riot going on, which usually happens when I play. It will be nice if they just sit down and watch the show. It's going to work. I know it. I can feel it in my water.'

He was right. But in September, just as the tour was gathering momentum and Rod was arriving triumphantly in New York, Rachel tragically lost the baby she had been carrying for six weeks. Only Rod, family and close friends, had been in on the secret that she was expecting another baby. Nothing had been announced publicly, partly because Rachel felt that all was not well.

Rachel later revealed that she had guessed something was wrong as soon as she had become pregnant. With Renee she had known after two weeks that she was expecting a baby, but this time round she had not felt sure. 'I kind of knew something was wrong. Call it women's intuition,' she said, and added that she had whispered a promise to the baby growing inside her: '"If you can't make it back this time, little one, you can come back next time."'

A scan revealed a haemorrhage near the embryo and doctors ordered Rachel to rest for two weeks. 'I did everything I could to help the baby,' she said, 'but the problem didn't go away. So I said to myself: "Listen, if it's not meant to be just let it go." In the end nature took its course.'

When she had another scan in New York her worst fears were confirmed. The baby's heart had stopped beating. Rachel told of her sadness and anguish: 'I cried and decided I wanted the baby induced, rather than wait for it to miscarry. My hormones were all churned up. I'd had something living inside me and now it had died. I just wanted to get it over with.'

That night Rod was due to perform in New York but he immediately offered to cancel the show if Rachel needed the operation straight away. She insisted that the show must go on, that the fans must not be let down, and allowed Rod to escort her to hospital and to remain with her until it was time for him to take the stage. Afterwards he rushed straight back to her clutching flowers from fans.

Naturally Rachel was heartbroken but, as she later revealed, Rod gave her tremendous comfort when the tears flowed and when she needed to talk to him about the baby. They had the rest of their lives together and they already had a beautiful little girl, he reminded her.

By the end of 1993 Rod was able to look forward to starting his 50th year, in January 1994, with several of the loose ends of his life tied up. The financial wrangle with Kelly was over and he was seeing Ruby on a regular basis. He had renewed his friendship with Ian McLagan, after a long period during which Mac's bitterness over Rod's abandoning the Faces had prevented him from speaking to Rod. And then to *Unplugged ... and Seated*, and a new direction in which to take his career.

Twenty years ago Rod Stewart fans would have considered it unthinkable that one day, the Rascal of Rock they admired so much, would have a hit with an old chestnut like 'Waltzing Matilda', and then have the audacity to give a concert perched on a stool wearing glasses. Remarkably the fans lapped it all up and welcomed his avowed intention to go on singing until he dropped.

After the heartbreak of Rachel's miscarriage, January 1994 brought Rod and Rachel the joyful news that she was expecting again. Their second child, a son they named Liam McAllister, was born in London at the same Portland Hospital as his sister Renee on 4 September 1994.

Liam's arrival heralded some of the happiest years of Rod's life. His young wife had a pigeon pair of a son and daughter, he was madly in love with her, and Rachel adored Rod. She was able simply to laugh at the answer Rod would trot out at interviews, when asked what he liked best in life: 'Shagging the missus.' Rachel was perfectly happy for Rod to continue with his routine of playing two games of football a week, plus one night spent on serious soccer training at Manhattan Beach. She also tolerated his football pals coming round to watch English soccer games on their giant TV screen, beamed in via a vast satellite dish perched on the roof. She even joined in Rod's excitement when the English and Scottish soccer scores were faxed through by his housekeeper in Epping, after league games.

Rod was not backward in coming forward about his new-found blissful existence with Rachel. 'I've never been as happy as I am now,' he stressed in a BBC Radio interview. 'Life is one long search for the right person. I'd given up hope three years ago and thought I was a confirmed bachelor for the rest of my life. I'd have been very unhappy because that was not the way I wanted to be, because I always wanted to make a commitment to somebody. Then that person came along, thank goodness. Up until now I'd never been in a meaningful relationship.

'Being a family man is something I welcomed. Rachel is patient. She gives me so much freedom. She's not possessive. I've always been used to really possessive women which can be flattering but can also be really annoying. She trusts me and I trust her.

'I wasted so much energy trying to find that perfect jewel to marry and I eventually found her. I went through a few but it's no more than what every other guy would do. Guys go from girl to girl until they find that one they want to be with.' Applying typical Rod logic, he explained that the only way he knew how to find the right girl was to go out with as many girls as he possibly could.

'The most important thing is that Rachel is on great talking terms with Alana and Kelly,' he stressed. 'It was hard for Rachel in the first two years.'

Very young as she was, Rachel at first was insecure enough and jealous enough of Kelly to say some less than flattering things about her. One was that she'd set her dogs on her if she came near their home, and there were some choice words about the settlement Kelly demanded from Rod as palimony. 'My heart starts palpitating when her name crops up. She makes me mad,' a flustered Rachel said then. 'I know I was awful,' Rachel had the good grace to admit later. 'I was so young. I was kind of insecure myself. Jealousy is such a wicked emotion and I was guilty of it. I said some pretty bitchy things about Kelly. But then I got to know and love all his kids and their mums and I thought: God, these women are the mothers of Rod's children, get real.'

Just about the only thing that rocked Rod's wonderful world with Rachel at this point was an earthquake that shook Los Angeles. 'It was a horrible experience,' Rod recalls with a shudder. 'I remember looking out from my house over California and all the lights had gone out and I thought: bloody hell, we're the only ones alive.'

The earthquake occurred just three days before Rod was due to be inducted into the Rock and Roll Hall of Fame. 'I couldn't go,' he says, 'the kids were too scared. I just couldn't leave them.'

It was a selfless gesture and eventually the induction ceremony was rearranged and Rod joined the rock 'n' roll greats. Perhaps unwisely, Jeff Beck was commandeered to carry out the induction, as Rod remembers all too well: 'He said: "We have a love-hate relationship. He loves me and I hate him."' Rod left everyone in no doubt that he felt Beck's words could have been better chosen.

When he returned to Los Angeles, Rod set up a simple earthquake early-warning system in his home. One downstairs mantelpiece contained a number of his Argyll and Sutherland

Highlanders toy soldiers, and Rod positioned one of the soldiers right on the very edge. Any tremor from the bowels of the Los Angeles earth would send the toy soldier toppling off the mantelpiece and falling noisily to the floor.

On the recording front, Rod continued to be prolific. The hugely successful record producer Trevor Horn was enlisted to mastermind and oversee the next Rod Stewart album, *A Spanner in the Works*. This was an interesting rather than a startling mix of songs by songwriters such as Bob Dylan, Tom Petty, Tom Waits and Chris Rea. It all made for pleasant, melodic listening, an album clearly made with the utmost dedication. Rod was astonished that for 'Lady Luck', Horn took the trouble to fly all the way over to Ireland just to put a penny whistle on the track.

During a trip to London to promote the new album, Rod reaffirmed that he had no wish to look at another woman now he was so blissfully happy with Rachel. 'There's still plenty of lead in the pencil,' he said, 'but I only write to one person now.' Rachel believed him, but when BBC disc jockey Simon Bates arrived at their Epping home with a gift of a little pair of tights for Renee, Rachel said very firmly: 'Those are the only tights he's going to get into in the future.'

In 1998 Rod released *When We Were the New Boys*, a gutsy album that harked back to his days as a rowdy rock 'n' roller. The title track had Rod singing his own composition about playing music in pubs, soccer on the green fields of England and the lessons he'd learned along the way. Cover versions of Oasis's 'Cigarettes And Alcohol', Primal Scream's 'Rocks' and Skunk Anansie's 'Weak' served as a nod from Rod to a new generation of rockers. The album was balanced with two ballads suggested by Elvis Costello: Ron Sexsmith's 'Secret Heart' and Nick Lowe's 'Shelly My Love'. During the recording of the album Ronnie Lane finally lost his long battle with multiple sclerosis, and Rod paid tribute to him by recording 'Ooh La La' which Lane had written with Ron Wood in their Faces days.

That same year Rod pocketed a cool $15 million by selling future royalties on his records to a Wall Street consortium. It was a way of raising instant cash for investment without being taxed.

CHAPTER TWELVE

ROD FORSAKEN

I think I will go to my grave feeling guilty and awful
that I hurt Rod so badly. It was hard hurting someone I
really cared about. Rachel Hunter

The first public indication that all was not well with Rod Stewart's marriage to Rachel Hunter was when the couple were snapped by a photographer outside Scalini's restaurant in Knightsbridge, London, towards the end of 1998.

There, for all the world eventually to see in their newspapers, was Rod cowering meekly like a naughty little boy as Rachel, towering over him in her pink stilettos and clearly boiling with anger, unleashed a screaming tirade at him. They had started arguing heatedly in the restaurant, continued the spat outside in the street and were then chauffeur-driven home to Epping, in silence, before storming off to separate rooms. It was hardly the way to celebrate their upcoming eighth wedding anniversary.

To the watching world, Rod and Rachel had, up to that telltale point, seemed the perfect couple. But, in the certainty of hindsight, there were signs that Rachel was becoming restless. She had begun taking acting classes, signing with a talent agent and landing a movie role. It was a first step towards a greater independence that she was beginning to find increasingly appealing.

Rachel later revealed she had spent sleepless nights plotting her escape from Rod. To the outside world, she said, she was a mother of two wonderful children, a glamorous, devoted wife to Rod and a hugely successful model with no financial worries. 'But inside I was in torment,' Rachel revealed. 'By the time I was 29, I had spent eight years with someone else's group of friends. In the nine years we were together I had never done anything for myself. It had a lot to do with me being very young when we first met, and I had a lot of growing up to do.' She felt she could no longer go on 'living a lie' as Rod's loving wife.

Rachel finally came to the conclusion she had to break free when she was shopping at a supermarket. She saw an old woman shuffling down the aisle with a shopping basket and realised that one day that could be her. 'I remember thinking: here I am, approaching 30, and oh shit, what am I doing with my life? I knew very definitely in that instant that I didn't want to get to that age and have any regrets about what I've done or not done. It gave me the impetus to move on.'

Alarm bells began ringing among Rod's till then unsuspecting entourage, when Rachel was noticeably absent as Rod stepped offstage after his British concerts. He was completing a successful British tour, in which he frequently dedicated Van Morrison's lyrical 'Have I Told You Lately That I Love You' to Rachel, and he generally liked his wife to be there for him at the end of every gig. Rod's brother Don immediately recognised all was not well with the marriage when he spotted Rachel at only one of Rod's 12 UK concerts.

The crunch came one night in London, when Rachel tellingly remained in her suite at the Dorchester Hotel and refused even to come down when Rod's chauffeur called for her.

On the night the break was to become permanent, Rod and

Rachel were barely on speaking terms at a pre-Christmas party at the Dorchester. When a very tall blonde in a sexy, tight black skirt wandered over to ask Rod for his autograph, he not only obliged but appeared to take more than a passing interest in front of his wife. His continuing interest in the girl, a budding photographer called Penny, was noted by several revellers at the party, one of whom pointed it out to Rachel – unnecessarily so, as she had observed it all.

The following day a car arrived to collect Rachel and the children, and they headed for the airport and flew off to the £5 million seafront home in Palm Beach, Florida, which they had bought in 1995. As Rachel fastened her seat belt, heaved a sigh and sank back into her seat, she knew she was flying away from nearly nine years with Rod and that their marriage was over. Rachel had fled by the time Rod's British tour had reached Earls Court, but gamely he went ahead with his remaining concerts.

The split remained secret for only a short while, even though the sight of a mournful Rod nursing a pint on his own in his usual corner in the Theydon Oak pub near his Epping home was a giveaway.

Within days the couple announced their split in a brief joint statement which caused shock waves around the world. It was issued through Rod's American management company, Stiefel Entertainments and read: 'After eight years of marriage Rod Stewart and his wife Rachel Hunter have formally announced their separation. There are no immediate plans for the couple's divorce.'

Rod's brother Don expressed the family's shock and sadness. 'What happened I just don't know,' he said. 'But I do know it will hit him hard. He will be completely stressed out, hit for six.'

The marriage split inevitably made headlines in newspapers in dozens of countries around the world, most speculating that the huge age difference was the contributing cause, that Rachel wanted to live it up while Rod wanted to stay in and play with his train set and watch the football on TV.

Social commentators correctly surmised that Rachel had got fed up living under Rod's superstar wing, and that after marrying so young and producing two children so quickly she now felt lost, had no identity and wanted to spread her wings, live for herself and find herself.

Rod was absolutely distraught, and utterly desolate. It was part of his relationship with Rachel that they were a team. She would go on tour with him and he would accompany her to a fashion shoot. Now he was alone. Losing Rachel was an excruciatingly painful hammer-blow for a man who had had his own way with women for nearly four decades. 'I was so sure she was the woman I was going to spend the rest of my life with,' he said. 'I hope and pray with all my heart that she will eventually come back.'

Rod and Rachel of course had had their differences, but Rod really had not imagined it had reached a point where his wife was prepared to walk out and leave him. 'It was like a bolt of lightning and I wasn't ready for that,' he said. 'Stunned isn't the word for it. I had my head cut off. I was totally unprepared for it. It hadn't happened to me before. No one had ever left me. It was totally unexpected and I was ill equipped for it.

'It was amazing that until then I hadn't been hurt by another woman. Maybe it would have been good if someone had got up and left and not put up with my nonsense, then I would have been ready for it. I don't think anything can prepare you for that heartbreak because it just goes so deep.'

For the first four months after his marriage collapsed, Rod says he went through absolute hell. He was so miserable he didn't know what to do. He turned to God, relied on prayers and meditation to lift his spirits and found his weight plummeting alarmingly due to worry. He eventually lost 14lb and found himself, incredibly, able to wear trousers with a 30-inch waist.

Friends who rallied round, full of sympathy, encouraged Rod to throw himself into his work and career and to keep playing his beloved football, to get through the pain and heartache. But he says: 'Work was the last thing on my mind, and I got into this surreal situation whereby I couldn't even play football with my mates cos I thought they didn't exist. It became like I was in a dream. I'd go and play football and it was like everyone else was a ghost. It was surreal, almost like walking two foot off the ground. It was so horrible. I literally fell to pieces and lost tons of weight.'

Rod says of his friends: 'They said: "It's going to take half the time you were in the relationship to get over it." I thought, oh no, I've got four and a half years of this. But I was OK after about eight months.'

In time Rod was able to come to terms with the fact that Rachel was simply too young for him when he married her. 'She was only 21 and I should have known better. Someone should have whispered in my ear: "Rod, you're making a complete dick of yourself." But I've no regrets whatsoever. It wasn't her fault, it wasn't my fault. It was the way it all came together.'

Somewhat surprisingly, but commendably in the eyes of his many fans, Rod eventually felt able to talk about his pain and anguish on national television. 'It was heartbreaking,' he told British chat-show host Michael Parkinson. 'I thought this was going to be the marriage of my life. I didn't look at any other woman, didn't mess about for nine years while I was married and it fell apart.' Again citing the age gap as the main reason, he added: 'She was too young. Someone should have said: "Rod, this is going to end in tears."'

Rod later learned of his sister Mary's warning to their brother Bobby at his wedding to Rachel, that one day she would break

Rod's heart. Rod's reaction was: 'Well, why didn't you tell me?' It was, of course, easier said than done.

Rachel had not taken lightly the decision to get out of the marriage and she knew how much she had hurt her husband. 'I'll take to the grave the pain that I caused Rod,' she said. 'I hurt the one person I loved and cared about, and that's a hard thing to live with on a daily basis.' She and Rod both knew what effect it could have on their children Renee and Liam, and both parents agreed to make it as painless for them as possible.

Rod knew he had been taught an extremely tough lesson. 'I learned: don't marry a 21-year-old girl when you are 45,' he said ruefully. 'But they were nine great years and I would rather have had nine years of bliss, which it was, than 30 years of hell with someone that you never loved.'

As Rod and Rachel got on with their separate lives, Rod was celibate for eight weeks before he began to be seen out with a succession of beautiful young women. He no longer had anyone to answer to and his dates included model Kelly Fisher, *Baywatch* beauty Angelica Bridges, *Playboy* model Kimberley Conrad, ex-wife of *Playboy* boss Hugh Hefner, model Tracy Tweed, and the blonde Wonderbra model Caprice.

But despite this beauty parade passing through Rod's life and Rachel's dating Michael Weatherley, an actor she had met while filming the low-budget movie *Winding Roads*, there was still much speculation that Rod and Rachel might get back together again once Rachel had enjoyed some of her 'own space'. They had spoken regularly on the telephone to each other about the children, often as many as five times a day, and their mutual concern about how each other was coping with the trauma of the break-up prompted members of their respective families to consider a reconciliation to be possible.

In London, while promoting his new album *Human*, Rod revealed: 'I never got down on my knees and begged her to come back. I just said to her when we broke up: "You're making a huge mistake," something which she probably realises now she has.'

But Rod, who by then was starting to become involved with new girlfriend Penny Lancaster, dismissed the idea of getting back with Rachel. 'I can't imagine it,' he said. 'Men have got so much pride and once they've been really hurt – unless it happens in the first eight or nine months – I think it's gone. I was so hurt.'

Around the same time, Rachel appeared on American shock DJ Howard Stern's show and also ruled out a reconciliation. 'I haven't been single since I was very, very young,' she said. 'I was married at 21. I didn't have time for much else. Before I knew it, I was married and having children. I missed my 20s. Now I'm ready to enjoy that time I missed. I'm revved up and ready to go.' Pointing out that she was now at her sexual peak, Rachel added: 'I need a stallion.'

The reality for Rachel was, as she admitted, that her fling with Michael Weatherley had simply been on the rebound. 'When you split up with someone who you have been with for so long, you look around for love and support and Michael was a very supportive guy.' The reality, too, was that she was now a single mother of two and there were nights when she sat at home with her sister Jacqui, wondering why neither of them had a man in their lives.

Like Rod, Rachel claimed they had been faithful to each other during their nine-year marriage, although she voiced doubts about his chastity before they wed. 'Yes, I heard the story about him and some woman in an elevator two weeks before our wedding,' she said. 'I didn't ask him about it. But I think anything before we were married was fair. As long as there was nothing during the marriage.'

While Rod's relationship with Penny Lancaster moved on apace, Rachel hooked up with British pop star Robbie Williams, though some doubted it was the great passionate romance the newspapers had the world believe. Piquantly, Rod said he approved of Rachel's new boyfriend and saw in Robbie something of a young Rod, in Robbie's passion for football and women.

With *Human* to promote and a long American tour looming so soon after the break-up, Rod had to pull himself together fast. As a first step, while he was in New York, he sought out a renowned tattoo artist in a body art parlour in the city's seedy East Village district, and went under the needle for his first tattoos. He wanted something to remember his father by and, after thumbing through books of designs of various thistles, he got the tattooist to come up with a good Scottish thistle design. Rod emerged with a chain of them around his upper right arm and a lion rampant.

In Nashville, some seven weeks after he had lost Rachel, Rod kicked off an American tour that was to criss-cross the country for the next few months. The crisis over Rachel, he decided, called for drastic measures over his alcohol intake during the tour. Determined not to drown his sorrows in bottles of booze, alcohol was banned from the tour. 'When you go through something as traumatic as that, you want to get right grounded,' he explained. 'Alcohol is only going to make it worse. So one night I went on in front of 18,000 people totally sober. How I had the strength to do that when I was so hurting inside was totally beyond me. Previously for 30 years when I was about to open my voice to sing I had to have a drink.'

Human, the 24th album of Rod's career, excluding his work with the Faces and the Jeff Beck Group, included 11 tracks he had selected from a batch of 30 he had recorded. For the first time there was no Rod Stewart composition on the album. The tracks were largely slow-paced, angst-ridden songs with a strong bias towards R 'n' B and included the Macy Gray song 'Smitten', a duet with Scottish songstress Helicopter Girl on 'Don't Come

Around Here', a warm version of Curtis Mayfield's 'It Was Love That We Needed', and a notable guitar break from former Dire Straits frontman Mark Knopfler on 'If I Had You'.

Rod described *Human* as 'a white boys R 'n' B album with a slight nod of the hat to hip-hop'. He claimed: 'It's the sort of album you can put on when you're driving, or having the first drink of the day or having a shag.' And he added: 'I am proud of this one. I wasn't that proud of the two previous.'

Significantly, *Human* was Rod's first album after switching from the Warner Bros label. His contract with Warner's was up and neither he nor the record company were jumping over fences to renew it. On Atlantic, Warner's parent company, Rod had joined a label that had produced hits for some of his early idols and role models like Otis Redding, Wilson Pickett and Aretha Franklin.

While he had been signed to Warner Brothers in the mid-1980s, Rod had suggested he take a complete change of musical direction and record an album of classic songs from the 1920s and 1930s. The record company turned him down flat, sniffily pointing out that their huge investment in a rock star did not encompass a collection of standards from 50 years ago.

Their reaction was much as Rod expected but the idea never left him. Rod even went on the TV channel CNN soon afterwards and openly expressed his desire to record such an album, proving the extent of his faith in the project. He also decided to put his money where his mouth was and invest in recording some demos, in the hope of generating enough interest to get the project off the ground.

Some two years later Clive Davis, the managing director of J Records, was interested enough to give Rod his head, and eventually enthusiastic enough to be a hands-on boss, working till the small hours to produce some of the tracks himself. Davis argued that Rod had a proven track record as one of rock's greatest interpreter's of other people's songs, and he was confident Rod would be able to stamp his own individual mark on songs that had become standards.

A meeting was convened with Rod, Clive, two producers and a member of Rod's management team to discuss exactly how recording should progress. 'We were a bit of a rudderless ship while recording,' Rod recalls, 'and suddenly in this meeting Clive got up to try and describe the feeling he wanted on the tracks. The only way he could do it was to start dancing around the room, pretending he was Fred Astaire and had Ginger Rogers in his arms. I did the same and so did two producers and my manager. So we had five men dancing round the room at 11 in the morning – and there was not a touch of alcohol in sight!'

The aim was for Rod to record a collection of songs with a consistent, romantic feel with nothing too up-tempo, and nothing too sad in the lyrics. Eventually, amid lush strings and traditional jazz arrangements, Rod tackled such challenging material as George and Ira Gershwin's 'They Can't Take That Away From Me', Cole Porter's 'Every Time We Say Goodbye', and other much-loved oldies including 'These Foolish Things', and 'You Go To My Head'.

When he went into the studio, Rod barely had to check the lyrics. These were songs he remembered his parents singing and consequently had come to know extremely well in his boyhood. He knew them all almost by heart. They had entered his subconscious in his youth and had stayed there.

The album was released, towards the end of 2002, under the title *It Had to Be You ...The Great American Songbook* and shot straight to number four in the American album charts. Rod was ecstatic, particularly when it went on to sell equally well in Britain. 'I thought it would go down the toilet,' said a genuinely delighted Rod. The CD's success was very timely, and more personally reassuring for Rod, who described his versions of the classics as a 'loosen up that pretty French gown' album. Rod Stewart fanatics remembered that was a line from his seductive 'Tonight's The Night' hit 24 years earlier. 'It's a nice album to put on when you're having your first drink of the day,' Rod commented. 'I don't like calling these songs standards, they're great classic songs of bygone years.'

Critical reaction was, however, mixed, but there was enough acclaim within the American record industry for *It Had to Be You ... The Great American Songbook* for Rod to be nominated for a Grammy award for Best Traditional Pop Vocal Album. Rivals in this category were Barbra Streisand, Bernadette Peters, Tony Bennett and Michael Feinstein. 'Some pretty big competition – and some pretty big noses!' joked Rod. 'I don't know how they are going to get us all on stage!'

It was while Rod was recording *It Had to Be You ...The Great American Songbook,* that his relationship with Penny Lancaster was growing stronger by the day. Rachel, meanwhile, was still clearly suffering, revealing that she was in deep therapy, seeing a female psychoanalyst two or three times a week. In an extraordinarily frank interview, Rachel admitted she had reached rock bottom and sometimes felt so low she had been unable to leave her house. Rod, by contrast, seemed strong, buoyed by Penny Lancaster's undemanding love for him.

Later in June 2003, Rachel surprised Rod by filing for a divorce in Los Angeles, only rather mysteriously to drop the petition a few weeks later.

CHAPTER THIRTEEN

A PENNY FOR YOUR THOUGHTS

*Rod likes me to wear sexy clothes. He says that if you
have got a nice figure you should show it off.*
Penny Lancaster

Rod Stewart was feeling anything but his usual cheery self on the
night in December 1998, when he relaxed with friends in the
nightclub inside London's elegant Dorchester Hotel. It was the
day he and wife Rachel realised their marriage was finally over
and both were understandably upset. But they were out in public together and Rod was doing his best to hide his heartache
behind that familiar smile. The singer has signed more autographs in his professional life than most stars and he always
prides himself on finding time for his fans. Normally he signs
with a grin and moves quickly on, but there was something
about the upfront approach of 28-year-old Penny Lancaster that
made Rod linger and talk a while.

A 6ft 1in blonde with a model-girl figure is very hard to
ignore. She was pushed into autograph action by a shy friend
who was yearning for Rod's signature in her book, long before
Penny had even noticed that the rock star was in the room.
Penny happily confessed later that she was never, ever a Rod
Stewart fan. She didn't possess even one of his singles and would

have found it difficult to name any of his hits but, like any good Essex girl about town, she knew exactly how famous he was.

Penny approached her prey with her customary outgoing confidence, and she was instantly impressed when Rod stood up like an old-fashioned gentleman to ask her to sit down. His politeness was possibly influenced by the very tight, very short black satin dress that Penny was wearing. There was an instant attraction between the two strangers as Rod asked Penny what she did for a living. Penny explained politely that she was studying photography and cheekily suggested that she would love to take his picture one day. Never one to reject an approach from a pretty girl, he suggested she come to his London concert the very next night. And as good as his word, he arranged for the beautiful blonde to be provided with a press pass, allowing her to move backstage and photograph Rod and his band in action. She enjoyed the evening very much but she did not get to meet Rod that night.

Rod admitted later that he had asked for Penny's phone number partly, at least, to annoy his wife because they were having such a bad time. The singer is a proud man and the humiliation of the highly public end of the marriage was hard for him to take. And the loneliness that followed was even worse. He was still on tour and, as he told the *Sunday Times Magazine*: 'The shows were not particularly cheerful. I dunno if you've ever broken up with someone you dearly love, but it's just not real. You feel as though you're in a dream. I had to finish the British tour, then go on to tour America, which took my mind off it a little. But some nights were so lonely. It's amazing how you can have 10,000 people out there and be making love to them, and then you come off-stage and it's the emptiest feeling because there's nobody in your life.'

So it was no surprise that Rod waited so long before telephoning the blonde with the gentle smile and the endless legs. Penny was very surprised some nine months later when she played back a message on her answerphone from Rod Stewart. At first she was sure it was one of her friends with a talent for impressions playing a joke. But after an hour or so she decided it was genuine and rang back. Rod invited Penny to come out and join him for dinner with a couple of friends that night.

Penny was thrilled. She was born in Essex in 1971, the year Rod Stewart reached number one on both sides of the Atlantic with 'Maggie May'. She was well aware of the yawning age difference between them, but the Rod Stewart she had met briefly was warm and witty and seemed like a lot of fun to be with. At the time Penny was in a long-standing relationship with a diminutive City trader called Micky Sloan, who had been her boyfriend for close to ten years.

But he was not the conventionally jealous type and he generously decided that dinner with Rod Stewart could be good for Penny's career, and he happily agreed that she should go off for the evening. She chose tight, but not too revealing, leather trousers for their first night out to show him her prized pictures of his Earls Court concert.

Penny tried to stay super-cool but when the chauffeur-driven Bentley arrived outside she was definitely impressed. Rod was again the gentleman and he jumped out of the car to open the door for Penny. They drove to a restaurant called Neil's in Loughton, where the couple nervously started to get to know each other. Penny was forced to admit she didn't really know that much about Rod's music, but he was much too down-to-earth and keen to get to know her that he didn't care in the least.

Penny found Rod charming and witty. She loved the way he took the mickey out of himself at every opportunity. And Rod's ever-present good manners impressed her, too. He insisted on pulling her chair out when she sat down and he jumped to his feet when she left the table. Rod had very publicly split from supermodel Rachel by then, but to Penny this first night did not seem so much romantic as simply getting on very well with an intriguing new friend. People looked and stared a little but the restaurant is one where Rod is well known so nobody made a fuss. She was frank and honest that she was in a relationship with a long-term boyfriend, but she said she was very happy to be friends. Rod was hardly looking for commitment and happily agreed that they would be just friends for a while.

When she got home Micky Sloan was relaxed about Penny's glamorous date for the evening. They both regarded it as little more than an interesting experience, and Penny was not considering a relationship with Rod. But the next day he asked her if she would take some photographs at a football dinner, and the friendship started to grow into something more promising. Rod invited Penny to come and enjoy some winter sunshine in Spain, and there they began to fall in love. Rod reflected how refreshing it was to go out with someone unconnected with the rock business, and he loved Penny's open enthusiasm for life as well as her stunning physical presence.

'Our first kiss was very natural,' said Penny. 'I didn't feel intimidated that he had been with lots of famous women and he was glad that I was not part of that world.' They had fun together in Spain and Penny knew her old life was over. When Penny returned from Spain she ended the ten-year relationship with a disappointed Micky Sloan, who generously wished her good luck after they parted. Rod was just the catalyst, insisted Penny: 'If it hadn't been him it would have been someone else.'

Experience told Rod to take things very slowly. He confided to friends that he had really fallen hard for the tall and blonde photographer, and he was anxious not to spoil things by moving too fast. But Rod Stewart in romantic mode is pretty irresistible for a girl. Penny was in her second year at Barking College and she was determined to finish what she had started. But sometimes it was hard to keep focused, when Rod was waiting outside in his Land Rover for lectures to be concluded for the day. Penny was staggered to receive gifts like a £1,500 Bronica camera and a £4,000 bed that she had casually approved of in Harrods. And in breaks from college, Rod would whisk Penny off first class to luxury holidays in Paris, Marbella or the Caribbean. It was more than enough to turn any girl's head.

Rod still took things very gently. He had to be in Los Angeles spending time with his children and attending to assorted business matters, but kept in touch with Penny through constant long and passionate telephone calls. Of course Rod was hardly living like a monk in California and he was frequently photographed with other women. He enjoyed a brief and highly publicised fling with the beautiful model Caprice, which did not exactly delight Penny back in England. But Rod insisted afterwards that it was her he wanted and the couple moved on. 'He said he was happy with me and he didn't want to see anyone else,' said Penny. And the relationship became more serious towards the end of the year.

After spending Christmas 1999 in England with her family, Penny flew out to Los Angeles to meet Rod's extended family. She met his ex-wife Rachel and the children. She was nervous at first but was soon put at her ease, and she quickly got on well with Rod's energetic and outgoing brood. 'They are great kids and every time they see me they become more relaxed. We get on well,' said Penny.

On New Year's Eve, Penny watched her lover give a highly successful concert in Las Vegas, and had to pinch herself that she was not dreaming. She was delighted that their relationship was still not hitting the headlines. She and Rod had secret meetings and kept a low profile. 'We just wanted to get to know each other without any outside pressure,' said Penny. Her parents, who are very close to Rod's age, were concerned for their daughter at first.

Lawyer Graham and hospital worker Sally are divorced and, while they were definitely not Rod Stewart fans, they were well aware of the colourful reputation of the rock star and were understandably anxious for their daughter's welfare. Both parents were concerned that Penny might get badly hurt, but when they separately met Rod and Penny together their fears were quickly eased. 'When they saw how much Rod means to me and how well he treats me they came to really like him,' said Penny.

But the spell of blissful privacy that nurtured the couple's romance was sadly running out. In January, Rod and Penny were holidaying in Barbados when they were snapped together on a beach. They were together lounging on the sands when they noticed a little boat out at sea, taking a little too much notice. They escaped the unwanted attention by slipping through a beachfront house, but they had been captured on film. At first Penny was identified as former *Baywatch* beauty Angelica Bridges, but Penny Lancaster's face and figure are much too distinctive to remain mistaken for another for very long. Penny's family and friends recognised the photos in the newspapers instantly and the secret was out. Reporters and photographers followed the couple in droves for a while, and Penny was shocked by how much her life changed once she was known to be Rod's love. 'It made the time we had enjoyed before so much more special and precious,' she told a friend.

Rod was only too wearily well aware of how irritating constant press attention can be, and he did his best to shield Penny from this unfamiliar new pressure. He was determined the media would not do anything to wreck this romance. 'Penny is fantastic,' he said. 'She's fresh and funny and so full of life. I'm a lucky guy.'

But Rod had more serious problems than romance on his mind in April 2000 when a routine scan at Los Angeles Cedars-Sinai Hospital revealed throat cancer. Rod was deeply shocked by the diagnosis and had emergency surgery to remove the growth. The operation also removed his famous singing voice for almost nine months. And he had to work hard and patiently for that period to restore the famous rasping tones to their former glory. It was a deep blow for Rod and he tried to keep the grim experience from as many of his nearest and dearest as he could.

He decided to let Penny fly back to Britain without knowing how seriously ill he was, and he was desperate not to burden his family with bad news. Rod was devastated when the scan picked up the growth on his thyroid gland. The doctors described it as a little spot, but they admitted it was cancerous. Rod was warned that it could become dangerous if not dealt with and he agreed to have the operation straight away.

Rod instantly felt grateful to trusted friend and long-time Rod Stewart aide Annie Challis, who persuaded him to agree to the routine checks. Annie had booked herself in for a health check and enthused to Rod afterwards how much better she felt, with the confidence of knowing that everything was working just fine. She felt great to receive the all-clear and Rod followed her good example.

Rod agreed to his operation instantly, but he never realised that it would have such a devastating impact on his voice. He was very scared when he discovered the surgeon would be cutting right through his neck. And when he woke up afterwards the famous voice was gone. 'Don't worry, your voice will be back in six months,' he was merrily advised. But it wasn't. He could talk normally after that time but he couldn't sing. And Rod was worried that his wonderful trademark tool, that has delighted millions of fans for four decades, might never return. In fact it took around nine months of dedicated training to get his voice back.

The doctors explained to Rod that the operation entailed cutting through the muscles, which then go through memory loss and literally forget how to sing. They shrivel up and have to be very slowly re-educated afterwards. For Rod it was a very difficult time. 'It was like learning to walk again,' he remembers. The operation was quickly over and he was in and out of the hospital in a day, but when he still could not sing about six months later it was hard to deal with. Rod's voice is his great gift. He sings for a living of course, but he also sings to express himself, and has always gained great pleasure from using his wonderful God-given instrument. But he realised that all his life he had taken his voice completely for granted. To have it taken away for such a long period was not easy.

The experience inspired Rod. He described it as a 'turning point' in his life, and has since devoted a great deal of time and money to the children's cancer charity, City of Hope. Rod has found his work with the charity both fulfilling and deeply humbling. As the father of five happily healthy children he is very moved when he sees the terrible effects cancer can have on kids. 'When you have a scare like this it puts everything into perspective,' says Rod. 'I thought: Jesus Christ, I'm lucky. This must have happened for a reason.' So now Rod has decided to support the City of Hope 'as long as I live'.

And his millions of fans can be reassured that the threat to the famous voice has been lifted. Rod believes the operation somehow even improved his voice: 'It has a new warmth to it. That's the upside. It's like I've gone back to the 1970s' rasp. My voice now is as strong as it ever was. Some of the songs I've had to drop down a key, but it's gained a bit of heart in the balance.'

Penny was deeply moved when she discovered that Rod had deliberately protected her from worrying about the operation. She wished she had been there to support him but appreciated his selfless strength. And Penny knew all about the kind of anxiety that her lover had been going through. She fought her own brave battle against cancer when she was 24. She was devastated when doctors found pre-cancerous cells in her cervix. The growths were blamed when Penny suffered a tragic miscarriage, and she endured the agony and anxiety of five operations in the last six years to remove those cells, and the two further cysts that developed on her ovaries and her appendix. The shock of being diagnosed with cancer when she was so young and apparently healthy was hard to handle. At the time Penny was still enjoying considerable success in her modelling career while training to be a professional photographer. It was the most difficult period of her young life, but it helped her to understand what Rod had been through.

The relationship between Rod and Penny has evolved from a strong friendship into something much more significant than either of them could have forecast. The beautiful Essex girl has certainly been strongly influenced by the charismatic rock star. For one thing she is a great deal blonder than she used to be. That comes partly from spending much more time in California with him. 'I think it suits the way I look,' declares Penny, 'and Rod likes it, too.'

Rod loves Penny's long legs to be shown off to their best advantage in very short skirts, and often buys her clothes for her. 'He likes me to wear sexy clothes,' says Penny. 'He says that if you have got a nice figure you should show it off. I used to dress more conservatively, but Rod has given me the confidence to dress more sexily. He doesn't like women in trousers. He prefers short, slinky dresses.'

Penny might be lucky to have been born with long legs and a slim figure but she works hard to stay in shape. She is a former county swimmer who still enjoys working out in the pool, and she goes walking. In Los Angeles she works out at the gym and with Rod's personal trainer. Every day she does an hour on the cycling and rowing machines or an aerobics class. 'I've always worked out,' says Penny. 'When I was younger I used to go to the gym with my mum. I also do a bit of weight training and am quite muscular. I have a fit-looking body rather than a thin-looking one. Exercise brings the blood to the surface and makes you look good.'

And she has even begun to learn the finer arts of football, under the expert instruction of her soccer-loving boyfriend. She is slowly gaining his enthusiasm for the sport and has been known to join in charity events.

And if Penny still does not share quite the same passion for football as Rod, her love of Scotland is growing fast. According to Penny: 'The reception he gets in Scotland is just unbelievable. He gets really excited about playing there. I think the Scots get the best out of him. In Glasgow he sang the first line of 'Flower Of Scotland' and the place went mad. I jumped down into the audience to join in. It's great meeting his fans. After all, they love him, too.'

Rod and Penny have not ruled out getting married at some point in the future, but at the moment they appear to be enjoying themselves too much to want to change anything. Rod famously hit the headlines in 2001 when he announced that marriages should be renewed annually, 'like dog licences', which produced the familiar flurry of overreaction. Penny defended him: 'Rod likes to have a laugh and a joke about things but sometimes it is taken seriously, and the next thing you know it is all over the newspapers. Of course Rod has been married twice and everyone knows he is not exactly enthralled by the idea of marriage, but he was just having a joke.'

Penny herself was very much against marriage as an institution for a time. Her parents' divorce was very painful. She found it terribly hard to be torn between the two people she loved most in the world who had decided they didn't want to be together any more. 'I was anti-marriage for a bit following my parents' divorce, but my dad was very comforting to me. He taught me how to love and trust again and to feel there is always a chance out there. If anyone is going to be my husband they've got to be at least as good as my dad. It's the maturity level. A woman needs to feel secure and an older man can give you that.'

It is clearly not always easy for Penny, sharing her life with a man with so much history. Rod works hard to maintain good relationships with the mothers of his various children, and echoes of previous relationships are all around. Penny's relationship with Rod's most recent ex, Rachel Hunter, is often fractious and difficult although Penny is always quick to deny any serious problems.

At an awards ceremony in Monte Carlo in 2002, the feelings between the two women appeared to surface, when Rachel was reported to have launched into an unprovoked outburst at the very mention of Penny's name: 'Is it a man or a woman? Have you felt its crotch? What the **** is he doing with her?' she is reported to have said.

Penny wisely made no comment. But she knows how hurt Rod was when Rachel walked out and left him, and many close friends hope that Rod and Rachel might one day get back together again. So Penny must have allowed herself at least a small smile, when Rachel was pictured in the tabloids cavorting topless on a sun-lounger with Robbie Williams.

But Penny started her own publicity storm with a highly controversial interview that appeared shortly after Rachel's raunchy photo-shoot. And Rod was less than delighted that the interview with Penny suggested she needed more sex than he could provide. In graphic detail, Penny was quoted as saying she was 'gagging' for sex all the time, and that Rod had difficulty keeping up with her demands to make love twice a day. The singer was mortified by this slur on his ability to enjoy his favourite activity, and his family were extremely upset.

He insisted that Penny had been misinterpreted. Naturally

the story was picked up and exaggerated to the maximum embarrassment of all concerned. Rod Stewart does not often lose his cool but he stormed that the story was absolute rubbish and so unfair. He spelled out his injured feelings to the *Daily Telegraph*: 'That caused so much upset because my family thought Penny really had said it and they took umbrage. It took a long time for it all to settle down. What she actually said, I believe, is that sometimes I play football in the morning and I had just done this tour. So I go off and do this two-and-a-half-hour concert in the evening and, naturally, I would be knackered when I came home. Sometimes I could manage sex, sometimes I couldn't. But that schedule would take it out of a 19-year-old.' Rod was livid and he insisted he was a romantic who liked to take his time with sex, and the older you get the better you become at it. Rod insisted that now it was a case of quality as opposed to quantity, and Penny was in full agreement.

But clearly the physical side of their relationship is very important, and Penny made it clear sex was still very good and very important to both of them. 'You could say my sexual appetite has changed a lot, for the better,' she stated. 'It's the 30s thing. It's all you've got on your mind when you're in love and have that passion for someone. And Rod's fitness level is incredible.'

In 2002 Penny was signed up to promote the Ultimo bra range, with Rod taking a particular interest in which pictures showed off her legs and body to best advantage. The marketing advantage of Rod Stewart's girlfriend being seen in her underwear did wonders for Ultimo, and the impact was instantly uplifting. Dynamic businesswoman Michelle Mone was delighted with her choice: 'Since we signed up Penny Lancaster sales have been incredible. The web sales alone are up 500 per cent in the space of six weeks over the Christmas period. Having someone like Penny has certainly helped. But you have to be careful. You need to find someone who is passionate about the product and looks good. People want to be inspired by what they see.' And it was clear Rod's pretty partner did not come cheap for the campaign; Michelle added pointedly: 'Of course there is a huge cost involved in having someone of that level.'

Penny is under no illusion that her relationship with Rod can only help her modelling career. 'Of course I can't deny that being with Rod has brought me more into the public eye,' she says. 'But I was a successful model and photographer before I met him and that is what I am doing now. I am not naïve and I talked this over with Rod. He agreed that I might get offers because of who I am, but if I wasn't any good they wouldn't come back. I have been given several photo assignments and no matter who I was, if the pictures were lousy, they would never ask me again and again. Rod is very supportive of me and he wants me to succeed in my own right. He likes to help and gives me huge encouragement. But he knows there are things I must do for myself and my career. Just in the same way I help and encourage him, but in the studio or on stage he is his own boss.

'Rod is 100 per cent behind everything I do. I couldn't have a more supportive boyfriend. It's amazing the doors that have opened for me, but I do feel the need to make sure I don't lose my identity. It does mean a lot to me when I get work off my own back, and in some ways it is a bit tougher because I have to work that little bit harder just to prove myself.'

An English friend who knows the couple well explains that Penny and Rod are very good for each other. 'On the surface they look like the typical golden couple, oozing cash and confidence and with the world at their feet,' he said. 'But the reality is much more complicated. Rod needs a woman he can trust as well as love. He has lots of fears and insecurities and he needs a friend as well as a lover.'

Penny was bullied at school and, although she has grown into a strong person, she has her vulnerable side. Penny recalls being picked on simply because she was different. She was tall and a little shy and that gave the impression that she was snooty and aloof. In Penny's opinion: 'Bullies pick on people who are different and I suppose I was in some ways. My nickname was "Lanky" Lancaster. At least that was one of the nicer things they called me. I was picked on because of my height and perhaps because of the way I talked. But I wasn't driven to despair like some poor kids. There was hair-pulling, some shoving and I remember some boys ramming their bikes into my legs and covering me with bruises.'

There were days when Penny came home and lay sobbing in her bedroom. But thankfully she had a very strong mother who helped pull her through and restore her confidence. She told her the other kids were just jealous of her and that the bullying was a result of something that was missing from their lives, not from hers. 'Mum kept telling me that the bullying was not my fault,' recalls Penny. 'I think it is important that bullied children realise that. And I am not the kind of person who retaliates. In the end, I would feel sorry for them rather than be angry with them. It was nearly always a jealousy thing.'

The English friend reports: 'Rod gets on really well with Penny's parents. Of course they are around his own age but they are good, kind people with a sharp sense of humour. Rod enjoys having a circle of people, like his own family, who are rooted in the real world and are not trying to hit on him for tickets or photographs or anything else. That is what has helped him to stay sane in this crazy business for so long. I have watched Penny really blossom since she met Rod. They seem to find something special in each other that is more than a healthy love life. She's the very best kind of Essex girl who understands how to look after her man. I think Rod relates to her so well because she was not part of the showbiz scene that is often so tacky and phoney.'

Penny is well aware of why their relationship works so well, and is fiercely supportive of her famous lover. 'He is unpretentious with a strong sense of family,' declares Penny. 'He is never happier than when he is in the local country pub. And he loves me precisely because I'm not "Hollywood". When he is at home in Essex he can relax and be himself, and I'm part of that. He says it is refreshing to meet someone who is caring and genuine.'

And Rod clearly dotes on Penny: when they were at a party recently he wrote on her arm, in a ballpoint-improvised tattoo, 'I love my Penny – Rod.'

Rod admits he has always suffered from chronic loneliness: 'It comes from nowhere and I can never rationalise it. My girlfriend is upstairs, my mates are round the corner, and yet I just feel so lonely. I was saying to Penny only the other night: "Do you ever, like, go to bed and still feel lonely, even if I'm here?" She said: "Yeah, course I do." Which was an amazing discovery after 57 years, that other people could feel that way too.'

CHAPTER FOURTEEN

DA YA THINK I'M SIXTY?

Bar none he's the best singer I've heard in rock 'n' roll.
He's also the greatest white soul singer.
Elton John on Rod Stewart

Rod Stewart is not one for looking backwards in life. He likes to live for the day. Next 10 January (2005), fully 12 years after he accepted a Lifetime Achievement Award, Rod Stewart will be 60. Conveniently for Rod, his 59th birthday fell on a Saturday, because he still likes to enjoy mad nights out and live it large on Fridays and Saturdays. 'Wonderfully working class,' he says. 'Can't stay in on Friday night, I've got to go somewhere. It never leaves you that old working-class thing of Friday, it's pay day, gotta go out.'

If the singer has his birthday wish, Rod's statuesque blonde girlfriend Penny Lancaster, with her 31-inch legs, will be standing on kitten stilettos by his side, literally watching over him as he blows out 59 candles on his cake and opens his gifts of additions to his beloved model train system. He will be surrounded by as many of his children as he can muster. There will be a song, or probably a dozen, in Rod's heart, and toasts a-plenty to the future from expensive bottles of wine – preferably a 1967 vintage he will have asked for to remind himself of the year Celtic won the European Cup. (A Celtic fanatic, Rod has an open ticket to the directors' box at Celtic Park.)

More than likely, a lushly romantic hotel suite will be booked for the night for himself and Penny, at some luxurious hotel where past experience has taught him that he won't have to complain about over-crisply laundered sheets. Hotels with bed sheets too stiffly starched are on Rod's list of pet hates. 'If you're having sex, they bring your knees up in a rash,' he complains in his wisdom, as a serial womaniser. He may be nearly 60, but the rascal of rock still likes good sex. 'I think in our lives we all need a good hobby, good sport and good sex,' he said recently. 'It's a fine balance.'

By that yardstick, with a truly magnificent, vast, computerised toy model railway system to play with, football twice a week plus his own soccer pitch in the garden of his Essex home, and a beautiful, young and adoring blonde model lover in Penny Lancaster, Rod believes his life is very well balanced indeed.

'We have a very good sex life,' he says of partner Penny. 'Quality sex is very important to a relationship. The older you get, the better lover you become. You pay more attention to foreplay and kissing, and girls like to be kissed.

'I used to tend to put girls up on a pedestal too much. That would be my weakness. I've learned not to do that now, to accept their weaker sides because there isn't the perfect female on this earth, and I was always looking for that perfect female. I'd get one that looks good, all the bodily shapes, have great sex and find out she picks her nose or something. You can't have it all.'

Rod Stewart never dreamed his singing career would last as long as it has. Incredibly, next year it will be 40 years since he cut his first single. Just as incredibly, he was performing on *Top of the Pops* when girlfriend Penny was in her mother's womb. Even harder to believe is that Margaret, the older woman who inspired Rod's first solo hit, 'Maggie May', back in 1971, would now be well over 60.

In every one of the past four decades Rod has filled concert halls and stadiums around the world, enjoyed a string of massive hit singles and albums and genuinely believes there are many more to come.

The extraordinary success of *It Had to Be You ... The Great American Songbook* is a pointer to the direction in which Rod's career is likely to go. At such a venerable age for a solo singer, songs from his past with titles like 'Attractive Woman Wanted', and 'Dirty Weekend' would these days sit uneasily in a set list at a Rod Stewart concert. Already 'Hot Legs', one of his greatest hits, could be deemed an uncomfortable inclusion in a live repertoire. Rod could appear absurd, belting out his tale of being worn out by a sexually insatiable 17-year-old schoolgirl with legs right up to her neck, who keeps coming round for more while promising all kinds of fun with her most persuasive tongue. Rod's 'Hot Legs' lyrics are not exactly the 'moon' and 'June' of *It Had to Be You ... The Great American Songbook*.

Despite the personally anachronistic words, when he sings 'Hot Legs' in the future, as he surely will, Rod will undoubtedly get away with it. As one of his intimate circle observes: 'Getting away with it is something at which Rod has always excelled. He's been getting away with everything all his life. When he got a girl pregnant in his teens, it could have ruined his life. It didn't. He got away with having two careers while with the Faces. He could have been killed in a hail of bullets in the restaurant shooting in Mexico, or when he was held up at gunpoint in his car in Los Angeles. He survived. His career could have finished when he sank into the disco depths of 'Do Ya Think I'm Sexy?'. Lester Bangs, the critic, wrote that in selling out to the mainstream, Rod executed the greatest betrayal of talent pop music had ever seen. But in the end he got away with it. He took a huge gamble with *It Had to Be You ... The Great American Songbook*. He more than got away with it.

'Rod has had a reputation for being tight and not buying his round, yet the manager at his local pub, the Theydon Oak, in Essex, refuses to let him ever pay for a drink! He hasn't had to pay for a drink there in 15 years. Rod's talent and hard work as a singer is undeniable. But he's gone out for a fun life of sexy women, fast cars, booze and footie – and he's got away with it. Big time. His hard-drinking days in the Faces could have irreparably damaged him. But he's really fit. The hotel fracas in Hawaii with the Faces is a classic example of getting away with it. Next time Rod went back there he was welcomed with open arms. Any other rock star who was revealed as having a penchant for wearing women's knickers and playing with train sets might have been laughed out of the business. But Rod somehow always gets away with it all. And good luck to him.

'Interestingly, I believe people love him for it. Getting away with it every time has always been part of Rod's blokey, Jack-the-lad appeal. Not only has he got away with it, but he's cashed in too and seemingly had it all: the most beautiful women, a fleet of the flashiest cars, loads of money and even his own full-size football pitch. Most guys would love to get away with it all like that, too – even if it meant your house being known as Spunk Towers, which Rod's was.'

Close pal Ron Wood's revealing insight is: 'He's just an insecure little boy with more front than Harrods.' And as for his escapades with women, Long John Baldry is direct: 'He's just a randy little sod – and he gets away with it every time.' Rod offers no excuses for his rampant past escapades with the opposite sex other than to say: 'That was just a young lad in a candy store in a different era before AIDS. It was a lot easier to have sex more often and that's when I took my sexual apprenticeship. I only did what any red-blooded British bloke would do who suddenly found himself with a lot of money: I spent it on cars, women, wine and song and football. That's what I am and I don't think

I'll ever change. I used to do OK with girls before "Maggie May" was a hit, always used to dress the best I could and have perfect chat-up lines. But it helps being famous.'

Rod, who once ostentatiously hung a Scottish flag from the window of London's highly desirable Savoy Hotel without reprimand from the management, himself recalls with relish two classic cases of his getting away with it. He was in the crowd at Wembley Stadium on the famous occasion when the Scotland football team beat England, who were then the World Champions. In their over-exuberance, the Scottish fans poured on to the pitch seeking clods of Wembley turf and more, as souvenirs of what for them was a historic win. Rod remembers: 'There was a pitch invasion and the Scots brought down the goalposts. I said to my dad: "I've got to get on the pitch." The police were trying to stop everyone going on. I was covering up my face, but when they saw me they said: "Oh go on, then," and let me on the field.'

On another very different occasion, Rod was performing at a small concert in Chicago to an audience of around 7,000 and remembers: 'There was one man I could tell I didn't want in the audience. He had about five cameras around his waist and had his feet up on the low stage. When I came on he started reading the newspaper. I couldn't believe it. So I set fire to his newspaper.'

The days of ultra-mad excess have long gone. But Rod still has his moments. Not so long ago a drinking pal showed Rod a photograph he had taken of him in high spirits on a night out. To this day Rod is still trying to work out how he came to be in that Monte Carlo nightclub, with a saucepan on his head and his trousers round his ankles.

Rod's friends will all vouch for his infectious sense of humour. Some years back, after a pre-Christmas shopping spree at Harrods, he and some pals enjoyed a few drinks and then decided to see if they could get back to Epping by bus, rather than by the usual de luxe, chauffeur-driven transport. Clutching their shopping bags and packages, they clambered on to the bus in high spirits and sang Christmas songs for the other passengers. 'We were all drunk and offering to pay everyone's fare,' Rod recalls. 'After three and a half hours and five different buses we finished up in the Blind Beggar pub in Mile End, and had to call a taxi because we'd given up trying to find the right bus.'

Another trait that has endeared Rod to fans and the press alike is his penchant for telling it like it is. He was never more searingly honest that when talking about his devastation when Rachel Hunter left him. He literally bared his soul. Rod has rarely ducked questions from the media and over the years he has become, if anything, ever more honest in his replies – even about what could be considered the most delicate of subjects: his nose. Seen from one side it can look like a huge banana, he says. Is he a big boy? one interviewer had the temerity to ask. Just averagely endowed, Rod replied without flinching. Memorable sexual experiences? Very good in the back of limousines, he said, but in elevators it's all over too quickly.

Rod sees no reason why he shouldn't go on singing for many years ahead: 'I still think I've got a great music career ahead of me. I think I can go on doing this for as long as I want to. I may not be jumping around the stage when I'm 60, but I'll always be able to make records.' As an extremely wealthy man, he is often asked why he needs to tour as much as he does. His answer is always the same: 'Because I really love it. People say well, then, why don't you do it for nothing? But it costs so much money to tour it's ridiculous.'

He believes there's now a warmth and depth to his voice that had never been captured before – probably as a result of the microphones he's been using. 'We experimented a lot with mikes to find the best for my voice, which I'd never done – I used to sing into everything.'

Over the years Rod has been one of the hardest-working live performers in rock music and, given good health, he expects to retain his enthusiasm. He feels fit and, in the words of one of his early hits, he's managed to wear it well. But then he insists he's always known when not to go too far. He has an inbuilt early warning system, he says, which tells him when he's had enough to drink and adds: 'I've never touched cigarettes or hash. I did take cocaine a few times but it wasn't excessive.'

As far as defying the years, it's all in the genes, he says. His father reached the ripe old age of 86, his mother 85. His brother Don, now 73, still regularly referees Rod's Sunday football matches, running up and down for 90 minutes on a full-size pitch. His brother Bobby, 68, still runs marathons. And, Rod points out, like him they both still have their hair.

As well as knowing when to call a halt to his drinking, Rod also learned that drugs messed him up for weeks and gave him terrible depressions. Surely the most infamous Rod Stewart story on this subject was an account of how he and Ronnie Wood took cocaine 'the same way the French take their medicines,' as Rod delicately put it in one interview; 'up the bum,' as he put it less delicately in another. He admitted to *Q* magazine: 'I had a terrible period taking cocaine about 1979.' But, in a manner that would have pleased his much-loved father, Rod added: 'Now I never touch it.'

On a side table in the sitting room of Rod's sumptuous mansion Wood House in Epping, Essex, is a framed photograph of his father Bob Stewart kicking a football. Behind it is another framed photo, of his funeral procession. Draped on top of the funeral car is a Scottish flag and floral tributes in the shape of footballs. At the front of the procession is a Scottish piper, playing one final tribute to one of Highgate's most popular figures: the late Bob Stewart.

The prominence given to the photograph reflects the esteem

Rod retains for his dad. He admits: 'I miss my dad tremendously. Not a day goes by without me thinking of him. I was very, very close to him.' And, he stresses: 'He was the Scotsman in the family.'

While countless beautiful blonde women have passed through Rod Stewart's life over the past 40 years, none of them will hold quite the special place in Rod's heart that Bob Stewart does. The same Bob Stewart who bought his youngest child Rod a guitar for his 14th birthday, who yanked his idle son out of bed by the ear to start his paper round, who burned Rod's filthy beatnik garb when he was deported from Spain for vagrancy, who told him he was too young to marry at 35, who still served tea for Rod and his friends on a Double Diamond tray long after his son was a multimillionaire. It's the same Bob Stewart for whom Rod was moved to tears publicly, for the first time, when he dedicated 'Every Beat Of My Heart' to his dad when he was playing Wembley Stadium. Complete with bagpipes, 'Every Beat Of My Heart' was his father's favourite song.

Bob Stewart was a principled man with a down-to-earth outlook; he was moralistic and a disciplinarian who has Rod's utmost respect. There had been many a time when Rod overstepped the mark of acceptable behaviour in Bob Stewart's eyes. None more so than when he found Rod had gone through a stage of photographing groupies in various stages of undress with a Polaroid camera. Bob was horrified and refused to speak to Rod, which wounded the singer deeply and put an end to such shenanigans.

These days there are times when Rod sees something of Bob Stewart in himself. 'I'm pretty strict with my kids,' he insists. 'I've got a cinema theatre at my house and I let the kids watch movies with their boyfriends. But I tell them: "Keep your hands to yourself, no fiddling about when the lights go down." I'm like an usherette at the Odeon!' Rod may have an annual income in a good year of around £8 million but he has told his children they cannot fly first class until they have earned it. Instead he makes them go business class.

Recently he admitted his priorities have changed drastically over the years. 'When you're 23, you just want to shag anything that's walking,' he told one interviewer. 'Now I want to be with my kids, my wonderful girlfriend. I want to be remembered as fondly by my kids as I do my father. That would be all I could want.'

Rod's eldest daughter Kimberley, by first wife Alana, has already enjoyed modelling success and has started her own clothes business, Pinkie Starfish. Ruby, his daughter by Kelly Emberg, has a beautiful singing voice which has several respected music judges predicting big things for her. Sean, Rod's son by Alana, has had problems with alcohol and narcotics and was jailed, convicted of assault. But Rod has been a supportive father through all his difficulties. Rod is an avid listener to a wide range of radio stations in LA but also relies on his children to keep him abreast of new sounds, new trends in the music world.

When Rod was a teenager, he couldn't wait to get as far away from his parents as possible. But in LA he's been surprised but delighted to find Kimberley and Sean taking him out to the best clubs.

Rod is adamant he is a much better father than he was 20 years ago. When Kimberley and Sean were young he was often away on tour because he thought that was what rock stars did. Kimberley hated her father going away and, in an effort to stop him leaving for his tours, she would hang round his neck telling him she had had a horrible dream that his plane was going to crash. It wasn't until Ruby was born, Rod's sister Mary believes, that he realised how much he had missed with his first two children. Now tours are planned around his offspring, to fit in with their schooling and holidays so they can be together as much as possible.

Rod has made every effort, too, to remain on good terms with the mothers of his children for the sake of the kids. 'When you've loved somebody as passionately as I have the three mothers of my kids, you don't want any harm to come to them,' he reasons. 'Even though a couple of them tried to sting me for loads of money. There's a feeling in your heart for them. Now that's all behind us, we're all great mates, all live within two minutes of each other, they all speak to each other and to me and I hope it stays like that.'

For the foreseeable future, Rod will continue to base himself in Los Angeles, returning to Britain for 90 days each year. 'I would come back tomorrow,' he sighs, 'for family, friends, the pubs, the English attitude, the papers, the weather, the humour. I love it all. But not until all the kids are 18 and gone their own way.'

On the musical horizon is a third CD of classic songs in the mould of *It Had to Be You … The Geat American Songbook,* and an oft-shelved album project with Ron Wood called *You Strum and I'll Sing.* Additionally, plans are in the pipeline eventually to take Ben Elton's hugely successful London stage musical 'Tonight's The Night' to other cities both at home in England and abroad. The success of the show and the international appeal of Rod Stewart songs has prompted enquiries from entrepreneurs in several countries overseas.

Musically Rod will probably be best remembered for his early solo albums. 'I had nothing to live up to then,' he says. 'I was fearless, I'd try anything.' His 'Maggie May', written with Martin Quittenton in 1970, is a pop classic that will last at least another 30 years. Still his crowning moment remains the week in 1971 when he topped both the singles and album charts on both sides of the Atlantic. 'For me, he's got that quintessential voice for rock 'n' roll and ballads,' says his old pal Elton John. 'He's got that marvellous rasp. Bar none he's the best singer I've heard in rock 'n' roll. He's also the greatest white soul singer.'

When assessing Rod Stewart's career, he will also assuredly be remembered for his cover versions of other people's songs. 'It's the one time I can blow my own trumpet,' he says. 'If anybody knows how to cover a song, it's me.' He's big enough to admit, however, that the one glaring exception is Free's 'All Right Now': Rod's version even featured an electric drum.

The one thing he is terrified of being remembered for is being tight with his money. It's a reputation that has clung to him for many years and Ron Wood, says Rod, hasn't helped by declaring he's as tight as two coats of paint. 'But I'm not,' says Rod. 'Anybody that knows me knows that I'm a very generous person. It's a reputation I got because of my Scottishness, but it's backfiring now.

'I am very careful with my money, but I'm certainly not tight. I keep a check on it every day: bonds, stock market, gold, everything I've got an investment in. Because in this business so many people go under because they don't keep an eye on their money. I've got good people working for me that I trust.'

While trying to teach his children the value of money and the importance of working for it, it's nevertheless his family who enjoy his bouts of generosity. Recently he paid out £11,000 to fly his two brothers and some mates up to Scotland on a private aircraft, with a stewardess on board to look after them. The excited faces of his brothers and their party, he said, was worth every penny.

It's been a long and extraordinary journey for Rod from north London's Archway Road to the mansions of Los Angeles and Epping. The often outrageous adventures along the way have been watched by the world with endless fascination, and by his brothers and sister Mary with awe and admiration, occasionally with some embarrassment, and always a desire to help him keep his feet on the ground. Mary, in particular, loathed the hotel-wrecking lifestyle of the Faces days.

Brother Don can remember their father Bob Stewart becoming seriously alarmed at Rod's rootless meanderings in his teens, so much so that he asked Don to have an urgent word with him: 'Dad said: "Why don't you have a chat with him. He might listen to you. Tell him to settle down and get a decent job." My talk did a lot of good, didn't it? Football, fast cars and faster women.'

Today Rod concludes: 'I've no regrets whatsoever. I'm one lucky bastard. I could still be digging graves. I've got everything, I've been so lucky. I've had such a charmed life I would not want to ask for anything else. If it should all end tomorrow, I'd be really pissed off, but I wouldn't complain or say I've missed out on anything – anything at all.'

CHAPTER FIFTEEN

TONIGHT'S THE NIGHT

*Rod's vast body of work would have been inspiring
enough to fashion a story from, even if the man himself
were a grumpy, self-important old git; the fact that he is
obviously so likeable and able to laugh at himself made
the whole experience a real joy.* Ben Elton

London's Victoria Palace Theatre has played host to a string of
smash hit musicals since it was built in the year 1910 for the then
hugely expensive sum of £12,000. *Annie, Barnum, Me And My
Girl, Black And White Minstrel Show, Fame, Jolson, Kiss Me Kate,
Grease,* and the Buddy Holly musical *Buddy,* are just a few of the
shows that have entertained audiences at the Victoria Palace over
the past 50 years.

Further back in time, it was at the Victoria Palace Theatre that
Lupino Lane did the Lambeth Walk more than 1,000 times from
1937 until war broke out. And it was in the autumn of 2003 at
the same Victoria Palace Theatre that Tim Howar did his distinctive Rooster Strut to a string of familiar numbers culled from
the catalogue of Rod Stewart.

Howar, a Canadian actor-singer from Edmonton, Alberta,
found himself breathing new life into Rod's songs as the star of
a brash, bright and breezy new musical called *Tonight's The*

Night, written by British comedian, playwright and novelist Ben Elton.

Ben Elton had first taken notice of Rod Stewart when his brother brought home a copy of the album *Every Picture Tells A Story* when Ben was just a boy back in 1971. Two years later Ben bought his own copy, and from then on he was a committed Rod Stewart fan. As time went by and Elton's writing talents flowered, first writing his own material for his stand-up comic routines, then as a TV scriptwriter, and latterly scripting stage musicals, he came to feel that Rod's hits would lend themselves perfectly to drama since they all told little stories.

Elton had previously collaborated with Andrew Lloyd Webber, writing the book and lyrics for *The Beautiful Game*. He then turned the songs by Queen into the stage musical *We Will Rock You* which, if far from universally critically acclaimed, became a huge commercial success. Now he turned his attention to Rod's back catalogue and set about weaving a story that would not be biographical but trade on many elements of Rod's personality and, of course, his music. 'So I decided I would almost make it a surrogate Rod by having this shy fella who sells his soul to get Rod Stewart's soul in order to find the courage to ask the girl he loves out.

'It's a very silly story,' Ben cheerfully admitted, 'but the best musical comedy, as P.G. Wodehouse observed, should be very silly. I based *Tonight's The Night* on the lure, the essence of Rod. I write comedy, and Rod's sense of fun is part of his life and work,' he explained. 'His body of work would have guaranteed him fame and success even if he was a grumpy self-important git, but the fact that he's obviously very talented and able to laugh at himself just make his music even more accessible.'

As the idea for *Tonight's The Night* began to take shape, Ben Elton met with Rod several times, both in London and Los Angeles, and instantly warmed to him. 'There's a sort of golden glow that emanates from Rod Stewart, as if a light bulb has been shoved up him,' he says. 'He's one of the few people I've met of whom it could be said that the sun truly does seem to shine out of his backside. People like Rod on sight. I know because I've been out drinking with him. There is a lightness about the man that people find uplifting. He lives his life with undisguised glee.'

In August of 2003 Rod, accompanied by his manager Arnold Stiefel, attended a workshop presentation of Elton's work in London, basically to see if Elton's project was viable. Stiefel, who has now been Rod's manager for 20 years, had been approached on numerous occasions to produce a musical revolving around the Rod Stewart catalogue but had never been tempted. The workshop was therefore a nerve-wracking experience for Elton, who had taken on the duties of the show's director as well as writer. He was especially tense because Rod had not read the script – he decided he didn't want to read it, he wanted to see it presented. Elton was even more anxious when Rod unexpectedly also brought Penny Lancaster along. He wondered just how Penny would react to the jokes he had written into the script which poked fun at Rod's reputation as a womaniser.

Although he was confident of Rod's ability to laugh at himself, Ben Elton was acutely aware of what was at stake if he didn't. 'It could have been two weeks on the workshop in vain,' says Elton, who gathered around 100 people in the audience to help the laughs along. 'But Rod did laugh, copiously, and he loved the show.' At the end, Rod turned to Elton and said: 'You've turned me into a legend.' Elton replied: 'Well, I think that job's already been done by you.'

Tonight's The Night, filled with 22 of Rod's hits, was scheduled to open at the end of October 2003 and, after a series of encouraging previews, word of mouth indicated that the musical was destined to be a big hit.

The show was launched with a first night gala which drew a

large and excited crowd outside the Palace Theatre at Victoria to see the arrival of Rod and Penny and other celebrity guests. Penny's entrance on Rod's arm was nothing less than breathtaking. There were audible gasps and wolf whistles at her £4,000, daringly short, see-through mini-dress revealing a tiny black G-string underneath. Rod, more formally and stylishly dressed, beamed with pride and said: 'Penny looks fantastic, I'm a lucky guy.'

In the Victoria Palace's 93-year history, rarely can any woman have made such an eye-catching entrance – either on stage or off. Extra tall in a pair of her very highest heeled shoes, Penny dazzled her way through the grey marble foyer with its old gold mosaic and pillars of Sicilian marble towards the auditorium. In deference to her lover's big night at the opening of a musical all about her man, Penny had deliberately mussed up her hair to wear it in spiky trademark rooster Rod fashion. 'I might as well look like Rod,' she said, 'but for one night only.'

Inside in the stalls, the celebrity audience – which included Twiggy, Roger Taylor of Queen, ex-Madness singer Suggs, comedy actor Harry Enfield, Radio 2 favourite Terry Wogan, nightclub owner Peter Stringfellow and the England football team manager Sven Goran Ericsson – broke into spontaneous applause as Rod and Penny entered the auditorium to take their seats. Seated near the front of the stage, next to TV's Pop Idol judge Nikki Chapman, was Rod's sister Mary, who clapped enthusiastically after every number.

Ben Elton's 'very silly story' centres on Stuart Clutterbuck, who works in a gas station in Gasoline Alley in Detroit. He's a bit of a nerd who never gets the girl and secretly he's in love with a local dish called Sweet Lady Mary. But although she's in his heart and she's in his soul, she is, alas, not in his arms.

Then one night, Satan, in the devilishly wicked shape of a long-legged blonde in tight-fitting PVC and leather bondage gear, appears and offers him a Faustian pact. She tells Stuart that she can get him a night of hot sex with Mary, but there is a price to pay: he must swap souls with Rod Stewart for eternity.

Young Stuart jumps at the chance, and next time he pulls on his jeans, they fit him like a rubber glove. Returning to the petrol station in his new hip persona, Stuart sings 'Tonight I'm Yours' to Mary and his impassioned outpouring and newly confident strut succeeds in wooing Mary into his bed.

Following his vagabond heart and troubadour leanings, Stuart next joins a band and, now he's the rocking Rooster Clutterbuck, freely indulging himself with the girls flocking around him.

Meanwhile, back at Rod Stewart's Hollywood mansion, Rod's manager Baby Jane (later revealed as having been born Maggie May) is aghast that her rock superstar client is going soft on her, even cancelling his subscription to the TV soccer channel and thinking about making an album of whale music. So there's only one solution: she'll pursue rising new star Stuart Rooster Clutterbuck and turn him into the new Rod Stewart rock god.

Also aiming to catch up with him is Stuart's real love Mary, who arrives at a gig in Los Angeles just as he's singing 'Do Ya Think I'm Sexy?' Appalled at Stuart's infidelities, Mary tells Stuart they are through, and how he broke her heart, by singing 'I Don't Wanna Talk About It'.

Stuart now has an affair with Baby Jane, but he's beginning to tire of his sleep-around lifestyle and Satan reappears to tell him that it is really God who creates rockers like Rod Stewart, not her. She gives Stuart back his soul and he proposes to Mary, just as word reaches a relieved Baby Jane that Rod Stewart hasn't gone soft after all – he's just punched Richard Gere on a visit to an Indian ashram.

The production winds up with its visual pièce de résistance. After Baby Jane receives a telegram from Rod Stewart offering his yacht to Stuart and Mary for their honeymoon, the set ingeniously turns itself from a petrol station into a magnificent white yacht, the RSS *Penny*, with the ensemble singing an extended all-join-in version of 'Sailing'. Night after night this flag-waving finale brought the entire audience to their feet, waving their arms from side to side and singing along to 'Sailing'. Just for good measure, two Scottish bagpipers entered stage left and stage right and marched up and down to the beat before the curtain came down.

On the opening night, Penny loyally jumped up out of her seat at the finale to lead the general euphoria by whooping and dancing in the aisle. Her spectacular solo gyrations on the dance floor at the after show party were even wilder, while Rod admiringly gazed down at her from a balcony. Late in the evening, however, Penny contrived to gash her shin while dancing and left the party with blood oozing from her leg.

The general verdict at the after show party was that Ben Elton had succeeded in his aim, of capturing the dominant traits of Rod Stewart in the show - great music, lashings of energy, gorgeous looking girls, brash excess, a good many laughs and some blatant vulgarity.

What surprised many was quite how far Rod had allowed Ben Elton to poke fun at him in the show – not least during the rendition of 'Hot Legs'. This was a number set beside the swimming pool behind the high walls of Rod's Los Angeles mansion, walls which were adorned with moulded figures of naked maidens, some with their nipples acting as coat hooks for poolside bathing robes. Dominating the gilded gates of the mansion gleamed a massive crest, bearing the initials RS against the background of the Scottish flag, blue with white cross, and flanked by statues of two blondes in the skimpiest of gold bikinis. The crest was topped off by a football and cans of beer, and underneath writ large was the motto Booze: Balls: Birds. Against this outrageously kitsch backdrop, a team of Rod Stewart's personal masseuses strutted their stuff in white mini nurses outfits and red high-heels to *Hot Legs*, one of Rod's most sexually explicit songs.

Timed to coincide with the opening of *Tonight's The Night* came the release of *As Time Goes By ... The Great American Songbook Volume II*, a follow-up album to Rod's 4-million selling CD of classic songs from days gone by. The new collection featured another batch of standards including 'Till There Was You', 'Smile', and 'I Only Have Eyes For You'. Among the 14 songs there were also two duets – Rod teaming up with Cher for a version of 'Bewitched, Bothered and Bewildered', and with Queen Latifah on 'As Time Goes By'. Once again, the lush arrangements and Rod's lovingly performed interpretations of songs so cherished by his parents' generation proved hugely popular. The album quickly shot high into the charts on both sides of the Atlantic.

It was while promoting the album in Britain that Rod gave a revealing interview to the listings magazine *Radio Times* in which he showed signs that the constant sniping at him for squiring the considerably more youthful Penny Lancaster was finally getting on his nerves. He expressed his irritation that he had been unfairly criticized for dating a younger woman, especially when ex-Beatle Paul McCartney escaped censure despite his taking a wife who was half the ex-Beatle's age.

Rod pointed out the difference was that McCartney, who at 60 was 26 years older than former model Heather Mills, had a knighthood. Rod, also 26 years older than Penny, however, did not have any such honour. 'What pisses me off is that they never have a go at Paul McCartney for marrying a younger woman', he told the magazine. 'He's 60 and Heather is 34, but they kill me because of Penny. Perhaps it's because he has a knighthood, a wonderful little honour to be bestowed on one. I don't know why I haven't got any honour. I do my bit for charity.'

Rod also complained he had regularly been passed over for the Grammy Awards, America's musical equivalent of the Oscars. 'It's astounding I've never won one. They tend not to give it to the British unless you're Sting,' he said huffily. 'The sun shines out of his arse – a pure jazz musician, Mr Serious, who helps the Indians.'

Rod's long-time rock buddy Elton John, another singer with a knighthood, also came in for some disapproval for not inviting him to his parties. And taking a swipe at 'Sharon's' appearance and weight, Rod said: 'My hair is nice and real and looks it, and hers doesn't. No, I take that back. He looks good at the moment, but he could lose a bit of timber.'

Nearly four years after his marriage collapsed, and with his relationship with Penny seemingly solid, it was something of a surprise to find Rod also openly declaring: 'I'm still shell-shocked about what happened with Rachel.' The hurt was clearly still there as he added: 'I've been a pretty good husband – totally faithful to Rachel for nine years, which was an astounding achievement for me, and then I got a smack in the head for it. I was devastated. I could never have left her like that. No one had ever left me before, so I didn't know what it was all about. I couldn't sleep and lost 15 lb. I went to bed with a hot water bottle on my chest because my heart really hurt.'

While Rod bared his grief, it became clear that he was by no means the only one who had been shell-shocked by Rachel abruptly walking out on their marriage. To coincide with the opening of the musical *Tonight's The Night*, Channel 5 broadcast *Rod's Girls*, a TV documentary (to which the authors contributed) in which several of Rod's former loves were persuaded to speak in the most intimate and explicit terms of their affairs with the rocker. And none spoke more tellingly – and even tearfully – than a ravishing beauty by the name of Ann Marie Ciccini. 'How anybody could leave him, I have no idea. He has sex appeal dripping everywhere,' Ann Marie said of Rod.

Ann Marie had met Rod at a time when he was footloose and fancy free after his break up with Kelly Emberg and she was working at the London Ferrari centre. 'One day I'm sitting behind my desk and here walks in this god of my life. There was like electricity,' she recalled of their first meeting. They started dating and it soon became a very passionate, highly physical affair. 'It was difficult to keep our hands off each other,' Ann Marie revealed. 'In a party situation we'd sneak off somewhere he'd seen earlier where we could take part in a little bit of love-making in private.'

But she says the most exciting passion she shared with Rod occurred after a meal at a country restaurant when he took her outside and they had sex on the back of his Lamborghini. 'We were in the country at a restaurant with his mate Ricky, and we went outside to have a cuddle. One kiss led to another and we made love on the back of his Lamborghini, which was incredibly sexy. I thought I'd died and gone to heaven.

'Lots of men are very, very selfish in bed but he's not a selfish man in the slightest. He always made me feel that I was the only one. But in my mind I knew that was one dream too far.'

Clearly still holding a torch for Rod 13 years after they parted, Ann Marie had to ask for a break in filming as her emotions got the better of her when she remembered how their affair finished in the autumn of 1990. 'I opened the paper,' she said after regaining her composure, 'and the headline was "Rod To Wed". He'd been away for a month about that time, so I called his mate Ricky and I said: "Is this a publicity stunt for the release of an album or single?" He paused, because he knew Rod wasn't going to see me again. It was left in his lap to bear me the bad news. He said: "I'm really sorry, yes it is true." I was shocked, really shocked.'

That Rod's womanising ways should merit one hour of prime time viewing on one of Britain's main TV channels was extraordinary enough. But the revelations from the lips of Rod's former lovers were remarkable. While Rachel Hunter, Alana Hamilton,

Kelly Emberg and other ex-girlfriends declined to take part, there were enough of Rod's former bedmates willing to spill the beans. And Rod's reputation between the sheets emerged from the programme thoroughly enhanced as virtually all of them chose to say good things about him.

Baronet's daughter Vicki Hodge, who once kiss-and-told about seducing Prince Andrew, recounted how she spent an afternoon enjoying hot sex with Rod after meeting him on the Kings Road in Chelsea. 'It was just like an afternoon shag,' she told the programme, 'so it was like good, hard sex, proper sex. Rod's a good lover, and the other thing I really liked about him is that he had masses of hair so that was good to pull and tug.' Asked how big was Rod's rod, Vicki said with a giggle: 'Ample – rather like bagpipes, when you blow it, it gets bigger!'

Dee Harrington commented: 'He had a very big sexual appetite and we spent a lot of time having sex. He was always wanting sex, he'd always be undoing my blouse if I was asleep. He liked me to show my legs and breasts. We used to just go about the house, and the grounds, and the fields and the barn having sex. He had quite a lot of time on his hands, so we had more sex.'

American Carole Mallory, once a top model and actress who had a two-year fling with Rod in 1976, claimed Rod would take her to bed at the Los Angeles mansion he shared with Britt Ekland while Britt was away. 'He liked me to be on top,' said Carole, 'and he liked to look at and talk to my breasts. He talked to my nipples – that's what he liked.

'Rod would see me on and off without Britt's knowledge. He was funny in bed and made me laugh. He wore a Sherlock Holmes hat and a Tam O'Shanter. He liked me in garter belts and all that stuff, corsets. He liked white. He was into white corsets. He put on Britt's boa once during sex. She had these damn awful fuschia boas. She had a make-up area that was out of the circus, and I would go in there and mess around with her make-up while she was away. Rod was well-endowed. I felt very sorry for Britt because she didn't know what was going on.'

Bebe Buell, her memories of Rod mellowed by time, gave an idea of how thoughtful a lover Rod can be. 'I had wonderful romantic times,' she said. 'He surprised me one time by having the bed in one of our hotel rooms, when we arrived, covered in rose petals and champagne and this beautiful antique negligee waiting for me to put on.'

Former *Playboy* model Marcy Hanson attested to Rod's sexual allure as a rock star by saying: 'There's nothing finer than seeing 200,000 women screaming for a man on stage to make you proud to go home with him.' Marcy, who met Rod when he was with Bebe Buell at a Playboy party in Los Angeles, also attested to Rod's sense of romance and of fun when they went to bed together in 1977. 'I don't think I've ever experienced a man more romantic than Rod,' said Marcy. 'He was very, very attentive and very playful. He put on my underwear and went running up and down the hotel room corridors,' she laughed. Quizzed about the size of Rod's rod, Marcy giggled: 'Quite a big man!'

American actress Teri Copley, whom Rod variously dated in 1984, 1989, and 1990, also gave a personal insight into Rod's sex appeal. 'The thing I really appreciate now, looking back, is that he is a man who really appreciated women,' said Teri. 'There are a lot of men who womanise who really don't like women and that underneath are quite mean to them and degrading and controlling. But Rod really appreciated women.'

Teri, however, did not appreciate the night she was on Rod's arm when he first met Rachel Hunter. 'I can remember the night he met Rachel,' she said downcast. 'He was on a date with me and I could see that he was flirtatious with her and I could see she was responding. I thought it was a little ... not nice. He could have waited until I wasn't there. And then she came back to the house and that was enough for me. I can't ... I won't even go there,' said Teri, her voice trailing off disconsolately. Then, offering a word of advice for Rod, Teri – who has found God – said: 'Let Him know you, let Him feel you.'

Among the bevy of beauties ready to assess Rod the lover on TV, only Britt Ekland cast doubts on Rod's ability to conjure up the correct chemistry all the time. 'It was definitely love-lust at first sight,' she said of their affair. 'He was very charming, very boyish, very playful and very cute. Rod liked sex very much, but we were not sexually compatible. We were very much in love and we were very affectionate but we were quite different sexually.' Interestingly, Britt added: 'I know why he married Alana Hamiliton – because she was pregnant. If I'd been pregnant he would have married me, but I was not prepared to do that and I told him that.'

Last word on the blondes who have passed through Rod's life without giving him true lasting happiness, came from his sister Mary Cady. 'Maybe if he changed and got someone a bit older with dark hair, not such long legs, not so thin, he might find love there,' she said. Quite what long-legged, thin, blonde Penny Lancaster thought of that remark has not been recorded.

While Rod basked in the stage success of *Tonight's The Night* and the acclaim for *As Time Goes By ... The Great American Songbook Volume II*, a Channel 4 TV programme researching the ultimate pop star, according to the UK singles charts over the last 50 years, totted up that Rod had sold 9,046,492 singles. This total placed him 11th in the all time singles sellers chart, above the Rolling Stones, Kylie Minogue, and Stevie Wonder. He had achieved this lofty position despite becoming predominantly an album artist over the past five years.

Penny, meanwhile, furthered her own career with the release of a keep fit video. It received many favourable reviews, which were in turn reflected by subsequent substantial sales. But try as

Penny Lancaster might to be her own woman and to prove she was a worthy incumbent of the prize position of being Rod's best girl, she was unable to shake off comparisons with Rod's former blonde lovers – notably estranged wife Rachel Hunter.

Sometimes Penny did not help herself, like the occasion she raised eyebrows as to whether the age gap with Rod was proving a problem by letting slip that she occasionally called Rod 'Dad.' But she also had to contend with the frequent, but misguided, press speculation that Rod and Rachel might one day get back together, and that did not help her cause. The newspapers continued to highlight what they perceived to be a thoroughly bitchy Penny v Rachel rivalry, and they had a field day when poor Penny humiliatingly had her modelling contract with the lingerie firm Ultimo cancelled after just one year and discovered her successor was to be ... Rachel Hunter. Rachel's two-year deal was reportedly worth £1 million, double what Penny was paid.

This galling news for Penny was made all the worse for her by new pictures emerging of Rachel now curvily clad in the very same clingy Ultimo swimsuit Penny had modelled the previous year. Ultimo claimed they ended Penny's contract because they needed a model with international appeal and Penny was not really well known enough outside the UK.

At first Rachel though it was a prank when she was asked to take over from Penny. When she realised it was for real, she could not turn it down. 'It was simply a business decision,' Rachel insisted. 'I'd prefer not to be the one replacing Penny. It's a very hard situation. All I can say is that she looked beautiful in the advertising campaign and she did a great job.' However hard Rachel tried to say that she took the Ultimo job because she was a working model and was simply accepting work offered, there was no denying that the ousting of Penny worked in Rachel's favour in more ways than one.

Rod was careful to stay out of the furore until he could no

longer stand the simmering hostility between the two. Gallantly he stood up for Penny, but much less gallantly laid into Michelle Mone, the boss of Ultimo, calling her 'a manipulative cow' for the way she had replaced his girlfriend with his wife.

'I hope she chokes on her profits,' he told a Scottish newspaper. 'Michelle really needs to be put in her place and, if this is revenge, so be it, I'm sticking up for my old lady. Penny doesn't want to admit it but she's been hurt by all this. She's been in tears. Penny is a beautiful girl, I love her and I hate to see her get hurt in this way. She did nothing wrong. Put yourself in her place. How do you think it feels to be told you're being replaced by Rod's wife?'

Clearly seething, Rod accused Miss Mone of using his girlfriend to gain more publicity for the company. 'I think Michelle Mone is a nasty piece of work, I really do,' he went on.

Rod protested that if a business had to come to an end, then everyone should remain friends. 'To get kicked in the teeth like this is horrible. Michelle was determined to rub Penny's nose in it. What an ungracious way to treat my girlfriend. I don't think Penny has got a single bad bone in her body.' Rod stressed that he had no axe to grind with Rachel. 'She's a single mum and it's up to her to earn a living,' he said.

Rod Stewart records continue to spin on personal CD players all over the world and still sell in their millions. The world appears never to tire of his voice. But it is a measure of the fascination the world has with Rod's public private life and the girls who so decoratively colour it that the Ultimo cat fight between two beautiful women garnered acreage of newspaper and magazine coverage around the globe.

Rod may be just a few months short of his 60th birthday. But this fascination with his women past and present is likely to remain and, of that, Rod's former publicist Tony Toon has no doubt. 'Believe me,' he told the nation on the TV documentary

Rod's Girls, 'Rod Stewart is woman-mad. He thinks about having sex day in and day out. And Rod Stewart's not faithful to anyone – apart from his bank manager, probably. But, 'added Toon, 'I've got to tell you, that man is magic.'

Days after celebrating his 59th birthday, Rod set off on a 44-city 'Maggie May To The Great American Songbook' concert tour of America, bravely trying to put over for his fans an evening which encompassed both his old rock numbers and his more recent mellow classics.

It was never going to be an easy mix to perform live and, in general, it was Rod's 90-minute first set of rock hits which went down better with audiences, some of whom were paying upwards of $100 a ticket, rather than his second set of standards like 'As Time Goes By'.

To reprise his rocking favourites like 'Some Guys Have All The Luck', 'Forever Young', 'You Wear It Well' and 'Stay With Me', Rod bounced around the stage looking the raffish bad boy rocker either in an orange jacket and orange-striped sneakers, or in a tangerine waistcoat, orange shirt and tight black jeans. Crowds at each venue greeted Rod's old hits with deafening approval.

Then there was a 20-minute intermission before Rod emerged in full white tie and tails to sing a selection of standards with a 16-piece orchestra. At one venue he seemed so unsure of the wisdom of trying to present an altogether different set from the first that he paused to tell the crowd almost apologetically: 'It's only going to be a half hour of this.'

Miriam Di Nunzio, reviewing the concert for the *Chicago Sun-Times* reported: 'By that time though, the crowd was eerily subdued, the applause only appreciatively polite. Stewart awkwardly navigated 'The Way You Look Tonight', 'As Time Goes By', 'I'm In The Mood For Love' and a few other standards while much of the crowd broke into conversations and made cell phone calls."

Rod knew he was never going to please everybody all the time, but his shows were crafted to bring the audiences roaring back. And at every venue when he finished up with a change of clothes for foot-stomping versions of 'Maggie May' and 'Do Ya Think I'm Sexy?' he once again had them eating out of his hands. 'I'm only getting better as I get older,' he allowed himself to tell the cheering crowd.

DISCOGRAPHY

Singles

With LONG JOHN BALDRY
You'll Be Mine/Up Above My Head (1964, United Artists. Rod featured on B side only)
With SHOTGUN EXPRESS
I Could Feel The Whole World Turn Around/Curtains (instrumental) (1966, Columbia)
With JEFF BECK GROUP Tallyman (instrumental)/Rock My Plimsoul (1967, Columbia) Love Is Blue (instrumental)/I've Been Drinking (1968, Columbia)
With PYTHON LEE JACKSON
In A Broken Dream/Doing Fine (1970, Youngblood)
With the FACES
Flying/Three Button Hand Me Down (1970, Warner Brothers)
Had Me A Real Good Time/Rear Wheel Skid (1970, Warner Brothers)
Stay With Me/Debris (1972, Warner Brothers)

Cindy Incidentally/Skewiff (Mend the Fuse) (1973, Warner Brothers)

Pool Hall Richard/I Wish It Would Rain (1973, Warner Brothers)

Cindy Incidentally/Memphis/Stay With Me/Pool Hall Richard (1974, Warner Brothers)

Memphis/You Can Make Me Dance, Sing Or Anything/Stay With Me/Cindy Incidentally (1977, Riva)

With the ATLANTIC CROSSING DRUM AND PIPE BAND

Skye Boat Song/Skye Boat Song (instrumental) (1976, Riva)

Solo Singles

Good Morning Little Schoolgirl/I'm Gonna Move To The Outskirts Of Town (1964, Decca)

The Day Will Come/Why Does It Go On? (1965, Columbia)

Shake/I Just Got Some (1966, Columbia)

Little Miss Understood/So Much To Say (1968, Immediate)

It's All Over Now/Jo's Lament (1970, Vertigo)

Handbags And Gladrags/Man Of Constant Sorrow (1970, Mercury)

Maggie May/Reason To Believe (1971, Mercury)

You Wear It Well/Lost Paraguyos (1972, Mercury)

Angel/What Made Milwaukee Famous (1972, Mercury)

Oh No Not My Baby/Jodie (1973, Mercury)

Farewell/Bring It On Home To Me (1974, Mercury)

It's All Over Now/Handbags and Gladrags (1975, Mercury)

Sailing/Stone Cold Sober (1975, Warner Brothers)

This Old Heart Of Mine/All In The Name Of Rock 'n' Roll (1975, Riva)

Tonight's The Night/The Ball Trap (1976, Riva)

The Killing Of Georgie/Fool For You (1976, Riva)

Sailing/Stone Cold Sober (1976, Riva) (Rereleased in UK when Sailing was adopted as theme tune for the BBC TV series *Sailor*)

Get Back/Trade Winds (1976, Riva)

Maggie May/You Wear It Well/Twistin' The Night Away (1976, Mercury)

First Cut Is The Deepest/I Don't Want To Talk About It (1977, Riva)

You're In My Heart/You Really Got A Nerve (1977, Riva)

Hot Legs/I Was Only Joking (1978, Riva)

Ole Ola/I'd Walk a Million Miles For One Of Your Girls (1978, Riva)

Da Ya Think I'm Sexy?/Dirty Weekend (1978, Riva)

Ain't Love A Bitch/Scarred And Scared (1979, Riva)

The Best Days Of My Life/Blondes (Have More Fun) (1979, Riva)

(If Loving You Is Wrong) I Don't Want To Be Right/Last Summer (1980, Riva)

Passion/Better Off Dead (1980, Riva)

My Girl/She Won't Dance With Me (1980/Riva)

Oh God I Wish I Was Home Tonight/Somebody Special (1981, Riva)

Tonight I'm Yours/Sonny (1981, Riva)

Young Turks/Tora, Tora, Tora (Out with the Boys) (1981, Riva)

How Long?/Jealous (1982/Riva)

Baby Jane/Ready Now (1983, Warner Brothers)

What Am I Gonna Do? (I'm So in Love with You)/Dancin' Alone (1983, Warner Brothers)

Infatuation/Three Time Loser (1984, Warner Brothers)

Some Guys Have All the Luck/I Was Only Joking (1984, Warner Brothers)

Love Touch/Heart Is On The Line (1986, Warner Brothers)

Every Beat of My Heart/Trouble (1986, Warner Brothers)

Another Heartache/You're In My Heart (1986, Warner Brothers)

Lost In You/Almost Illegal (1988, Warner Brothers)

Forever Young/Days Of Rage (1988, Warner Brothers)

Downtown Train/The Killing Of Georgie (1989, Warner Brothers)
Rhythm Of My Heart/Moment Of Glory (1991, Warner Brothers)
The Motown Song/Sweet Soul Music (1991, Warner Brothers)
Broken Arrow/I Was Only Joking (1991, Warner Brothers)
Your Song/Broken Arrow (1992, Warner Brothers)
Tom Traubert's Blues (Waltzing Matilda)/Holding Back (1992, Warner Brothers)
Ruby Tuesday/You're In My Heart (1993, Warner Brothers)
Shotgun Wedding/Sweet Soul Music (1993, Warner Brothers)
Have I Told You Lately/Gasoline Alley (1993, Warner Brothers)
Reason To Believe/It's All Over Now (1993, Warner Brothers)
People Get Ready (1993, Warner Brothers)
You're The Star (1995, Warner Brothers)
Lady Luck (1995, Warner Brothers)
Purple Heather (1995, Warner Brothers)
f We Fall In Love Tonight (1996, Warner Brothers)
Da Ya Think I'm Sexy? (1997, Globe)
Ooh La La (1998, Warner Brothers)
Rocks (1998, Warner Brothers)
Faith Of The Heart (1999, Universal)
I Can't Deny It (2001, Atlantic)

Albums

With STEAMPACKET
The First Supergroup (1968, Charly Records)
With JEFF BECK
Truth (1968, Columbia)
With the FACES
First Step (1970, Warner Brothers)
Long Player (1971, Warner Brothers)
A Nod is as Good as a Wink to a Blind Horse (1972, Warner Brothers)

Ooh La La (1973, Warner Brothers)
Coast to Coast/ Overture and Beginners: Live Album (1974, Mercury)

Solo Albums

An Old Raincoat Won't Ever Let You Down (1970, Mercury)
Gasoline Alley (1970, Mercury)
Every Picture Tells a Story (1971, Mercury)
Never a Dull Moment (1972, Mercury)
Smiler (1974, Mercury)
Atlantic Crossing (1975, Warner Brothers)
A Night on the Town (1976, Riva)
Footloose and Fancy Free (1977, Riva)
Blondes Have More Fun (1978, Riva)
Foolish Behaviour (1980, Riva)
Tonight I'm Yours (1981, Riva)
Absolutely Live (1982, Warner Brothers)
Body Wishes (1983, Warner Brothers)
Camouflage (1985, Warner Brothers)
Every Beat of My Heart (1986, Warner Brothers)
Out of Order (1988, Warner Brothers)
Storyteller (1989, Warner Brothers)
Vagabond Heart (1991, Warner Brothers)
Lead Vocalist (1992, Warner Brothers)
Unplugged and Seated (1993, Warner Brothers)
A Spanner in the Works (1995, Warner Brothers)
If We Fall in Love Tonight (1996, Warner Brothers)
The Best of Rod Stewart (2001, J Records)
Human (2001, Atlantic Records)
It Had to Be You/The Great American Songbook (2002, J Records)
As Time Goes By ... The Great American Songbook (2003, J Records)

PICTURE CREDITS

INDEX